The Little Web Cam Book

Elisabeth Parker

Illustrations by John Grimes

Peachpit Press
Berkeley ▼ California

Peachpit Press
1249 Eighth Street
Berkeley, CA 94710
510 524 2178
fax 510 524 2221
Find us on the Web at http://www.peachpit.com

The Little Web Cam Book

Peachpit Press is a division of Addison Wesley Longman

Editors: Carol Henry, Simon Hayes
Production Coordinator: Amy Changar
Compositor: Owen Wolfson
Interior Design: Robin Williams
Cover Design: TMA Ted Mader & Associates
Cartoon Illustrations: John Grimes
Indexer: Carol Burbo

ISBN 0-201-35420-9

0 9 8 7 6 5 4 3 2 1
Printed and bound in the United States of America

To my husband,
Richard Grace.

Acknowledgments

I'd like to thank the many people who helped while I was writing this book:

- **John Grimes, Illustrator**: For drawing all the wonderful cartoons and friendly hardware illustrations. Who'd 'a thunk computer innards could look so cute?
- **Marjorie Baer, Managing Editor**: For helping me stay on track (and remain reasonably sane) when things got crazy. I couldn't have finished this book without her.
- **Carol Henry, Editor**: She kept the book consistent, caught quite a few boo-boos, and raised a few technical questions that helped me make the book more user friendly.
- **Simon Hayes, Editor**: He came up with the basic idea for *The Little Web Cam Book.*
- **Amy Changar, Production Coordinator**: For getting this book through production, coping with my never-ending changes, and making the book look so great!
- **Rich Grace**: My husband (and live-in hardware/multimedia consultant): He knows just about everything about hardware, multimedia, and networking—which sure came in handy for this book. He also writes computer books (**http://www.byteit.com/rgrace/**) and helped write Chapter 12.

I'd also like to thank the many cammers and software company people who gave me their time and contributed lots of helpful information. They include: Betty Skov at Logitech; Franzisca Marks at Phase2 Strategies; Willy Wiegler at White Pine Software, Inc.; Brad Lowe and Helen Boltson of Rearden Technology; Susan Walton and Terry Weissman of Netscape Communications Corporation; Maggie Acuff of Dubl-Click Software; and Lisa Violet of Lisa Violet's Cat House. And let's give a hand to the shareware developers who create inexpensive, downloadable programs so you can do way-cool stuff with your cam! You'll learn about many of these programs as you read this book.

About the Author

Elisabeth Parker is the author of several computer books, including *The HotDog Pro Visual QuickStart Guide* (Peachpit Press); *The Complete Idiot's Guide to FrontPage 2000* (Macmillan); *The Microsoft Word 97 Exam Cram* (Coriolis); and *Home Page Improvement* (IDG Books Worldwide). She lives in San Francisco with her fellow computer-book author and husband, Richard Grace, and Puddy the fat, lazy cat. For more information, or just for grins, drop by Elisabeth's home page at **http://www.byteit.com/**. You can also visit the Little Web Cam Book site at **http://www.byteit.com/Cam/**.

Contents

Read Me First

You've bought a cam, or you're thinking about getting one. So now what? The *Little Web Cam Book* will get you started with creating, communicating, and having fun with your cam. So get ready to make your own screen savers, movies, and Web pages. Set up a Web cam of your very own. And start videoconferencing with friends, family, and coworkers. All you need are a cam, an Internet connection, a Web site, some inexpensive (or free) software that you can download and use right away, and this book!

What's In This Book?

Guess what? I really, really *hate* computer books. Oh, you too? Not to worry. We've organized the *Little Web Cam Book* so you always find what you're looking for quickly and easily. Feel free to use this book like a tutorial, and read through each chapter if you want. But we've also included a detailed table of contents, easy-to-find headings, and plenty of illustrations so you can skip around to topics that interest you, and quickly find whatever information you need.

This book uses the following visual cues to guide you along:

Keywords and Headings

Keywords and headings in the outside margins, like the ones you see on this page, tell you the main topic for each paragraph or task.

Boldface words and phrases make it easy to find definitions for keywords that you may be looking for.

Special icons and graphic illustrations

This book uses icons and little illustrations in the margins and other key spots to get your attention. They point out useful facts, advice to keep you out of trouble, topics that relate only to Windows or Macintosh users, and important screen elements.

> **Tips** call attention to shortcuts for getting things done, interesting software features, fun stuff you can try, and other facts that will make you a better cammer.

Danger, Will Robinson! Warning icons alert you to keep you from accidentally doing something that will prove annoying or inconvenient.

Windows only

Macintosh only

Platform Alerts. I may be a cross-platform floozy, but I also know that nobody likes to read about stuff only to find at the end of the paragraph that they can't do it on their computer anyway. The Windows and Macintosh icons you see here point out platform-specific information, so you can skip what doesn't apply to your computer system.

Part One: Getting Acquainted with Your Cam

The first part of this book tells you what stuff you need to get to start camming, and how to get your cam up and running. It also walks you through the basics for using the image- and video-editing software that comes with your cam.

Chapter 1 **Before You Begin**

The first chapter has the basics: what hardware and software you need to get started, computer/cam fundamentals, how to download files from the Web, and how to compress and decompress files with WinZip and StuffIt Expander.

- To download WinZip, go to **http://www.winzip.com/**
- To get StuffIt Expander, visit **http://www.aladdinsys.com/**

Chapter 2 **Setting Up Your Cam**

Whether you've purchased a cam product (like QuickCam), or you're planning to hook up and use your video camera, Chapter 2 shows how to set up your equipment and get acquainted with video capture software. This chapter also gives you Web sites for various hardware companies and online computer stores so you can get everything you need.

Part Two: Beautifying Your Desktop

Before you start Web camming, try some warm-up exercises. Sure, you can do fun and creative things with your cam on the Web and over the Internet. But you can also use your pictures to spiff up your desktop with custom screen-savers, icons, splash screens, and more.

Chapter 3 **Creating Your Own Screen Savers**

A+ Screen Saver for Windows and Photos4us for Macintosh make it easy to create screen savers using your favorite pictures taken with your cam.

- You can download A+ Screen Saver from **http://www.regsoft.com/**
- To get Photos4us, visit **http://www.zoetech.com/entrance/Photos4us/**

Designing the Picture-Perfect Desktop

Chapter 4

Imagine displaying a favorite photo on your desktop, instead of one of those boring patterns that everyone else uses. Or turning your pictures into icons to use on your desktop and folders. Your computer system comes with software for changing your desktop. And with MicroAngelo for Windows and IconMania! for Macintosh, you get fun and easy ways of customizing your icons.

- You can download MicroAngelo from **http://www.impactsoft.com/** and take it for a spin
- IconMania! is available in stores for $69. Or you can download and purchase the electronic version for only $39 at **http://www.dublclick.com/**

Part Three: Instant Multimedia

Having fun with your cam? Share your pictures and movies through e-mail, or put them on a Web page for the world to see. Chapters 5–7 show you some exciting applications for your photos and videos, like building GIF animations, creating and editing your own movies, and putting stuff on your home Web page.

Making GIF Animations

Chapter 5

In this chapter you'll see how to use a GIF animation program to turn favorite cam pictures into a simple animation. You can then put your creation on a Web page, e-mail it to your friends, or display it on your own computer for enjoyment.

- Windows users can try out WWW Animator by downloading it from **http://stud1.tuwien.ac.at/~e8925005/**
- Macintosh users can use GIF Builder, available at **http://iawww.epfl.ch/Staff/yves.Piguet/clip2gif-home/GifBuilder.html**

Roll 'Em! Creating and Editing Movies

Chapter 6

With the QuickEditor software, you can assemble photographs and video clips into movies and multimedia slide shows, and add audio and special effects.

- Windows and Macintosh users can get QuickEditor from **http://www.wild.ch/quickeditor/**
- Since QuickEditor makes QuickTime movies, you also need to download the latest version QuickTime for Windows and Macintosh from **http://quicktime.apple.com/**

Chapter 7 **Putting Pictures and Movies on Web Pages**

What can you do with all of your cam pictures, GIF animations, and movies? Show 'em off on the Web, of course! Chapter 7 provides a concise introduction to how Web pages work. You'll see how to place images on a Web page, link to files, embed a movie, and create a Web-page slide show.

Part Four: Web Cams

Just about anyone can set up a Web cam that automatically takes pictures of something every half hour (or however often you want), then uploads the pictures to a server and displays them on a Web page. Chapters 8–10 show you some Web cam examples and tell you how to get one up and running yourself.

Chapter 8 **Web Cams: Examples, Ideas, and Inspiration**

You can take pictures of just about anything for your Web cam. Show people how your garden's coming along, let them watch your coffee brew, or whatever else you want to expose to the big wide world. This chapter begins with a brief discussion about Web cams and then gives a quick tour of some cool Web cams for ideas and inspiration.

Chapter 9 **Setting Up Your Web Cam**

Once you get to Chapter 9, you'll be full of great ideas for Web cams and ready to get started. First, you'll need to download ISpy for Windows or SiteCam for Macintosh. You can then learn how to set up your Web cam and use the software.

- Windows users can download ISpy from **http://www.ispy.nl/**
- Mac users can grab SiteCam from **http://www.rearden.com/**

Chapter 10 **How Do They Do It? Interviews with Web Cammers**

Meet the people behind three of the Web's most popular cams, hear their stories, and learn their camming secrets. At Netscape Communications, Terry Weissman's Netscape Engineering Sign Cam displays an electric bus sign with messages from visitors to the Web site. Brad Lowe, creator of SiteCam (the Macintosh Web cam software explained in Chapter 9), offers a panoramic view of San Francisco. Lisa Violet has 18 cats—and you can probably see one of them lounging in the comfy chair right now!

Part Five: Cams and Videoconferencing

You can use your cam to keep in touch with friends and coworkers, talk face-to-face, and save on phone bills. Part Five's chapters cover videoconferencing basics, popular programs, and incorporating audio with your cam.

Chapter 11

Videoconferencing with White Pine CU-SeeMe

White Pine's CU-SeeMe is the videoconferencing program recommended in this book. It's easy to use, feature-packed, works on both Windows and Macintosh, lets you conference with groups and individuals, and gives you access to a community of millions of users around the world. Chapter 11 explains basic videoconferencing concepts while taking you through the steps of setting up the program, exploring video chat rooms, and calling up your friends.

- Windows and Macintosh users can purchase CU-SeeMe or download a trial version from White Pine's Web site at **http://www.wpine.com/**

Chapter 12

Videoconferencing Freebies

Although I recommend CU-SeeMe, there are also a few freeware videoconferencing programs out there. They don't have White Pine CU-SeeMe's range of features or its large community of users, but they're still very popular and well worth consideration. Chapter 12 introduces you to BoxTop Software's iVisit, Microsoft's NetMeeting, and the freeware version of CU-SeeMe.

- Windows and Macintosh users can download iVisit from **http://www.ivisit.com/**
- Windows users can download NetMeeting from **http://www.microsoft.com/netmeeting**
- Windows and Macintosh users (and Linux, Amiga, and OS/2 users, too!) can get the freeware version of CU-SeeMe at **http://www.rocketcharged.com/cu-seeme/**

Chapter 13

Troubleshooting, Online Help, and Fun Stuff

Most videoconferencing programs are easy to set up and use, once you get started. But sometimes they just don't work right! This chapter helps you troubleshoot when glitches occur, points you to helpful and fun videoconferencing and camming resources on the Internet, and tells you about some excellent software that you can download to make videoconferencing even more fun.

Chapter 14 **Cams and Audio**

When you think about camming, audio issues may not come immediately to mind. But if you want to videoconference, or add sounds to your movies, Web pages, and screen savers, then it helps to know how to work with sound files. Chapter 14 introduces you to digital sound basics, tells you how to record and convert audio files, points you to sound files available on the Web, and more.

List of Resources and Glossary

The List of Resources in Appendix A provides a complete catalog of all the fun and useful Web sites mentioned in this book. This list is organized by category and includes URLs and brief descriptions to jog your memory.

And if you forget what a particular technical term means, not to worry! You can look it up in the Glossary.

Ch-Ch-Changes

In the world of technology, things keep changing faster and faster these days. It's hard to keep up! I've mentioned prices for various products in this book, but they may go up or down at any time. In addition, software makers frequently update their programs to make them easier for you to use, and Web pages often change and move to different locations. If the fast pace throws you off, not to worry. I've set up a companion Web site for this *Little Web Cam Book*, and I'll be adding links, news, and updated information from time to time. Drop by **http://www.byteit.com/Cam/**, and feel free to e-mail me at **eparker@byteit.com** to ask me questions or tell me what you think.

Have fun!

Part One
Getting Acquainted with your Cam

1 Before You Begin

You've got a cam, or maybe you're thinking about buying one and setting it up. So now what? It's time to create, communicate, and have some fun. How would you like to set up a Web cam, design screen savers with your favorite photos, build animations, create movies, and videoconference face-to-face with friends and colleagues? This book tells you how to do all this and more.

Whether you're a complete novice looking for the basics or a power user who wants to add to your savvy, this book cuts straight to the chase. Headings, lists, and short paragraphs make it easy to find the information you need and skip over the stuff that doesn't interest you. You'll also find plenty of tips, warnings, and illustrations to help you along the way. So feel free to use *The Little Web Cam Book* as a handy reference, or read it cover to cover. And I promise not to ruin the fun with unnecessary computer jargon and boring technical discussions.

This chapter tells you about the following:

- Cams and Web cams—what are they?
- What you need to get started
- How to figure out what you have on your computer
- Online shareware and freeware, and how it works
- How to download files from the Web
- WinZip and StuffIt Expander, why you need them, and how to get and use them

What's a Cam?

Cam is affectionate slang for a product or combination of products that let you use your computer to take pictures, record video, and do videoconferencing. Products such as Logitech's QuickCam (shown in **Figure 1.1**), VideoLabs's FlexCam, CompPro's Dcam, and Kodak's DBC323 digital video camera are all especially made for easy camming. They plug into your computer and come with all the software and hardware that you need to get started.

Figure 1.1
Logitech's QuickCam sits on your computer.

And what's a Web cam?

I used Logitech's QuickCam for the projects described in this book because of its popularity, affordability, and user-friendliness. But you can employ any cam to do the projects explained in this book. If you already own a video camera, it's easy and inexpensive to set it up as a cam. Chapter 2 tells you more about the various types of cams, how to set them up, and how they work.

A **Web cam** automatically takes pictures and uploads them to a Web site, so visitors can meet your pets, check out your office, enjoy your view, watch your fish swim around, or see whatever your cam sees. Chapters 8 through 10 show you some cool Web cam pages and tell you how to set one up yourself.

"Web camming" is also used to describe the many things you can do with your cam on the Internet, including videoconferencing and sharing your pictures and movies via e-mail or your Web pages.

What You Need to Get Started

Do you have an Internet account and did you buy your computer within the past couple of years? If so, then relax. You probably already have most of what you need to get yourself started with camming. Newer PCs running Windows 95 or 98, and Macintosh computers running System 7.0 or higher are designed to easily handle graphics and multimedia.

A Cam-Friendly System

Before you begin, make sure you have the following system components and software:

- **A Current Operating System**: *The Little Cam Book* was written with Windows 95/98 or Macintosh System 7.0 and higher in mind. You need a computer that runs one of these systems in order to work with most of the programs discussed in this book.
- **Recent Computer Hardware**: Ideally, you should have at least a 120 MHz processor (although a 75 MHz processor will do), a minimum of 16MB of RAM, and a monitor that displays at least 256 colors. Windows users should have a 486, Pentium, or more advanced processor with a sound and video card (most computers made within the past couple of years come with video and sound capabilities). Macintosh users should have a 68040, PowerPC, G3, or more advanced processor. And finally, since you'll need to install some software and because video takes a fair amount of room, you should have at least 200-300MB available disk space.

More Hardware

- **A Cam**: To do the projects in this book, you need a cam product, such as QuickCam, that can take photographs and record video and sound. These cam products come with all the hardware and software you need. You can also use a video camera, but you'll first need to purchase some inexpensive parts to connect it to your computer. For more about connecting your cam or video camera to your computer, see Chapter 2.
- **A Microphone**: For videoconferencing and recording videos with sound, you'll need to purchase a microphone for your computer. Fortunately, microphones cost as little as $35. Windows users may also need to purchase speakers, but many computers come with speakers built in. Macs often come with a microphone as well.

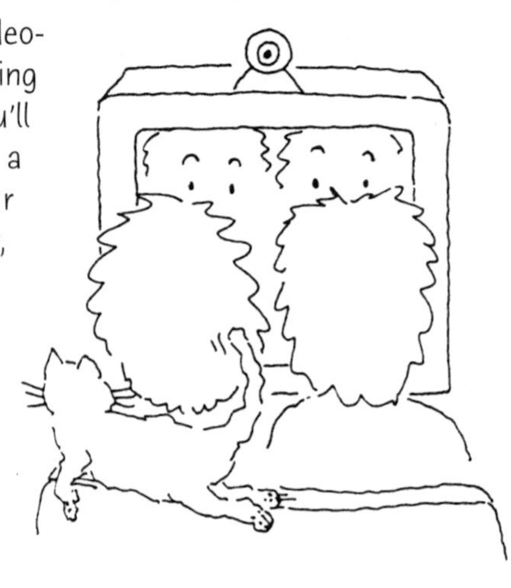

Access to the Web

- **An Internet Connection**: In order to download software, set up a Web cam, and do video conferencing, you need an Internet account. You should also have at least a 28.8 Kbps (kilobits per second) modem. Luckily, most computers come with built-in modems these days, but if you aren't wired yet, not to worry. U.S. Robotics modems are affordable, reliable, and easy to set up and use. As for getting an Internet account, companies like Earthlink, America Online, and local Internet service providers (ISPs) are ready to give you all the software you need for signing on, surfing the Web, and getting your e-mail.
- **Web Stuff**: If you want to set up a Web cam, you also need to have a program that lets you create Web pages, a working Web page, and an FTP (File Transfer Protocol) program for uploading your Web pages to the server. Most Internet service providers give you space on their server for Web pages when you sign up with your account. For creating your Web page, you can use Netscape Communicator's Composer program, or any word processing or text editing program.

For a quick tutorial in writing HTML—the markup language used for creating and formatting Web pages—and help with working with Web pages, read Elizabeth Castro's *HTML for the World Wide Web, 4th Edition, Visual QuickStart Guide* (Peachpit Press, 1998). Peachpit's *Visual Quick Start Guide* books can also get you up and running with a variety of popular Web tools.

Download Tools

- **A Web Browser**: Naturally, you need a recent version of Netscape Navigator (**http://home.netscape.com/**) or Internet Explorer (**http://www.microsoft.com/**). Most computer systems come with a Web browser—maybe even two. Most Internet service providers also include a browser with their setup software.
- **Software**: You can do most of the projects in this book with software that comes with your system or cam, or with inexpensive software that you can download from the Web. The following sections tell you where to get the software you need. If you're still new to the Web, never fear. The "Downloading Files from the Web" section of this chapter tells you how to download files.
- **WinZip (Windows) or StuffIt Expander (Macintosh)**: You can download most of the software discussed in this book from sites on the Web. But before you can install your downloaded programs, you'll need to ***decompress*** them with WinZip or StuffIt Expander. Don't worry if this doesn't make sense right now. Using compression/decompression utilities is covered in the "WinZip, StuffIt Expander, and Why You Need 'Em" section.

Are you mystified by all this?

If you're a relative newcomer to the whole wonderful world of computers, the foregoing list of components and software might sound like a lot of technobabble. What does it all mean, and how do you figure out what you've got on your system? The "Finding Hardware and System Information" section explains it all in greater detail.

Attention iMac Users

If you have an iMac, keep in mind as you read this book that the normal Macintosh rules may not apply when it comes to camming. QuickCam and other cam products plug into a printer or modem port; video cameras and camcorders, on the other hand, plug into the RCA Video or S-Video port. Alas, iMacs don't come with these types of ports. Instead, they have USB (Universal Serial Bus) ports. Make sure you buy a USB cam so you can plug it into your computer!

USBs offer numerous advantages. They let you attach up to 127 devices to your computer, and they're much easier to work with. Logitech's $129 QuickCam VC supports USB, and other manufacturers, as well, are catching up. Stay on the lookout for USB-compliant cam products and special USB-to-serial port adapters, so you can plug in your existing cam or video camera. Chapter 2 tells you more about cams and USB ports.

Finding Hardware and System Information

Yikes! A few more RAMs, Kbps, and MHz, and we'll have a nice tasty bowl of alphabet soup! I've told you what hardware and operating system you need to do the camming thang. And as promised, I won't leave you stranded trying to figure out what you've got, and what you should use it for. So let's begin with some basic computer definitions.

Terms to Know

- **Operating System**: The operating system tells your computer how to run, and also determines which programs will work on your particular computer. For example, you cannot run a Windows program on a Macintosh, and vice versa. Newer operating systems can usually run programs that were created for an older version of the same operating system. For example, Windows 95 software works on Windows 98, and Macintosh System 7 software works with System 8. However, programs created for newer operating systems won't always work on older operating systems.

  A particular operating system will have a particular **interface** that determines how you work with the computer. For example, you may have to enter text commands in order to do things (as with DOS and UNIX), or you may be able to click on **icons** and select information from **menus** and **dialog boxes** (as with Windows and Macintosh).

- **Processor**: The *processor*—shorthand for central processing unit (CPU)—is a piece of hardware in your computer. It determines how fast the computer can run. The faster the processor, the more quickly you can launch applications and do things on your computer. Types of processors include 486 (short for 80486), Pentium, and MMX for Windows; and the 68040, PowerPC, and G3 for Macintosh. The 486 and 68040 are the oldest and slowest processors that you can get by with these days. The Pentium and PowerPC processors are faster and perfectly adequate for most people; the newer MMX and G3 processors are superfast. Processor speeds are measured in *megaHertz* (MHz). The more MHz, the faster the processor.

Upgrades: Many computer systems allow you to upgrade your processor. Processor upgrades cost a couple of hundred dollars and up, depending on the kind of processor you want. You can go to a local computer store, ask how much the processor costs, and have a technician install it for you.

- **RAM**: RAM stands for **Random Access Memory**, which determines how many tasks a computer can handle at once without slowing down or crashing. The more programs you intend to have running at once (for example, your Internet dialer, your Web browser, and an e-mail program), and the more complex the data you work with, the more memory you need. Videos, for instance, are very complex; they involve images, motion, and often sound. Therefore, video player and videoconferencing applications require a substantial amount of RAM to run well. I recommend at least 32MB of RAM for happy camming.

Adding Memory: Most computer systems let you add more memory when you need it. Memory is very inexpensive these days. Memory chips come on a board that you can insert in a special memory slot inside of your computer. If you prefer not to mess around with your computer's innards, go to your local computer store and have them take care of it.

- **Color Display**: Computer monitors generally come in three flavors: 256 colors, thousands of colors, and millions of colors. Most people these days have at least a 256-color monitor.
- **Free Disk Space**: Think of your computer as a room that has only so much space. Just as you would measure your living room before buying another couch, you should measure your hard disk to make sure you have enough room to install more applications and store your pictures and movies. Disk space is measured in **megabytes** (MB). Each MB is equivalent to about one floppy disk full of information.
- **Modem**: You need a *modem* in order to connect to the Internet, and you need a modem that's fast enough to surf the Web, download software, and do videoconferencing. The modem connects your computer to a phone line. Modem speed is measured in **kilobits per second** (Kbps). A 14.4 Kbps modem is the minimum required for using the Web. More typical are 28.8 Kbps, 33.6 Kbps, and 56 Kbps modems. In addition, speedier connections are possible through special types of connections such as ISDN and cable modems. The more Kbps per second, the speedier the modem.

- **Network Connection**: If you access the Internet through work or school, then you probably dial up through a local area network (LAN) rather than with a modem. Network connections offer lots of advantages when it comes to video-conferencing and Web cams, including faster connections and direct access to the server. However, you should talk to your department head and your network administrator before you start camming.

So now, with these definitions under your belt, how do you find out what you've got?

What's My CPU?

To determine the type and speed of your central processing unit (processor), look on the computer casing. The label should say something like Pentium/266, or Power Macintosh 7600/132. The first part tells you the processor model, and the second part with the three-digit number tells you the processor speed. In other words, Pentium/266 means a 266 MHZ Pentium processor.

Windows Version and RAM

Windows only

To determine which version of Windows you're running and how much RAM you have, follow these steps:

1. Click the My Computer icon with the *right* mouse button (**right-click**) to display the pop-up menu. (If there is no My Computer icon on the desktop, then you're running Windows 3.x and need to upgrade.)
2. Select Properties to display the **System Properties** dialog box.
3. Make sure the General tab is selected. The General tab of System Properties displays the operating system version at the top, and the amount of RAM toward the bottom of the displayed information. To close the System Properties dialog box, click the Close button (X).
4. To determine how much disk space you have available on your hard drive, double-click on the My Computer icon on the desktop.

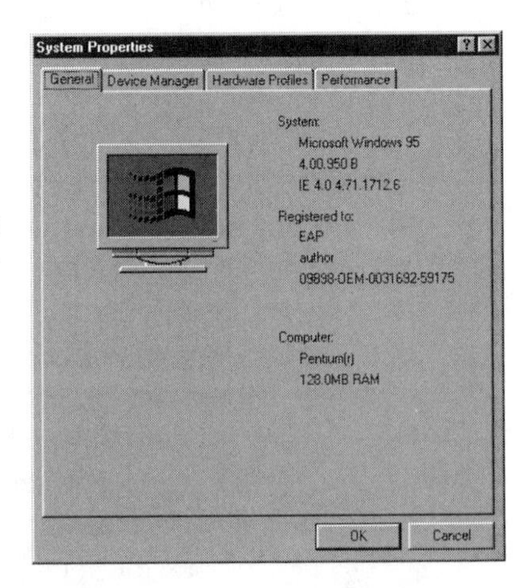

5. In the My Computer window, right-click on the icon representing your hard drive (in most cases, the C: drive) to display the pop-up menu.
6. Select Properties, and make sure the General tab is selected. The amount of space available (Free Space) is displayed in both bytes and megabytes. To close the Properties dialog box, click the Close button (X).

Mac Version and RAM

Macintosh only

Follow these steps to determine which version of Mac OS you're running, and how much RAM and free disk space you have:

1. From the Apple menu, select the **About This Computer** option.
2. The About This Computer dialog box displays the operating system version on top.
3. To see how much memory (RAM) you have, look at the number next to Built-in Memory. 
4. To see how much disk space you have available, look at the number next to the Largest Unused Block item.
5. To close the dialog box, click the Close box at the top-left on the title bar.

Shareware and Freeware on the Web

What's one of the coolest things about the Web? Downloadable goodies! You can find all kinds of cool pictures, multimedia, documents, snazzy fonts, shareware, and more on the web. To do the projects in this book, you'll first need to get your shareware programs.

What's **shareware**? It's the same thing as regular software, except that you get to try before you buy. Some software makers refer to their downloadable shareware as an "evaluation version," because you get to evaluate the program. If you like the software, you can pay for it. If you don't find the software very useful, you can remove it from your computer. Shareware programs generally come with some sort of documentation (instructions for use), even if it's just a plain old text file with no pictures. We'll be downloading a few shareware programs to do the projects in this book.

You can also find lots of **freeware** on the Web. Yes, *freeware*. You don't have to pay for it. Some of the best things in life really *are* free! Including CU-SeeMe, a videoconferencing program that you'll learn how to use in Chapters 12 through 14.

What's the deal on freeware?

Why would anyone distribute programs for free? Some people simply love programming and offer their work out of the goodness of their hearts. Many companies, as well, offer freeware to promote their other marketed products. For example, Apple allows its QuickTime movie viewer to be downloaded free by both Windows and Macintosh users from **http://quicktime.apple.com/**. Why? Because without QuickTime nobody would be able to see all these wonderful movies. And Microsoft (**http://www.microsoft.com/**) and Netscape (**http://home.netscape.com/**) offer their Web browsers free of charge to promote their Web server and development products.

Using and Registering Shareware

How does shareware work? It depends on the software maker. Some programs display a "nag screen" every time you launch the program. The nag screen reminds you to pay for and register the software. Some programs stop running after a certain period of time (generally 14 to 30 days) unless you register and pay, and other programs won't let you use certain features without a valid registration code. On the other hand, many applications never pester you or stop working, because the programmer trusts you to be nice and pay up eventually.

With most shareware programs, you can either pay online with a credit card, or mail the authors a check or money order. Some programs even provide a built-in feature that helps you register and pay online. When the software maker receives payment, they will e-mail you a registration code and instructions for ***unlocking*** the program. Once you enter your registration code to unlock the program, it will function normally—without nag screens and with all the features fully enabled.

Web registration

Many shareware authors offer a registration form on their Web site that you can fill out. When you provide your contact and payment information and submit the form, your browser may display a scary-looking security warning. Don't worry. The browser just wants to let you know that you're about to send off your information, in case you want to change your mind. Most people who sell products and software online use a **secure server** to keep your credit card information safe.

Support Shareware!

If you try out a shareware application and you like it, please pay the programmer so he or she won't starve!

Downloading Files from the Web

When you visit a software maker's Web site, it will display a link to the page that gives information about their software, and a link for **downloading** the file. Links to downloadable shareware programs will usually say something like "Evaluate," "Get It!" or "Download." Some software makers—even the ones who offer freeware—will often want you to fill out a form at the Web site and provide your name and e-mail address before you can get your goodies.

"But I don't know *how* to download files!"

No problem—we'll fix that right now. Depending on your browser and operating system, menu items and dialog boxes used for downloading may vary slightly, but the basic steps are the same.

Steps for downloading files:

1. In Windows, click your right mouse button (right-click) on the link to the file. On a Macintosh, click your mouse on the link to the file and hold the mouse button down to display the shortcut menu.
2. Select the Save Link As or Save Target As option from the shortcut menu.
3. When the Save As dialog box appears, as shown in **Figure 1.2**, browse for the folder you want to use as the location for your downloaded file.
4. Click the Save button.

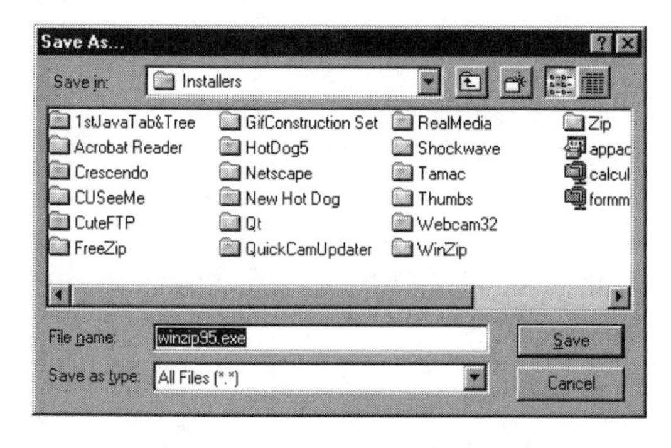

Figure 1.2
A Save As dialog box as displayed in Netscape Communicator for Windows. (Similar dialog boxes appear in Internet Explorer and on Macintosh browsers.)

A status dialog box appears, telling you approximately how long the file will take to download and displaying the progress of the download. Download time depends on the file size and your connection speed.

Don't Lose That Download

"Whoops, where did my download go?"

You know the file is there somewhere, because it took five minutes to download. But where is it? **When you click a link instead of displaying the shortcut menu** and selecting the Save Link As or Save Target As option, your browser may download your file without asking where you want to put it. If only we always knew where the browser's default folder is!

If you're ever caught unawares in this situation, there are two ways to deal with the problem. You can continue with the download, make note of the filename, and then search for it with your system's Find function. Or you can cancel the download and then force the Save As dialog box to appear, as I explained in the "Steps for downloading" task list earlier in this chapter.

What's a Beta?

When you download shareware and freeware, you may notice that some Web sites feature links to a **beta version** of the software. *Beta* is ancient computer geek-speak for "software that doesn't really work." Just kidding. The term comes from the ancient Greek word for "second."

When software makers are working on a new version of their software, they first create an alpha (Greek for "first") version as a prototype. Then they move on to the beta phase—a more complete version of the software. Software developers like to promote the upcoming release and get feedback from potential customers by letting people download and try out the betas. Betas generally run fairly well but still have bugs (software glitches) and lack instructions.

Sneak preview!

Think of a beta as a sneak preview of an upcoming movie. The producers have almost completed the movie and plan to play it in theaters within the next few months. But they may change some of the scenes based on feedback from the audience. **Beta downloads give you the chance to try out programs** that are often only available in stores. There's nothing seriously risky about downloading and using beta programs, but more often than not they can act a little flaky. If you feel comfortable with computers, go ahead and dive off the cutting edge. Otherwise, stick with established programs with a user manual.

Where to Get Shareware and Freeware

If something can be done on a computer, chances are someone has written a shareware or freeware program that does it. But how do you find them? Well, you can pick up a book like this one that tells you about some cool programs. Or, you can visit one of the many shareware/freeware megasites on the Web. These Web sites have huge collections of shareware and freeware, which you can search through by keywords or browse by category.

Here's a handy list of Web sites that offer downloadable software:

Web Sites for Downloadable Software	Description
The Ultimate Collection of Winsock Software (TUCOWS) *http://www.tucows.com/*	Despite the name of this site, TUCOWS has Macintosh programs, too. The site is well organized and offers quick reviews of various programs with ratings on a scale of one to five cows.
Shareware.Com *http://www.shareware.com* **Download.Com** *http://www.download.com*	Hosted by C|Net (http://www.cnet.com), which offers all sorts of information about computers and cutting-edge technologies on the Web. You can find just about anything under the sun at these sites; however, not all of the programs are reviewed and rated.
HotFiles.Com *http://www.hotfiles.com/* **Macdownload.Com** *http://www.macdownload.com/*	Hosted by Ziff Davis (http://www.zdnet.com/), publishers of computer magazines such as *PCWeek* and *MacWeek*, these sites have tons of shareware accompanied by meaty reviews and ratings. HotFiles is for Windows users, and Macdownload is for Macintosh users.

Decompression Utilities: Why You Need 'Em

You can download most of the software discussed in this book, and all kinds of other neat stuff, from the Web. But to put the programs to work, you need to **decompress** them.

Software makers **compress** their files to make them smaller so you can download them faster. Otherwise the file transfers take forever (and sometimes they seem to take forever anyway!). Once you've downloaded the files, you have to decompress them in order to use them. If that doesn't make sense to you, think of instant soup. You buy it in a small package that you can store or carry around easily. But when you add hot water to "decompress" it, voilà! You have a whole cup of soup.

__Compressed File Types__: Compressed WinZip and StuffIt files are also called __archives__. WinZip files have the .ZIP filename extension and StuffIt files have the .HQX, .SEA, or .SIT filename extension, as in file.zip and file.hqx.

Windows developers often compress files with Nico Mak's WinZip, and most Macintosh developers compress files with Aladdin Systems's StuffIt. You'll need to have the decompression utilities—WinZip for Windows or StuffIt Expander for Macintosh—to decode compressed files.

Getting WinZip

Windows only

WinZip is a $29 shareware program that you can download from Nico Mak's Web site at **http://www.winzip.com**. You can try out the program for 30 days, but it's a very good idea to go ahead and purchase it, because just about everyone in the "Wintel world" (Windows operating system, Intel processors) zips their files before distributing them on the Web or sending them as e-mail attachments. The WinZip site's main page has a link to the download page, and also provides information about the program.

Installing WinZip

Once you've downloaded WinZip (it'll take about 15 minutes to a half hour, depending on your connection speed), it's easy to install. At the time of this writing, Niko Mac was not yet offering a WinZip for Windows 98, but the Windows 95 version should work just fine if you're running Windows 98.

Steps for installing WinZip:

1. Display the Setup dialog box by clicking the WinZip installer icon (it looks like a yellow file cabinet clenched in a vise and is named **WinZip95.exe** or **WinZip98.exe**). Then click the Setup button.
2. When the second Setup dialog box appears, click the OK button. The WinZip installer unzips the files, creates a WinZip folder on your computer, and installs the program.
3. Another Setup dialog box appears. Click the Next button to display the License Agreement And Warranty disclaimer, and then click Yes to agree and return to the Setup dialog box. (You can also click the Read The Agreement button if you want to take a look.)
4. The next dialog box tells you that the WinZip Wizard option is easier to use. But Wizards can get pretty annoying when they do things automatically without asking you. So for now, click the Start With WinZip Classic radio button and then the Next button to move on to the next Setup dialog box.
5. Click the Express Setup radio button and then the Next button.
6. Click the Finish button. The WinZip application window now appears, so you can start using the program.
7. To close the program, click the Close box (X) on the title bar, or select Exit from the File menu.

Creating a Shortcut

Shortcuts help you keep your programs handy on the Windows desktop. You can launch an application by double-clicking the shortcut icon instead of clicking the Start button and walking through all those menus.

When you install WinZip, the installation program should automatically create a shortcut to the application window and put it on your desktop for you. If you don't see the shortcut, you can easily create one.

To create a shortcut for WinZip (or any application), follow these steps:

1. Open the application's program folder (usually located in the C:\Programs folder).
2. Right-click the application icon.
3. Select Create Shortcut from the shortcut menu.
4. Drag the shortcut icon to your desktop.

Unzipping Files with WinZip

Now, with WinZip installed, you can **unzip** downloaded files that were compressed with WinZip. Here are the steps:

1. Launch WinZip. First click the Start button, click Programs, choose the WinZip folder from the cascading menu, and then select WinZip.

   The first time you use the program, a dialog box appears and asks whether you want to use the WinZip Wizard or WinZip Classic. Select the WinZip Classic option.

You can also launch WinZip by simply double-clicking a .ZIP file in any folder.

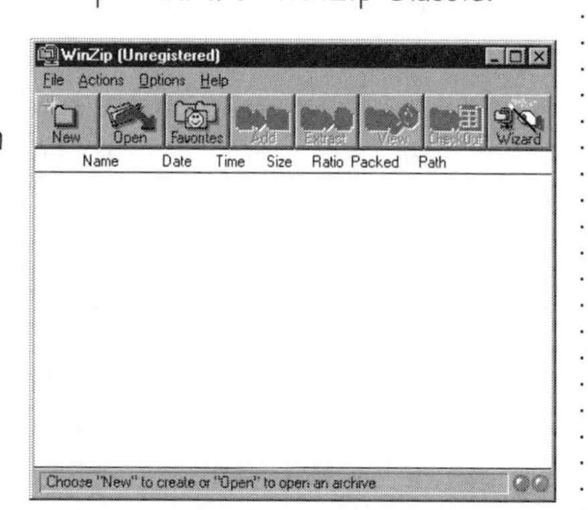

2. When the WinZip application window launches, click the Open button on the toolbar.
3. When the Open Archive dialog box appears, browse for the zipped file you want to open. Select the file and click OK.
4. In the list of files contained in the archive, choose Select All from the Actions menu to select all the files. Then click the Extract button in the toolbar.
5. In the Extract dialog box, browse for the folder in which you want to put the unzipped files. Then click the Extract button.

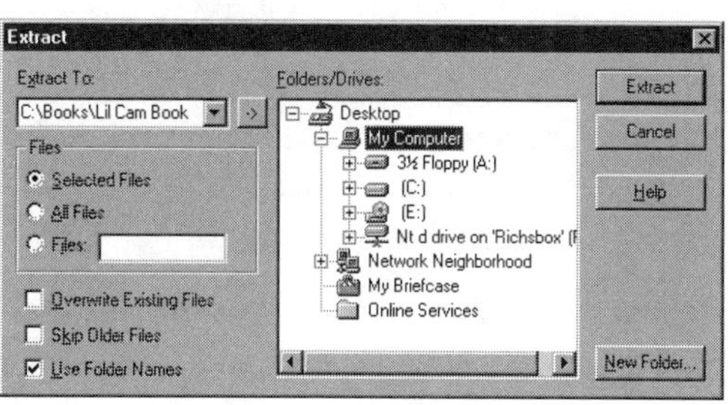

The unzipped files appear in the folder you select. There, now wasn't that easy?

You can also open stuffed Macintosh (.HQX) files with WinZip.

Zipping Files with WinZip

You can also compress **large files or groups of files** and zip 'em up with WinZip. This comes in especially handy when you want to send someone a few photographs or a movie by e-mail.

1. Start up WinZip by clicking the Start button, then Programs, and then WinZip. From the cascading menu, select the WinZip application.
2. When the WinZip application window launches, click the New button in the toolbar.
3. In the New Archive dialog box, browse for the folder in which you want to create the new zipped archive, or click the New Folder button to create a new folder. Type a name for the file in the File Name text box, and click OK.
4. The Add dialog box appears. Select the file or a group of files to zip (you can select more than one file by holding down the shift key while selecting them). Then click the Add button.

   WinZip compresses the files, returns you to the WinZip application window, and displays the files you selected on the list.
5. To compress and add more files to the archive, click the Add button and repeat step 4.
6. When you finish adding files, select Exit from the File menu.

After you've registered your WinZip program, you'll be able to create **self-extracting zip files**. These zip files don't require WinZip to unzip them, which means you can send them to anyone you want, without worrying about whether they have a copy of WinZip available.

StuffIt Expander

Macintosh only

Most people in the Macintosh world use Aladdin Systems's program, StuffIt, to compress files. In order to open or use these files, you need to decompress them with StuffIt Expander. Fortunately, StuffIt Expander is free and you can download it from Aladdin's Web site at **http://www.aladdinsys.com/**.

Compressed Macintosh files are **binhex encoded** and have either the .BIN or .HQX filename extension. Files compressed with StuffIt also sometimes have the .SEA or .SIT filename extension. StuffIt Expander can handle all of these file formats.

> **StuffIt Deluxe.** If you want to compress files yourself (and this does come in handy when you want to send pictures and movies to your friends and family), or open zipped files from your Windows-using associates, then you need to buy StuffIt Deluxe. It costs $79.95, and you can order it on Aladdin's Web site or buy it in a computer store.

You may already have StuffIt Expander

Because StuffIt Expander is so popular, you might already have it on your computer. It may have come bundled with your system, or on your ISP's CD-ROM, or as part of another software package. If you use a computer at school or work, your network administrator may have installed it on your machine. Go to your desktop and select Find from the Edit menu to launch the Find File utility. Enter the keyword **Expander** to see if you have the program already. If you do, then you're all set.

Updating an Existing Version

Even if you have StuffIt Expander, it's a good idea to visit the Aladdin Systems Web site at **http://www.aladdinsys.com/** and download the latest version. When you get to the Web site, follow the instructions, fill out the registration form (they want your name, e-mail address, and zip code), and download the file.

MacBinary version downloads faster

Aladdin Systems lets you choose the **BinHex** or the **MacBinary** version. I recommend the MacBinary file because it takes less time to download. Once you've got the file, you can use your older version of StuffIt Expander to unstuff the new file.

What's the filename?

The MacBinary version of the StuffIt Expander file is named stuffit_exp_45_installer.bin. The number 45 may change depending on the current version of StuffIt Expander. For example, when StuffIt Expander 5.0 comes out, Aladdin Systems will name the file stuffit_exp_50_installer.bin.

For instructions on expanding files, see "Unstuffing Files with StuffIt Expander," coming up.

Catch 22?

If you don't already have an older version of StuffIt Expander, then you've got a little bit of a quandary. The downloadable file is **binary** (.BIN) encoded, which means you need an existing version of StuffIt Expander to open it! I find this extremely annoying. But there are a couple of ways to get around it.

The easiest solution is to ask a Macintosh-savvy friend or colleague to simply give you a copy of StuffIt Expander. Since the software is freeware, this is perfectly legal. The other solution is to ask Aladdin Systems to send you StuffIt Expander via e-mail. They'll send you the binary-encoded (.BIN) version of the program, but most Macintosh e-mail programs automatically decode binary files.

Getting StuffIt Expander via e-mail

To receive a binary-encoded version of **StuffIt Expander by e-mail** so your e-mail program can automatically decode it:

1. Send an e-mail message addressed to **info@aladdinsys.com.**
2. In the Subject line of the message, enter **getexpander**. Do *not* write anything in the body of the message.
3. Within 48 hours (often sooner), you'll receive StuffIt Expander via e-mail.

Your e-mail program will store the StuffIt Expander installer in its attachments, cache, or temp folder, depending on which e-mail program you use. Some e-mail programs display an icon for the attachment as part of the e-mail message. If so, you can double-click the icon to launch the installer straight from the message.

Installing StuffIt Expander

Once you've decompressed the StuffIt Expander file, the StuffIt Expander Installer icon appears—either on your desktop or in the folder you selected for your file.

To install StuffIt Expander:

1. Double-click the StuffIt Expander Installer icon. A dialog box appears, with Aladdin Systems application and contact information.
2. Click the Continue button. The Welcome message and installation instructions appear. You can read this file, and save or print the document for future reference by clicking the Save or Print button. When you finish, click the Continue button.
3. Next you'll see the License agreement. Read it and click the Agree button.
4. In the next dialog box, you can begin installing StuffIt Expander. Click the Install button, and you'll see the dialog box shown in **Figure 1.7**, suggesting a folder in which to install StuffIt Expander. If you're comfortable with computers and want to use a different folder, you can browse for it and select it; otherwise, don't change anything.

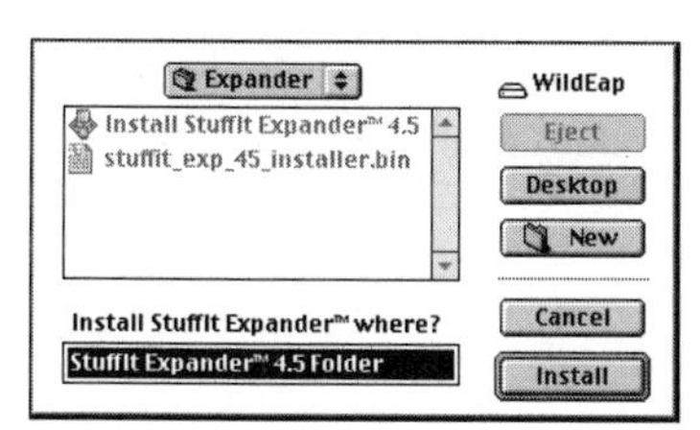

Figure 1.7 *The StuffIt Expander install program chooses a folder in which to install the program. You can also browse for a different folder.*

5. Click the Install button.
6. The Installing dialog box appears and tells you which files are being installed. When the installation finishes, you'll see a message to this effect; click OK.

Creating an Alias

Now, you may want to do one more thing: Make an alias and put it on your desktop so that you can easily find StuffIt Expander when you need it. Or, you can put the alias in your System\Apple Menu Items folder so it appears on your Apple menu. An **alias** is an icon that represents an application. You can put the alias anywhere you want on your computer.

To make a StuffIt Expander alias:

1. When you install StuffIt Expander, it automatically opens the application folder for you, as shown in **Figure 1.8**. Click the StuffIt Expander icon.

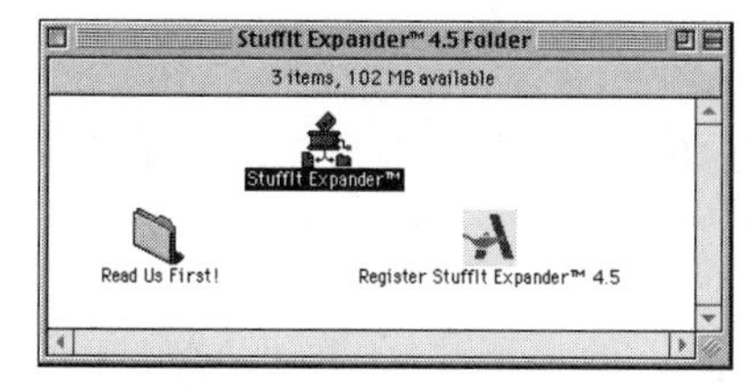

Figure 1.8
StuffIt Expander application folder

2. Select Make Alias from the File menu, or press ⌘M.
3. When the Stuff It Expander alias appears, drag it to your desktop. You can close the StuffIt Expander folder now if you want.
4. If you want the alias to appear on your Apple menu, open the System folder and drag the alias into the Apple Menu folder.

Unstuffing Files with StuffIt Expander

Decompressing—or **unstuffing**—files is easy with StuffIt Expander. You can even set up your Web browser to automatically launch StuffIt Expander whenever you download a .BIN, .HQX, .SIT, or .SEA file.

- To expand a stuffed file, simply double-click on the file, or select it and drag it onto the StuffIt Expander application icon or alias.

Alternate method

- On occasion, you may find that double-clicking or dragging the stuffed file's icon doesn't work. But don't worry. Unless the file is damaged (which does happen once in a while), you can still expand the file by **opening it from within the StuffIt Expander application.**

Here are the steps to expand a file from within the StuffIt Expander application:

1. Double-click the StuffIt Expander application icon or alias. You will not see an application window, but the menu bar will change.
2. Select Expand from the File menu.
3. The Expander dialog box appears. It works similarly to the Open dialog box in most applications. Browse for your file, select it from the list, and click the Expand button.

To close StuffIt Expander, select Quit from the File menu.

Stuffing Files with StuffIt Deluxe

If you have a version of StuffIt Deluxe installed, then you can also compress files for sending to other people or so you can offer the files for download from your Web site. You can also open WinZip-compressed files!

When you install StuffIt Deluxe, it creates a **DropStuff icon alias** on your desktop. When you want to stuff a group of files, place the files in a folder, drag the folder onto the DropStuff icon, and voilà! StuffIt compresses the files.

Summary

Okay, maybe this chapter wasn't terribly exciting. But before you can start camming and unearthing the Web's many treasures for cammers (including the shareware programs covered in this book), you do need an adequate computer system and knowledge of how to download files.

- **Cam** refers to a setup that lets you take pictures and record movies on your computer. You can buy a stand-alone cam product like Logitech's QuickCam, or use a regular video camera with a video card or inexpensive adapter.
- A **Web cam** is simply a cam that takes pictures and uploads them to a Web site. The term also loosely covers the many ways you can create, communicate, and share pictures with cams over the Internet.
- **Camming** requires a computer with a recent operating system (Windows 95, Windows 98, or Macintosh system 7.0 and higher), a color monitor, a speedy processor, sufficient RAM and free disk space, and an Internet connection. You also may need to purchase speakers and a microphone if you want to videoconference with audio.
- If you don't know what you've got on your computer, it's easy to find out. Check the label on your computer case, and bring up the dialog box on your computer that tells you your **system information**.
- **Shareware** is software that you can download from the Web and take for a spin before you pay for it. Some programmers also offer **freeware**, which you don't have to pay for. You'll need to download a few shareware and freeware programs to do the projects in this book.
- To **download** software from a Web page, right-click the link (Windows) or click the link and hold down the mouse button (Macintosh). When the shortcut menu appears, select Save Link As or Save Target As (depending on your browser) to display the Save As dialog box. You can then choose where you want to save your file.

- It is customary for software developers to let people take **betas** for a spin. Betas are prerelease versions of upcoming software. This gives you a chance to try out cool programs—new or updated—that are often only available in stores.
- Programmers usually **compress** their applications so you can download them faster. In order to **decompress** the applications so you can install and use them, you need a decompression utility like **WinZip** for Windows or **StuffIt Expander** for Macintosh.

Now that we've gone over the basics, let's move on to Chapter 2, which tells you how to unpack, set up, and start using your cam.

2 Setting Up Your Cam

So, you've got a cam. Or you're thinking of getting one. Either way, read this chapter first! Fortunately, today's cams are quite simple to set up and use. Most people can get one up and running without a hitch, and in a matter of minutes to boot. Then again, some people have rotten luck. They unpack their cam at two in the morning, only to find out that they need some silly adapter or thingamabob. Unless you've got a computer store in your area with 24-hour delivery, a little reading may save you time and trouble.

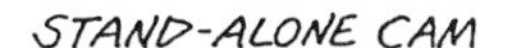

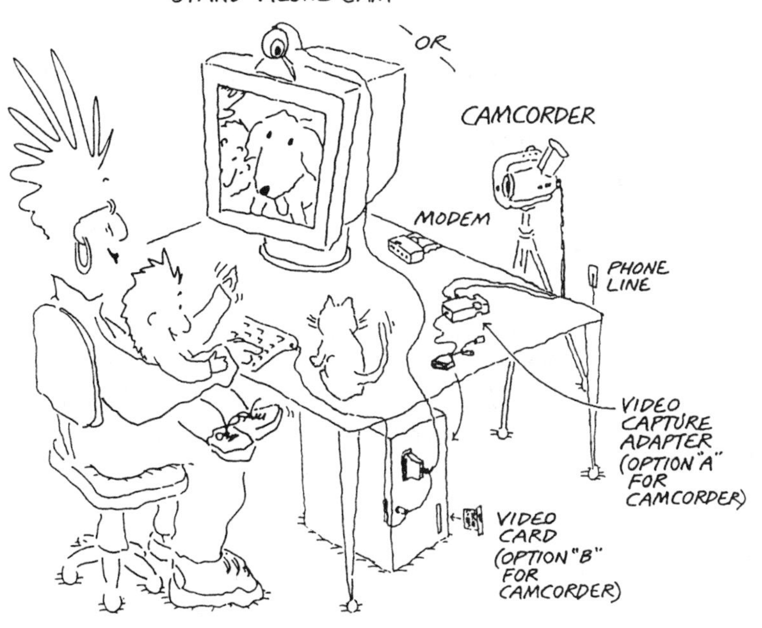

Whether you're looking into buying a cam, or you have one and want to set it up, I aim to make it as quick and painless as possible. This chapter tells you about different types of cam setups. It also introduces you to typical cam video and image settings, so you can can get your pictures and movies to look the way you want them to. Feel free to skip over any boring hardware stuff—you can always flip back to this chapter if you need to.

This chapter tells you how to do the following:

- Unpack your cam.
- Connect your cam to your computer.
- Add more ports so you can connect more stuff to your computer.
- Use a handheld video camera as your cam.
- Get acquainted with your cam software and basic imaging and video settings.
- Find image and video editing programs so you can get creative with your pictures and movies!

Prices keep changing! The prices I've given for the hardware products in this chapter were accurate when I wrote this book. But they change all the time and often vary with different stores. Fortunately, prices go down more often than up!

What's Available?

There are many decent, inexpensive cams around, and you can pick up a good one for between $100 and $300, depending on the features you want. **Creative Labs**, **VideoLabs**, **Connectix**, **Logitech**, **ARS Innovations**, and several other companies compete, offering their own versions of these affordable and quirky devices. Some of these companies even manufacture a variety of cams with assorted features, priced for different budgets.

A Few Cam Products

- **QuickCam by Logitech**: I recommend Logitech's Color QuickCam ($199) and I use it in the examples throughout this book. Why? It gives you the most bang for the buck, works with just about every type of computer and video/imaging program, and over one million people already happily use QuickCam. If you're on a budget, you can get the older, grayscale QuickCam for less than $100. Or you can try the $139 QuickCam VC for parallel ports and USB. For more information, visit **http://www.quickcam.com/**.

But I Thought Connectix Made QuickCam Well, they used to, but Logitech bought QuickCam from Connectix in summer 1998. Logitech's a much bigger company, so you can look forward to more support and more availability of QuickCam products in more stores.

- **Compro Dcam**: ARS Innovations's cam enjoys modest popularity. It works with many software programs and costs about $100. For more information, visit **http://www.ascompro.com/**.

- **VideoBlaster WebCam II**: Creative Labs, maker of high-end digital video products, has now stepped into the camming market with their $99 Video Blaster WebCam II for Windows. Mac users can get the Video Blaster Web Cam Color Video Camera for $149. For more information, visit **http://www.cle.creaf.com/**.

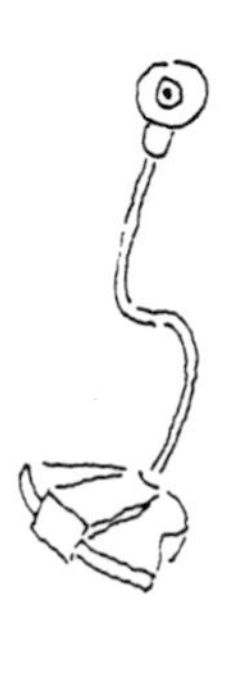

- **VideoLabs FlexCam and Planet View**: The $199 FlexCam for Windows makes for great camming. VideoLabs's line of cams offer superior image quality, and the cam sits atop an 18-inch gooseneck that you can swivel around. If you're looking into a videoconferencing system for the office, you may also want to give the $399 Planet View for Windows and Macintosh a serious look. Yes, it costs more, plus you have to buy a video card. But you get flexibility, crisp pictures at various distances, and professional videoconferencing software. For more information, visit **http://www.FlexCam.com/**.
- **CU-SeeMe Cam Kit for Windows**: If you plan to do a lot of videoconferencing, check out White Pine's $124 CU-SeeMe Cam Kit for Windows (**http://www.wpine.com/**). It even comes with CU-SeeMe videoconferencing software, covered in Chapter 11.

Unpacking Your Cam

So, what's in the box? When you unpack your cam, you'll find the cam itself, some means of connecting it to your computer, a manual, and a CD-ROM or a floppy disk or two with the cam software that you'll need to install.

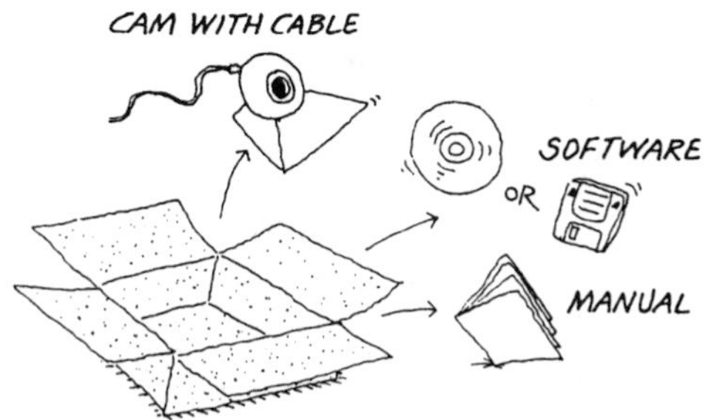

The Camera

What does a cam look like? That depends. Logitech's QuickCam looks like a billiard ball with a lens. The VideoBlaster WebCam II is shaped like an egg, and ARS Innovations made its Compro Dcam to look somewhat like a conventional camera.

For the most part, cams are rather small critters that fit easily in the palm of your hand. They sit obediently on top of your computer, or you can move them anywhere you want—as far as the connection cable will stretch! You can buy a serial extension cord, but alas, that may not help—some cams lose their power when they wander more than about 12 feet from your computer.

A Way to Connect It

The way your cam connects to your computer depends on what kind of computer you have. It'll hook up in one of three ways:

- Through your parallel port **(Windows)**
- Through your printer or modem serial port **(Macintosh)**
- Through a USB port **(newer versions of Windows 95, Windows 98, or Macintosh System 8.5)**

If this sounds like a mess of gobbledy gook right now, don't worry. When you finish reading the following sections, you'll know what kind of connection you've got.

If your cam connects through the parallel port or serial port, it may also come with a **keyboard adapter** (also called a **keyboard pass-through**). One end of the adapter plugs into the keyboard port (you need to unplug your keyboard connector first), and the other end provides a port so you can plug your keyboard back in again. Why bother playing musical plugs? Your cam needs electricity from the port in order to run.

When it comes to cams, taking a picture is often called ***capturing a frame****, and recording video is called* ***capturing video****.*

USB ports work as power sources, as well, so you can plug a USB camera straight into your computer without worrying about the power supply.

We'll look more closely at the various types of connections in upcoming sections.

Cam Software

Cams come with software so you can take pictures, record video, and tweak your image and video settings a bit. The software also tells your computer to recognize the cam.

These cam programs only give you the basic tools. If you plan on getting more creative with your pictures and movies, you'll need a couple of decent image- and video-editing programs. I recommend a few of them at the end of this chapter.

Cams and USB Ports

USB (Universal Serial Bus) provides a new way to connect stuff like cams and printers to your computer. In fact, the Macintosh iMacs *only* have USB ports. When you have a USB cam, like Logitech's QuickCam VC, you don't have to worry about your cam hogging up your printer and modem ports, or your parallel port. Recent Pentium II and MMX PCs even come with USB ports built in—look at the back of your computer and you'll see them.

Plugging in Your USB Cam

To plug in your USB cam, grab the rectangular USB connector and put it in the rectangular USB port on the back of your computer. That's all there is to it! Oh, you don't have USB? Keep reading...

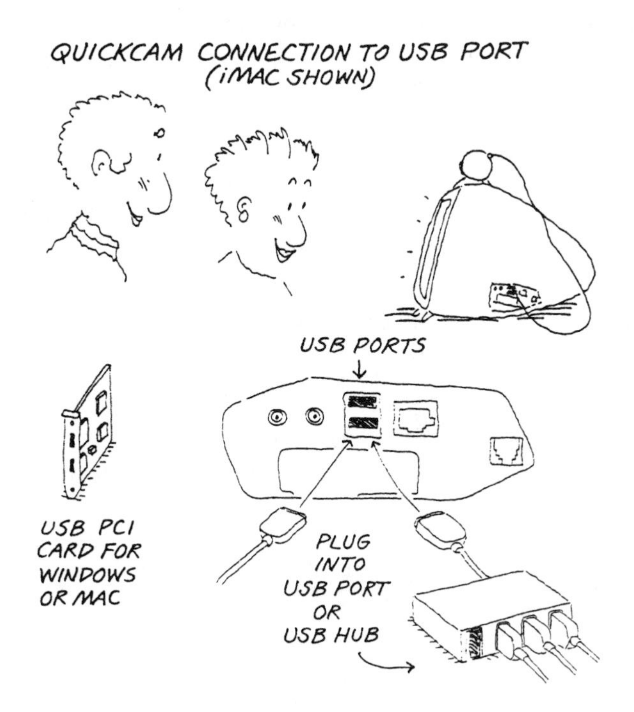

Attention iMac Users: If you use an iMac and have a serial port cam, don't panic. Buy a USB-to-serial-port adapter. UConnect sells one through MacMall (**http://www.macmall.com/**) for $59.

Getting on the (Universal Serial) Bus

If you've got an older Pentium PC running Windows 98, or a PowerMac 7200 or above running System 8.5, you don't have to buy a whole new computer just to use USB. That's like throwing the baby out with the bath water! Instead, you can buy a **PCI-based USB card** and slip it into your computer. PCI stands for Peripheral Component Interconnect. Invented by Intel, PCI has become the standard way to add hardware capabilities to your computer.

Most of the PowerMacs also use PCI cards. Unfortunately, iMacs do not come with PCI slots, but that's okay because they have USB ports built in.

Belkin Components (**http://www.belkin.com**) offers a $79 USB card for Windows, and Keyspan (**http://www.keyspan.com/**) makes a $59 USB card for Macintosh.

Need More USB Ports?

Hold everything. What if you need more USB ports? You can buy a **USB hub**. It turns a single USB port into many ports, usually four or eight. You can find USB hubs at almost any computer store for well under $100. Some of the newer computer monitors build a USB hub into their base.

Watch for hub quality. The inexpensive ones may not work as well. Windows and Macintosh users can purchase the Belkin and Keyspan products mentioned just above. Macintosh users can also get the $79 Macally iHub at **http://www.macally.com**.

USB Caveats

After all this enthusiastic talk about USB, I hate to poop on the parade. But keep in mind that USB is a highly promising technology that still has a ways to go. Let's see what that means.

First of all, if you want to use USB ports, you'll have to upgrade to Windows 98, Windows 95 with USB support, or Macintosh System 8.5, because older operating systems don't support these ports.

Second, unless you've got an iMac (which was made for USB), you may have trouble getting your computer to recognize your USB ports.

Finally, many hardware manufacturers still need to jump on the USB bandwagon so they can offer you more choices of products. But as USB grows more popular, this is bound to happen.

Cams and Parallel Ports for Windows

Windows only

If you use Windows and you didn't get a USB cam, then your cam will plug into your **parallel port** and your keyboard port, as explained earlier in this chapter. To plug in the cam, take the parallel port connector, slip it into the parallel port in the back of your PC, and make sure it fits snugly.

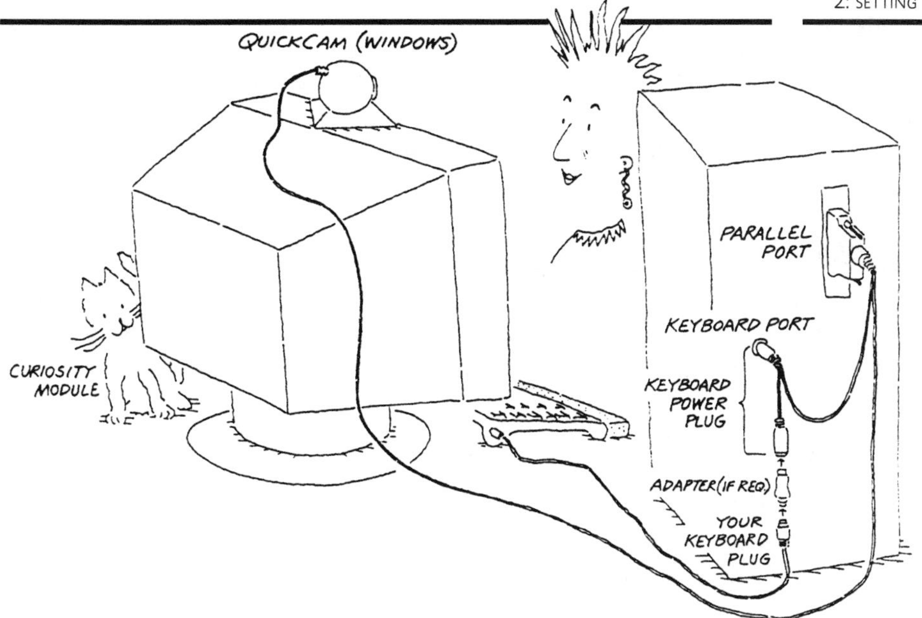

Keyboard plugs and adapters

Your cam will also come with a keyboard adapter attached to the cam, and two **keyboard plugs**. That's because there are two types of standard keyboards. Plug in the keyboard plug that fits your keyboard connector, then plug the keyboard connector into the adapter, and then plug the keyboard connector into the keyboard port.

Parallel Port Switchers

There's a common problem with parallel-port cams (which is why USB is catching on): You might already have something like a scanner or another device plugged into your parallel port.

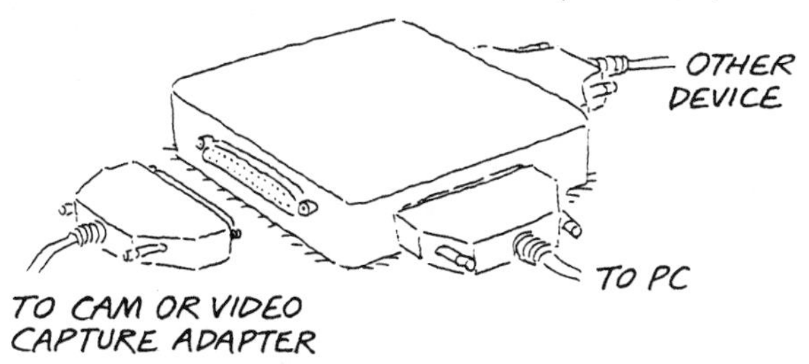

The best way to solve this is to buy inexpensive **A/B switch boxes,** which are available at any computer store. Costing about 30 bucks and up (depending on the quality and the number of devices it can accommodate), a switch box lets you share a parallel port among two or more devices. Unlike a USB hub, however, a switch box doesn't let you use more than one thing at once—all you can do is switch the port between one device and another. You can try Belkin's Bitronics Data Switch Kit for $49 (**http://www.belkin.com/**), or get a recommendation from someone at your local computer store.

If you use a switch box, remember to turn the switch when you want to use your camera!

Cams and Modem/Printer Ports on Macs

Macintosh only

If you're a Macintosh user but don't have an iMac or a USB port, then your cam plugs into your printer or modem port and may also plug into your keyboard port. Take the serial port connector and plug it into the back of your Macintosh. Look carefully, and you'll see that the printer and modem ports are labeled with tiny lettering, or with little telephone and printer icons. Now unplug your keyboard, plug in the cam's keyboard adapter (if your cam came with one) and plug the keyboard connector into the other end of the adapter.

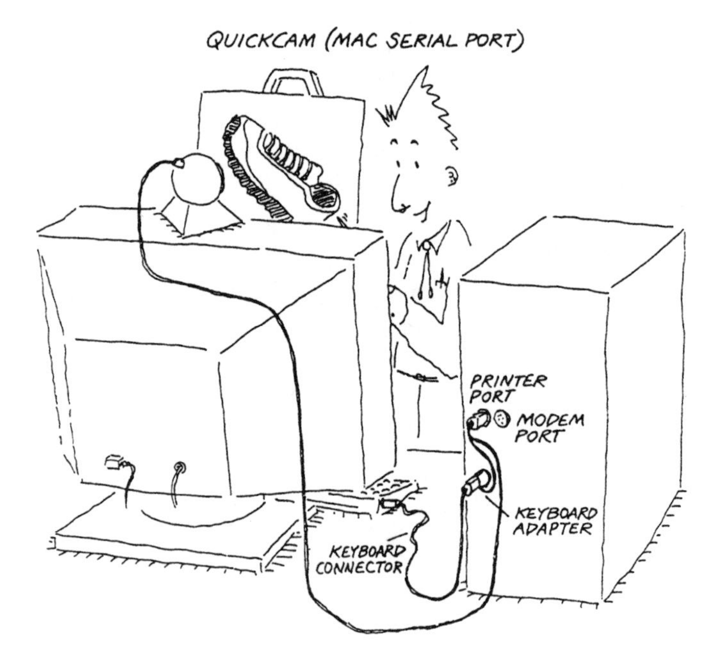

Plug your cam into your printer port! You need to use your modem and cam at the same time in order to videoconference or set up a Web cam.

Help! I Need My Printer and Modem!

Since your Mac has only one printer port and one modem port, you can run out of ports pretty quickly! Not to worry; having a cam doesn't mean you have to cramp your computing style. Get Macally Peripheral's Port Xpander for $59.99, and voilà—you can switch among three devices on a single port. I recommend that you plug Port Xpander into your printer port, because camming on the 'Net requires using your cam and your modem at the same time.

For more information about Port Xpander, visit **http://www.macally.com/**.

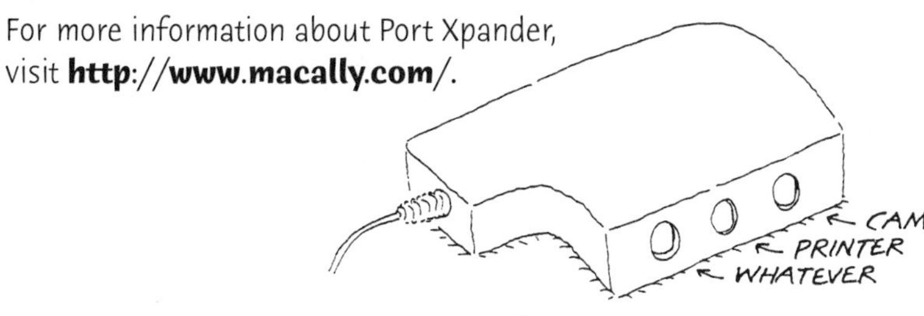

"PORT XPANDER"

Got a Video Camera?

Use it! Huge numbers of people already own handheld video cameras. If you've got one, you can connect it to your computer and use it as your cam. Video cameras give you much better image quality, and they adjust better to bright light and darkness. Plus, if you set up your computer to capture video, you can also plug in your TV or VCR and grab a few frames from them.

Video cameras come in all shapes, sizes, and price points. The cheapest are the ones that use normal VHS tapes; they cost around $300 and work just fine for basic computer-based camming.

Digital Video Cameras

If price is no object, consider going digital. Digital video cameras offer stunning quality and speed, and there's no messing around with VHS tapes.

These high-tech devices are among the more expensive toys in any media junkie's arsenal. Fortunately, **prices keep dropping**—still, digitals are far more expensive than a cam or regular video camera. On the low end, JVC's GR-DVM5 Digital CyberCam is feature packed, comes with great software, and lists for a little over $1,200. On the other end of the scale, all the major brands offer digitals, including Sony and Hitachi. As good as these are, they're overkill for basic camming.

Connecting Your Video Camera

There are many different ways to plug a video camera into your computer. As discussed in the following sections, you may need an adapter or another card. Let's see how it works.

Video Capture Cards

Very few computers offer built-in video capture. That's why cams are so great. But if you want to go beyond the limitations of basic Web cams, you'll need to go shopping for a **video capture card** in order to plug an existing video camera into your computer. Some video capture cards can be plugged into a PowerMac, G3, or Pentium PC system's PCI slot.

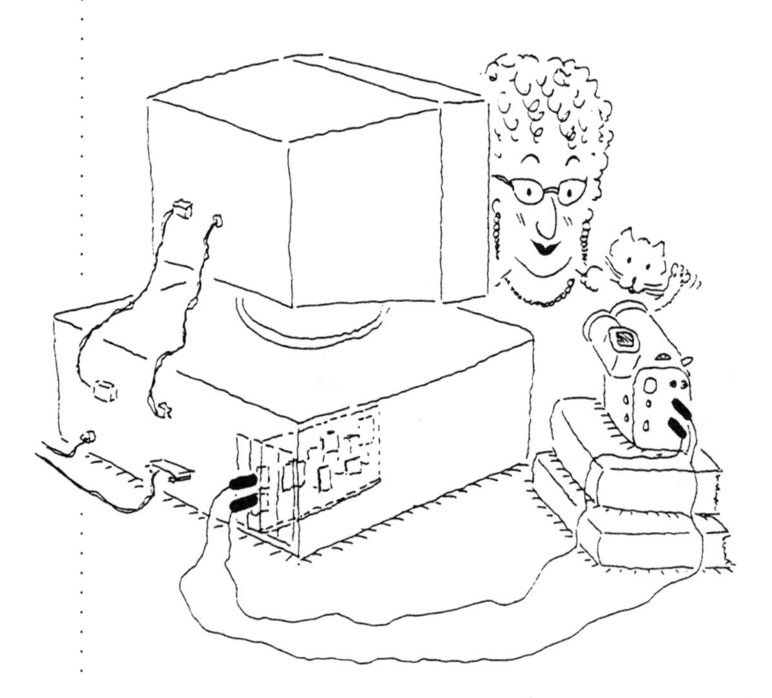

VIDEO CARD WITH VIDEO CAM (OR CAMCORDER)

IdeaMedia's Miro DC20, DC30, and DC40 video cards for Windows and Macintosh range from $700 to $1,650 and provide professional-quality video and high-end video editing software. For more information, visit IdeaMedia's Web site at **http://www.ideamedia.com.au**.

Low-Budget Choices

If you're on a budget, try the $179 Intel Smart Video Recorder III for Windows: **http://www.pentium.com/product/multimedia/svr3/** or ATI Technologies' $269 Xclaim VR for Macintosh: **http://www.atitech.ca/**.

These products have received rave reviews and should work just fine for most people's camming needs.

Got a Mac?

If you use a Power Macintosh, you may be in luck. Many Macintosh models come with **video ports.** If you've got 'em, go buy a video cable from a computer or video store for about $10. Plug two ends into the computer's video ports and the other two ends into the camera, and that's it. You can then use AppleVideo (which comes with the Macintosh) to record movies and take pictures, which you can use in the projects described in this book. SiteCam software for Web cams, as covered in Chapter 9, also works great with video cameras.

Mac Issues

CU-SeeMe, the freeware videoconferencing program discussed in Chapters 11–13, may not work if you plug a video camera into the video ports on your Mac. That's because Apple's built-in video software doesn't support grayscale, and CU-SeeMe doesn't support color. But don't give up the ship! CU-SeeMe version 1.0 offers color video, and the Mac release is on the way. You can also go to Chapter 13 to read about workarounds and other videoconferencing options.

Macs with Video

A typical video-capable Macintosh desktop system offers **two sets of video-in ports:** the standard RCA ports, and the S-Video (SuperVHS) ports. Most consumer-grade video cameras use standard RCA cables. If you're not sure what you've got, call the store that sold you the video camera, or the camera manufacturer.

Among the Macintoshes that offer built-in video capturing are the following:

- Power Macintosh 7500, 7600, 8500, 8600, 9600
- Some Power Macintosh G3s (but not all models)
- Macintosh Quadra 660AV, 840AV

Sad to say, the iMac does not have built-in video-in ports.

Low-Cost Adapters

So, you've got video camera tastes and QuickCam pockets? Try plugging your video camera into your computer with a low-cost adapter. Like cams, these adapters plug into your parallel port, USB port, or printer/modem port, depending on your computer.

Here are three popular low-cost adapters:

- **Snappy Deluxe:** Play Inc.'s $139 Snappy Deluxe for Windows at **http://www.play.com** is a great example. Connecting to your computer's parallel port, Snappy

does an amazing job. Snappy comes with very good image- and video-editing software to help you get creative with your pictures and movies once you get them onto your computer.

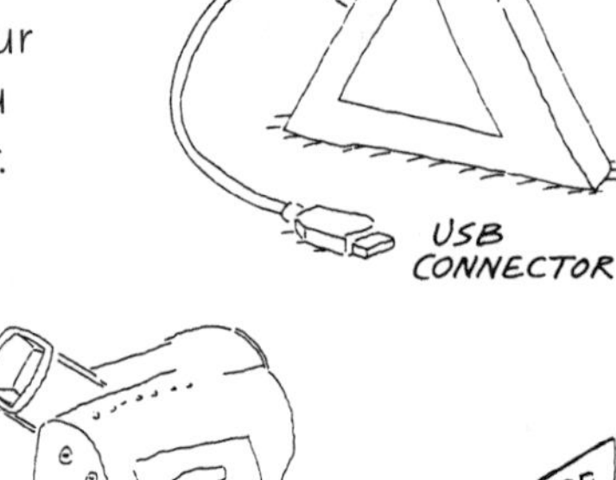

- **QuickClip**: If you're on a truly slender budget, Windows 98 users can try Logitech's USB adapter, QuickClip, for $99: **http://www.quickcam.com/**.

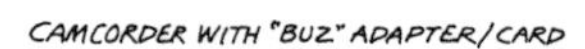

- **Buz**: Windows and Macintosh G3 users may want to take a look at Iomega's $199 Buz. The product comes with a PCI card, Buz box, video editing software, and audio software. Visit the Iomega Web site: **http://www.imoega.com/buz/**.

Get QuickTime 3.0! If you want to cam, if you plan to use some of the shareware discussed in this book, or if you just enjoy other people's movies, then you should download QuickTime 3.0. This popular movie player comes built into Windows 98 and Macintosh System 8.5. Otherwise, you can download QuickTime from Apple's Web site at **http://quicktime.apple.com/**.

If you run into problems there, try a shareware Web site such as: Download.com (**http://www.download.com/**) or Tucows (**http://www.tucows.com/**).

When Things Go Wrong

Although all kinds of neat things can be done with simple cams, it's also true that plenty can go wrong. If you follow all the rules and still have a blank image, there are a few ways to start hunting the problem down.

Read the Manual! Most cams are simple beasts requiring a minimum of setup time. (The Connectix QuickCams are good examples.) Simply connect the camera, turn the computer on, install the software, and reboot. When your computer comes back, you should be able to start up the cam software and immediately get a video image. It's unlikely that you'll experience difficulty with either setup or use, but read the manual to make sure you don't miss anything.

Get the Latest Software or Driver. If your computer refuses to recognize your cam, a new software edition or driver upgrade might help. For example, if you've just upgraded to a new version of your operating system, the people who made your cam have probably published a corrresponding upgrade to your cam software. Most of the time, you can get these upgrades on the Web. Which brings us to...

Check the Web Site. The Internet is a real boon for any computer user. If something goes wrong with your cam, support and software updates are usually just a modem connection away. (A lot of us take this for granted, but a few short years ago, none of this existed!) Every major cam company offers new software and updated information that you can download in a few minutes. Keep checking the Web site for your cam's company. Watch for updated drivers. Many sites offer FAQ pages or special tech support pages where you can get questions answered and find out if anyone else has run into the same problem you have.

Call Tech Support. After you've tried everything, and you're still having trouble with your cam, call the company's Tech Support line. They can take you through some troubleshooting steps and help you figure out what's wrong. However, it often pays to check the Web site first, since it sometimes takes a while to get a real human on the line.

Where to Buy Hardware

You can purchase the hardware mentioned in this chapter at your local computer store. Or you can order over the phone or on the Web. The following list points you to a few mail-order computer stores where you can get hardware—and software, too.

- **PC Connection**: http://www.pcconnection.com/ (for Windows and Macintosh)
- **The PC Zone and the Mac Zone**: http://www.zones.com/ (for Windows and Macintosh)
- **PC Mall**: http://www.pcmall.com/ (for Windows)
- **Mac Mall**: http://www.macmall.com/ (for Macintosh)
- **Cyberian Outpost**: http://www.outpost.com/
- **Computer Discount Warehouse**: http://www.cdw.com/ (for Windows and Macintosh)

Starting Up Your Cam

Some cam programs have separate modules for taking pictures and recording movies. Or you may be able to just click a button to switch back and forth between making pictures and movies.

For example, with QuickCam, a program called QuickPict takes still pictures (**Figures 2.1** and **2.2**). A separate program called QuickMovie records movies (**Figures 2.3** and **2.4**). The QuickCam's software displays a preview window that shows you what the cam sees, and you click a button to take a picture or start recording a movie.

Figure 2.1 *QuickCam's QuickPict for Windows.*

Figure 2.2 *QuickCam's QuickPict for Macintosh.*

Figure 2.3 *QuickCam's QuickMovie for Windows.*

Figure 2.4 *QuickCam's QuickMovie for Macintosh.*

Image and Video Basics

Before you start actually taking pictures and recording movies with your cam, you should get acquainted with some fundamental principles and characteristics of image and video files. Your cam software provides menus and dialog boxes containing settings for working with your pictures and movies. The other applications covered in this book provide similar options. But all these choices don't do you much good if you don't know what they mean! The following sections introduce you to concepts that you'll encounter while camming—including size issues, color settings, special effects, frame rates, compression, and more.

In most situations, you'll tweak your pictures and movies with the goal of getting the **highest possible quality at the smallest possible file size**. Why? Well, you want your pictures and movies to look good. But you don't want them hogging up space on your computer or taking forever to download from your Web page.

> **Manual Camera Adjustments.** Some cams, including QuickCam VC, allow you to improve your picture by adjusting the camera lens manually. To do this, preview your picture with the software that comes with your cam, while rotating the lens to the left or right.

Image and Video Formats

When you save a picture or movie with a cam or image program, the Save As dialog box may ask you to choose an image format. So how do you know what to select? That depends on your operating system and how you plan to use the files. Your cam software will probably allow you to save files only in your system's default image or video format, or as JPEG files.

Image and Video Formats

Format	Usage
JPEG	Most cam programs provide the option to save your pictures as JPEGs. In fact, you should always do this because you can use JPEGs on your Web pages and for just about anything else.
GIF	This format is also used on the Web, but many cams don't support it. When it comes to photographs, JPEGs look much better than GIFs. But you can do some neat stuff with GIFs, including creating GIF animations (covered in Chapter 5).
Bitmap (BMP)	Windows default image file type. If you use Windows, you may have to save pictures as BMPs if you plan to import them to a program that doesn't support JPEGs.
PICT	Macintosh default image file type. If you use Macintosh, you may have to save pictures as PICTs if you plan to import them to a program that doesn't support JPEGs.
AVI	Windows format for movies (also known as VFW, Video for Windows). All Windows cams record and save movies as AVI files.
QuickTime	Apple's format for movies. All Macintosh cams record and save movies as QuickTime movies. QuickTime is also very popular with Windows users.
MPEG	Another popular video format that offers excellent video and sound quality, and smaller file sizes, too.

Picture and Movie Size

If you like to paint with oils or watercolors, you can use any sized canvas you want. But when it comes to camming, you've only got three choices: **full-screen, half-screen,** and **quarter-screen.** The larger the image or movie, the larger the file size. Cam software, and image- and video-

And what's a pixel? *In the computer world, people use them as a unit of measurement. Everything on your computer screen is made up of tiny dots. Each of those dots is a pixel.*

editing programs generally provide a menu or a dialog box with a list of sizes to choose from.

Full-screen pictures measure at 640x480 pixels—way too big for most of the things you'll want to do with your cam. Full-screen pictures look great in presentations or when printed out, but they don't work well on the Internet. Cammers generally stick with the smaller half-screen (320x240 pixels) and quarter-screen (160x120 pixels) sizes.

When you preview a picture or movie with your cam software or another application, the preview window's size changes when you select a different option.

Color Depth

Color depth refers to the **number of possible colors** that can be used in an image or movie. Pictures and movies with higher color depths look more realistic but also weigh in at heftier file sizes. Most cam software and image/video programs provide a menu or dialog box with a list of available color depth options. For example, **Figure 2.5** shows the Image Size and Quality dialog box from QuickCam for Windows. It lets you choose settings for the image size, color depth (Colors), zooming, special effects, and sharpness.

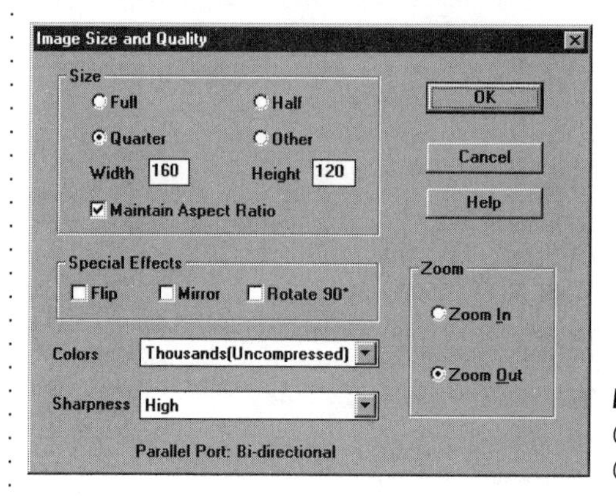

Figure 2.5 *Image Size and Quality dialog box in QuickCam for Windows.*

Color Depth Options

Color Depth Setting	Usage
256 grays (8-bit color)	For grayscale (black-and-white) images. This option can help speed up your online videoconferencing. Also, if you like black-and-white photography, grayscale images look great and don't take very long to download.
256 colors (8-bit color)	Maps the colors in your picture or movie to a 256-color palette stored in your system. Although the colors don't look as realistic as they do in 16- or 24-bit mode, 8-bit color is suitable for recording decent-looking movies and reduces the file size.
Thousands of colors (16-bit color)	In some situations, this is the ideal compromise. Thousands of colors can provide you with great image quality, yet the files for 16-bit pictures and movies aren't as large as their 24-bit cousins.
Millions of colors (24-bit color)	The 24-bit setting gives you the best-looking images and videos, with the accompanying hefty file sizes.

Brightness/ Contrast

Most cams automatically adjust for **different levels of light**. However, you can also choose settings to affect the brightness and contrast if your picture looks too light, too dark, or is indistinct. Most cam and image programs provide a dialog box with sliders for making brightness, contrast, and color adjustments. Take a look at the QuickCam for Macintosh Video dialog box shown in **Figure 2.6**. You move the sliders to the right to increase the brightness or contrast, or to the left to decrease the brightness or contrast. **Note**: You'll also need to deselect your cam software's Auto Brightness checkboxes when making these adjustments.

Some programs let you adjust the **white level** or **black level**, too. Lowering the white level (or increasing the black level) helps you manage the problem of **blooming**, which happens when a light source overwhelms your picture with bright light.

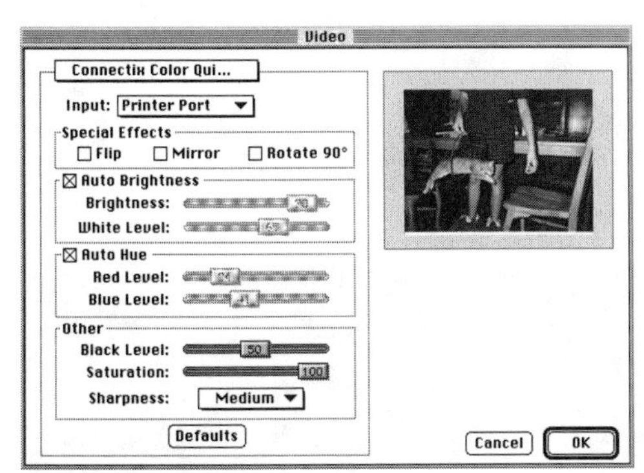

***Figure 2.6** QuickCam for Macintosh's Video dialog box with brightness, contrast, and color settings.*

Hue/Saturation

Hue and saturation are **elements of color and intensity of color.** As it does for the brightness and contrast settings, your cam software automatically adjusts for various levels of color. However, you may want to override these settings for some reason. You can adjust the hue and saturation settings by moving sliders to the right or left. More red tones make your pictures look warmer; blue tones make your pictures look cooler. More saturation makes colors look more intense, and less saturation tones your colors down.

Special Effects

Most cam and image programs let you apply special effects. With cam software, this is generally limited to **mirroring** the image (reversing it horizontally), **flipping** the image so it's upside-down, or **rotating** it in 90° increments.

Sharpness: Medium

Some cam programs also let you adjust the **sharpness.** In some situations, you can make adjustments that emphasize the details of the shot, while in other situations adjusting the sharpness makes the objects' edges look jagged.

Video Frame Rates

When recording movies or doing videoconferencing, you can change your cam's **frame rate**. The frame rate determines how many images are captured per second. Each image is a frame in a movie. Lower frame rates result in smaller file sizes and faster transfers over the Internet, but the product looks "choppy." Faster frame rates make your movies look more fluid, but they also result in larger file sizes.The standard for recording decent-quality video is 30 frames per second; one frame per second is the slowest possible rate for most cams. And keep in mind that 30 frames per second means that your cam takes 30 entire pictures every second! That can *really* slow down your system. Some programs let you select a frame rate from a list. In others you'll enter a number in a dialog box.

Frames per second:
✓ Best
8
10
12
15
24
25
29.97
30

Compression

Fortunately, your cam software (and other image and video programs, too) gives you options for compressing your pictures and movies—which means **making them smaller**.

With JPEG images, you can adjust the compression level by moving a slider or choosing an option from a list. Options generally range from Least Quality to Highest Quality (or Best); the higher the compression factor, the less quality your image has. Your cam software generally lets you specify a setting for JPEG images through a menu or dialog box. In image programs, a dialog box appears when you save a picture as a JPEG.

When it comes to video, you generally have a variety of compression options. And none of them makes any sense whatsoever to the camming novice! When you save a movie, a dialog box asks you to choose a compression method. I recommend that you select either **Intel Indeo** or **Radius Cinepak**. These types of video compression are standard—which means most people's computers and video programs can handle your movies.

> **Watch Out for Proprietary Compression Schemes.** Most cams come with proprietary compression schemes that only work with certain hardware and/or software. So if you want to share your movies with people who don't use the same type of cam as yours, *don't* use your cam manufacturer's compression method. For example, QuickCam ships with Videc. When you compress a movie by choosing Videc, you wind up with a great-looking video that fills up surprisingly few megabytes. But only people with QuickCam will be able to view your Videc-compressed movie.

Zoom

Some cams, including QuickCam, provide options for **zooming** in and out. This lets your cam zoom in on the subject for a close-up, or zoom out to show the subject in context. With QuickCam for Windows, the Zoom options (**Figure 2.7**) appear in the Image Size and Quality dialog box. With QuickCam for Macintosh, you can zoom in or out by selecting Angle of View from the Settings menu, and then choosing Constant when the cascading menu appears (see **Figure 2.8**).

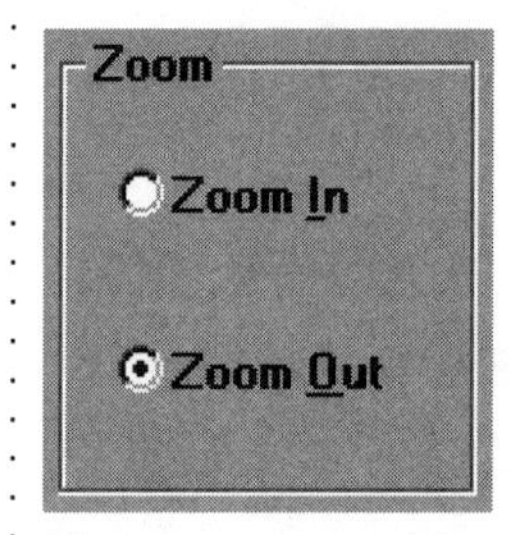

Figure 2.7 *Zoom options in QuickCam for Windows.*

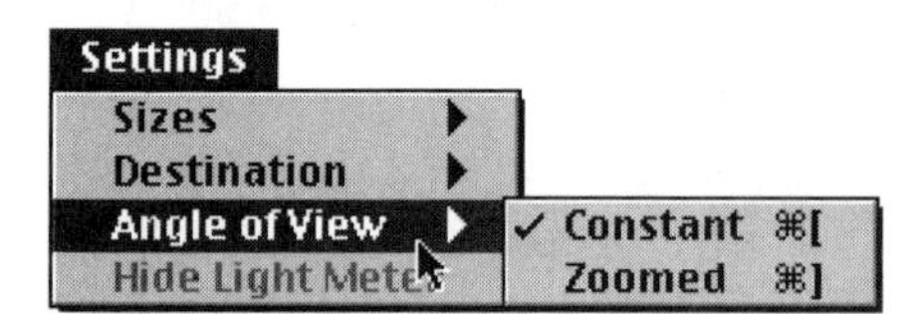

Figure 2.8 *Zoom options in QuickCam for Mac.*

Taking Pictures and Recording Movies

How exactly do you take pictures and record movies? That depends on your cam. But it's usually as easy as clicking on a button.

Take Picture

Record

With some cams, including Color QuickCam, the image and video software are individual applications (QuickPict for pictures and QuickMovie for video). Other cams, like the QuickCam VC, let you switch between the image and video functions seamlessly by clicking a button or selecting options from a menu.

If you're recording a movie, don't forget to click the Stop button when you're done!

Some Programs to Try

Face it—the software that comes with your cam does have its limitations. If you want to do more creative things with your pictures and videos, you'll need to invest in a little software. Fortunately, it doesn't have to cost a bundle. The Web abounds with shareware programs and trial software that you can take for a spin.

Imaging Programs

Would you like to convert pictures to different file formats, add special effects, or start creating your own graphics? The PaintShop Pro and Graphics Converter programs can get you started.

- **PaintShop Pro** by Jasc gives Windows users a bundle of great features for only $129. You can download a 30-day trial version from Jasc's Web site at **http://www.jasc.com/**.
- **Graphics Converter** by Thorsten Lemke is a nifty little Macintosh shareware program that makes it easy to convert and touch up your pictures. It also comes with some drawing tools. The program costs $25 and you can download it from **http://members.aol.com/lemkesoft**.

Both PaintShop Pro and Graphics Converter also support popular PhotoShop plug-ins that help you add exciting special effects to your pictures—Alien Skin Black Box, Eye Candy, and Kai's PowerTools are a few. For example, you can make photos look like oil paintings, add textures, age them with sepia tones and torn edges, or distort them in a variety of ways.

Video Programs

Fancy video editing requires big bucks and imposes a steep learning curve. But you can still use Mathias Tschopp's **QuickEditor for Windows and Macintosh** to do some pretty imaginative work, such as compositing movies, turning a series of pictures into a movie, adding sounds, editing existing movies, and more. Chapter 6 tells you how. QuickEditor costs $35 and you can get it from **http://www.wild.ch/quickeditor/**.

In addition, Apple's $29 QuickTime MoviePlayer Pro offers a variety of editing features. For more information visit Apple's QuickTime Web site at **http://quicktime.apple.com/**. And pick up *The QuickTime and MoviePlayer Pro 3; Visual QuickStart Guide* by Judith Stern and Robert Lettieri (1998, Peachpit Press).

The Crème de la Crème

If you decide to get *really* serious about images and video, then you'll want to invest in **Adobe PhotoShop** (for imaging) and **Adobe Premiere** (for video editing). Yep, these programs cost a pretty penny. PhotoShop lists for $895 and Premiere lists for $495. But they're popular among multimedia developers for good reason—nothing beats the features and performance in these two programs. For more information, examples, and sometimes a free trial download or two, visit Adobe's Web site at **http://www.adobe.com/**.

Keeping Track of Your Stuff

Yikes! Cams are so much fun… all those pictures and movies can pile up pretty fast. How do you keep track of them all? Some **multimedia cataloging software** can help you stay organized. These programs display thumbnail views of your pictures, movies, and other types of files so you don't have to open each file to remember what it is.

Windows users can download Dryad Software's **Media Blaze** from **http://www.dryad.com/**. At $14.95, you can't beat the price. Macintosh users can visit Script Software's Web site at **http://www.scriptsoftware.com/** and download **iView**. If you like it, iView costs $25.

Summary

Whew! We've sure gone through a lot of stuff in this chapter.

- I recommend Logitech's Color **QuickCam**, but there are many other good, affordable cams. Cam products come with all the software and hardware you need.
- Cams **connect** to your computer through the parallel port (Windows), printer or modem serial port (Macintosh), or USB port (Windows 98 or Macintosh System 8.5).
- Parallel port and serial ports also get **power** from the keyboard port through a keyboard adapter. USB ports also work as power sources and don't require adapters.
- If you run out of parallel, serial, or USB ports, you can buy a **switchbox** or **hub** so you can keep using your printer, scanner, or other device.
- If you have a **video camera,** you can use it as your cam. Inexpensive adapters and video cards are available. With some Macs, you can buy a video cable and plug your video camera right in. Digital video cameras also offer flexibility and excellent image quality, if you don't mind spending $1,000 or more.
- Most people can get their cams up and running in a matter of minutes. But **if you run into trouble**, read the manual carefully, check the manufacturer's Web site, or call the technical support line.
- Windows cams usually capture BMP and JPEG pictures and AVI movies. Macintosh cams generally capture PICT and JPEG pictures and QuickTime movies. JPEG and QuickTime are the more popular **image and video formats.**
- You can adjust the size and quality, color depth, brightness, contrast, hue/saturation, frame rates, and compression options for your images or movies with your **cam software**. Many cams also offer a few special effects.

Now that your cam is plugged in and you're familiar with its software, let's take that cam for a spin. Chapter 3 tells you how to create your own screen savers.

Part Two
Beautifying Your Desktop

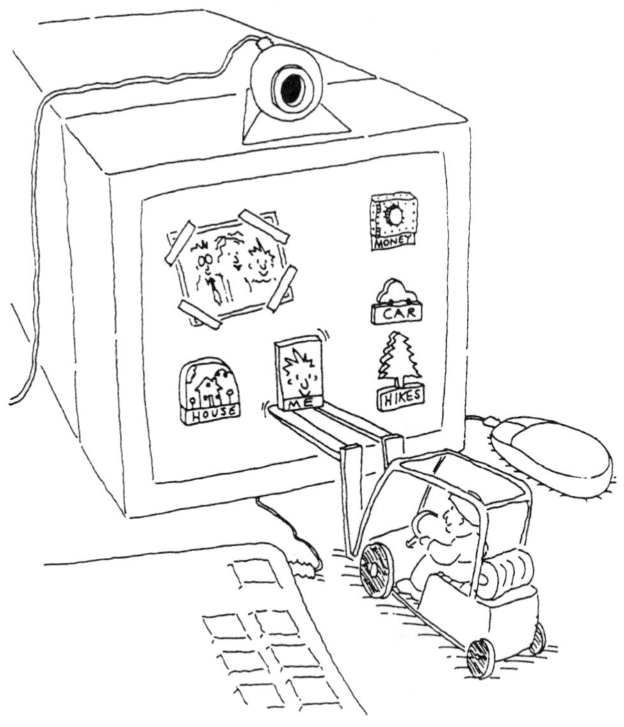

3 Creating Your Own Screen Savers

Screen savers are the programs that display those cool pictures and games on your computer screen when you go to lunch or stop working for a few minutes. Back in the not-so-good old days, screen savers kept your monitor from going on the fritz. Nowadays, nobody actually *needs* screen savers, because today's computers come with software that keeps monitors from burning out. But everyone still likes screen savers because they're fun.

So how would you like to create your own screen-saver slide shows starring your friends, family, coworkers, and pets? You can even add sounds if you want. All you need are a few pictures that you can take with your cam, a little creativity, and one of these programs:

- **A+ Screensaver Creator (for Windows)**
- **Photos4us (for Macintosh)**

① TAKE COOL PICTURES

② DOWNLOAD SOFTWARE

③ UNLEASH CREATIVITY

Getting the Software

You can download one of these programs from the Web and take it for a spin right now. Because A+ Screensaver Creator and Photos4us work very differently, this chapter has **separate sections for each program** to take you through all the steps. Just look for the Windows and Macintosh icons to find the sections that apply to the computer you use.

A Web cam warm-up!

Creating a screen saver is also a great warm-up for making GIF animations and movies for the Web (you'll be reading more about this in Part Three). Making screen savers gives you an easy introduction to working with **multimedia**—a catch-all word referring to files that combine different types of data (in this case, images and sound).

This chapter covers the following:

- A screen saver "recipe"
- Getting and installing your screen-saver program
- Turning on your screen-saver control panel
- Adding pictures to your screen saver
- Applying special effects
- Adding sound files to your screen saver
- Editing the screen saver
- Getting image files from the Web

Recipe for a Screen Saver

To design your own screen saver, you'll follow the general steps outlined in this section. As you work through the chapter, you'll find the details for each step.

Step 1

Get your pictures together: You can take pictures with your cam, scan photographs (if you have access to a scanner), or use images from a CD-ROM clip-art collection. You can also grab pictures from the Web, as explained in the later section, "Grab It! Getting Images from the Web."

Step 2

Format your images: A+ Screensaver Creator for Windows requires JPEG or bitmap (.bmp) files, and Photos4us for Macintosh requires PICT files. You can set up your cam to save your pictures to the correct file format, or you can convert pictures with an image program. File formats, cam settings, and image programs are covered in Chapter 2.

Step 3

Download, install, and activate your screen saver program: Screen-saver programs are **control panels**—special settings that let you customize the look of the desktop and add features to your computer system. This chapter tells you where to get your screen-saver program, how to set it up, and how to activate it through your computer's control panels.

Figure 1.1 *Windows users display control panels by clicking Start|Settings|Control Panel. Double-click the Display icon; then access A+ Screensaver Creator from the Screen Saver tab of the Display control panel.*

> ***Where Are My Control Panels?***
> *Windows users can view their control panels by clicking Start|Settings|Control Panel. Macintosh users can access their control panels by selecting Control Panels from the Apple menu.*

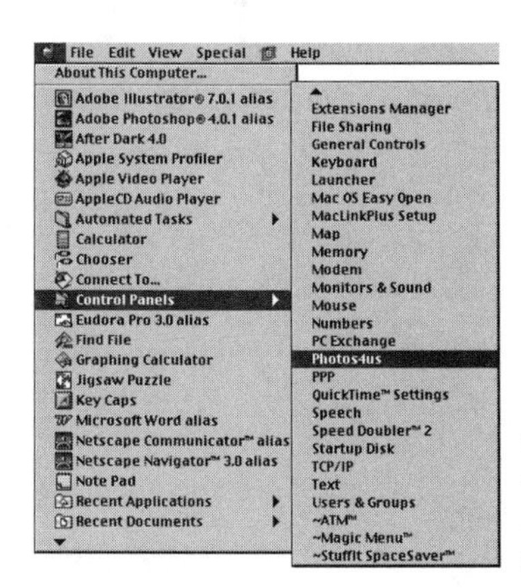

Figure 1.2 *Macintosh users display control panels by selecting Control Panels from the Apple menu; then select Photos4us.*

Step 4

Create a picture list: Screen-saver programs *cycle* (display) pictures based on a list that you create. You can choose to cycle your pictures in a certain order, or randomly. This chapter takes you through the steps of creating a picture list with A+ Screensaver Creator and Photos4Us.

What Size Should My Pictures Be? Your screen savers will look best if you use the **half-screen** (320x240) or **full-screen** (640x480) settings when taking your pictures. Most cams support these standard settings. Full-screen images are generally too large for Web pages, Web cams, and videoconferencing—a pity, since full-screen images look pretty impressive on your computer. Screen savers give you a great excuse to use the full-screen setting.

Step 5 **Apply special effects**: A+ Screensaver Creator and Photos4us both provide settings for special effects that you can apply to jazz up your screen saver. For example, with A+ you can display a picture within a picture or show four pictures at once, and Photos4us provides an assortment of exciting transitions including fades, wipes, and dissolves.

Step 6 **Add sounds**: Add a sound track to the screen saver by creating a list of sound files. You can loop a single audio track over and over again, play a sound or a narration for each picture, or display pictures and play sounds at random.

For more about audio, see Chapter 14.

A wealth of interesting sound effects and music can be downloaded from the Web. If you have a microphone (many computers come with them, or you can purchase one inexpensively) you can also record sounds with software that comes with your system. Many cams, including QuickCam, can also record sounds along with movies. You can then open the movies in QuickEditor (a video editing application covered in Chapter 6) and export the sound track as a separate sound file.

Step 7 **Preview your screen saver**: Before activating it, preview your screen saver and make sure you like it.

Step 8 **Activate your screen saver**: When you've activated your screen saver, the slide show will play whenever you take a break from your computer.

Got After Dark and QuickCam?

After Dark by Berkeley Systems is a popular screen-saver program for Windows and Macintosh users. Some versions of QuickCam come with the **QuickSaver** and **Full-ScreenQuickSaver** modules of the After Dark program. If you have these modules, they'll appear as options on your AfterDark control panel. These modules record what your cam sees, and display the pictures on your desktop as a live-action screen saver.

The Full-ScreenQuickSaver module displays large pictures that demand more from your system. The QuickSaver shows smaller, less resource-hungry pictures.

- **To use QuickCam with AfterDark,** display the AfterDark control panel, select QuickCam from the list, and choose an option.

If you want to purchase After Dark or get more information about it, visit Berkeley System's Web site at **http://www.berksys.com/**.

If you have After Dark but no QuickCam

You may have After Dark installed on your computer, but your cam does not come with the screen-saver modules. Don't let that ruin your fun. It's likely that you can still use photos taken with your cam to personalize your screen savers. Several popular AfterDark screen-saver modules, including Art Critic and Slide Show, have options for adding your own pictures to the mix.

Introducing A+ Screensaver Creator

Windows only

A+ Screensaver Creator by RegSoft helps Windows 95, 98, and NT users whip up a cool screen saver in minutes. A+ can handle both JPEGs and bitmap (.bmp) pictures, which are supported by QuickCam and most other cam products. If you need to convert pictures from some other file format, then you can use an imaging program like LView or PaintShop Pro, as discussed in Chapter 2.

Once you've downloaded and installed A+ Screensaver Creator, you can take it for a spin right away, but your screen savers will display a nag message every 20 minutes or so until you register and pay for the program.

Downloading and Setting Up

To download A+ Screensaver Creator, visit **http://members.aol.com/softdd/screens/index.htm**. There you can read more about the program and then download it by clicking the "Download Here!" link. When you finish downloading the file (which is named aplus.zip), unzip it with WinZip as explained in Chapter 1.

To set up A+ Screensaver Creator, double-click the Setup.exe icon and follow the setup instructions. Unless you specify otherwise, the Setup program automatically puts your files in the directory C:\softdd\.

Registering A+ Screensaver Creator

If you like the A+ program and want to continue using it, you can register it for $14.95. To do this on the telephone with a credit card, call 1-888-reg-it-80 and tell them you'd like to register Product ID number 4876. People outside of the United States can call 1-770-497-9126. If you want to order online or by mailing a check or money order, follow the instructions given on the download Web site.

Turning On the A+ Control Panel

Like most screen-saver programs, A+ Screensaver Creator works as a control panel that you can get to via your Display Properties settings.

1. Click the Start button to display the Start menu, select Settings, and choose Control Panel.
2. When the Control Panel folder appears, double-click the Display icon to launch the Display Properties dialog box.
3. Click on the Screen Saver tab and activate the Aplus program by selecting it from the Screen Saver pull-down list, as shown in **Figure 3.3**.
4. Click the Settings button to display the A+ Screensaver Creator Settings dialog box.

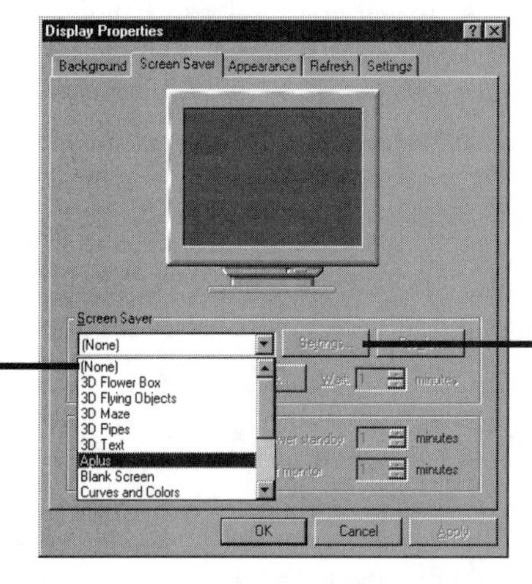

Figure 3.3 *Activating the A+ Screensaver Creator control panel from the Display Properties dialog box.*

Try the Shortcut Menu! There's gotta be an easier way to get to the Display Properties dialog box... and there is! Right-click on the desktop and select Properties from the shortcut menu.

"Um...Where Are My Files Again?" Don't let this be you! To help you keep track of files you're using in your screen saver, create a new folder, name it something like "Screensaver," and move all relevant files into it.

Creating a Picture List

Okay, enough about setting up the program—let's get to the fun stuff. The next step is to tell A+ Screensaver Creator which pictures you want to use. Your **picture list** designates the order in which your screen saver's pictures will appear (unless you choose to display them randomly, as explained in the "Settings and Special Effects" section).

To create a picture list with A+ Screensaver Creator:

1. From the Screen Saver tab of the Display Properties dialog box, click the Settings button to display the A+ Settings dialog box (**Figure 3.4**).
2. To begin adding your first picture, click the Add Picture button. The Open dialog box appears (**Figure 3.5**).

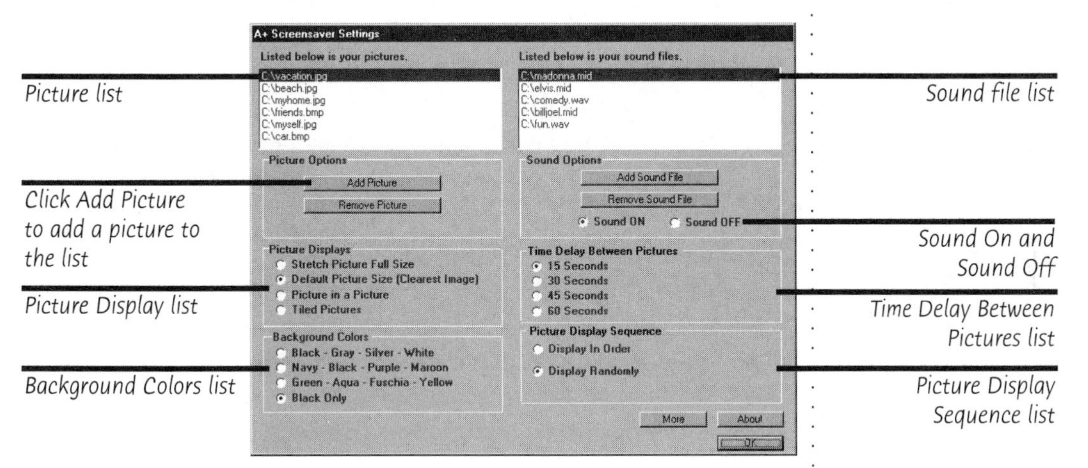

Figure 3.4 *The A+ Screensaver Creator Settings dialog box.*

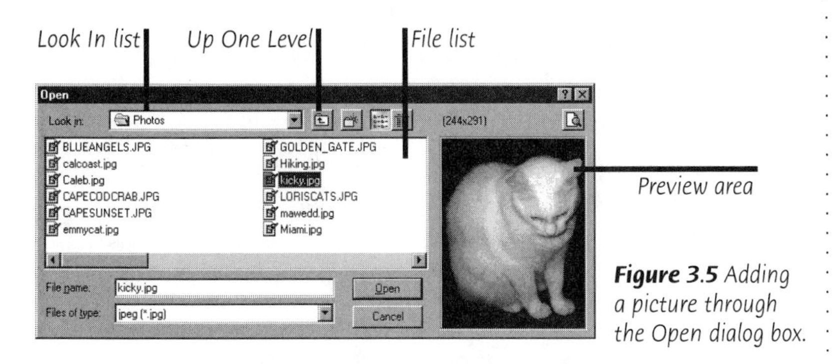

Figure 3.5 *Adding a picture through the Open dialog box.*

If you have an older cam, it may only support the bitmap image format.

3. From the Files of Type list, select the file type of the picture you want to add. Choose JPEG (*.jpg) or bitmap (.bmp). Most of today's cams can save images as either bitmaps or JPEGs.
4. Browse for the folder that contains your pictures, and click on its filename. The selected image appears in the preview box.
5. Click Open to add the picture to your slide show and return to the A+ Settings dialog box. The directory path and filename for the picture appear under Listed Below Is Your Pictures List.
6. To add more pictures, repeat steps 2 through 5.

Picture Settings and Special Effects

A+ Screensaver Creator offers a few special effects that you can try. The A+ Settings dialog box also contains options for specifying how your pictures display when the screen-saver slide show runs.

A+ Screensaver Creator Settings and Special Effects

- **Stretch Picture Full Size** enlarges your pictures to fill the size of your monitor. Be careful—large images do look better stretched to full size, but this setting can also cause smaller pictures to look distorted.
- **Default Picture Size**: This is A+'s default, and I recommend that you leave it selected. This setting cycles your images one-by-one and shows your pictures at their real sizes.

- The **Picture in a Picture** option gives you one enlarged image with a different picture displayed in the middle of the enlarged image. The images cycle through the screen saver's routine so that each picture takes its turn as a large picture and a small picture.

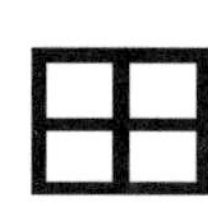

- The **Tiled Pictures** option displays four images at a time on the screen and cycles through the images.
- **Background Colors**: You can pick a color or a combination of colors to display behind your pictures.
- **Time Delay Between Pictures**: Specify the length of time each picture displays before the next one appears.
- **Picture Display Sequence**: To cycle your photos (and sounds if you include any) in the order they are listed in the picture list, click the Display Pictures in Order radio button. To cycle your pictures in random order, select the Display Pictures Randomly radio button.

Adding Sound Files

So, how would you like a **soundtrack** to go with your screen saver? A+ Screensaver Creator supports both WAV and MIDI files. You can list your **sound files** the same way you listed your pictures. Since cams only record audio along with movies, you'll need to record audio separately. Or you can export a sound track from a movie that you recorded with your cam in QuickEditor. Chapter 6 tells you more about QuickEditor, and Chapter 14 covers audio files and cams.

In choosing your sound setup, consider the end-product you want to wind up with:

*You can get **sound files** on the Web. Check out Chapter 14.*

- If you want your screen saver to play a sound or a tune **over and over again,** then you should include only one audio file on your sounds list.
- To designate an audio file **to accompany each picture** in the slide show, add the sounds to the list in the same order as the pictures appear, and then select the Display Pictures in Order radio button in the Settings dialog box. This method is ideal for setting up a continuing narrative.
- Or you can play sounds and display pictures **randomly,** by creating the sounds list and then selecting the Display Pictures Randomly radio button in the Settings dialog.

To create a list of sound files:

1. From the Settings dialog box, click the Add Sound File button to display the Open dialog box.
2. Browse for and select a MIDI or WAV file, and click the Open button. When you return to the Settings dialog box, the directory path and name of your audio file appear under Listed Below Is Your Sound Files.
3. Repeat steps 1 and 2 to add more sounds.
4. In the Settings dialog box, click the Sound On radio button.

How to Drive People Batty. Want to drive your coworkers, family, or roommates absolutely nuts? Leave the Sound On radio button selected all the time, so your computer beeps, squawks, and sings the live-long day. Otherwise, for a more peaceful environment, go back to Settings and select Sound Off after you've finished showing off your new screen saver.

Action! Running Your Screen Saver

Ready to see your screen saver in action?

Preview it first. To preview your new screen saver, click the OK button in the Settings dialog box. This takes you back to the Display Properties/ Screen Saver tab, as shown in **Figure 3.6**. Now, click the Preview button.

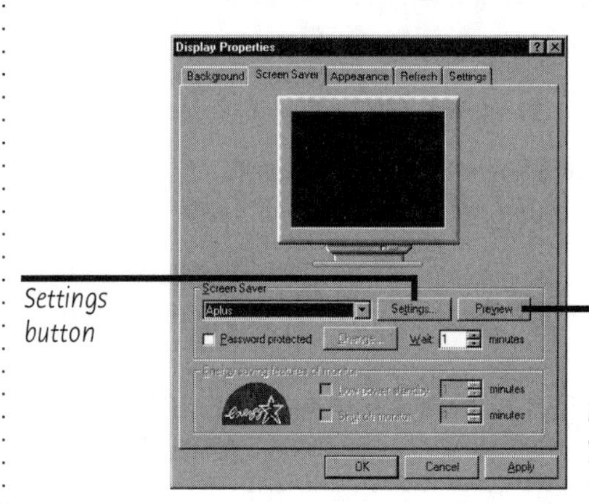

Figure 3.6 *You can preview your screen saver from the Display Properties dialog box.*

How does it look? Have a look and a listen at your creation. Then, if you want to make any changes, click the Settings button to return to the Settings dialog box.

Activating Your Screen Saver

Once you've added all your pictures, sounds, and special effects from within the Settings dialog box, you can start showing off your new screen saver. To activate it, click the OK button to return to the Display Properties dialog box. From there, you can click the Preview button to check out everything in the screen saver one last time, or click the OK button to return to your desktop. The next time you take a break from your computer, the screen saver will launch.

Turn your movies into screen savers! When you register and pay for A+ Screen Saver, you'll also be able to record movies with your cam and turn them into screen savers, too.

Editing the Screen Saver

You can change your screen saver any time you like by removing the current files and re-creating the lists of pictures and sounds.

1. Go to the Display Properties dialog box Screen Saver tab and click the Settings button to return to the Settings dialog box.
2. To remove picture or sound files, select them one at a time from the Listed Below Is Your Picture Files or Listed Below Is Your Sound Files list. Click the Remove File button, and repeat until all of the files are gone. (Sorry, you can't remove them all at once.)
3. Now, you can create your new lists.

Disabling a Screen Saver

Yikes! When your fastidious boss or Aunt Millie comes to town, you might want to hide those wild party pics for a while. No problemo. You can disable your screen saver temporarily. Go back to the ol' Display Properties dialog box, open the Screen Saver tab, and select a different screen saver from the drop-down list. When the snooper leaves, you can open go back to Display Properties and reactivate your screen saver.

Trashing A+ Screensaver Creator

Well, so screen savers aren't for everyone. If the thrill goes stale, you can easily **uninstall** the A+ Screensaver Creator program.

1. Go to your Control Panel folder and double-click the Add/Remove Programs icon.
2. In the Add/Remove Programs dialog box (**Figure 3.7**), select A+ Screensaver Creator in the list of programs and click the Add/Remove button.

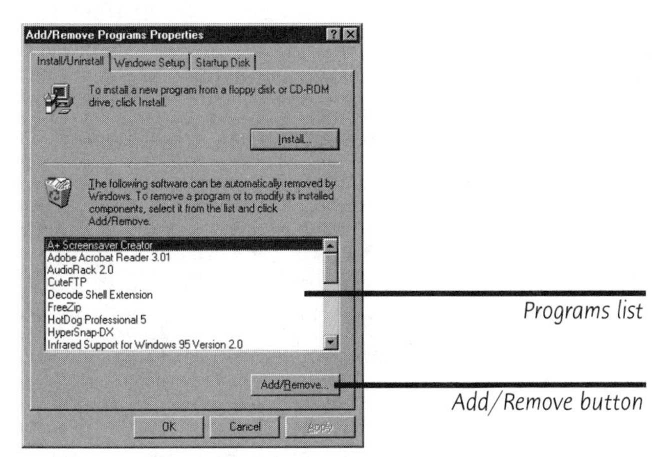

Figure 3.7 *Use Add/Remove Programs to uninstall A+ Screensaver Creator.*

3. When the program finishes uninstalling, click OK to return to your desktop.
4. Proceed with file clean-up as described in the next section.

File Clean-up After Uninstalling

After uninstalling A+ Screensaver Creator, you also need to clean out a few files, named aplus20.ini, aplus.scr, and aplus.dat. They're located in your C:\Windows directory if you want to dig around for them. But doing a search is much easier.

1. Click the Start button, choose Find from the Start menu, and select Files or Folders from the cascading list.

2. In the Find dialog box, enter **aplus** in the Named box and click the Find Now button.
3. When the Finder locates the files and displays them in a list, as shown in **Figure 3.8**, select those sneaky little files—aplus20.ini, aplus.scr, and aplus.dat—and drag them to the Recycle Bin.
4. When you finish, click the Close box (X) to return to the desktop.

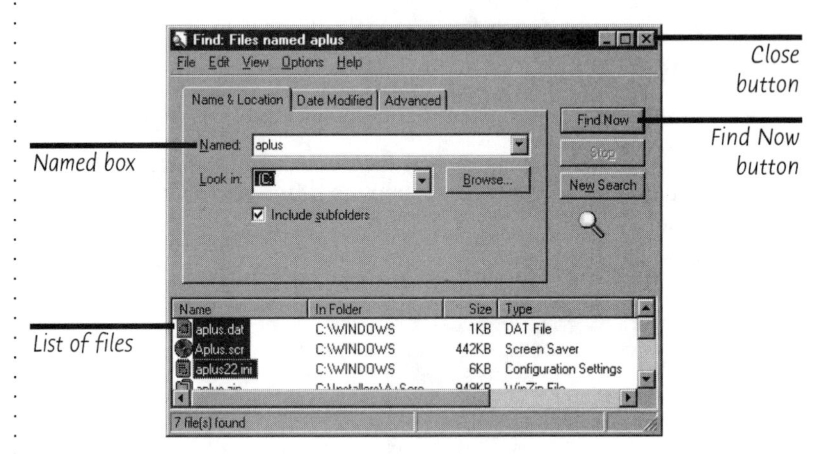

Figure 3.8 *File clean-up after uninstalling A+ Screensaver Creator.*

Remember How to Remove Files! I hope you'll be completely enchanted with every shareware program you ever try. But since life doesn't always work that way, you'll want to remember the procedures for "Trashing A+ Screensaver Creator" and "File Clean-up After Uninstalling." These procedures will work for removing just about any program and its proprietary files (as long as you change the filenames you select or enter).

Introducing Photos4us

Macintosh only

Photos4us by Eric Iverson is a $10 shareware program that helps you put together your own screen saver in no time. With Photos4us, you can only use images formatted as PICT files. Fortunately, however, you can set up most cams to save snapshots as PICTs, as explained in Chapter 2. If you have other types of pictures that you would like to use, you can convert them to PICT files with an imaging program (Chapter 2 recommends a couple).

You can download the free **Photos4us Lite** and try it out right away. The Lite version lets you include up to ten pictures and ten sounds in your screen saver. With the full (paid for) version of the program, you can include all the pictures and sounds your heart desires.

Downloading and Setting Up

So, you want to check out Photos4us? To download the program, visit **http://www.zoetek.com/entrance/Photos4us/**. There you can read more about Photos4us, and download the Lite version by clicking the "Try It!" link (the filename is Photos4us_sea.hqx).

After you unstuff the file, double-click the photos4us_lite_1.02 folder (the "1.02" part of the filename may change with upgrades). Then double-click the Photos4usLite icon to display the contents of the Photos4usLite folder, as shown in **Figure 3.9**.

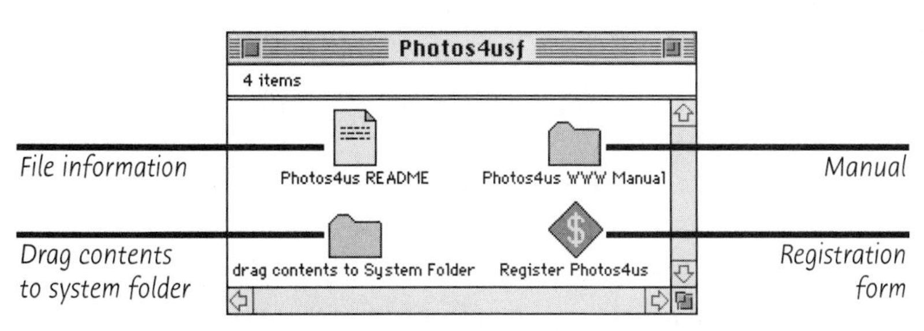

Figure 3.9 *Inside the Photos4usLite folder.*

Do you see the folder named Drag Contents to the System Folder? Do what it asks—open the folder (see **Figure 3.10**), select the Photos4us control panel and the Photos4us Items folder, and drag them into your System folder. Your computer will automatically recognize the Photos4us control panel and put it in your Control Panels folder. Then restart your computer so it will recognize the new control panel.

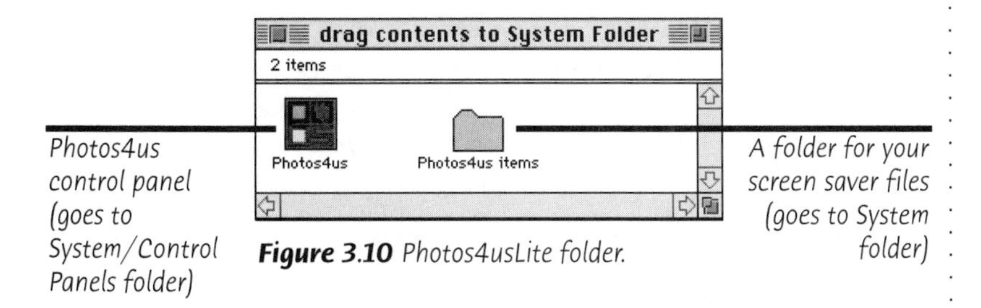

Figure 3.10 *Photos4usLite folder.*

Registering Photos4us

If you like Photos4us, you can register it for $10. Double-click the Register icon located in the Photos4usLite folder to display the registration form. Fill out your information and select a payment method. You can then print out the form and save it as a text file.

To send your order form by e-mail with a credit card number, e-mail the registration file as an attachment addressed to sales@kagi.com. To fax your order form with a credit card number, print out the form and fax it to Kagi at 510-652-6589. You can also snail-mail a check or cash payment to Kagi, 442-A Walnut Street #392-G1, Berkeley, California 94709-1405. In three or four days, you'll receive an e-mail response with your registration number.

Activating Photos4us

Once you restart your computer, you can activate Photos4us and get busy creating a screen saver. First, though, set your program options.

1. Select Control Panels from the Apple menu, and select Photos4Us from the cascading list.
2. When the Photos4us control panel appears, as shown in **Figure 3.11**, choose your options as follows:

Photos4us Control Panel Options

   - **On/Off**: Select the On radio button to activate the Photos4us screen-saver program. To disable your screen saver (once you create it), select the Off radio button.
   - **Activate after __ minutes of no activity**: Screen savers launch after a certain amount of time passes without your doing anything on the computer. To specify how many minutes you want to elapse before the screen saver launches, enter a number in the box.
   - **Sleep Now Corner**: No, Photos4us isn't telling you to take a nap! The Sleep Now Corner feature lets you drag your mouse to a corner of your computer screen to launch the screen saver, so you can preview it and change your special effects and other settings. You can either leave the current Sleep Now Corner selected, or pick a different one. You should also make sure that the Sleep Now Corner is turned on. Once you've created your screen saver, you can launch it any time you want by moving your cursor into your Sleep Now Corner.
3. When your options are set, click the Close box to activate the settings and close the control panel.

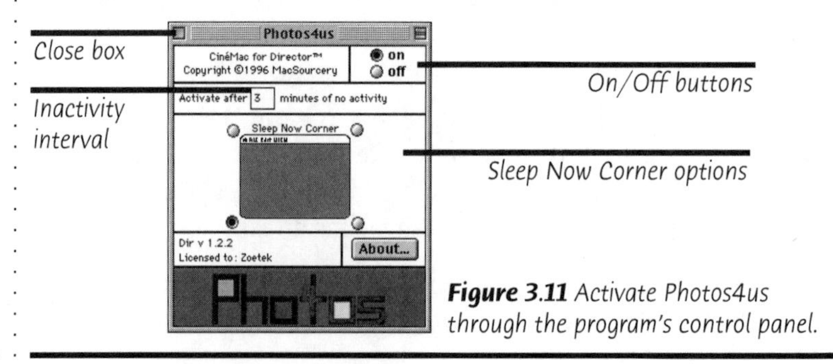

Figure 3.11 *Activate Photos4us through the program's control panel.*

Creating a Picture List

Creating a picture list takes two easy steps:

1. Open the Photos4us Items folder in your System folder.
2. Move your images to the Pict folder, as shown in **Figure 3.12**.

Changing the order of the pictures

Photos4us then finds the pictures and displays them in alphabetical (or numerical) order by filename. If you want your pictures to display in a particular order, you can rename your files.

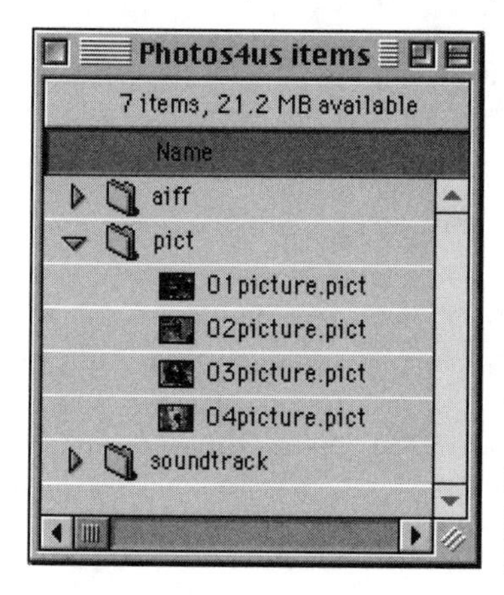

Figure 3.12 *Creating a picture list in the Photos4us Items folder.*

Adding Sound Files

Photos4us gives you two choices for adding audio to your screen-saver slide show:

- The **SoundTrack** option loops a single audio file over and over again. It works well for songs, or atmospheric sounds such as a babbling brook or the tones of wind chimes.
- The **Narration** option lets you play a sound file for each picture. You can include random noises or record a narration for each picture if you want.

Photos4us only supports the **AIFF** sound file format, but you can download files from the Web, convert your existing sounds, or record sounds with your system software. You can also record audio with your cam along with your movies. You can then open the movie in QuickEditor (a video application covered in Chapter 6) and export the sound track as a separate file. **Chapter 14** tells you more about cams and audio.

You create your sound file list the same way you created your picture list: by moving the sound files into a folder. Use the AIFF folder for a narration; use the SoundTrack folder for a single-sound-file screen saver.

Creating a Narration

1. From the System folder, open the Photos4us Items folder.
2. Move your AIFF sound files into the AIFF folder, as shown in **Figure 3.13**. You should have a sound for each picture.
3. If you want your sounds to play in a particular order, rename the files to correspond with the files on your pictures list.

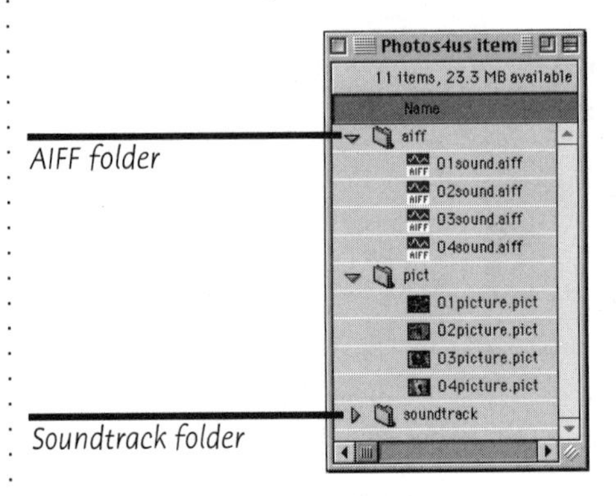

Figure 3.13 *Creating a sound file list for a slide-show narration in the Photos4us Items folder.*

Creating a Sound Track

1. Open the Photos4us Items folder from the System folder.
2. Move one AIFF sound file into the Soundtrack folder.

The Best of Both Worlds. Can't decide whether you want to include a soundtrack or to have a sound play with each picture? Go ahead and create a file list for your narration in the AIFF folder, and put the sound file that you want to use for your soundtrack in the SoundTrack folder. No, you can't play your screen saver in both Narration and SoundTrack modes. But once you've put your files in the right folders, you can decide how to use them as explained in "Settings and Special Effects" coming up. And you can change modes any time you want.

Action! Previewing Your Screen Saver

Why wait when you can **preview** your screen saver right now? Go to your desktop, and move the arrow cursor with your mouse into the special Sleep Now Corner and hold it there for a minute. If this doesn't start the screen saver, move the mouse as far into the corner of your screen as it will go. If your screen saver *still* doesn't launch, display the Photos4us control panel and make sure that it's turned on, and that you're correctly remembering which corner you selected.

Settings and Special Effects

Now that you've created your lists of image and sound files, you can customize the way your new screen saver will run. With Photos4us, you can display cool transition effects between pictures, set up a soundtrack or a narration (or no sound at all), and more.

To display the Options dialog box, as shown in **Figure 3.14**, press the Option key while your screen saver is running. (You can either wait for the screen saver to launch, or force it into action by moving your mouse into the Sleep Now Corner.)

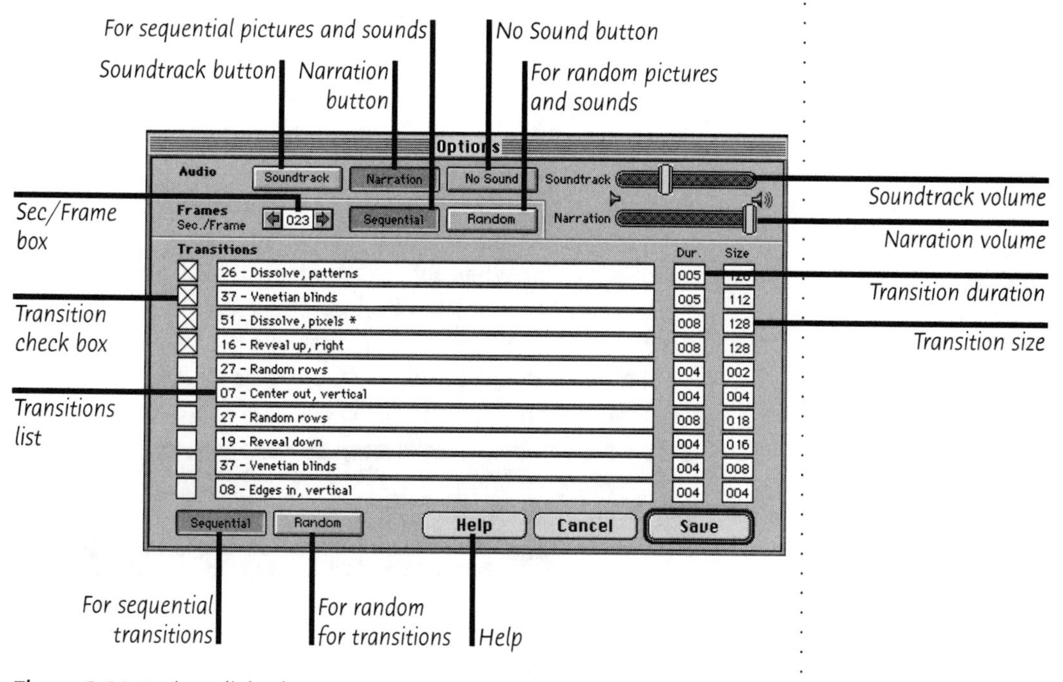

Figure 3.14 *Options dialog box.*

Photos4Us Options

- **Audio**: To loop a sound over and over again, click the SoundTrack button. To play a sound file with each picture, click the Narration button. To keep your sound files from playing, click the No Sound button. (You cannot select more than one Audio option.)
- **Volume Controls**: You can turn the volume up or down for your soundtrack or narration by moving the SoundTrack or Narration slider to the right or left.
- **Frames**: Designate the display time for each picture by clicking the Sec./Frame box and then the right or left arrow to

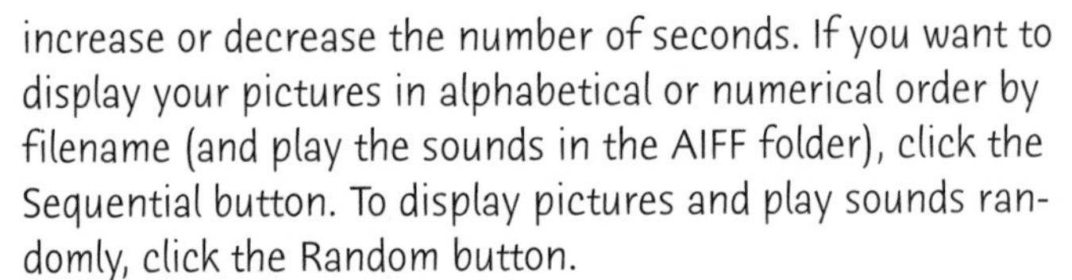

increase or decrease the number of seconds. If you want to display your pictures in alphabetical or numerical order by filename (and play the sounds in the AIFF folder), click the Sequential button. To display pictures and play sounds randomly, click the Random button.

Synchronizing Pictures and Sounds. With Photos4us, getting your sounds in sync with your pictures isn't too hard. If you've selected the Narration button, each picture displays until its corresponding sound file finishes playing, regardless of the number you select in the Sec./Frame box. If you want to accompany pictures with specific sounds, make sure to click the Sequential button in the Frames options.

- **Transitions**: You can use up to ten transitions in your screen saver but should probably stick with one or two, so people don't get dizzy. To pick a transition, click to select the first checkbox on the Transitions list, and then click the selection box to the right. When the right and left arrows appear, use them to scroll forward and backward through the list of effects. To designate whether transitions play in the order listed or at random, click the Sequential or Random button at the bottom of the Options dialog box.

***Transitions** are animated special effects that appear as your slide show moves from one photo to the next. Photos4us comes with over 58 types of transitions, including a variety of fades, wipes, and dissolves. Try 'em all!*

- **Duration and Size**: You can also determine the duration of a transition (how long it takes to move from one picture to the next) and its size (the number of steps it takes to close over one picture and reveal the next one). Click the Dur. (Duration) or Size box next to the selected transitions. When the arrows appear, click them to increase or decrease the number.
- **Save/Cancel**: Click the Save button to save and apply your changes, or click Cancel to return to the desktop with your settings unchanged.

Wanna Drive People Nuts? If you're feeling evil, then go ahead and set up your screen saver to beep, squawk, and sing the live-long day. Before everyone hates you forever, you can go back into the Options dialog box and turn off the sound (*after* showing off your new screen-saver slide show, of course).

Editing Your Screen Saver

You can edit your Photos4us screen saver any time you'd like, by replacing and rearranging the files in the Photos4us Items folder. Or, you can display the Options dialog box to change your settings and choose various transitions.

Disabling Your Screen Saver

Yikes! Grandma and Grandpa (or the big boss) are coming to town and they probably won't like your Wild Party screen saver pics. Don't fret—just turn off the screen saver. To disable it temporarily, go back to the ol' Photos4us control panel and click the Off button. When the coast is clear, you can turn your screen saver on again.

Trashing Photos4us

If you get tired of your screen saver, you can easily **uninstall** the Photos4us program. First, turn off the Photos4us control panel. Then find all your Photos4us files and drag them into the trash. Here are the steps:

To get rid of Photos4us:

1. Go to the Photos4us Items folder in your System folder and move the pictures and sounds to another folder so you don't lose them.
2. Go to the desktop (the Finder) and select Find from the File menu.
3. When the Find dialog box appears (**Figure 3.15**), enter **Photos4us** in the text box and click the Find button.

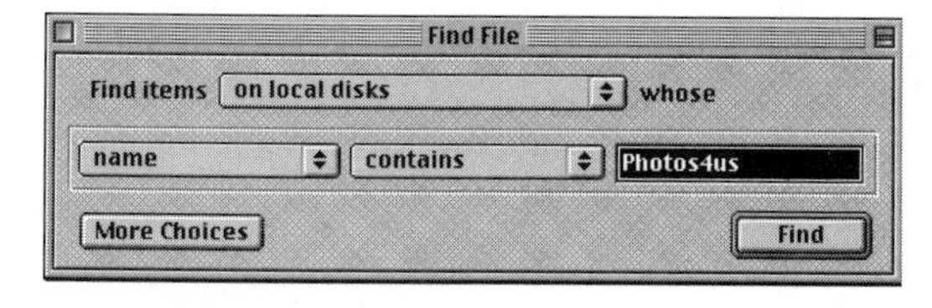

Figure 3.15 *Searching for the Photos4us files in the Find dialog box.*

4. In the Items Found list of files and folders, select items one by one and drag them into the trash. (Or, if you're not sure yet about ditching the program, you can drag them into any folder you want.) To close the Items Found list, click the Close box on the upper-left corner.
5. Restart your system, then empty your trash.

Remember How to Remove Files! I hope you'll be completely enchanted with every shareware program you ever try. But since life doesn't always work that way, you'll want to remember the procedures for "Trashing Photos4us" section of this chapter work for removing just about any program (as long as you change the text you enter in the Find dialog box!).

Grab It! Getting Images from the Web

Cams are great, and it's fun to share your photos and use them for creative projects. But sometimes you'll prefer (or require) other types of images for use in your GIF animations (Chapter 5), movies (Chapter 6), or Web pages (Chapter 7). Maybe you want some textured backgrounds for your desktop (Chapter 4) or your Web page. How about some clip art?

So—let's go shopping! Since all of the Web sites in the following list offer their artwork for free, you can't beat the price. One caution: Be patient when waiting for these pages to load in your browser. It can take a few minutes to load all the images.

Where to find free images on the Web

Site	What's There
Iconz - The Ultimate Site for Free Images http://www.geocities.com/Heartland/1448/	Pages and pages of buttons, backgrounds, icons, and more.
Virtual Free Clip Art http://www.dreamscape.com/frankvad/free.clipart.html	An extensive list of free picture Web sites, including eclectic categories such as backgrounds and textures, icons, animal art, and Mother's Day.
Icon Bazaar http://www.iconbazaar.com/	An enormous, well-organized collection of all sorts of pictures, with a search engine.
Rain Frog's Web Art http://www.rainfrog.com/	Free, original art with a touch of whimsy, plus links to other art collections and tips for creating your own pictures.
Fun with Clip Art http://www.nauticom.net/www/jillrh/clipart.htm	Links to all sorts of clip-art related Web sites (GIFs, JPEGs, and more).

Downloading an Image File

1. Right-click the image (Windows), or click the image and hold down the mouse button (Macintosh) to display the shortcut menu.
2. Select Save Image As, and proceed as you would when downloading other types of files.

Summary

Screen savers give you a fun way to use your cam, enjoy your favorite photos, and impress your coworkers, friends, and family. And when you start creating your own screen savers, you get an easy introduction to working with images and sound.

- **Screen savers** are programs that launch when you aren't using your computer. They display a series of pictures and play sounds on your computer until you start working again.
- You can take pictures with your cam and use them in your own screen savers. **A+ Screensaver Creator for Windows**, and **Photos4us for Macintosh** are inexpensive user-friendly programs that you can download from the Web and build your own screen savers.
- For best results, use the **full-screen** (640x480) or **half-screen** (320x240) settings when taking pictures for your screen saver. Most cams support these standard settings. Since image file sizes aren't an issue with screen savers (as they are with Web pages and the Internet), creating screen savers gives you a great opportunity to take full-screen pictures with your cam and use them.
- A+ Screensaver Creator for Windows can display **BMP** and **JPEG** images and play **WAV** or **MIDI** audio files. Photos4us for Macintosh supports **PICT** images and **AIFF** sound files.
- This chapter mostly covers A+ Screensaver Creator and Photos4us, because they don't cost much and you can download them from the Internet and use them right away. In addition, some cams come with **After Dark's** screen-saver modules (from Berkeley Systems) that record pictures with your cam and display them on your desktop as a live-action screen saver. Many of After Dark's modules also provide options for using your own pictures in a screen saver.
- **To create a screen saver,** gather your favorite pictures into a folder, activate the control panel from A+ Screensaver Creator or Photos4us, and create a picture list. You can also add special effects and sounds if you want. Chapter 14 tells you more about cams and sounds.
- You can **edit your screen saver** and change your picture list, sound file list, and special effects at any time through the screen-saver program's control panel.

- If you like A+ Screensaver Creator or Photos4us, you should register and pay for the program. **Registering** unlocks additional program features—and it's also the nice thing to do. If the thrill wears off quickly, you can always uninstall the program.
- Sure, you can take pictures with your cam and use them for the projects in this book. But you may also want to use other types of graphics in your GIF animations, movies, and Web pages. **The Web** offers treasure troves of free patterns, textures, and clip art that you can download.

When you're ready, Chapter 4 will tell you about more ways to spiff up your desktop, using pictures that you take with your cam.

4 Designing the Picture-Perfect Desktop

Chances are, you spend an awful lot of time at your computer every day. So why not make your desktop look as pleasant as possible?

In Chapter 3 you learned about creating custom screen savers with pictures that you can take with your cam. You can also use snapshots of people, pets, toys, collectibles, patterns, textures, and any old thingamabob to change the whole look and feel of your computer's display. This chapter gets you started with **three easy and fun projects** for making your computer environment a friendlier place:

- Putting your own photos on the desktop
- Turning your favorite photos into icons
- Creating your own startup screen

Putting a Photo on Your Desktop

What's the easiest and most inexpensive way to show off your favorite cam photo du jour? Put it on your desktop where you and everyone else can see it. Windows and Macintosh both come with control panels that let you change the look and feel of your computer screen. You can display a single photo, as shown in **Figure 4.1**, or tile a picture into a pattern, as shown in **Figure 4.2**.

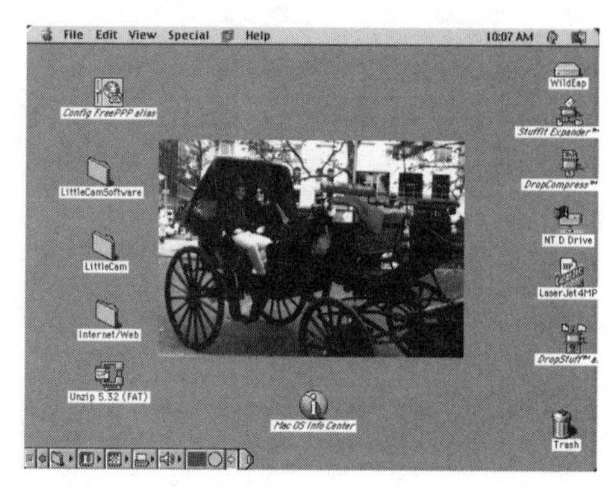

Figure 4.1 *A photo centered on the Macintosh desktop.*

It's time to put your image programs to work

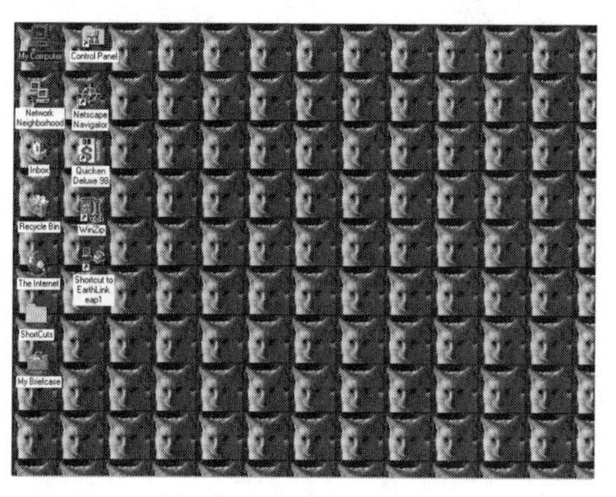

Figure 4.2 *On this Windows desktop, the photo is "tiled."*

Remember the image editing programs we covered back in Chapter 2? You'll need them to do the projects in this chapter. Don't worry if you don't think you know a lot yet about image programs. At this point, you won't have to do anything too difficult—just a little resizing, cropping, and converting.

For more about setting up your video camera as a cam, see Chapter 2.

As you can see, we were outdoors when we took the photo shown in **Figure 4.1**. When you use a regular video camera as your cam, you can take pictures and record movies anywhere you want!

Tiling

Tiling pictures works a lot like tiling the kitchen floor (only it doesn't take *nearly* as much hard work). Your computer takes a single image (tile) and repeats it across the screen over and over again so it looks like a pattern. Tiled images on the desktop are generally referred to as **wallpaper** on Windows, and **desktop patterns** with Macintosh.

Don't get carried away with tiling. Tiled backgrounds can look awfully busy if you don't watch out. When you're planning to tile an image on your desktop, fiddle around with it first, using the image editing programs discussed in Chapter 2. Try adjusting the brightness and contrast (the less contrast, the better) and experiment with some filters.

Acceptable Image Formats

What image formats can you use on your desktop? Windows 95 users need to use bitmap (BMP) files. Windows 98 users can use bitmap, GIF, and JPEG files. On the Macintosh, you can use PICTs, JPEGs, TIFs, and GIFs.

Most of today's cams, including QuickCam, can save images as JPEGS and BMP files on Windows and JPEGs and PICTs on the Mac. When you save a picture with your cam software, you can choose an image format from the Save dialog box. If you plan to use an image on a Web page as well as on your desktop, make sure to save a copy as a JPEG or GIF.

Using Patterned Backgrounds

Textures make great **desktop patterns**! Although you can find plenty of textures and patterns on the Web (as covered in Chapter 3), you can create your own textures with your shiny new cam. Set your image size to quarter-screen (160x120), zoom in on your subject, and take the picture, as explained in Chapter 2.

With some cropping and touching up, you can even turn parts of your images—such as leaves, sand, water, flowers, and pebbles—into a patterned background. If, like many people, you can't take your cam outside, look around your house or office. You can take close-up snapshots of indoor items like fabrics, carpets, furniture surfaces, and other stuff to build up a collection of attractive textures.

Patterns on the Web. Patterned backgrounds on Web pages work the same way as desktop patterns. Only instead of tiling a single image across your desktop, the browser tiles the single image across a Web page. For more about putting your pictures in a Web page, see Chapter 7.

Smaller is better!

When you use your cam to take pictures for desktop patterns and icons, choose the quarter-screen (160x120) image size. Smaller images work better when it comes to desktop patterns and Web page backgrounds because they demand less from your system. And since you have to crop and reduce pictures before you can use them as icons, that's another reason to start off with smaller images.

Now let's look at the steps to follow for getting a photo onto your desktop.

Making a Desktop in Windows

Windows only

To put a photo on the Windows desktop:

1. Right-click the desktop to display the shortcut menu, and select Properties.
2. In the Properties dialog box, select the Background tab (see **Figure 4.3**).
3. Click the Browse button to display the Browsing for Wallpaper dialog box.
4. Browse for your file (.bmp only), select it, and click OK to return to the Properties dialog box.
5. If you want to tile your image, click the Tile radio button; or choose Center if you want your picture centered on the desktop.
6. Click Apply to apply your new settings without leaving the dialog box, or click OK to apply your settings and return to the desktop.

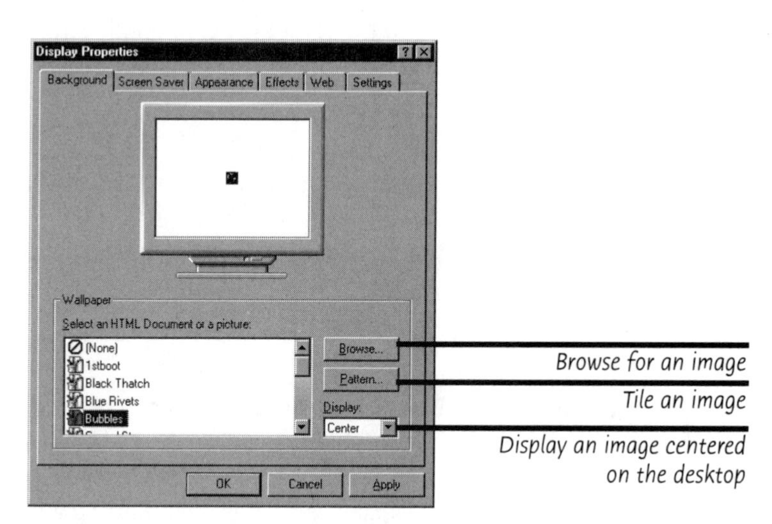

Figure 4.3 *The Display Properties dialog box Background tab.*

Making a Desktop on the Macintosh

Macintosh only

To put a photo on the Macintosh desktop:

1. Select Control Panels from the Apple menu, and select Desktop Pictures. The Desktop Pictures dialog box appears (**Figure 4.4**).
2. Click the Picture icon to indicate that you want to insert your own pictures. Then click Select Picture to display the dialog box that lets you browse for your files.
3. Select a picture and click Open to return to the Desktop Pictures dialog box.
4. You'll see a preview of the picture, as shown in **Figure 4.5**. Choose a display option from the pull-down list. You can tile an image, center it, or fill the entire screen with it (this last one works best with horizontally oriented images).
5. Click Set Desktop to preview the picture on your desktop.

   You can also click Remove Picture to try a different picture. To leave your desktop unchanged, click Pattern after removing the picture.

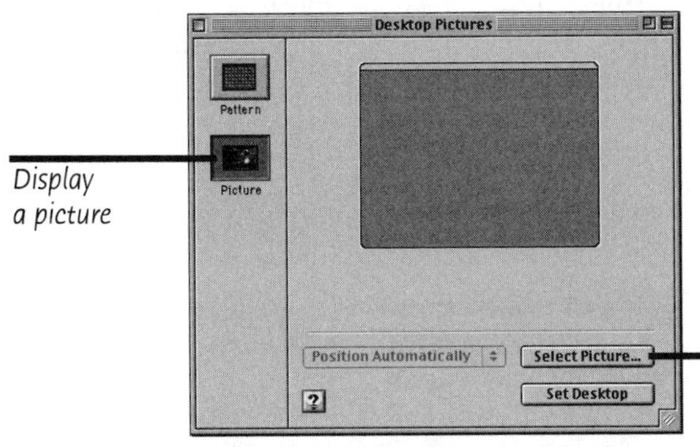

Display an Open File dialog box so you can pick an image file

Figure 4.4 Desktop Pictures dialog box.

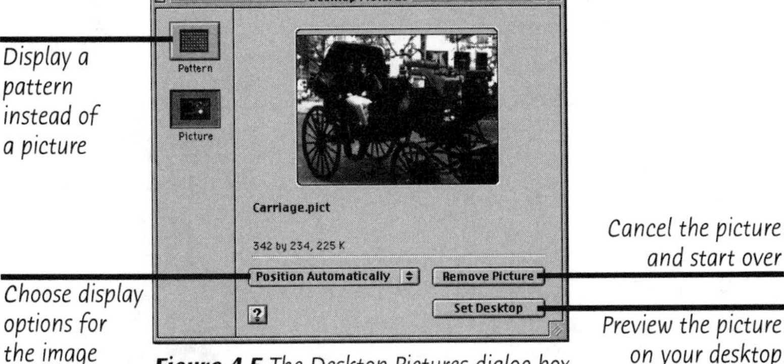

Figure 4.5 The Desktop Pictures dialog box after selecting an image.

6. When you're finished, click the Close box to close the dialog box and return to the desktop.

Creating Your Own Icons

Icons are the little pictures on your computer screen that represent applications, drives, and folders. The artists who create them try to come up with simple designs that make it easy to figure out what each icon does. When you double-click on a folder, a window opens to show your list of files. Double-click on an icon that looks like a page with text typed on it, and your word processing application launches.

But enough of that newbie stuff. Savvy users like you are ready to get more creative. With **MicroAngelo** (for Windows) and **Icon Mania!** (for Macintosh), you can turn your own cam pictures into icons. So go ahead and put Junior's face where that dreary old My Computer or Macintosh HD icon used to be.

This is just the beginning!

We're just scratching the surface here—MicroAngelo and Icon Mania! are sophisticated tools with lots of features. You can even use them to draw your own icons from scratch or do advanced touch-ups. All the possibilities of these tools are far beyond the scope of a single chapter, but you'll find built-in help systems in both of these programs that you can use to learn more.

Making Pictures Icon-Ready

Right now, you're probably saying something like, "But my pictures are so much larger than my computer's icons!" And you're right. You need to use one of the image-editing programs described in Chapter 2 to touch up your photos and convert them to the correct file formats. It also helps to plan ahead. When taking pictures that you plan to use as icons with your cam, select the Zoom In and quarter-screen (160x120) settings, and make sure to center your subject in the middle of the picture.

Crop, resize, and reformat

First, because your cam takes rectangular pictures, you need to **crop** your picture to a square to make it ready to become an icon. If your image editor doesn't come with a cropping tool, you can select a square area of your image and copy it into a new image.

Next, **resize** the images you plan to use, to 64x64, 48x48, 32x32, or 8x8 pixels. I recommend using the 64x64, 48x48, and 32x32 sizes, because 8x8-pixel images are *way* too tiny for most uses. **Pixels,** by the way (short for Picture Elements and sometimes abbreviated as **pels**), are the main unit of measurement in the computer graphics world.

Finally, you need to get your image in the right **format**: Windows users should convert pictures to the bitmap, JPEG, or GIF format, and Macintosh users should convert to the PICT file format.

Note to Macintosh Users: With a Mac, you have more flexibility with image sizes, but you should still keep the recommended icon measurements in mind. For best results, crop your pictures so the main subject fits into a perfect square, like the examples shown in **Figure 4.6**.

Figure 4.6 *Examples of ordinary pictures, cropped and resized to be used as icons.*

Don't Ruin Your Originals! Before making a picture icon-ready, select File|Save As and save a copy of your image with a different filename. This way, you can still use the original.

Getting Started with MicroAngelo

Windows only

With Impact Software's MicroAngelo, you can import GIF, bitmap, and JPEG files and turn them into icons for standard system elements like drives, folders, and your Recycle Bin. MicroAngelo has five separate components—integrated applications that let you do various things. The program costs $59.95, and you can get it from **http://www.impactsoft.com**.

The installer application is called MicroAngelo.exe, and you don't have to unzip it. Just double-click it to launch the Setup program, and follow the instructions.

Before you begin, gather the pictures you've taken with your cam and reformatted with your image editing program into a folder so that you can find them more easily.

Registering MicroAngelo

You can try out MicroAngelo for 30 days without registering; after 30 days the program stops working. To pay for MicroAngelo so you can receive a registration key, click the How to License button on the startup screen (it appears when you first launch a MicroAngelo component). Or, you can select About from the Help menu to display the About MicroAngelo dialog box; then click the Next button.

This displays a dialog box that provides options for registering online and paying with your credit card, or printing out a form so you can fax your order or mail a check. When you receive your registration key by e-mail, you can register the program. If you have no patience for registration forms, you can order by phone at 1-800-777-7687.

MicroAngelo's Components

The MicroAngelo program gives you the following five components:

- **Animator**: You can change the graphics for the various types of cursors used by your system and applications. Since you have to use very small files, and the Animator is an advanced utility, this chapter does not cover Animator.
- **Engineer** is used for changing your icon and desktop settings.
- **Explorer** lets you browse for icon files and install them.
- **Librarian** helps you locate all the icons on your system and organize them into libraries.
- **Studio** is used for converting images (like the photos you've taken with your cam) to icons.

To launch a MicroAngelo component:

1. Click the Start button, select Programs, and click the MicroAngelo folder to display the list of components. Then select a component.
2. When you first launch one of MicroAngelo's components, a somewhat startling File Associations Have Changed dialog box appears, with an ominous "Files no longer associated with MicroAngelo" message. Not to worry. Just click Yes and you'll never see it again.
3. The startup screen appears. If you haven't already done so, you can register and pay now by clicking the How to License button, or click the Quit button to leave the program. Or (and this is the part you're waiting for!), click the I Agree button to start using the program.

What am I agreeing to?
*All software comes with a **licensing agreement** that explains the terms of use—such as whether you can run copies of the program on more than one computer, how long you can use the program before you have to pay for it, etc.*

Changing MicroAngelo Display Settings

Before you start changing your icons, you should first establish your display settings in the **MicroAngelo Engineer**. The Engineer offers more options than the Display control panel that comes with your system, so you'll be able to make your icons look as good as they possibly can. Once you've created your icons, you can also use the Engineer to quickly change the standard icons, as explained later in this chapter.

To change your display settings with the Engineer:

1. Launch the Engineer by clicking Start | Programs | MicroAngelo | Engineer.
2. When the Engineer launches, as shown in **Figure 4.7**, make sure the System tab is open (it should already be displayed).
3. Choose your options (descriptions coming up), and click the Apply button to apply the settings.
4. If a dialog box appears and tells you that your new settings will not take effect until you restart your system, go ahead and click the OK button.

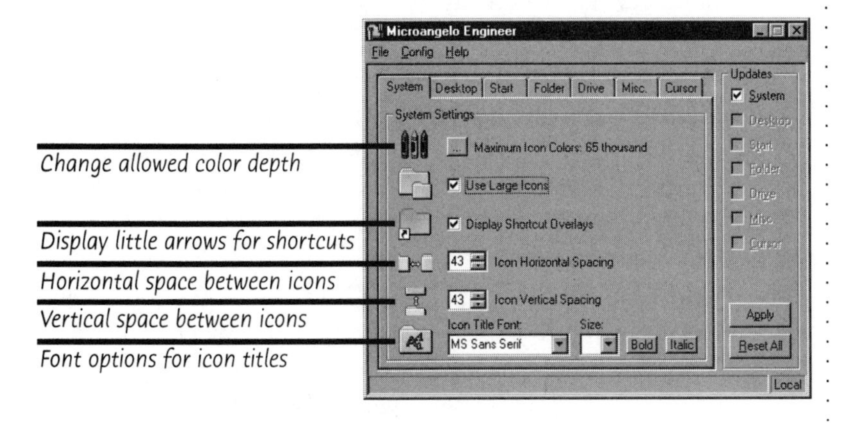

Figure 4.7 *Changing the settings in the MicroAngelo Engineer.*

MicroAngelo Engineer Options

- **Maximum Icon Colors:** This is the most important setting for our purposes in this chapter. Your system defaults to displaying icons in 4- or 8-bit color. This works fine for simple line-art drawings, but not for the photos you're going to be using. Cams normally take pictures in 16- or 24-bit color. Click the button next to the crayons to display the Icon Color Depth dialog box (**Figure 4.8**), select the 16-bit option, and click OK to return to the Engineer. (You can also select 24-bit, but 16-bit should work fine and doesn't demand as much from your system resources.)

For more about color depth, see Chapter 2

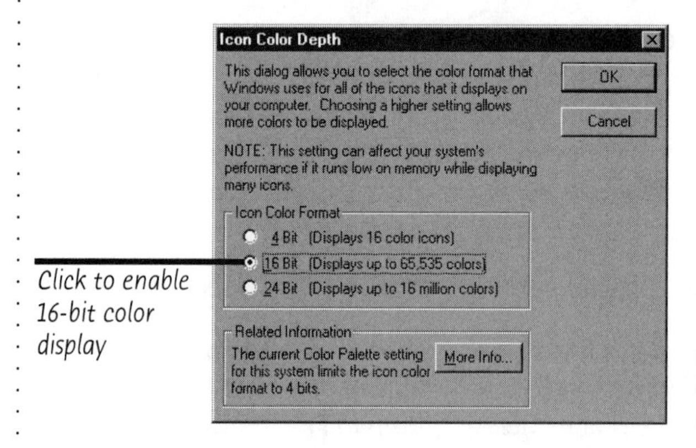

Click to enable 16-bit color display

Figure 4.8
Adjusting your icon color display.

- **Use Large Icons**: Select this checkbox only if you plan on customizing *all* your icons. This option is ideal for displaying your photographs in a slightly larger size, but it will make the rest of your icons look distorted.
- **Display Shortcut Overlays**: Windows shortcuts appear with **overlays**—those little curvy arrows that distinguish shortcuts from real icons. Leave this checkbox selected so your icons will behave the way all Windows icons do.
- **Icon Horizontal and Vertical Spacing**: Enter numerical measurements (in pixels) to designate the space between adjacent icons. The spaces create a horizontal and vertical buffer around each icon. I recommend leaving these settings as is.
- **Icon Title Font**: This is the font style used in the text below your icons to tell you what they represent ("My Computer," "Recycle Bin," and so on). You can select a different font from the Icon Title Font list. You can also make the font larger or smaller by selecting a number from the Size list (the default is 8 points, and it's best not to go any larger than 10 points). You can also select the Bold and Italic buttons to add these attributes to your icon titles.
- **Apply/Reset**: Click the Apply button to apply your changes, or Reset to cancel your settings and start over.

Converting Pictures to Icons

Windows icons are stored as icon resources with the .ico filename extension. Ordinary image programs cannot save pictures to this file format, which is why you need a program like MicroAngelo. To turn your image into an icon, you need to import and convert it with the **MicroAngelo Studio**. The Studio, shown in **Figure 4.9**, has lots of tools and settings for editing icon files; you can even draw icons from scratch.

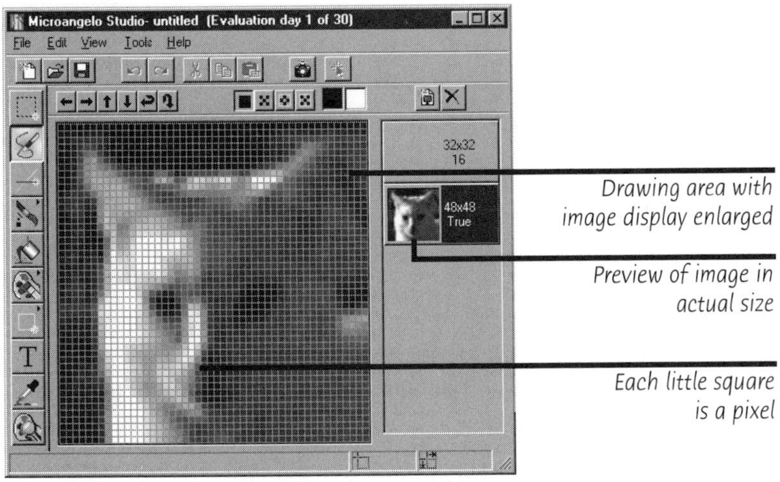

Drawing area with image display enlarged

Preview of image in actual size

Each little square is a pixel

Figure 4.9 *Image file displayed in MicroAngelo Studio.*

To convert a picture to an icon:

1. Launch MicroAngelo Studio by clicking Start|Programs|MicroAngelo, and (finally!) selecting Studio.
2. Open your file.
   - To open a **GIF** file, select File|Open. When the Open dialog box appears, you can browse for a file, select it, and click the Open button.
   - To open a **bitmap** or **JPEG** file, select Edit|Open Bitmap as Image and browse for your file from the Open dialog box. If you're opening a JPEG file, select All Files from the Files of Type list.

   When your photograph displays as an enlargement in the drawing window and at actual size in the preview area, you can proceed.

3. To save your image as an icon, select File | Save As to display the Save As dialog box (**Figure 4.10**).

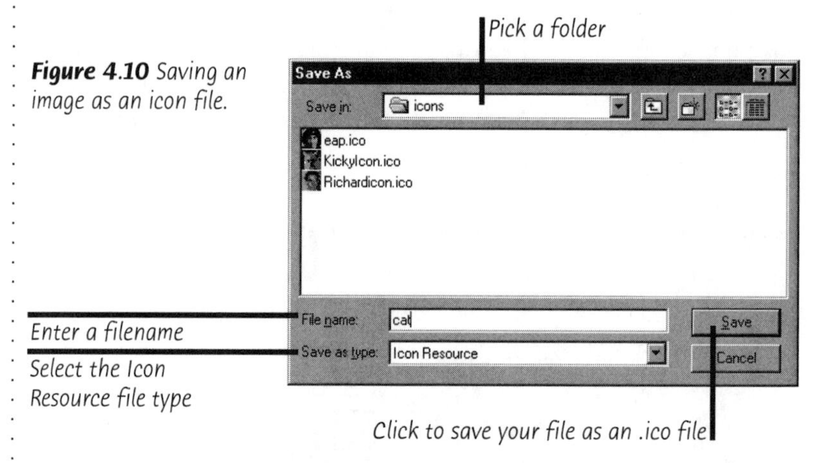

Figure 4.10 *Saving an image as an icon file.*

4. Choose the folder where you want to keep your icon files by selecting it from the Save In list. Enter a name for this icon file in the File Name box (Windows automatically provides the .ico filename extension). Select Icon Resource from the Files of Type list, and click the Save button.
5. You can now open and convert additional files, or click the Close box (X) to exit the Studio.

Hey, My Picture Looks Funny

Since you're not yet familiar with the wunnerful world of icons, your images may look odd to you when displayed in the Studio. Have you ever seen a pointillist painting, in which the artist has painted images with tiny dots? Pointillist paintings look realistic from far away, but when you look at them closely, you can see all the dots that compose the image.

Computer images work this way, too. Everything you see on your computer screen is made of those tiny little **pixels**—including the pictures you take with your cam. But you never notice the pixels unless you look *really* closely. MicroAngelo Studio enlarges your image and **displays each pixel**, so you can edit icons and even create them from scratch.

Creating and editing icons takes a lot of work and practice. I don't recommend touching up your photos this way, because photos are extremely detailed and it could take *hours*.

Creating Your Icon Library

Having a cam is sure to bring out the shutterbug in you. If you take lots of snapshots and convert them to icons, you might need some help keeping track of them all!

Once you've created a few icons, you'll want to create an **icon library** so you can store them together and find them easily. The **MicroAngelo Librarian** component makes it easy to organize all the icons you create. The Librarian searches for files in folders you select, and displays a list of the files it finds so you can save your list as a library.

To create an icon library:

1. To launch the Library, click Start|Programs|MicroAngelo, and select Librarian. From the Library window, select File|Search.
2. When the Search dialog box appears, as shown in **Figure 4.11**, go to the Folder list and select the folder or drive that contains your icons. In the Files of Type list, select Icon Files. (If you also want to search folders *within* the selected folder or drive, check the Include Subfolders checkbox, as well.) Then click the Search button.

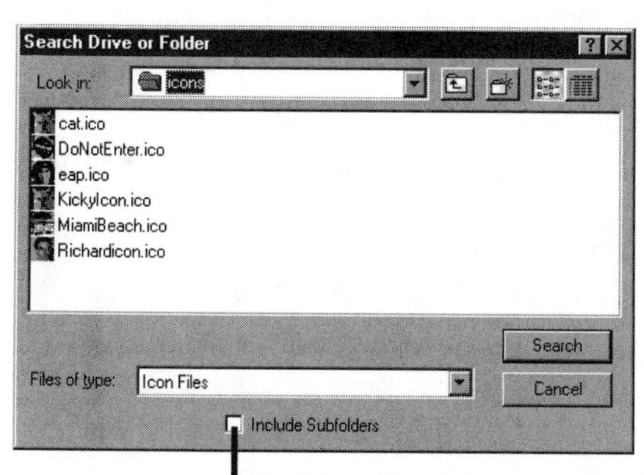

Figure 4.11
Searching for icon files.

3. When the Library finishes searching for your icons, it displays them as shown in **Figure 4.12**.
4. To save your new library, select File|Save to display the Save As dialog box.
5. Browse the Look In box for the folder that will store your library, enter a name for your library in the File Name box, select Library (*.ICL) from the Files of Type box, and click the Save button.

Keep your libraries in one folder.

Figure 4.12 *Displaying an icon library.*

Working with Libraries

Adding Icons: As you take more pictures with your cam, you may want to convert them to icons and include them in your library. You can add more files to your library by searching folders, as you did when you first created the library. If the Librarian finds new files that weren't in the folders the last time you did a search, the new files are added to the library. You can then select File|Save to save your updates.

Opening a Library: Now that you've created a library, you'll probably want to use it again sometime soon. Open your library by launching the Librarian, and then clicking the Open toolbar button to display the Open dialog box. You can then browse for your library file.

Closing a Library: You should leave the Library open for now, so you can customize your icons (as explained in "Installing Your Icons," coming up). But you can exit the Librarian at any time by clicking the Close (X) box.

Creating a New Library: After you've accumulated lots of icons—whether you created them yourself or downloaded them from the Web—you can create as many libraries as you want. Whenever you launch the Librarian, it opens a New File window for you, and you can follow the steps in the preceding section for creating a library. If you're already in an open library, you can display a New File window by clicking the New button.

Want More Than One Library? The Librarian creates libraries by searching existing folders for icons. If you want to create multiple libraries organized by category, then you should store your icons in separate folders. You can then create a single folder in which to store all your library files.

Installing Your Icons

Now that you've converted some images into icons and built your library, you're ready to install those icons. **Installing your icons** is MicroAngelo's phrase for turning those boring old system icons into the fabulous pictures you've taken with your cam.

Change your desktop and drive icons! *After all, these are the items you probably look at most often. Wouldn't it be fun to look at your pictures instead?*

Windows Icon Categories: You can install icons—that is, replace existing icons with a created or downloaded icon—for a variety of categories:

- **Desktop**: Items that appear on your desktop, including My Computer, the Recycle Bin, and My Briefcase.
- **Start Menu**: Items that appear on the Start menu, such as Find, Settings, and Help.

  Since the Start menu only uses the smaller 8x8 icons, I don't recommend putting photos on the Start menu.

- **Folder**: Various types of folders, including Open, Closed, and Program Group.
- **Drive**: Icons for your computer's drives, including the floppy drive, CD-ROM drive, removable storage devices, and computers on your network (if you're connected to one).
- **Misc**: Icons for miscellaneous standard items that don't fit into the other categories.

Steps for Installing

To install your icons:

1. Open your icon library.
2. Right-click the icon you wish to use, to display the shortcut menu.
3. Select Install From System to display the Install Icon dialog box (**Figure 4.13**).
4. Click a tab for an icon category, and select an icon from the list. (The icon you select here is the icon you are replacing with the icon you chose in step 2.)
5. Click the Apply button to install the special icon and return to the Librarian window. (Or click Cancel to return to the Librarian window without making any changes.)

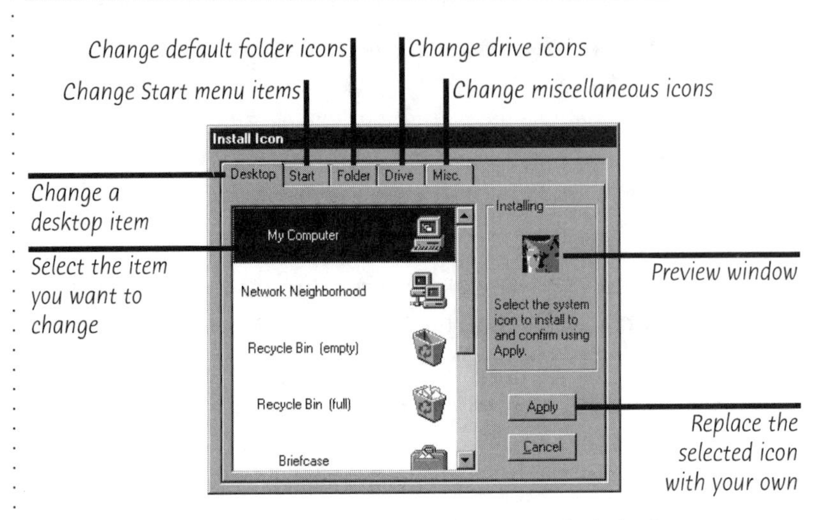

Figure 4.13 *Installing your own icons lets you customize the look of your computer environment.*

Don't Limit Yourself to Photos. The Free Themes Web site mentioned at the end of this chapter can hook you up with all kinds of cool icon collections. You should also take a look at the Icon Arcade at **http://members.xoom.com/webwork/index.html**.

Changing File Type and Application Icons

You can also apply your icons to file types and applications. For example, you might want to use your pictures to represent the files you create with your cam—including JPEGs, BMPs, GIFs, AVI movies, and QuickTime movies. Another option is to use your own icons to replace the ones for your camming software and other applications.

To change the icon for a file type or application, follow these steps:

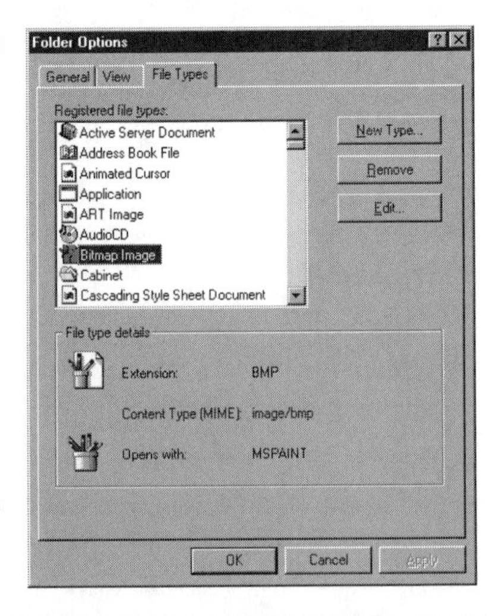

1. Launch Windows Explorer by selecting Start|Programs|Explorer.
2. Select View|Folder Options.
3. In the Folder Options dialog box, click the File Types tab.
4. Select a file type from the scrolling list (an image file format like BMP, or an application). Click the Edit button to display the Edit File Type dialog box.

5. Click the Change Icon button to display the Change Icon dialog box, where you'll see the standard system icons for the file type display. But naturally, you probably want to use your own.

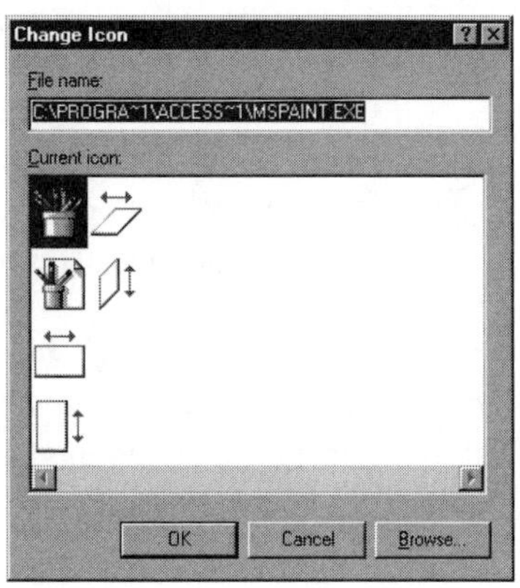

6. Click the Browse button to display a second Change Icon dialog box that allows you to search for your icon files.
7. Browse for your icon, select it, and click the Open button to return to the first Change Icon dialog box.
8. Close all of the dialog boxes by clicking the Close buttons.

Removing MicroAngelo

If you decide not to keep MicroAngelo, you can **uninstall** it through the Windows Add/Remove Programs control panel. Chapter 3 takes you through the steps of removing a program (see the "Trashing..." sections).

> Before you remove MicroAngelo, you might want to **remove any custom icons** you've installed and restore the standard ones. Otherwise you won't be able to change them back again!

Restoring Standard Icons

To **restore standard icons,** go back to the Librarian, open a new library, and search your entire hard drive for icon resources. (Make sure to select the Include Subfolders checkbox in the Search dialog box.) This takes a few minutes. Once the Librarian has displayed all of the icons on your system, you can scroll through the list, locate the standard icons, and re-install them over your custom icons. You won't be able to save this library (too many files), but at least you can use it to get your desktop back to normal.

You can also restore many types of icons through the Windows Explorer, as covered in "Changing File Type and Application Icons" section earlier in this chapter.

Using Icon Mania!

Macintosh only

Icon Mania! by Dubl-Click Software Corporation is a versatile, user-friendly little program that makes it easy to turn PICT files into icons. You can apply these custom icons to any folder, application, drive, alias, or file on your computer. The program also comes with a great clip-art collection, so you can put Oscar the Grouch in your trash can if you want, or replace the hard drive icon with a miniature *Mona Lisa.*

Though, of course, it's much more fun to use the pictures you take with your cam!

Folders for Everyone! If you share your computer with family members or coworkers, you can create a folder for each person and use their picture for the folder icon.

Icon Mania! costs $39.95 if you order online and $69.95 in computer stores. You can download and order the program through Dubl-Click Software Corporation's Web site at **http://www.dublclick.com/** (see the section that follows). Or download the **demo version** and check it out. The demo version lets you run through the steps explained in this section, but you won't be able to save the changes to your icons. If you decide to purchase Icon Mania!, double-click the How to Buy file in the Icon Mania! Demo folder and follow the instructions.

Ordering Icon Mania!

To get a fully functioning copy of Icon Mania!, visit Dubl-Click Software's Web site at **http://www.dublclick.com/** and click on the "Products" link. When the list of Dubl-Click software products appears, scroll down to Icon Mania! From here you can either download the demo or purchase the full version.

When you first launch Icon Mania!, you'll get an Unlock This Product dialog box with various options for registering. You can order by phone, e-mail, or fax with your credit card, or you can print out the form and mail a check. For more information, call Dubl-Click Software Corporation at 541-317-0355, or visit their Web site.

More Treats: You can download additional icon libraries for Icon Mania! from **ftp://empnet.com/pub/DublClick/Icon Mania/**.

Getting Started with Icon Mania!

Before you start using Icon Mania!, bear in mind that the program only works when you set your monitor to 256 colors. Once you create your icons, you can change back to your normal display settings. So you'll need to take these setup steps before you start using the program:

Important monitor setup steps

1. Select Control Panels from the Apple menu, and then Monitors & Sound to display the Monitors & Sound control panel (**Figure 4.14**).
2. Click the Monitor button. Make sure the Colors radio button is selected, and pick 256 in the Color Depth list.
3. Click the Close button to apply your settings and exit the control panel.

There, you're all set. When you're done using Icon Mania!, you can go back and change your monitor to the millions of colors setting.

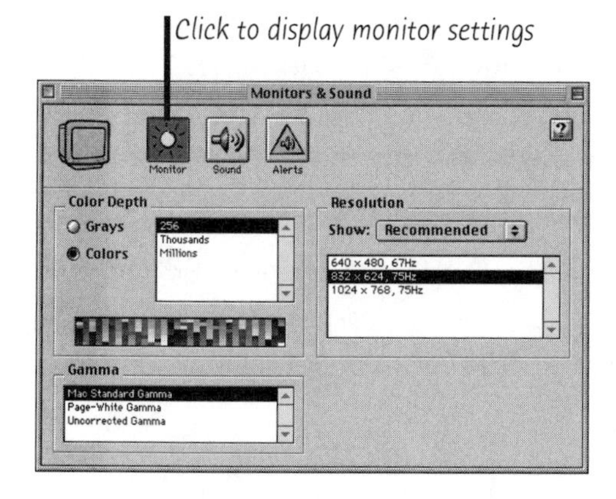

Figure 4.14 *You have to change the display to 256 colors when using Icon Mania!.*

You can use the Macintosh Control Strip—that tiny row of buttons in the lower-left corner of your screen—to change the monitor color settings, in addition to basic settings for many of your control panels. To change a control panel setting, click a Control Strip button, and select a new setting from the pop-up list.

Launching Icon Mania!

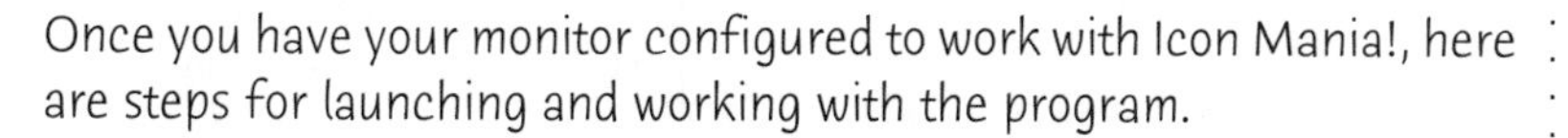

Once you have your monitor configured to work with Icon Mania!, here are steps for launching and working with the program.

1. Double-click the folder for Icon Mania! or Icon Mania! Demo to display the contents (**Figure 4.15**). Here, the Icon Libraries folder contains groups of icons, the Icon Mania! manual provides instructions and an overview of the program, and the Icon Mania! item launches the application.

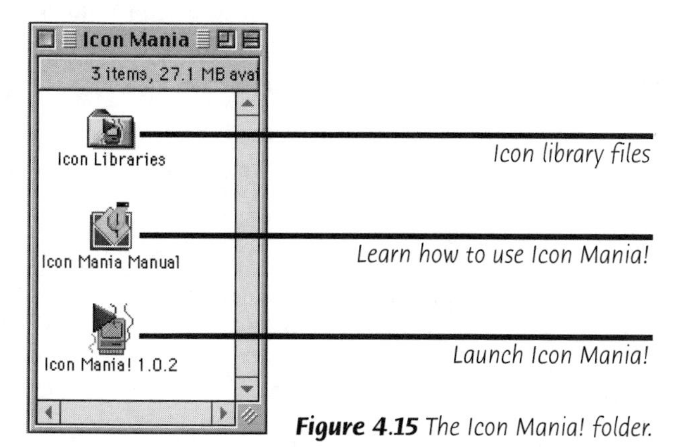

Figure 4.15 *The Icon Mania! folder.*

2. Double-click the Icon Mania! icon to launch the application.

   The first time you start Icon Mania, a dialog box appears asking you to personalize your copy of Icon Mania! Go ahead and enter your name and your organization (if applicable).

3. When the Icon Mania! window appears (**Figure 4.16**), you can start making your icons. Icon Mania! displays the following three panels:

Icon Library	The contents of the current icon library.
Drive/Folder	The contents of the currently selected folder.
Pasteboard	If you're artistically inclined (and very patient), you can edit or draw your own icons from the Pasteboard.

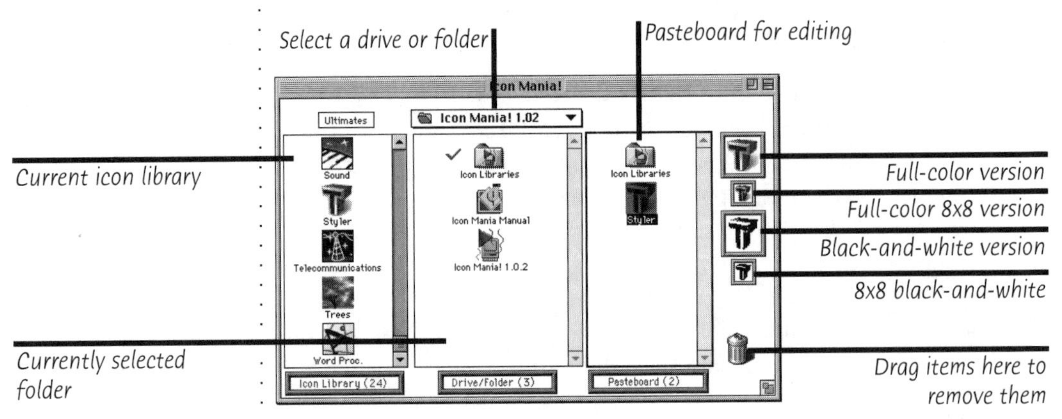

Figure 4.16 *The Icon Mania! application window.*

Working with Icon Libraries

Icon Mania! uses **libraries** to organize images used for icons, so you can keep track of files more easily. That's a darned good thing, because taking pictures with your cam and turning them into icons can get addictive! Libraries are groups of images organized by category. You can categorize your libraries and images however you like.

Icon Mania! comes with some libraries already jam-packed with great-looking artwork you can use. The library files are located in the Icon Libraries folder in the Icon Mania! folder.

Before you import your pictures and turn them into icons, it's a good idea to create a library for them. Otherwise you might have trouble finding them later!

To Create a New Icon Library

1. Select New from the File menu.
2. When the Save dialog box appears, as shown in **Figure 4.17**, browse for the folder in which you want to save your library. (I recommend saving it to the Icon Libraries folder, so you can keep all your libraries together.) Enter a name for your library in the Save New Library As box.
3. Click the Save button. When you return to the Icon Mania! application window, the name of your library appears above the Icon Library list.

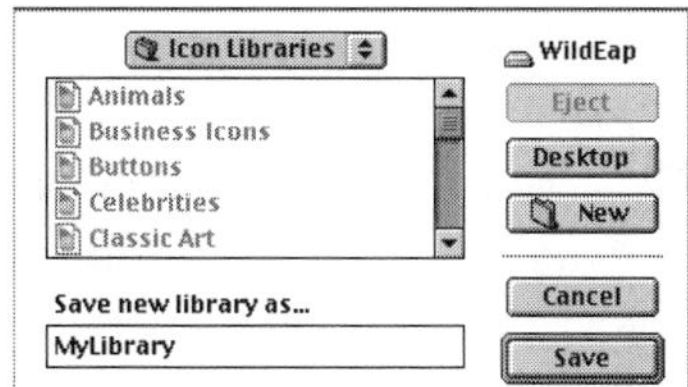

Figure 4.17 *Creating a new library.*

"But my library is empty!" Don't worry, it won't stay empty for long. Pretty soon, you'll be filling it with your own icons.

Adding Pictures

When you're ready to bring your pictures into an icon library, follow these steps:

When files on the Drive/Folder list can be used as icons, Icon Mania! marks them with a ✔.

1. Move all the images you want to use as icons into one folder.
2. From within an Icon Mania! library (you just created one in the preceding steps), select the folder that contains your images.
3. When Icon Mania! displays your image files in the Drive/Folder column, select a picture and drag it into the Icon Library column, as shown in **Figure 4.18**.
4. You can include as many pictures as you like in your library, and you can also add pictures from other folders. Icon Mania! automatically saves changes that you make to your library.

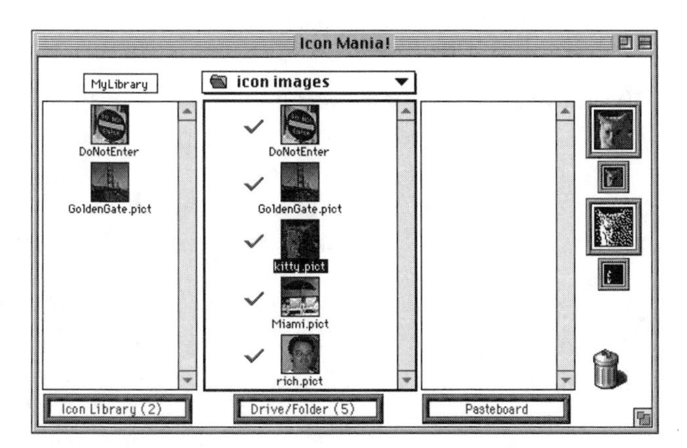

Figure 4.18 *Creating a new library.*

Open an Existing Library

When you want to open your library, or check out the libraries that come with Icon Mania!, just select File|Open. When the Open dialog box appears, browse for a folder, select a library file, and click the Open button.

Removing a Picture

To remove a picture from a library, just select it from the Icon Library list and drag it to the trash can in the lower-right corner of the Icon Mania! application window. ***Note:*** This just removes the picture as an item in your library; it does not delete the real image file!

Changing Your Icons

Once you know how to work with libraries, changing your icons is the easy part. First open a library. In the Drive/Folder list, display the items you want to customize. Now select a picture from the Icon Library list, and drag it onto an item on the Drive/Folder list. Icon Mania! immediately replaces that item's icon with your picture, as shown in **Figure 4.19**.

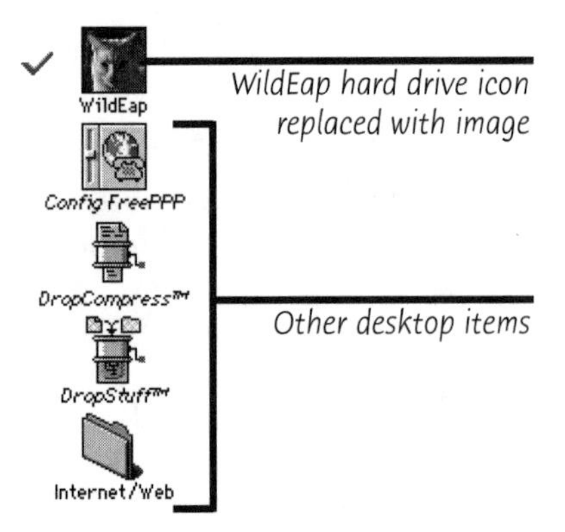

Figure 4.19 *Replacing a desktop item in the Drive/Folder list.*

Changing Default System Icons. You can display lists of your Default System Icons, Alert Icons, and Trash icons on the Drive/Folder list by selecting them from the pull-down list at the top of the Icon Mania! application window. These changes do not take effect until you restart your system.

Editing and Drawing Icons

If you're artistically inclined, you can use **Icon Mania's image editor** (shown in **Figure 4.20**) to edit icons and even create them from scratch. Creating and editing icons takes a fair amount of work and practice, but with some time and determination, you can get the hang of it.

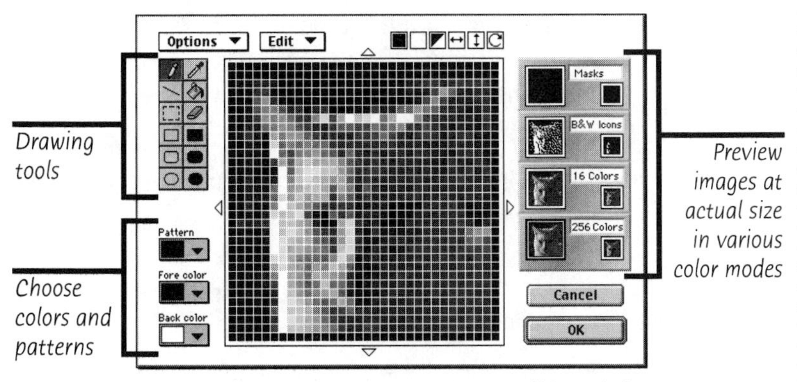

Figure 4.20 *Editing an icon in Icon Mania!'s image editing window.*

Working Pixel-by-Pixel

First, you should understand that because icons are so small, they must be created and edited pixel-by-pixel. That's why the cat picture in **Figure 4.20** looks kinda funny.

Have you ever seen a pointillist painting, in which the artist has painted images with tiny dots? Pointillist paintings look realistic from far away, but when you look at them closely, you can see all the dots that compose the image. Computer images work this way, too. Everything you see on your computer screen is made of those tiny little pixels. But you never notice the pixels unless you look *really* closely, as you will do with Icon Mania!'s image editor.

To edit an icon:

1. Select an image from the Icon Library list.
2. Drag the image to the Pasteboard list.
3. Double-click the image.

To draw an icon from scratch:

1. Create a blank image with an imaging program, and size it to 8x8, 32x32, or 48x48 pixels.
2. Save the image as a PICT file.
3. Open the PICT file from Icon Mania!, and drag the image to the Pasteboard list.
4. Double-click the image to launch the image editor.

Restoring Standard Icons

Icon Mania! has libraries that contain standard icons for system components and many applications. If you ever want to restore your computer's standard icons, you can search for them in these libraries.

If you've changed an icon associated with an application and want to restore the original icon, you can usually find the default image files on the CD-ROM or disk used to install the application.

Exiting Icon Mania!

To exit Icon Mania!, select Quit from the File menu. The program automatically saves any changes you made.

Removing the Icon Mania! Demo. Did you take the demo for a spin? If you have decided to upgrade to the "real" version, or to pass on the program, you can drag the Icon Mania! Demo folder into the trash.

Creating Your Own Startup Screen

Tired of looking at the Windows or MacOS (sounds like a new cereal!) logo every time you turn on your machine? Replace your system's **startup screen** with one of your cam pictures, instead, like the one shown in **Figure 4.21**. It's easy to do and it only takes a few minutes.

Figure 4.21 *You can use your own cam picture as a screen saver or opening screen.*

As with creating screen savers (Chapter 3), designing your own startup screen gives you a great opportunity to use the full-screen setting when you take a picture with your cam. Most of the projects in this book work better with half-screen and quarter-screen images and movies, because large images don't transfer well over the the Internet.

When it starts up, your operating system is programmed to look for an image named logo.sys (Windows) or StartupScreen (Macintosh). But you can rename one of your pictures so your computer displays that instead. (Windows users will first need to use one of the image-editing programs mentioned in Chapter 2 to format their image.)

Following are the steps to set up a picture as a startup screen.

Take a Picture

Step 1: Since you want a picture that will fill up your screen, you should set up your cam to take a snapshot at the largest size (640x480). Macintosh folks can use any image size they please (though it should be large enough to display well when you start up your system), but a Windows startup screen *must* start out at 640x480. Luckily, just about every cam has a full-screen (640x480) setting that you can use when you take a picture.

If you want to use an existing picture that doesn't fit the 640x480 dimensions, you can fix that with one of the image programs described in Chapter 2. Create a new image with the correct dimensions, paste your picture into the new image, and color in the border, as I did for **Figure 4.21**.

Format the Picture

Step 2: Format your picture as a 256-color bitmap file (Windows) or as a PICT file (Macintosh).

> **Note to Windows users**: You also need to resize the 640x480 image to 320x400 pixels with an image-editing program, as shown in **Figure 4.22**. (Make sure to uncheck the Maintain Aspect Ratio option so the picture resizes correctly. This distorts the image, but don't worry—it will display correctly as a startup screen.) I know this doesn't make any sense, but you'll have to trust me on this one!

Horizontal measurement (320)

Deselect this, to force your measurements to 320x400

Resize

Select new size

320 x 200
640 x 350
640 x 480
800 x 600
1024 x 768

Custom size:
320 x 400

Maintain aspect ratio
of 1.33333 to 1

OK Cancel Help

Vertical measurement (400)

Figure 4.22 *Resizing a Windows bitmap file to 320x400 in PaintShop Pro, a popular image editor. Most image-editing programs offer similar resizing options.*

Maintaining Proportion

When you're resizing an image, you normally leave the **Maintain Aspect Ratio** option selected to ensure that your image is resized proportionately. (But see the Warning just above, for Windows users.) You enter a horizontal or vertical measurement, and the image program automatically enters the other measurement.

A caution about unit of measurement

Some image-editing programs provide options for choosing the unit of measurement (such as inches). For the purpose of this book, however, you should *always* use pixels.

Save the Picture

Step 3: Select File|Save As in the image-editing program to display the Save As dialog box.

Windows only

If you're a Windows user, select the C: drive from the Save In list, enter "**logo.sys**" in the File Name box (as shown in **Figure 4.23**), select BMP from the Save As Type box, and click Save. *Do not omit the quotation marks* around the name—this prevents Windows from adding the .bmp filename extension. You must name the file correctly and save it to your root directory (the C: drive) in order for your startup screen to work.

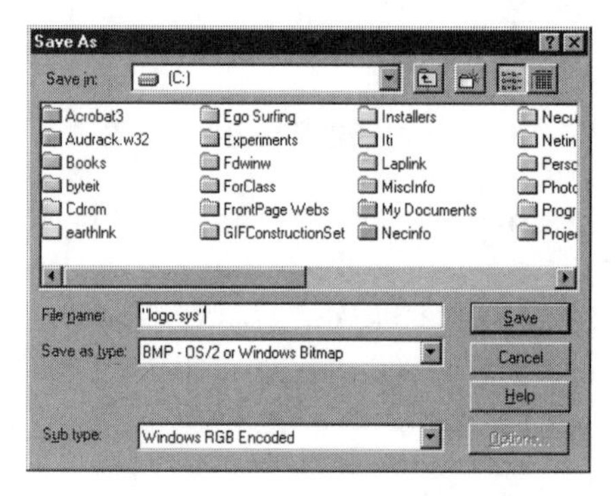

Figure 4.23 *Saving the startup screen image to the C: drive as* "**logo.sys**" *from an image program in Windows.*

Macintosh only

If you're a Macintosh user, select System Folder from the Save In list, enter **StartupScreen** in the File Name box, select PICT file from the Format list (as shown in **Figure 4.24**), and click Save. You must name the file correctly and save it to your system folder in order for your startup screen to work.

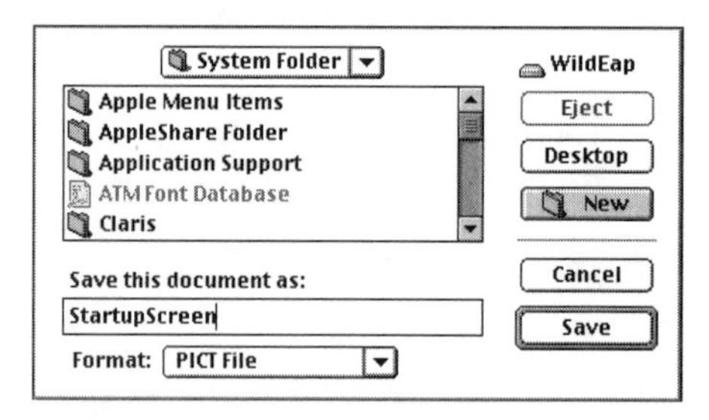

Figure 4.24 *Saving the startup screen image as StartupScreen and a PICT file on the Macintosh.*

Start It Up!

Step 4: Now you can restart your system to try out your new startup screen.

Going Whole Hog

There are lots of ways to beautify your desktop: screen savers, custom startup screens, downloadable icon collections, patterns, and themes. The following two Web sites offer a wealth of virus-free **shareware, free stuff, and tips** for jazzing up your desktop, working with icon files, and creating screen savers:

- **Free Themes** (for Windows) at **http://uzoom.freethemes.com/**
- **GUI Junky** (for Macintosh) at **http://www.kindground.com/gui_junky/index.html**

By the way, GUI stands for graphical user interface—which describes operating systems like Windows and Macintosh that let you do things by clicking on graphics. With pre-GUI operating systems like UNIX and DOS, you have to memorize and enter text command lines in order to get anything done.

Summary

Wow, we've sure covered a lot of ground. By now, you know a great deal about cams, computers, and images!

- Use your cam to make your computer a friendlier place! You can **decorate your desktop** with photographs, patterns, and icons, and substitute a picture for your system's boring old startup screen.
- Windows and Macintosh systems both have **control panels** for putting a picture on your desktop and for using smaller images as desktop patterns. On Windows: Right-click the desktop, select Properties, and view the Display Properties control panel. On the Mac, select Control Panels from the Apple menu, and choose Desktop Pictures.
- Your computer displays desktop patterns by **tiling a single picture** across your computer screen to form a pattern. Your home or office probably has many objects within reach of your cam that would make for interesting photos, patterns, and textures.
- Want to use your own pictures as icons? Take some **snapshots with your cam.** For best results, use the quarter-screen (160x120) image size, select your cam's Zoom In setting, and position your subject in the center of the photo.
- Stick with the 64x64, 48x48, or 32x32 sizes for icons, because 8x8 is awfully small. This means you'll need an image-editing program to **crop** and **resize** your pictures, and **reformat** them as bitmaps, JPEGs, GIFs (Windows), or PICTs (Macintosh).
- Once you've formatted your pictures, download **MicroAngelo** for Windows or **Icon Mania!** for Macintosh. These programs help you convert your images to icon files and replace existing icons. If you don't like the results, you can change your icons or restore the original ones any time you want.
- MicroAngelo and Icon Mania! store icon files in **libraries.** Libraries are easy to create and they help you keep track of all those icons. To stay organized, you should create a special folder for your custom icons.

- You can experiment by editing your icon files to improve the way they look, or even draw icons from scratch. When you **edit icon files**, your icon program displays them *really* close up so you can see and work all the **pixels** (those tiny dots) in your picture.
- How about a picture of your friends, kids, spouse, or pet as a **computer startup screen**? Take a picture with your cam, resize and reformat as needed, and save the picture over the existing startup screen file.

Now we can move on to Part Three. The next three chapters tell you how to create GIF animations, produce your own movies, and put your pictures and multimedia on the Web.

Part Three
Instant Multimedia

5 Making GIF Animations

Hey—want to do something really cool with some of your favorite cam pictures? Turn them into GIF animations that you can put on your Web page or e-mail to your friends. Once you download and set up your GIF animation program, animating your pictures only takes a few minutes. Really!

In this chapter:

- What are GIF animations?
- Downloading WWW Gif Animator (Windows) or GifBuilder (Macintosh)
- Launching your GIF animation program
- Creating a GIF animation
- Importing and converting pictures
- Mapping pictures to a color palette
- Selecting frame rates and looping options
- Applying special effects and transitions
- Previewing and saving your animation

What's a GIF Animation?

A **GIF animation** is a special kind of GIF image that cycles through a group of pictures when you open the file in a Web browser. GIF animations are a great way to liven up your Web pages without making visitors wait for huge multimedia files, or take time to download a plug-in.

Just about any browser that can display graphics can also run your GIF animations. They download pretty quickly, too—unless you use an awful lot of pictures. So grab five to ten of your favorite pictures and copy them into a new folder for easy access, and you're ready to get started with GIF animations.

Do your friends cam? Ask them to e-mail some pictures, so you can use them in your GIF animations and movies (we'll talk about editing movies in Chapter 6).

Downloading a GIF Animation Program

Oh, yeah—before we start building GIF animations, you need to download a **GIF animation program.**

- **Windows** users can visit **http://stud1.tuwien.ac.at/~e8925005/** and get **WWW Gif Animator** by Irmgard Wasinger and Ramin Nourbakhch. If you choose to register the software, it costs $20. You'll need to unzip the file (see Chapter 1) before installing it on your system.
- **Macintosh** users can drop by **http://www.epfl.ch/Staff/Yves.Piguet/clip2gif-home/GifBuilder.html** to pick up **GifBuilder** by Yves Piguet. And you'll love GifBuilder's price—it's free! You don't need to install GifBuilder. Once you unstuff it, you can move the folder to an appropriate place on your computer and go to work on your animations.

Having trouble getting your program? Yikes! Those long URLs for WWW Gif Animator and GifBuilder aren't very easy to remember. Save yourself some typing! Go get your program from one of the many popular shareware collections on the Web. Try one of these:

http://www.tucows.com/

http://www.shareware.com/

http://www.download.com/

You can browse for files by category, or use the handy search engines to locate your file.

Starting Your GIF Animation Program

When you're ready to start up your GIF animation program, see some examples, and maybe get some help, you'll find everything you need in the program's folder.

- **Macintosh users**: Open the GifBuilder folder (**Figure 5.1**), and double-click the GifBuilder icon to launch the application.

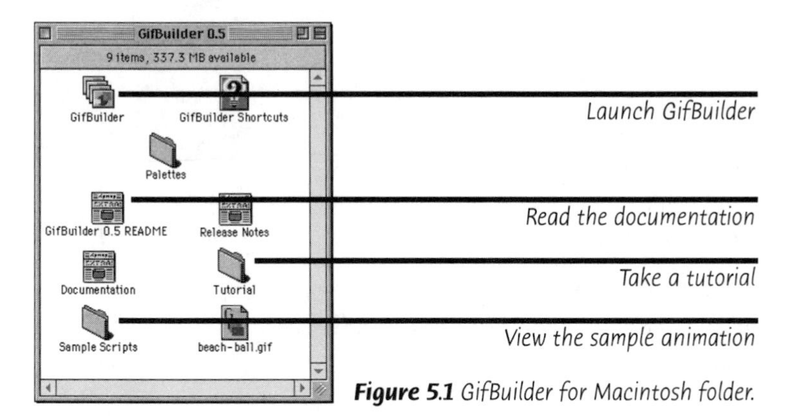

Figure 5.1 *GifBuilder for Macintosh folder.*

- **Windows users**: WWW Gif Animator for Windows creates a folder called Graphics on your system, and then installs itself in the C:\Graphics\WWWGifAnim folder. To launch the program, open the WWWGifAnim folder (**Figure 5.2**) and double-click the Wwwgifa.exe icon. Or you can launch Wwwgifa.exe from the Programs folder on the Start menu.

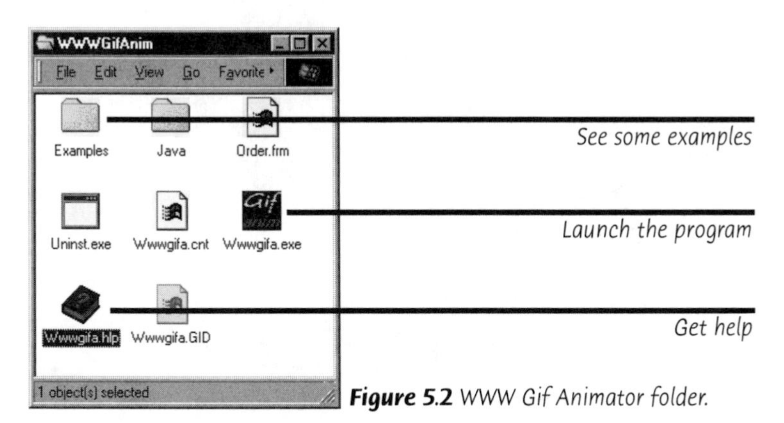

Figure 5.2 *WWW Gif Animator folder.*

When the WWW Gif Animator registration reminder appears (**Figure 5.3**), click the "I Consider Registering" button (and pardon the funny syntax—English isn't the programmer's first language!).

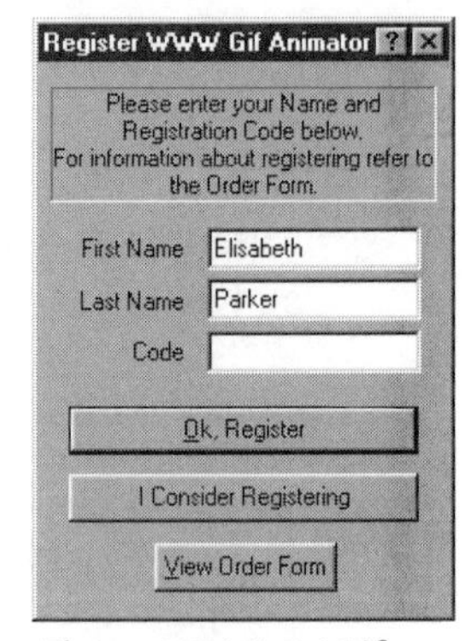

Figure 5.3 *WWW Gif Animator for Windows registration reminder.*

Building the Animation

When WWW Gif Animator and GifBuilder launch, they both look kind of, well, empty. That's because you haven't added any pictures yet. Once you've done that, a list of pictures appears when you start the program, with a preview of the selected picture. See **Figures 5.4** and **5.5**.

Frames and cells

The individual pictures that compose an animation, movie, or other multimedia file are called **frames** or **cells** by animation and multimedia pros.

The following sections take you through the steps of importing your pictures.

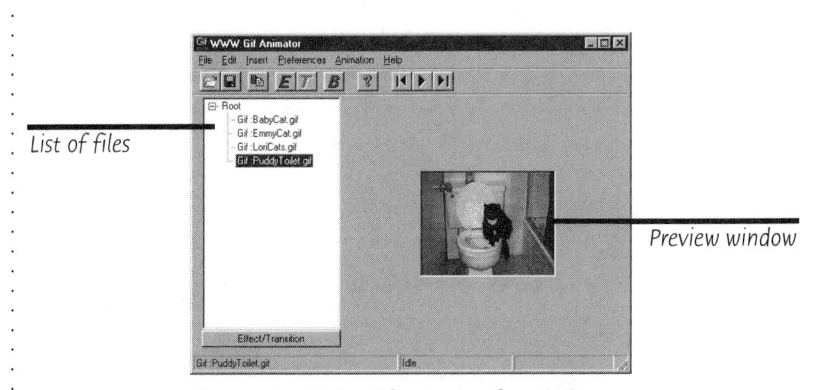

Figure 5.4 *WWW Gif Animator for Windows.*

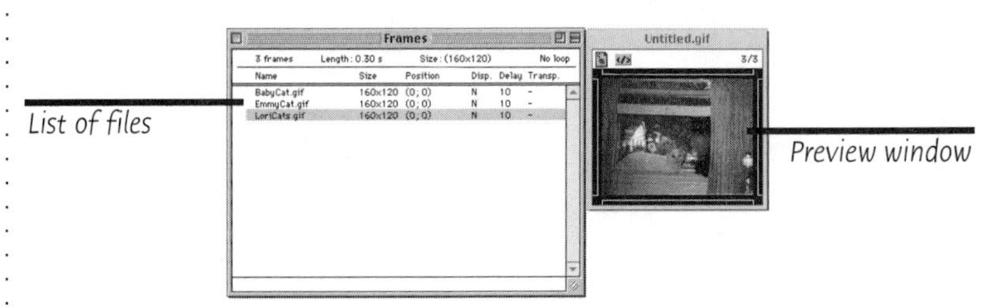

Figure 5.5 *GifBuilder for Macintosh.*

Importing Pictures

Adding pictures is easy—it's just like opening a file.

Get the size and order right!

Make sure that all your pictures are the **same size** (in width and height), or you might run into problems with the final animation. I recommend using the quarter-screen (160x120) image size when you take pictures with your cam, because larger files take longer to load from your Web page. Chapter 2 tells you how to adjust your image size settings when taking pictures with your cam. Also, make sure to add your pictures in **the order you want them to be seen**, because GIF animations display pictures in the same order as the picture list.

- **Windows users**: Add a picture to the list by selecting File | Open. When the Load Image dialog box appears (**Figure 5.6**), select an image and click the Open button.
- **Macintosh users**: Add a picture to the list by selecting File | Add Frame. When the Open dialog box appears (**Figure 5.7**), click the Open button.

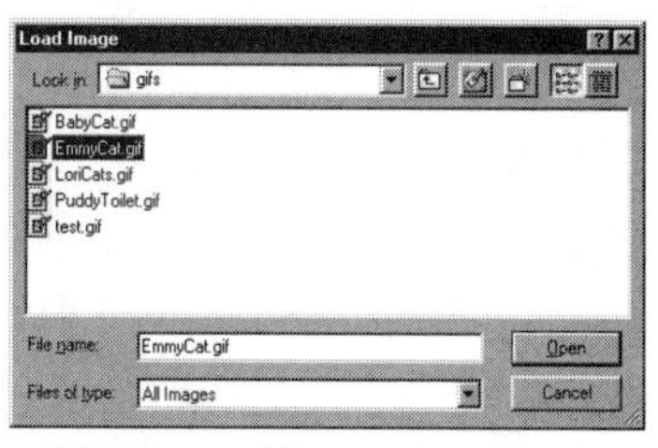

Figure 5.6 *Adding a picture with WWW Gif Animator.*

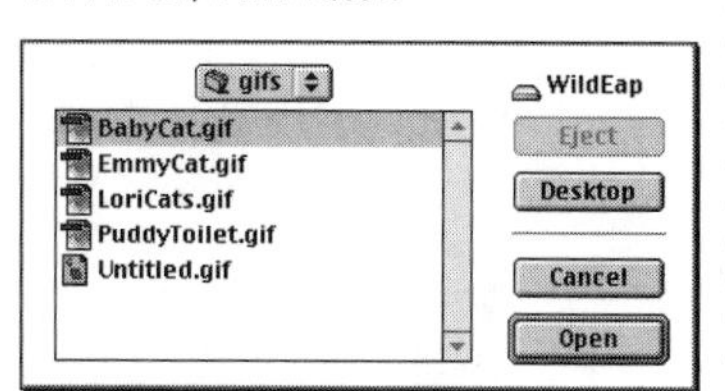

Figure 5.7 *Adding a picture with GifBuilder.*

Go easy on the pictures! Use no more than 10—or 15 at the most—in your GIF animation. More than that, and the file will take an awfully long time to download.

Converting Images

Oh, you don't have any GIF images or a program for converting them? No problem. Both WWW Gif Animator and GifBuilder can open a variety of image file formats and convert them to GIFs for use in your animation. Some cam software comes with an option for saving your pictures as GIFs, but many cams let you save pictures as bitmaps and JPEGs (Windows) or PICTs and JPEGs (Macintosh) only.

- **Windows users**: Convert a file to a GIF by simply adding it to the animation, as explained in the preceding section. The conversion will take place when you save the animation file.

- **Macintosh users**: Convert an image file to a GIF by selecting Convert from the File menu. When the Open dialog box appears, choose a file and click the Open button. Then go ahead and add the converted animation as explained in the preceding section.

Mapping Pictures to a Color Palette

GIF files are 8-bit images that map to a 256-color palette. But GIF *animation* files contain several images, probably all with different colors. Out of all these colors, you can only use 256 of them for the entire animation!

Fortunately, you don't have to choose the colors yourself. Your GIF animation program can fix everything for you. Although your pictures won't look quite as good as they do at millions of colors (as explained in Chapter 2), it's a small price to pay for way-cool animations and faster downloads.

- **Windows users**: Create a color palette for pictures by selecting Optimize Images from the Edit menu, as shown in **Figure 5.8**.
- **Macintosh users**: Map pictures to the same color palette by selecting the images, then selecting Colors from the Options menu, and choosing Best Palette from the cascading menu shown in **Figure 5.9**.

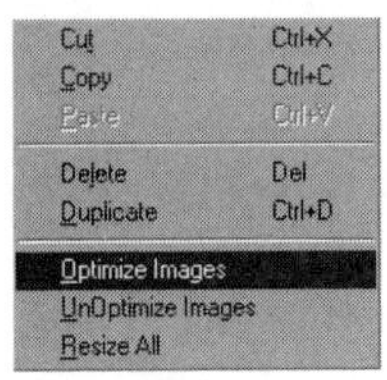

Figure 5.8 *Mapping images to a color palette in WWW Gif Animator for Windows.*

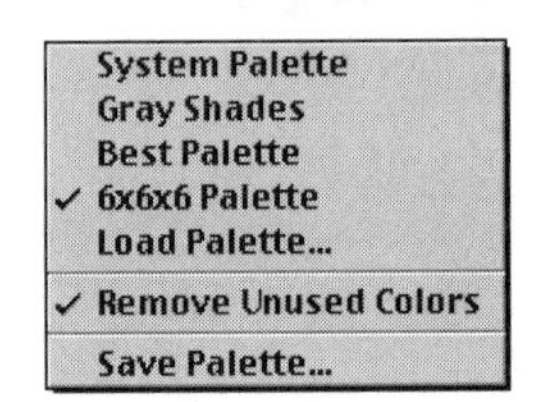

Figure 5.9 *Mapping images to a color palette in GifBuilder.*

Hold your horses—if you plan to add special effects to your GIF animation, as explained later in this chapter, don't map your pictures to a color palette until *after* you add the special effects.

Frame Rates and Looping

Once you've got some pictures imported, you can decide how fast your animation will run (the **frame rate**) and how many times to play it (**looping**).

Since frame rates are measured in 100ths of a second, you should enter a frame rate value of at least 50 (half a second) to ensure that each cell displays long enough to be seen.

As for looping, you can play your animation infinitely (over and over again) or have it run just once or twice. And bear in mind; Web pages with animations that never stop moving can make people dizzy.

Windows only

To set the frame rates and looping in WWW Gif Animator:

1. Choose Parameters from the Preferences menu.
2. When the dialog box appears (**Figure 5.10**), enter a number in the Global Delay box to adjust the frame rate.

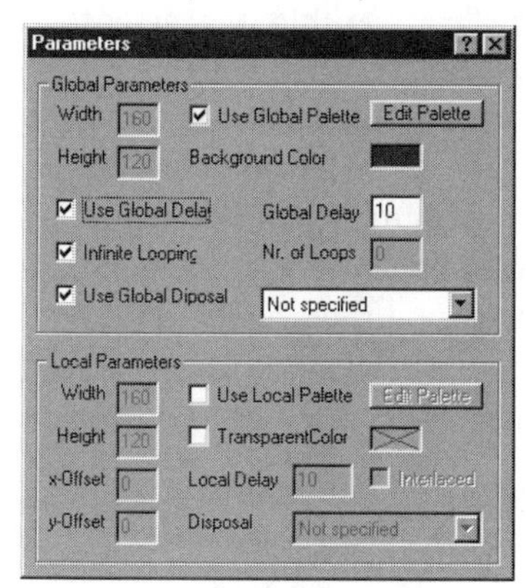

Figure 5.10 *Parameters dialog box for WWW Gif Animator.*

3. Set up the looping. You can loop your animation forever by leaving the Infinite Looping checkbox turned on. Or, turn it off and enter a number in the Nr. of Loops box.

Macintosh only

To set the frame rates and looping in GifBuilder:

1. To tell GifBuilder how many times to loop your animation, select Loop from the Options menu.
2. When the Looping dialog box appears, as shown in **Figure 5.11**, click the Forever radio button to play your animation infinitely, or click the Number of Times radio button and enter a number. When you finish, click OK.

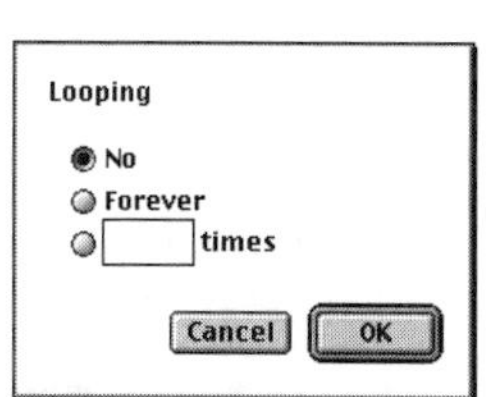

Figure 5.11 *Looping a GIF animation in GifBuilder.*

3. To set your animation's frame rate, select all of the files on your Frames list.
4. Select Interframe Delay from the Options menu.
5. When the Interframe Delay dialog box appears (**Figure 5.12**), enter a number. ***Note:*** I do not recommend selecting the As Fast As Possible option.

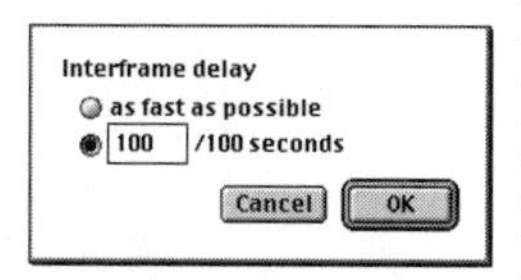

Figure 5.12 *Setting the frame rate in GifBuilder.*

GIF Movies, Anyone? Some cams, including QuickCam (see Chapter 2), enable **time-lapse photography**; for which you take a bunch of sequential, rapid-fire snapshots. With time-lapse photography, you can import your pictures and create a GIF animation that runs sort of like a movie—for example, a sequence of pictures of yourself waving hello. If you do this, set your frame rate to 10 (hundredths of a second). GIF movies do take longer to load in the browser, but even so, they're usually faster than real videos!

Special Effects and Transitions

When watching a TV program, have you ever noticed those nifty **transitions** that display while the show moves to a different scene? Ricky's singing "Babaloo" at the night club, confident that Lucy won't try to appear on his stage (for tonight, anyway). Suddenly, animated vertical blinds close on the scene and then open again on the living room back at the apartment. There's Ethel calling a cab while Lucy puts the final touches on her disguise.

You can use these slick special effects in your GIF animations, too! WWW Gif Animator gives you 20 to choose from, including **Blinds**, **Spiral**, and **Fade Out**. GifBuilder offers a select few. The **Peel**, which peels back one image like a page to reveal the next, is my favorite.

Keep in mind that those spiffy transitions do make your file larger. In order to create a transition, your GIF animation program generates additional images and adds them to your animation.

WWW Gif Animator

Windows only

To apply special effects and transitions in WWW Gif Animator:

1. Select a picture.
2. Click the **E** toolbar button to create a special effect, or click the ***T*** toolbar button to create a transition. The Special Effect/Transition dialog box appears, as shown in **Figure 5.13**.

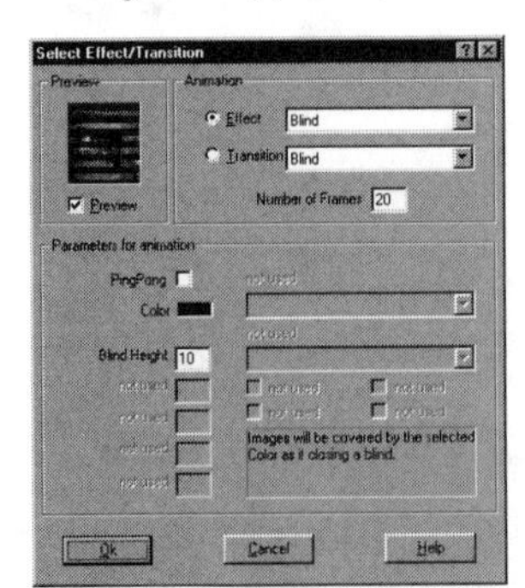

Figure 5.13 *Adding special effects and transitions in WWW Gif Animator.*

3. Select the Effect or Transition radio button and pick an item from the list. If you'd like, you can experiment with various options for each effect and see them in the preview box.
4. When you're satisfied with the effect, click OK.

GifBuilder

Macintosh only

To apply special effects and transitions in GifBuilder:

1. Select an image.
2. Pull down the Effects menu (**Figure 5.14**), and select Transitions. A cascading menu appears, with a list of transitions and simple illustrations of each transition (**Figure 5.15**).

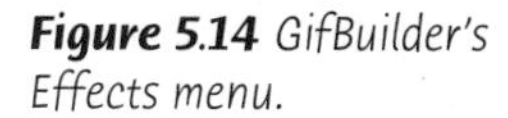

Figure 5.14 *GifBuilder's Effects menu.*

Figure 5.15 *GifBuilder's Transitions menu.*

3. Choose an option, and release the mouse to display a dialog box with additional options for the special effect.
4. Enter a number of steps to determine how long it takes to reveal the next picture (I recommend 4 steps). With some effects, you can also select a Direction to determine where the transition begins (for example, the transition can move from the left, top, right, or bottom of your picture).

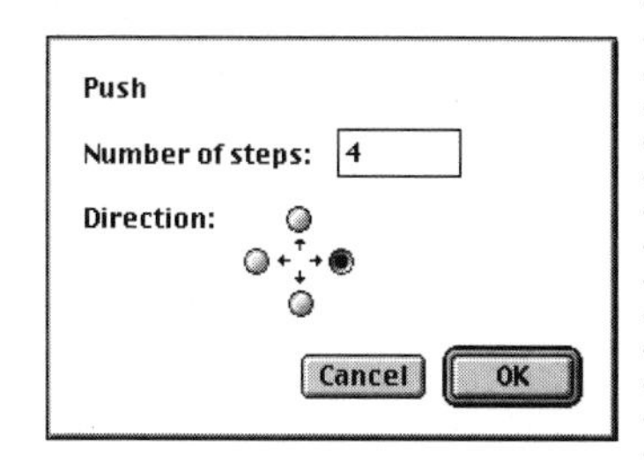

5. Click OK to apply your transition and return to your animation.

And there's more!

GifBuilder's Effects menu also offers **Static Filters** and **Dynamic Filters**. You can use the Static Filters options to apply special effects to a single cell. The **Blur** comes in handy for smoothing out jagged edges in a picture. Dynamic Filters work the same way as transitions—you can select Blur to make a picture appear blurry before it displays, or choose **Tiles** to display your image as blocky squares that shift into focus.

Previewing Your Animation

Now that you've created your GIF animation, let's take it for a spin! WWW Gif Animator and GifBuilder both let you **preview** animations, and the steps are the same in both programs. Pull down the Animation menu and select Start to run your fabulous creation in the preview area. When you get tired of admiring your work (or feel dizzy), go back to the Animation menu and select Stop.

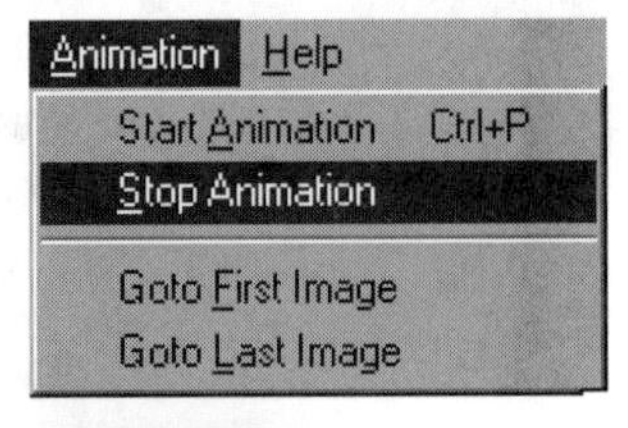

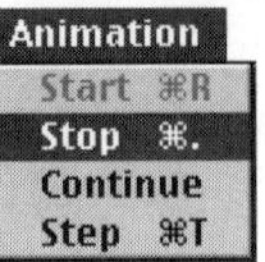

Saving Your Animation

Don't forget to save your animation file! Save it just the way you save any other file—by choosing File | Save. You can now put it on a Web page as an image, as discussed in Chapter 7, or e-mail it to a friend.

Windows only

Note: With **WWW Gif Animator,** that pesky old registration reminder will appear after you save your file. This might make you worry about whether it was saved or not. Don't worry—your file is fine.

Animated Greetings!

Want to send **animated greeting cards** to friends and relatives? Take some pictures with your cam, and use one of the image editors mentioned in Chapter 2 to type a text message on one of the pictures. Then build your GIF animation—and there you are. Now you can send your fabulous creations by e-mail. When Grandma receives your message, she can open the animation in her Web browser and enjoy the show! Most e-mail programs make it easy to send file attachments along with your messages.

When taking pictures for animated greeting cards, **use your cam's half-screen** (320x240) image size so your friends and relatives can see the pictures better. Since they won't have to wait for the files to download from your Web page, you don't have to worry as much about small file sizes (though you still shouldn't overdo it!).

Send as an Attachment

You can attach an animation file with Eudora, Netscape Mail, Internet Mail, and Outlook Express. Here are the steps (although the toolbar button and dialog box names may vary slightly, depending on your e-mail program):

1. Launch your e-mail program and compose the message to which you will attach the animation file.
2. Click the Insert Attachment button to display the Insert Attachment dialog box.
3. Browse for your file and click the Attach button to attach the file and return to your e-mail message.
4. Send your message.

Summary

GIF animations are a great way to turn the pictures you take with your cam into instant multimedia that you can put on your Web pages or send to people as e-mail attachments. WWW Gif Animator for Windows and GifBuilder for Macintosh help you whip up GIF animations in a jiffy.

- **GIF animations** are a collection of GIF images that play as an animation when launched in a **Web browser**. Most Web browsers (including Netscape Navigator and Internet Explorer) that display graphics can also run GIF animations.
- **WWW Gif Animator** for Windows and **GifBuilder** for Macintosh make it easy to create GIF animations.
- To begin building your GIF animation, launch your program and import your pictures in the order you want them to appear. Some cams provide options for saving images as GIF files; others let you save images as bitmaps (Windows), or PICTs (Macintosh), or JPEGs. Luckily, your GIF animation program **converts your bitmap, PICT, and JPEG files to GIFs when you import them**.
- You also need to apply a **color palette** to your animation. GIF files are 8-bit images that map to a 256-color palette. Since GIF animation files contain several pictures, you can only use **256 colors** for the whole animation. To ensure the best possible image quality, choose Edit|Optimize in WWW Gif Animator, or in GifBuilder select Options menu|Colors|Best Palette. If you plan to add transitions to your animation, wait until you finish that task before mapping the animation to a color palette.
- You can set **looping** and **frame rate** options to determine the number of times your animation plays and how quickly each picture displays.
- WWW Gif Animator and GifBuilder come with an assortment of **transitions** that you can apply to pictures in your animation. Transitions are animated special effects that reveal pictures gradually. When you add transitions, your GIF animation program creates new frames and adds them to your file.
- Once you create your animation, you can **preview it**. When you're happy with the results, save it as you would save any other type of file.

- You can put GIF animations on your **Web page**, as explained in Chapter 7, or send them out as **e-mail attachments**. If you have one of the image programs mentioned in Chapter 2, you can even type text on your pictures and turn GIF animations into **animated greeting cards**.

If you enjoy getting creative with your cam, read on! The next chapter tells you how to make your own QuickTime movies.

Roll 'em! Creating and Editing Movies

6

So, you like recording movies with your cam? In this chapter you'll learn how to edit those movies. **QuickEditor** by Mathias Tschopp, in both Mac and Windows versions, puts you in the director's chair. And for $35, you can't beat the price. So go ahead and get creative. Mix your movies together, add some pictures and sounds, and throw in some snazzy transitions for good measure. You can even import individual pictures and make them into movies.

In this chapter:

- Getting started with QuickEditor for Windows and Macintosh
- Opening movies and clips
- Navigating through movies and clips
- Creating and saving movies
- Selecting frames from a clip
- Adding image clips, movie clips, and sound clips
- Applying transitions to movie clips
- Compressing and saving movies

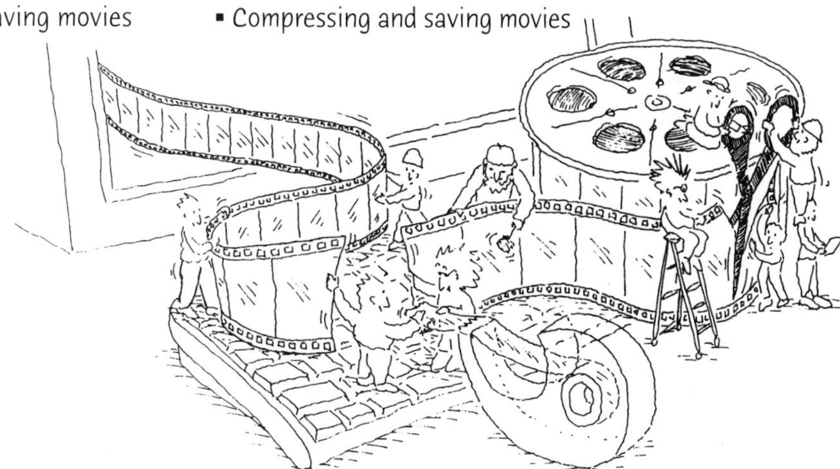

Getting QuickEditor

Both Windows and Macintosh users can download **QuickEditor** from **http://www.wild.ch/quickeditor/**.

Oh, and if you don't yet have the latest version of QuickTime, go download it from Apple's QuickTime Web site at **http://quicktime.apple.com/**. (Macintosh System 8.5 ships with this version.) You need QuickTime version 3.0 or higher in order to run QuickEditor.

Important Update Note: As this book was going to press, QuickEditor was upgraded to version 6.0. The program may work a little differently from what I've described in this chapter. Visit the *Little Web Cam Book* Web site at **http://www.byteit.com/Cam/** for updated information.

Try QuickTime Pro! Apple distributes a freeware version of QuickTime, but they also offer a beefier QuickTime and MoviePlayer Pro version for $29. QuickTime Pro plays just about every video format and comes with a variety of editing features. For more about working with QuickTime and MoviePlayer Pro, read the *QuickTime and MoviePlayer Pro 3: Visual QuickStart Guide* by Judith Stern and Robert Lettieri (Peachpit Press, 1998).

Starting Up QuickEditor

Once you've unzipped or unstuffed QuickEditor, you can launch it by double-clicking the QuickEditor icon in the QuickEditor folder, as shown in **Figures 6.1 (Windows) and 6.2 (Macintosh)**. Windows users can also start up the program by clicking Start|Programs|QuickEditor.

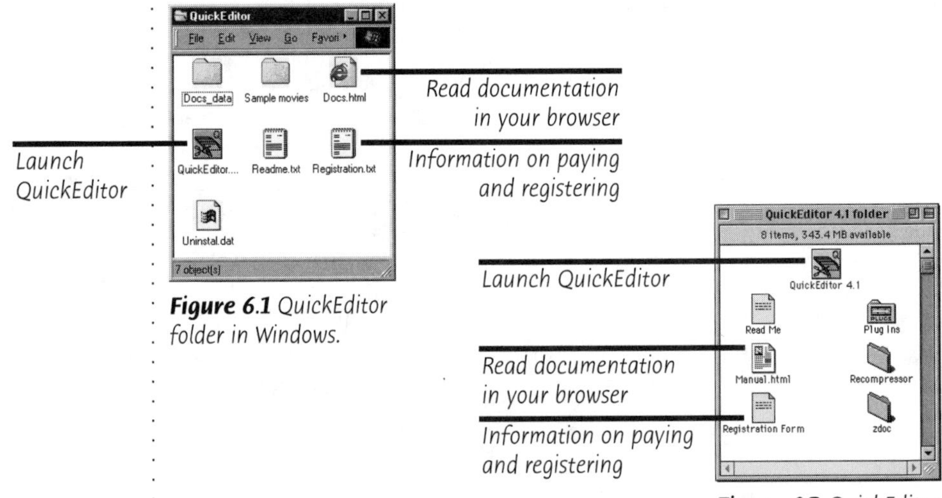

Figure 6.1 *QuickEditor folder in Windows.*

Figure 6.2 *QuickEditor folder for Macintosh.*

If you decide to **register and pay** for the software, read the registration document in the QuickEditor folder.

If you get stuck, you can get **online help**: QuickEditor comes with a set of Web pages with information about using the program. (If a nag screen appears and reminds you to register, click OK.)

Getting Acquainted with QuickEditor

Whew! QuickEditor's interface may look kinda complicated, as shown in **Figures 6.3 (Windows) and 6.4 (Macintosh)**. Not to worry—it's easier than it looks.

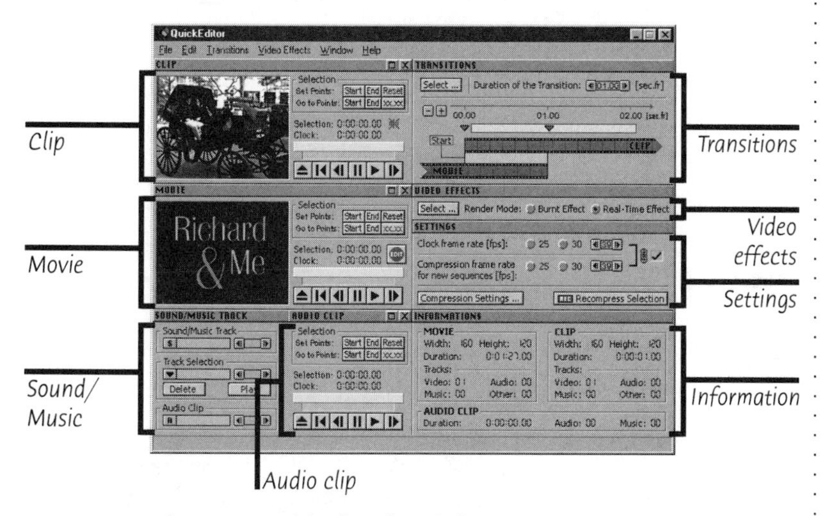

Figure 6.3 *QuickEditor for Windows.*

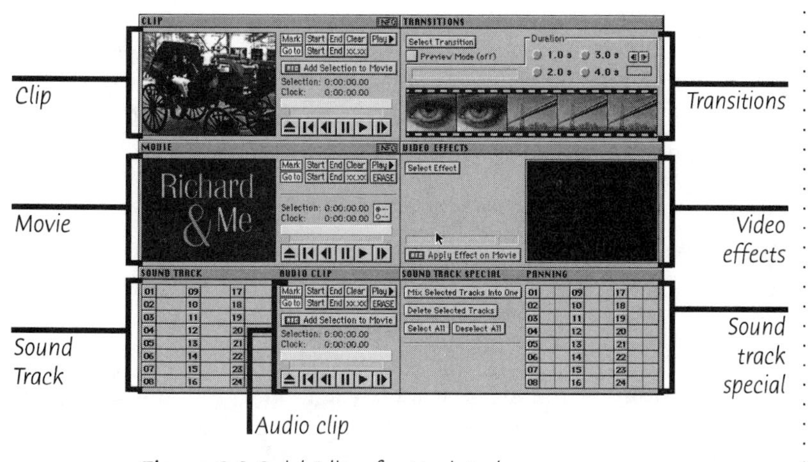

Figure 6.4 *QuickEditor for Macintosh.*

What's an interface?
The interface is everything you see on the screen—buttons, menus, work areas, toolbars, Web links —everything you see and use to view and interact with a program or Web site on your computer.

I'm not going to try and tell you *everything* about creating and editing movies, but this chapter will give you a good start. First, let's take a fast tour of QuickEditor's interface. With a few minor differences, the Windows and Macintosh versions of the program look very similar.

QuickEditor Interface Elements

Window Element	Purpose
Clip	For inserting a movie or image in the current movie. If you click on the preview, the movie opens in a separate window.
Movie	Displays the movie you're working on. If you click on the preview, the movie opens in a separate video window.
Sound/Music Track	Lists all the audio files in the movie.
Audio Clip	For inserting audio clips of sounds to be synchronized with frames in your movie.
Transitions	For applying fades, wipes, and other effects to a frame as it moves forward to the next frame.
Video Effects	For correcting colors and applying special effects to pictures in the selected frames.
Settings	For compressing the movie and adjusting frame rates. (*Macintosh:* You can display and change these settings by selecting Edit|Compression.)
Information (Windows only)	Displays information about the movie and selected clips, including the height, width, and duration (length).
Sound Track Special (Macintosh only)	For mixing and arranging sound tracks.

Opening a Movie

Although QuickEditor creates QuickTime movies only, it does allow you to **open and import AVI movies.** That's a nice convenience; yesterday's shareware video editors could open files in only one format or the other.

To open a movie file that you want to edit:

1. Choose Open Movie from the File menu.
2. When the Open dialog box appears, browse for your file, select it, and click the Open button to return to QuickEditor.

The first **frame** of the movie will be displayed in the Movie preview box. But don't confuse this with opening a movie **clip**—we'll get to that next.

Opening an Image, Movie, or Audio Clip

Sound files, frames from other movies, and pictures are what make up your movie. How do you add them? By first opening the files as **clips**. QuickEditor supports JPEG, GIF, BMP, and PICT images, along with the most popular sound formats WAV, AIFF, and AU. (If you need to review these file formats, go to Chapter 3.)

1. To open a movie or image as a clip, select Open Clip from the File menu.

   Macintosh only

   Mac Note: If you're using a Mac and you want to open a PICT file as a clip, select Import Pict as Clip from the File menu instead of Open Clip.

2. Proceed as though you were opening a movie, as explained in the preceding section. Browse for your image or sound file in the Open dialog box, select it, and click the Open button to return to QuickEditor.

3. When you open a picture or import a PICT file as a clip, you'll see one of the dialog boxes shown in **Figures 6.5 (Windows) and 6.6 (Macintosh)**. Here you enter a number of seconds for the duration of your clip. You should give your picture least one or two seconds—otherwise, it will speed by so fast you can't see it.

   Figure 6.5 *Import Picture dialog box in Windows.*

   When you finish opening your clip, it appears in QuickEditor's Clip preview box.

   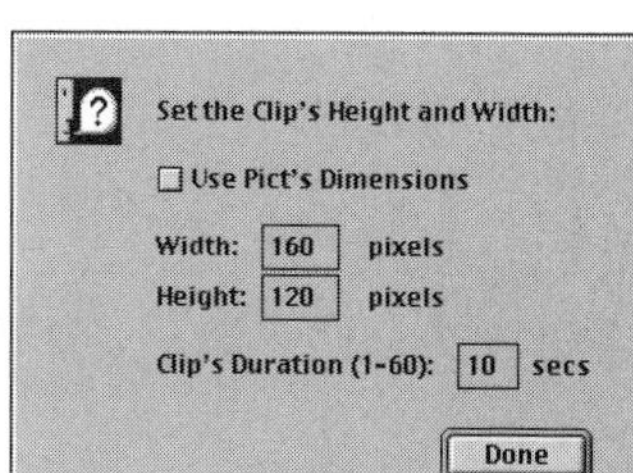

   Figure 6.6 *Import PICT dialog box on the Macintosh.*

Movies and clips should be the same size. Before you open pictures and movies as clips, be sure to consider their size. The files should have the same dimensions as the movie you're working on (either 320x240 pixels or 160x120 pixels). Otherwise, QuickEditor automatically reformats the clip to your movie's dimensions—which might cause the clip to look distorted.

If you have one of the image-editing programs mentioned in Chapter 2, you can also create images with text captions for frames in your movie. Or you can type text on your pictures before you insert them as clips in a movie.

Opening an Audio Clip

Opening a sound clip is similar to opening a picture or movie clip.

1. First, select Open Audio Clip from the File menu.
2. On **Windows**, you can browse for a sound file when the Open dialog box appears.

   On a **Macintosh**, there's one extra step: You'll get a cascading menu with various sound file types. After you choose a format, the Open dialog box appears so you can hunt for your audio clip.

Where do you get audio clips? You can record them yourself, download them from the Web, or use QuickEditor to export the sound track from another movie as a sound file that you can insert in the current movie. Chapter 14 tells you more about cams and audio.

Moving Through a Movie or Clip

The movie, clip, and audio clip areas all have their own set of player buttons, like the set shown in **Figure 6.7**. These buttons help you move through a file to select frames and edit them. Many multimedia players and applications have similar buttons, so these should look pretty familiar.

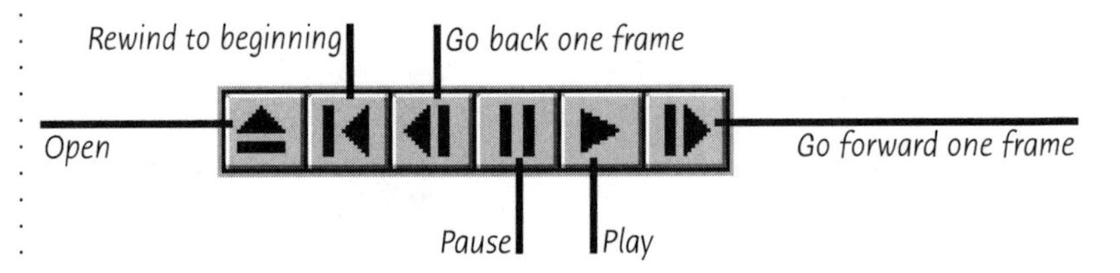

Figure 6.7 *QuickEditor player buttons.*

Creating a New Movie

Let's say you have some pictures and maybe some sound files or even other movies, which you'd like to put together and turn into a movie. Rather than edit an existing video file, you can create a brand-new movie and open the other files as clips.

To create a new movie, choose New Movie from the Edit menu.

Editing a Movie

OK, now that you can find your way around QuickEditor, let's do some real editing. But first, you have to get used to the way QuickEditor thinks.

First: Find the frame

Here's how it works: Each frame in a movie occupies a particular moment in time. Take the frame shown in **Figure 6.8**, for example. The clock above the progress indicator says **0:01:27.00**. This indicates a point within the movie. Translated into English, it means the movie has progressed to the frame that occurs at 0 hours, 1 minute and 27 seconds, frame 0 for the 27 second mark. In order to edit movies, you need to locate and mark moments in time on a movie or a clip.

Selecting Frames

What's the first thing you normally do when you want to edit something in a computer program? You select it, of course. Frames in a movie are no exception; you have to select them to edit them. But when you're selecting frames, it works a little differently—you have to think in terms of **Start points** and **End points**.

Start Point and End Point

QuickEditor's interface might throw you off a little until you get used to it. You're accustomed to selecting things by clicking on them or dragging your mouse over them, but you can't select frames in a QuickEditor movie that way. After all, there isn't enough room on your computer screen to display all the frames in your movie!

With QuickEditor, you select frames in a movie, movie clip, or audio clip by inserting a Start point and an End point. In **Figures 6.8** and **6.9** you can see the progress indicator marked with Start and End points.

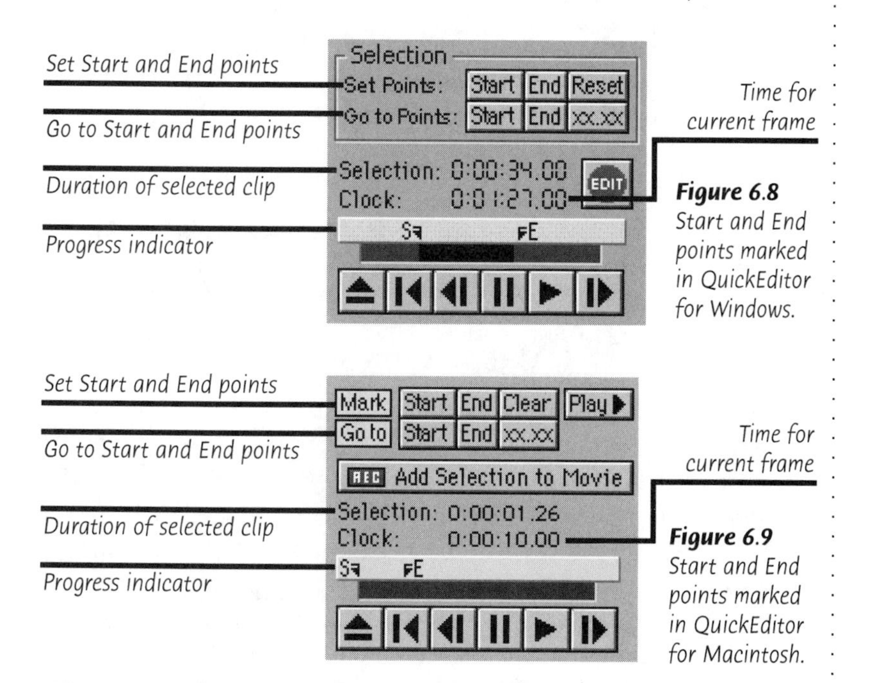

Figure 6.8 Start and End points marked in QuickEditor for Windows.

Figure 6.9 Start and End points marked in QuickEditor for Macintosh.

Macintosh only

Mac Note: Macintosh users can also move through a movie or clip by clicking the progress indicator and dragging it to the right or left.

To create a Start point:

1. Hold down the **One Frame Forward** button until the first frame you want to select appears in the preview box. This will be the Start point. (If you want the first frame in your movie to be the Start point, you can skip this step.)

   Easy does it

   Moving forward and backward just **one frame at a time** is easy: Just click the One Frame Forward (or Backward) button *without* holding the mouse button down.

2. Above the progress indicator, you'll see two rows of buttons for Set Points and Go to Points. Click the Start button on the Set Points row, and a tiny arrow appears above the progress indicator to mark your Start point.

To create an End point:

1. Use the One Frame Forward button to move to your ending frame. As discussed just above, you can click the button to move one frame at a time, or click and hold it to move forward more quickly.
2. When you reach the frame you want as your ending frame, click the End button on the Set Points row.

Oops—If you mark the wrong Start and End points by mistake, you can click the Reset button and start over. Or you can move to different frames and re-mark the points.

Going to a Particular Frame

There are other ways to navigate in your movie or clip.

- Once you've created your Start and End points, you can go to either point by clicking the **Start** or **End** button in the Go to Points row.
- You can move to a **specific frame** if you remember the clock time for the frame *and* the frame number. Click the Go to Frame button (marked **xx.xx**). When the Go To dialog box appears (**Figures 6.10** and **6.11**), enter a time and click OK (Windows) or Done (Macintosh).

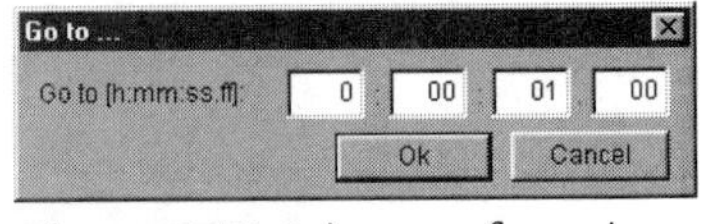

Figure 6.10 *Going to a frame in QuickEditor for Windows.*

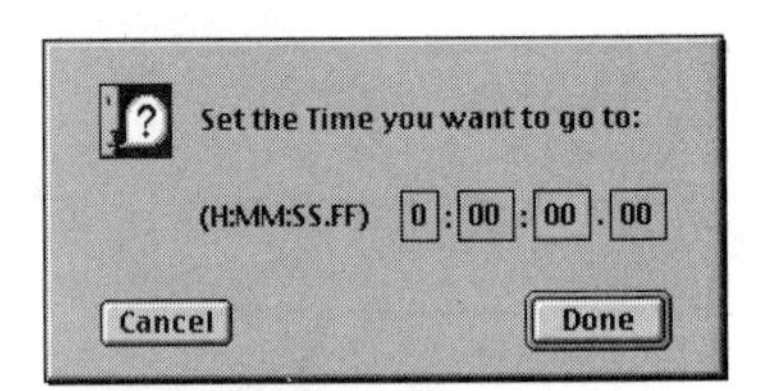

Figure 6.11 *Going to a frame in QuickEditor for Macintosh.*

Clock indicator

Remember—the clock time indicator means, from left to right: Hours, Minutes, Seconds, and Frame Number for that particular second.

Adding a Clip to a Movie

Once you know how to create Start and End points, placing a clip in your movie is easy.

1. Open a movie or create a new movie. The movie displays in QuickEditor's Movie area.
2. Open a movie, image, or sound file as a clip. Movie and image files display in the Clip area. Audio clips are loaded into the Audio Clip area.
3. Create a Start point in the movie; this is the place where you want to insert the clip. (You don't need to create an End point in this case—unless you want to replace the selected frames with the clip, as I'll explain shortly.)
4. Create a Start *and* End point for the clip you are adding.
5. Add the clip:

   Windows only

   In **Windows**, click the Edit button. In the pop-up menu **(Figure 6.12)**, select Insert to display the cascading menu shown in **Figure 6.13**. Then choose either Clip Selection in Movie (to insert a movie clip or a picture as a clip) or Audio Clip Selection in Movie (to insert an audio clip).

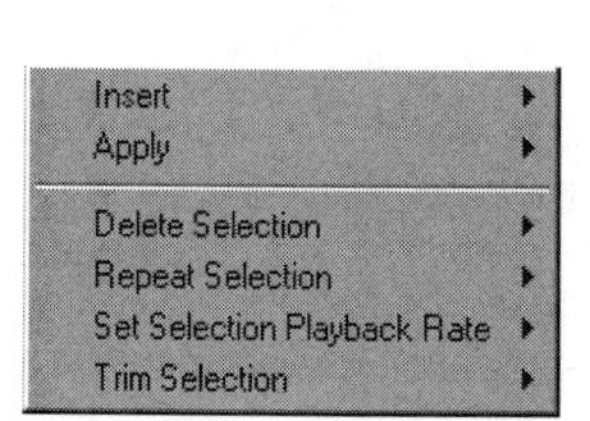

Figure 6.12 *Pop-up Edit menu in QuickEditor for Windows.*

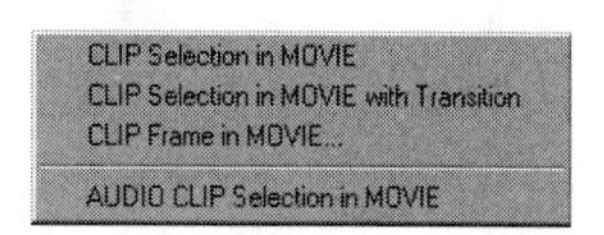

Figure 6.13 *Insert menu in QuickEditor for Windows.*

   Macintosh only

   In **Macintosh**, life is easy. Just click this button to add the clip: REC Add Selection to Movie

Ripple editing

When you add a movie clip this way, QuickEditor adds the selected frames and moves the rest of the frames in your movie forward. In the video biz, that's called **ripple editing**.

When you add an audio clip, QuickEditor adds the sound as a **new layer** that plays along with the movie's frames.

Want to save a movie frame as a picture? Move to the frame you want to save, and select File | Export. This comes in handy when you see something you like. You can also export a frame as a picture—so you can touch it up or add a text caption with an image program—and then import that frame again as a clip for your movie. Chapter 2 suggests some good image-editing programs.

Replacing Frames

When you replace frames in a movie with frames from a video clip, that's called **insert editing**. To do this, mark the range of frames you want to replace by adding a Start point *and* an End point. You can then insert your movie clip in that range, as explained in "Adding a Clip to a Movie."

Of course, you can't replace frames in a movie with an audio clip, because sounds play *with* the movie.

Deleting Frames from a Movie

It's easy to get rid of a frame or two in your movie. First, create the Start and End points for the movie frames you want to delete. Then:

- In **Windows**, click the Edit button, choose Delete Selection from the pop-up menu, and select In Movie.
- On a **Macintosh**, click the Erase button.

A dialog box appears asking you to confirm that you want to remove the frames; click OK to process the deletion.

You can only delete frames from a movie. QuickEditor won't let you delete frames from clips. After all, you may want to use them for other movies.

Transitions

QuickEditor comes with over 25 transitions for spicing up your movies. Transitions are animations that reveal pictures (frames) as the transition progresses, like the programs that do screen savers and GIF animation, covered in Chapters 3 and 5. With QuickEditor, you don't apply transitions directly to your movie. Instead, you apply them to movie clips *before* you put them in the movie. To apply a transition to a clip:

Adding a Transition

1. Open a movie clip (or import a picture as a clip) and create the Start and End points for the clip.
2. Click the Select Transition button in the Transitions area, as shown in **Figures 6.15** and **6.16**. If you use Windows, this launches the Select Effect dialog box. If you use Macintosh, a list of transitions appears.

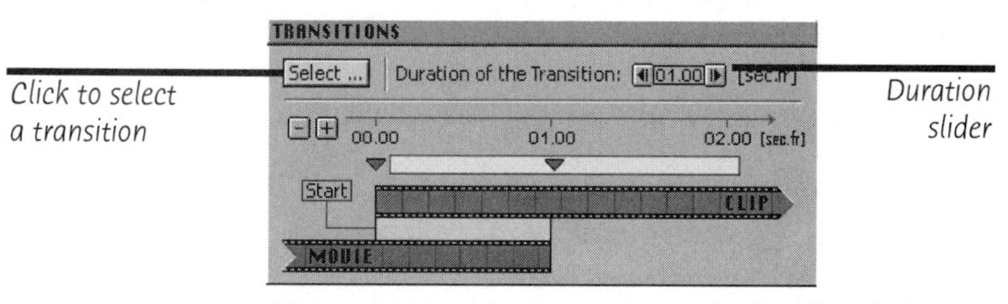

Figure 6.15 *Transitions area in QuickEditor for Windows.*

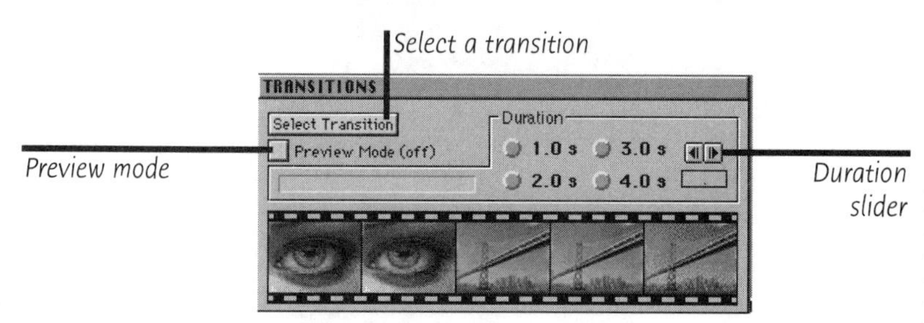

Figure 6.16 *Transitions area in QuickEditor for Macintosh.*

3. Choose a transition, as follows:

   Windows: In the Select Effect dialog box (**Figure 6.17**), choose a transition from the list and preview it. With some transitions, additional settings appear in the area on the right so you can do a little fine-tuning. When you have the transition you want, select it and click OK.

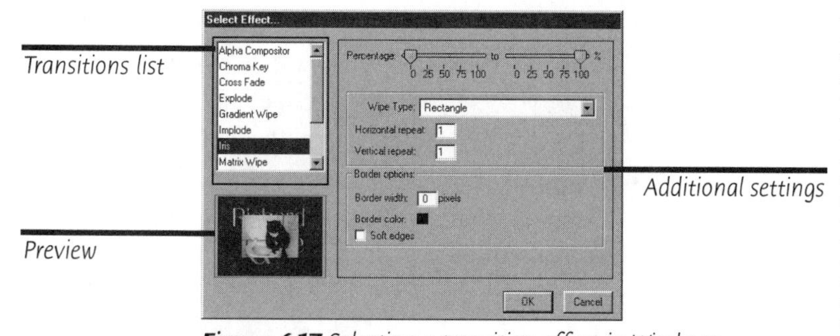

Figure 6.17 *Selecting a transition effect in Windows.*

Adding a Transition
(cont.)

Macintosh: In the menu (**Figure 6.18**), select a transition. From the cascading menu that appears, choose the transition options you want to use.

4. Set the length of the transition, as follows:

   Windows: Move the Duration slider to the right or left (the number of seconds is indicated in the Duration of Transition window).

   Macintosh: Move the Duration slider to the right or left. To preview your transition, click the Preview checkbox. When the preview is displayed (see **Figure 6.19**), you can move the slider to progress through the transition.

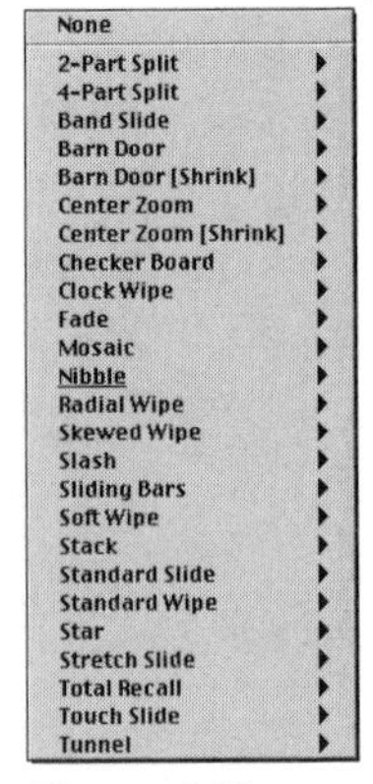

Figure 6.18 *Transitions menu for Macintosh.*

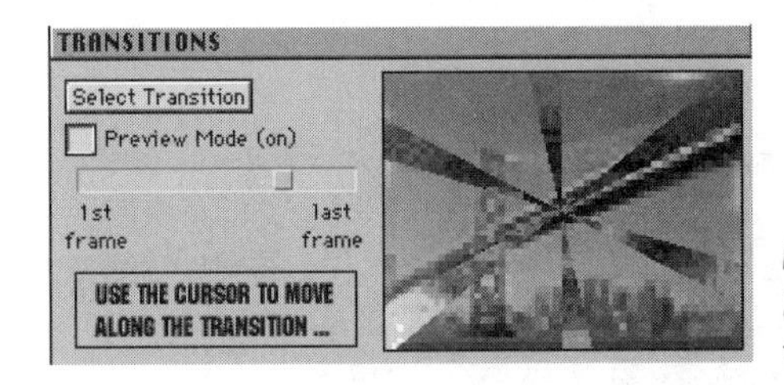

Figure 6.19 *QuickEditor for Macintosh with preview of transition displayed.*

5. Add the clip and transition to the movie, as follows:

   Windows: Click the Edit button, select Insert, and choose Clip Selection in Movie with Transition.

   Macintosh: Click the Add Selection to Movie button.

Applying Video Effects

Adding video effects to your movie works a lot like creating transitions, except that you apply the effects directly to your movie rather than adding them to a clip first.

1. To apply a video effect, create Start and End points for the movie frames, and then click the Select button in the Video Effects area.
2. When the Video Effects dialog box (Windows) or menu (Macintosh) displays, you can choose an effect and apply it to your movie, as you would apply a transition to a clip.

Before you apply a video effect to a lot of frames, experiment with a single frame first! Video effects can take several minutes to apply and you don't get to preview them first!

Compressing Your Movie

Naturally, you'll want to compress your movies to make the file sizes just a *little* less huge. Movie files are large because each frame is a picture and even the shortest movies contain many frames.

- **Windows**: Click the Compression Settings button to display the dialog box shown in **Figure 6.20**.
- **Macintosh**: Select Compression Settings from the Edit menu to display the dialog box shown in **Figure 6.21**.

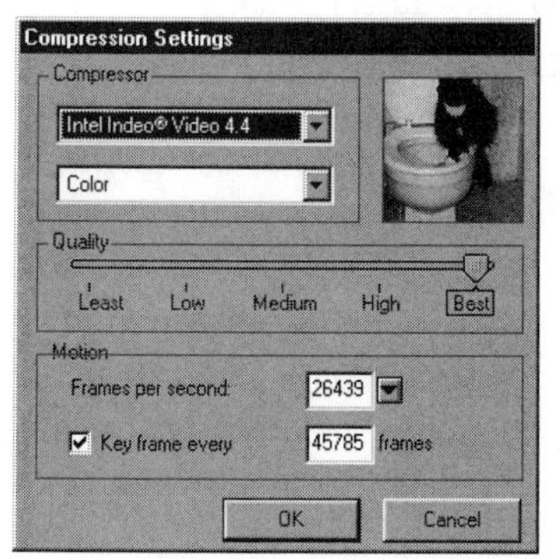

Figure 6.20
Compression Settings dialog box in Windows.

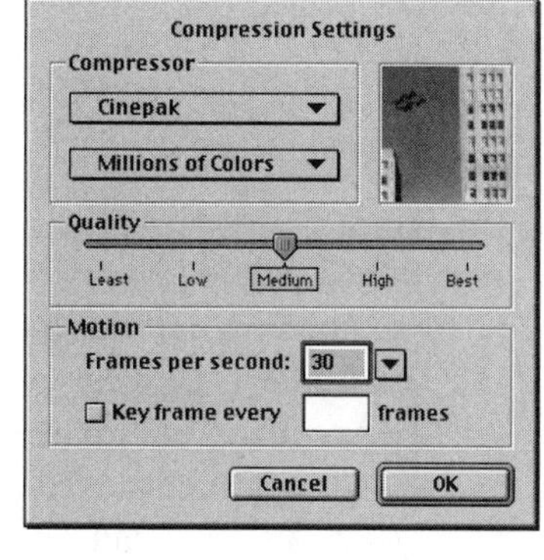

Figure 6.21
Compression Settings dialog box in Macintosh.

Choose a compression option and a color depth, and click OK when you're done. (if you need a review, Chapter 2 explains the compression and color-depth settings.)

Making the Most of Compression: I recommend that you choose a standard compression option such as Cinepak, Intel Indeo, or plain old Video, to make sure other people can view your movies. If your movie file is still too large after you compress it, you can also try reducing the number of colors. However, this may deteriorate the image quality.

Saving Your Movie

Are you happy with your movie? If so, you can save it as you would any other file—by selecting File|Save.

Getting your movie just right may take some time and some trial-and-error. It's a good idea to select File|Save As and save a copy of your movie-to-be under a different name. This way, if you change your mind about something as you're working, you've still got the original file.

Don't forget the filename extension! When you save and name your movie, remember to include the **.mov** filename extension. You need filename extensions in order to put files on the Web or share them with Windows users. (Windows users don't have to worry about this; good ol' Windows adds extensions automatically.)

Showing Off Your Movies

What's the best way to show off your movies? Put them on your **Web page**, as explained in Chapter 7 coming up. You can then e-mail your Web page URL to your friends, family, and coworkers. You might also want to try your hand at creating exciting **multimedia greeting cards** for birthdays, holidays, and other special occasions. For these projects you'll need QuickEditor, an image-editing program, sounds, and pictures taken with your cam. Or, you can **create a movie** for a presentation, report, or a small gathering if you know there will be a computer in the room (make sure the computer has a recent version of QuickTime installed). Save your movie on a Zip disk and take it with you.

Think before you attempt to e-mail a movie to someone as an attachment! **Video files weigh in at a hefty 1–2 MB or more,** even after you compress them. Some people's connections can't handle such large files. You're better off creating a special Web page for your movie and then sending your pals an e-mail with the Web page's address.

Summary

Sure, it's fun to record movies with your cam—but add QuickEditor to your computer and cam, and you have a virtual movie studio! QuickEditor helps you edit existing movies or start a movie from scratch, and import videos, pictures, and sounds as clips.

- **QuickEditor** is a $20 shareware video-editing program for Windows and Macintosh. Before you can use QuickEditor, you need to also download the latest version of **QuickTime** (3.0 or higher) for Windows and Macintosh.
- The different parts of the QuickEditor application window let you work with **clips, movies, audio, transitions, and video effects**.
- In QuickEditor, the **movie** is the file that you create or edit in the program. **Clips** are other movies (or pictures or sounds) that you open and insert in the current movie.
- To navigate through a movie or clip, use the **player buttons** next to the movie or clip.
- **Frames** are the individual pictures that together make up a movie. Each frame represents a moment in time. To select frames from a movie or clip, locate the first frame in the sequence you want to select and create a **Start point** for that frame. Then locate the last frame in your sequence and create an **End point**.
- **To add a clip** to a movie, create a Start point where you want to insert the clip. Then open the clip, create Start and End points for the frames you want to add, and click the Edit button (Windows) or the Add Selection to Movie button (Macintosh). This is **ripple editing**—it inserts your clip in the movie and moves the subsequent frames forward.
- **To replace frames** in a movie with a clip, create a Start point and an End point for the frames that you want to replace. Then open the clip, create the Start and End points for the clip, and add the clip to your movie. This technique is called **insert editing**.
- **To remove frames** from a movie, create the Start and End points for the frames you want to remove. Then click the Edit button and select Delete Selection from the pop-up menu (Windows), or click the Erase button (Macintosh).

- **Transitions** are animated special effects that gradually reveal frames as the movie plays. You can add a transition to a clip before inserting the clip in the movie, but you can't add a transition directly to a movie. To apply a transition to a clip, create the Start and End points for the clip, click the Select Transition button, and choose a transition. You can also preview your transitions before you apply them. With some transitions, you can apply custom settings.
- **Video effects** work similarly to transitions, except that you can apply them directly to a movie.
- Since video files are enormous, you'll need to compress them. Click the **Compression Settings** button to display the Compression Settings dialog box, then choose a compression option and color depth.
- Save your movie with File|Save. You also might want to save a working copy with different filenames. That way, you can experiment while leaving your original movie intact.

Once you've created a movie, you can strut your stuff and put it on the Web, as covered in the next chapter.

7 Putting Pictures and Movies on Web Pages

Now that you've got all these cool pictures, GIF animations, and movies you took with your cam, how do you show them off? Put them on your Web page, of course. I can't tell you everything about Web pages here, but this chapter does get you started and offers a few handy tips and tricks. Getting comfortable with Web pages and images will also help you get prepared for setting up your own live Web cam, as covered in Part Four.

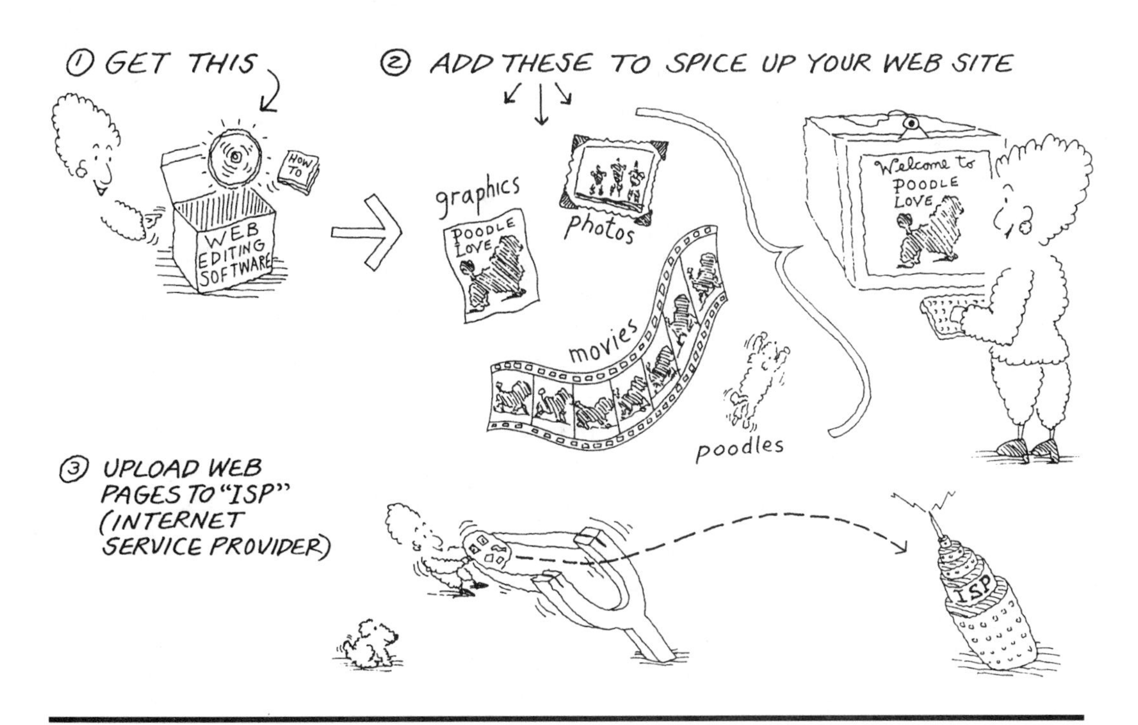

In this chapter:

- Web basics: Getting a Web site, uploading pages to a server, and Web page editors
- Web Images 101: Web-friendly image file formats, and how to put images on Web pages
- Image tricks: Low-res images, thumbnails, and Web-page slide shows
- Linking to movie files and embedding movies
- Fun with DHTML

Why Use a Web Page?

Sure, there are other ways to share your files with your friends, families, and coworkers—you can send 'em as e-mail attachments or even on a floppy disk through "snail mail." But some people have trouble with e-mail attachments, and the popular iMac doesn't even *have* a floppy drive. It's much easier for everyone (including you) if you put all your nifty stuff on a Web page, and then e-mail the **Web page address** out to everyone. Then they can go to your page and view your files at their leisure.

Web site addresses

A Web site address is a **URL** (Uniform Resource Locator) that points to a Web site or a Web page, as in **http://www.byteit.com/Cam/index.htm,** which is my Web Cam site.

Got a Web Site Yet?

If you don't have a Web site yet, that shouldn't be a problem. When you sign up with a local **Internet Service Provider (ISP)** for your Internet account, or join up with one of the big services like Earthlink (**http://www.earthlink.com/**), America Online (**http://www.aol.com/**) or Microsoft Networks (**http://www.msn.com/**), they give you Web space with your account.

Most ISPs and other Web-page hosting services also provide all kinds of helpful tools for building your Web site, including step-by-step instructions and downloadable shareware. Check your ISP's home page or call them for details.

Free Web Sites

If you've got free Internet access through school or work but you don't have Web space, don't let that stop you. GeoCities (**http://www.geocities.com/**) and other companies on line offer **free Web space,** a permanent e-mail address that you can keep after you graduate or change jobs, and all the information you need to get started.

The catch? They make their money from paid **advertising.** This means you have to set up your page so they can run ads from it. To see how this works, go to GeoCities, read their information, and explore their online communities.

HTML and Web Page Editors

As you may already know, Web pages are created with **HyperText Markup Language (HTML)**, a set of special tags that tell browsers how to display the pages. As you work through this chapter you'll get a look at some of these tags. You don't even need a special program to write HTML—you can use a text editor like Windows Notepad, or any word processing program in Text Only mode.

There are plenty of inexpensive (and sometimes free) programs available out there to help you create Web pages. Some can be downloaded; some can be purchased in computer stores.

Text HTML Editors

Take a look at **Figure 7.1**, which shows you Sausage Software's HotDog Pro for Windows. This program and other **text-based HTML editors** have toolbar buttons, dialog boxes, and other powerful features for coding Web pages. Most of these programs come with tutorials and help options to get you started.

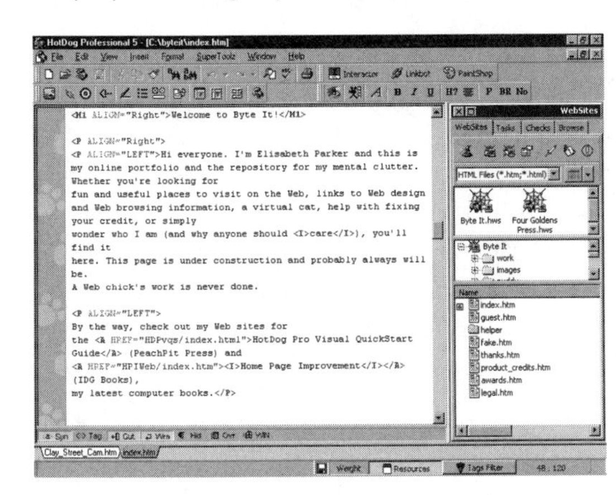

Figure 7.1 *Web page shown in HotDog Pro, a text HTML editor for Windows.*

Graphical HTML Editors

If you don't feel like working directly with HTML code, you can use a **graphical HTML editor** like Macromedia's Dreamweaver (for Windows and Mac), as shown in **Figure 7.2**. These applications display your Web page as it looks in the browser and behave more like a word processor or page layout program—so you can work more intuitively and see your results in an online-like setting.

Want to Learn HTML? Getting a page up and running isn't rocket science. Pick up the *HTML for the World Wide Web Visual QuickStart Guide* by Elizabeth Castro (Peachpit Press, 1998). You can also find helpful tutorials on the Web. Start with your ISP's Web page—it should have some information and links. Or visit Earthlink's Web tutorial at **http://www.earthlink.net/assistance/support/member/**.

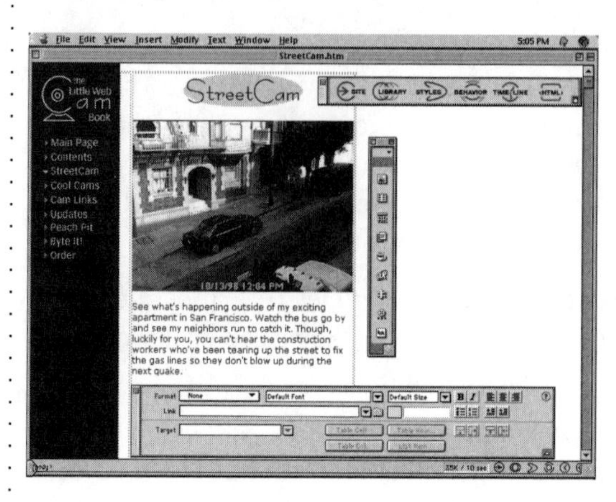

Figure 7.2 *Web page shown in Dreamweaver, Web authoring software with a graphical HTML editor for Macintosh and Windows.*

Recommended Web Authoring Programs

Here are some popular **Web authoring programs** that will help you get your page designed, created, tested, and up and running:

- **AOL Press**: A free, easy-to-use graphical Web page editor for Windows and Macintosh users, go to **http://www.aolpress.com/**.
- **Microsoft FrontPage**: No-fuss Web design and development; you can add features that would normally require programming... *if* your server offers FrontPage support. For more information, go to **http://www.microsoft.com/frontpage/**. And if you like this *Little Web Cam* book, you might also find *The Complete Idiot's Guide to FrontPage 2000* helpful—I wrote that one, too.
- **Macromedia Dreamweaver**: The perfect tool for graphics designers who are picky about their pages. Dreamweaver also comes with fully functional text editors (Allaire HomeSite for Windows, and BBEdit for Macintosh). To get started, try the *Dreamweaver Visual QuickStart Guide* by J. Tarin Towers (Peachpit Press, 1998). For more information, visit **http://www.macromedia.com/**.
- **HotDog Pro by Sausage Software**: A feature-packed Web tools suite and text editor for Windows users. Try out the 30-day trial version at **http://www.sausage.com/**. If you need more help, you can pick up the *HotDog Pro Visual QuickStart Guide* (PeachPit Press, 1997), by yours truly.
- **Allaire HomeSite**: Another popular text editor for Windows users. Take a run with the trial version at **http://www.allaire.com/**.

- **BBEdit**: A powerful text editor for Macintosh users. You can also try out the slimmed-down freeware version. Go to **http://www.barebones.com/**.
- **Go shareware "shopping"**: The Web has more than a few sites for downloading and trying out shareware for Web editing, fooling around with images, and just about anything else. TUCOWS provides an extensive, well-organized collection of cool downloads and reviews for Windows and Macintosh users. ZDNet's Hotfiles.com for Windows users and MacDownload.com for Macintosh users also offer extensive, well-organized collections and reviews. You can also try Download.com, Shareware.com, and Filez.com. Here are all the relevant URLs:

  http://www.tucows.com/
  http://www.hotfiles.com/
  http://www.macdownload.com/
  http://www.download.com/
  http://www.shareware.com/
  http://www.filez.com/

What's Suitable for the Web?

Web browsers can only display two types of image files: **GIFs and JPEGs**. Most cam programs can save images to your computer system's primary image-file format (BMP for Windows and PICT for Macintosh) and as JPEGs. Make sure to save your pictures as JPEGs, because Web browsers cannot display Bitmap or PICT files. You can also use one of the image-editing programs covered in Chapter 2 to convert pictures to Web-friendly file formats.

Think twice about full-size. When you take pictures and make movies with your cam, they normally come in only two sizes: half-screen (320x240 pixels) and quarter-screen (160x120 pixels). Sure, you can also capture photos and video at the full-screen size (640x480). But if you do, you'll wind up with whopping huge files that take *way* too long to download.

Pictures on Your Web Page

Just about every HTML editor, whether text or graphical, has image toolbar buttons for **inserting pictures**. When you click the toolbar button, a dialog box appears so you can look for your image file. With some programs, you can also enter settings for your image from the same dialog box. Other programs insert the image first, and then give you an image properties dialog box where you can manage the image settings.

GIF Animations on a Web Page. *Since a GIF animation is a type of image, you can insert it the same way as any other image: by clicking your Web page editor's Insert Image button or by entering an HTML <IMG> tag.*

Figures 7.3 and 7.4 show the Insert Image options for HotDog Pro for Windows. Most of today's HTML editing programs offer the same options, though they may be arranged and/or accessed differently.

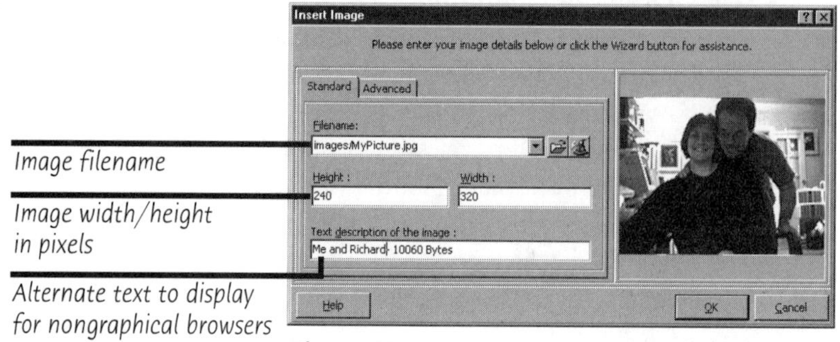

Figure 7.3 *HotDog Pro's Insert Image dialog box with Standard options displayed.*

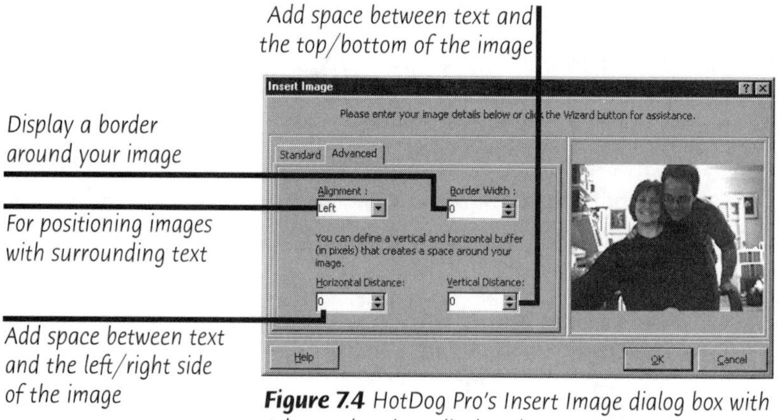

Add space between text and the top/bottom of the image

Display a border around your image

For positioning images with surrounding text

Add space between text and the left/right side of the image

Figure 7.4 *HotDog Pro's Insert Image dialog box with Advanced options displayed.*

Image Options

Let's look at these image options.

- **Image filename**: Naturally, you need to tell your HTML editor where the image is located in relation to your Web page. You can do this by clicking the folder icon to browse for the picture, or by entering a directory path such as **images/MyPicture.jpg**.
- **Image height and width**: The image's height and width settings tell Web browsers to hold a place for your picture while your page loads. A good Web page editor automatically figures out the height and width dimensions for your picture in pixels.

***Image Options** (cont.)*

- **Alternative text**: Be nice to people whose Web browsers only display text, as well as folks who can't see as well as you do—enter a brief text description of your picture. When someone can't view the image, the text displays instead, or a voice recognition program reads the text to the user so they'll know what's there.
- **Alignment**: You can choose from a variety of options to determine how your image lines up with the surrounding text. The most popular options are Left, which positions the image to the left of the text and flows the text around the right side of the image; and Right, which positions the image to the right of the text and flows the text around the left side of the image.
- **Border width**: You can display a border around your image by entering a number in pixels, such as 1 or 2. Or you can choose not to have a border by entering 0. If you create a link around the image, the border will take the same color as the link. Otherwise, the border is displayed in the same color as your body text (or with no border at all in older browsers).

What's a Pixel? *On the Web, pictures and other Web page elements are measured in* ***pixels****—the tiny dots used to display everything on your computer screen. For more about pixels, see Chapters 2 and 4.*

Lookin' Smooth as Buttah... In most design situations, images look much nicer *without* borders. To create a smoother look for your pages, specify 0 for the Border Width option when you insert pictures. Some Web editors automatically enter this setting for you.

- **Horizontal distance (space)**: If you choose to wrap text around your image, use the Horizontal Distance option to create a little space between the text and the right/left sides of the picture. Enter a value in pixels. Something between 5 and 10 pixels usually looks great.
- **Vertical distance (space)**: Since the browser automatically puts space between lines of text, you don't need to create as much of a cushion at the top and bottom of your picture. Try a value between 3 and 5 pixels for the space between the picture's top/bottom edges and the surrounding text.

You can use pictures for Web page backgrounds. Remember how we talked about desktop patterns back in Chapter 4? You can also take pictures of textures and patterns around your house or office and use them as patterned backgrounds for your Web pages. With most Web editors, you can choose background images as well as text and link colors from the Properties dialog box (Edit|Properties).

The HTML Source Code

You might be wondering what all this stuff looks like in HTML. Let's take a peek under the hood. If you enter settings for all of the image options we've just discussed, the HTML code will look similar to the following example. This is how it appears in the graphical Web editor, Dreamweaver, shown in **Figure 7.5**:

```
<IMG SRC="images/MyPicture.jpg"
WIDTH="320" HEIGHT="240"
ALT="Picture of Richard and Me"
ALIGN="LEFT"
BORDER="0"
HSPACE="6" VSPACE="3">
```

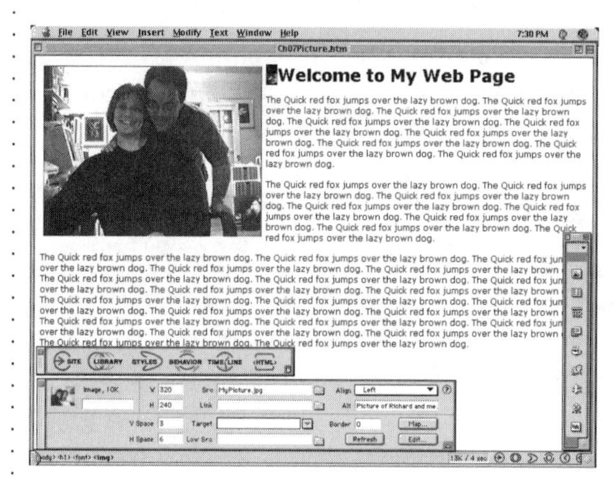

Figure 7.5 *Picture, text, and image options displayed in Dreamweaver.*

Translated into English, this HTML relays the following info:

- The image source file is in the **images** folder and is called **MyPicture.jpg**.
- The picture is **320** pixels wide and **240** pixels high.
- If someone can't see the image, display **Picture of Richard and Me** instead.
- Align the picture to the **Left** so the text wraps around the right side, and do not display a **Border** around it.
- And, oh, yes, please be so kind as to insert **6** pixels between the side of my picture and the text, and **3** pixels between the top and bottom of the picture and the text.

"Low-Res" Images

The Web is a great place to show off your pictures, but those images often take too long to download on many computers in use today. For example, a 320x240 pixel, high-quality JPEG file shot at millions of colors (24-bit) takes up about 59K.

So how do you keep impatient visitors from giving up and clicking their browser's Back button before your image finishes loading? Create a **low-res version** of your picture that displays while the "real" image is downloading. Low-res stands for low resolution, describing lesser-quality images with smaller file sizes that download more quickly.

Creating Low-Res Images

Grayscale (black-and-white) image files are much smaller than images with millions of colors. When you use your cam to take snapshots for your Web pages, make it a point to take both a full-color and a grayscale version of each picture. You can then **use the grayscale picture** as your low-res image.

If you have an image program such as PaintShop Pro for Windows or Graphic Converter for Macintosh (described in Chapter 2), you can put their special tools and filters to work creating interesting effects for your low-res images. For example, compare the low-res and regular images in **Figure 7.6.** I copied the original photo, converted it to grayscale, and then applied a filter that makes the picture look like a charcoal drawing.

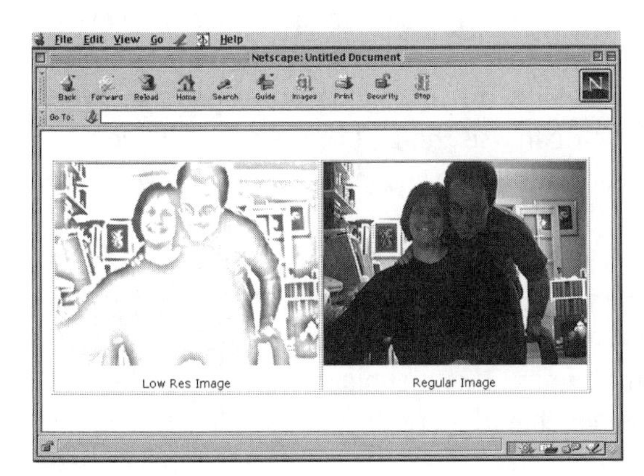

***Figure 7.6** The low-res and regular versions of an image.*

Displaying Low-Res Images

Web browsers must be told to display the low-res image first. Newer Web editor programs know about low-res images, and provide options in their Image Properties dialog boxes so you can specify low-res for the current picture.

Alerting the browser is important

But if your Web authoring program doesn't do this, you'll need to **alter your Web page's source code**. Don't worry—this is very easy to do. View the page's source code, and locate the <IMG SRC> tag for your picture. You'll enter code like the following:

```
<IMG SRC="images/MyPicture.jpg"
WIDTH="320" HEIGHT="240"
ALT="Picture of Richard and Me"
ALIGN="LEFT"
BORDER="0"
HSPACE="6" VSPACE="3"
LOW SRC=
"images/MyPictureLowRes.jpg">
```

The <IMG SRC> tag's LOW SRC attribute tells the browser to display the low-res image on your Web page first, and then replace it with the better image when it's finished downloading.

Are My Pages Too Fat?

A Web page—and all the pictures that you put into it—should take no longer than **20 seconds to load**. Otherwise there's a good chance your visitors will get impatient and leave your Web site. As a rule of thumb, every 2K of data take about a second to download in a Web browser for a visitor with a 28.8Kbps or 33.6Kbps modem. That means a 30K image displays in about 15 seconds.

Luckily, many Web editors come with tools that conveniently tell you how long your Web page will take to download at various modem speeds. Most people these days have 28.8Kbps or 33.6Kbps modems—but the 56.6 modems are becoming more popular. When a page gets too heavy, you can use the ol' low-res trick. Or, you can move a larger image to a different page and make a link to it. We'll cover links next.

Making Links to Pictures and Movies

You may want to use **links** to your images and movie files, rather than including them in your page. The images and movies will be displayed when someone clicks their links. This technique works well when you want to display large images that don't fit in your page layout and that take a while to load. When you link to your movies, people can play them back with whatever browser **plug-in** or **video player application** they have on their computer.

How do you link something in your page to a picture or a movie? The same way you would link to a regular Web page: Select the text or image from which you want to link, click your Web authoring program's Link button, and browse for your picture or video when the Link dialog box appears. You can also enter the link code by hand. Here's an example:

```
<A HREF="video/MyVideo.mov">
My QuickTime Movie</A>
```

and here's another example:

```
<A HREF="video/MyMovie.avi">
My Avi Movie</A> or
<A HREF="images/MyPicture.jpg">My Picture</A>
```

> ***What's a Plug-In?***
> *Plug-ins are applications that work with your browser to extend its capabilities. For example, the QuickTime plug-in lets you play movies straight from a Web page.*

Give Your Visitors the Scoop

When you provide links to large image files and movies, it's nice to give visitors a little **information on the Web page** to help them decide whether or not to download the file. You can give them a brief description of the file, the file size and format, and what plug-in launches the file—something like "Watch my cat jump up on the bed—1.2MB QuickTime movie. If you don't have QuickTime, you can get it from http://quicktime.apple.com/."

Use Thumbnail Images

To encourage visitors to view your linked pictures and movies, you can provide **thumbnail images** on the Web page and link them to the larger files. Thumbnails are miniature pictures that let visitors preview the larger image or movies, as shown in **Figure 7.7**. When a visitor clicks the thumbnail image, it displays the original image or launches the movie.

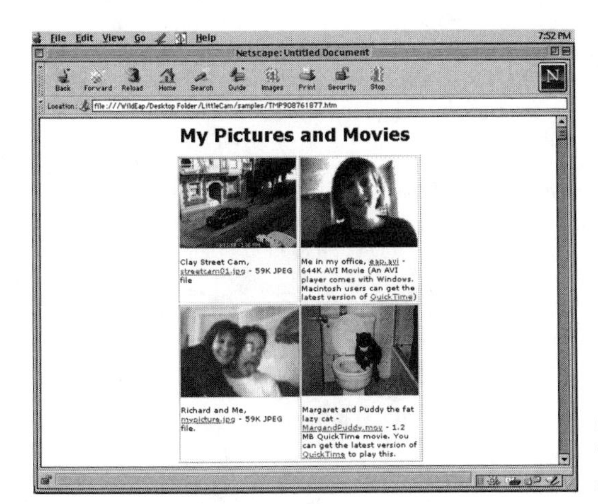

Figure 7.7 *Web page with thumbnails to images and movies.*

In order to add thumbnails to a Web page, you first need to create miniature versions of your pictures. Use one of the image programs discussed in Chapter 2. You can then arrange these little pictures on your Web page (tables work great for presenting them) and create links for each of the thumbnails.

Grabbing Pictures from Movies. QuickEditor, discussed in Chapter 6, lets you open a movie, move to your favorite frame in the movie, and save it as a BMP (Windows) or PICT (Macintosh) file. You can then use an image program to convert the picture to a JPEG file that you can display on your Web page.

The Importance of Filename Extensions

When you are creating and saving files that you plan to put on the Web, don't forget to add the **filename extension**—a period followed by three or four letters, as in .gif or .jpeg. Filename extensions identify the files for browsers, and tell the browser what application should launch to open the file. Windows 95 and 98 computers automatically add the correct extensions when you save files. But **Macintosh users** need to remember to make sure this gets done.

Macintosh only

Filename Extensions

Extension	File Type
.jpeg or .jpg	Joint Photographic Expert Group, the organization that developed the JPEG file format. Most cam software programs save pictures as JPEGs because this image format compresses down to small file sizes and supports millions of colors (24-bit).
.gif	Graphic Interchange File format. Until JPEGs came along, Web browsers could only display GIFs. GIF files can only display 256 colors, and photographs usually look better as JPEGs. But you can do some cool things with GIF files, including turning them into animations as explained in Chapter 5.
.mov	QuickTime movie files. QuickTime comes with Macintosh computers, and Windows users can download a compatible version of the player and plug-in. For the latest version of QuickTime, visit http://quicktime.apple.com/.
.avi	Audio Video Interleaved, the standard video format for Windows. All Windows systems come with an AVI movie player. Macintosh users can play back AVI movies with QuickTime 3.0 and higher. AVI movies are also sometimes saved with the .vfw extension, which stands for Video for Windows.
.mpeg	Motion Pictures Expert Group, the organization that developed this video format. QuickTime supports MPEG movies in addition to its native .mov format.

Embedding a Movie

Browsers display pictures as **inline files**—meaning that the pictures appear on the Web page as part of the page layout. You can make movies display as inline files, too, by **embedding** them on your Web page, as shown in **Figure 7.8.** If the visitor has the correct plug-in (QuickTime, in most cases), embedded movies will play straight from your Web page.

Control buttons

Figure 7.8 *Web page with embedded movie.*

Most Web authoring programs these days have options that help you embed movies and other types of files. However, since people don't embed files as often as they make links, insert images, and format text, your particular Web editing program might not have a toolbar button for embedding files. You may have to pull down a few menus to find the command you need. Try the Insert menu first, and look for a command like Embed File or Plug In.

Good things come in small packages: When recording movies for the Web, stick with the small 160x120 movie size. Even 320x240 movies are usually too large for the average page. Think about it—a high-quality image with millions of colors can be about 59K. And movies show about 30 pictures *per second*. For a half-minute movie, that's over 5MB! Oof.

Movie Properties

If your Web editing program supports embedding, you'll get a Plug-In Properties dialog box similar to the one shown in **Figure 7.9.** You'll have access to some or all of the following options:

- **File Source (or Data Source):** The name and location of your movie, as in video|MyMovie.mov.
- **Alternate Message:** You can designate a message to be displayed for browsers that do not support plug-ins. Although

most people use browsers that can handle embedded files, it can't hurt to display a message just in case.

- **Size**: When providing the width and height dimensions for your movie, you must add 18 pixels to the movie's height to leave room for the player application's control buttons. This means a 160x120-pixel movie becomes 160x128 pixels, and a 320x240-pixel movie becomes 320x258 pixels.

- **Alignment, Horizontal Spacing, Vertical Spacing, and Border Thickness**: These options are similar to the ones described for the Image Properties dialog box, covered earlier in this chapter.

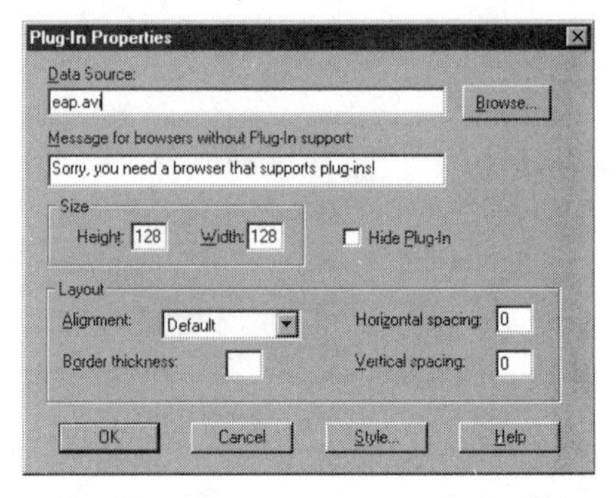

Figure 7.9 *Plug-In Properties dialog box in FrontPage 98 for Windows.*

In addition, some HTML editors offer the following options:

- **Loop**: Determines the number of times the movie automatically plays. I recommend entering 1, to play the movie only once. If visitors want to see your movie again, they can click the Play button.

- **AutoStart**: Select Yes (or True) to play the movie automatically when the page loads, or No (False) to play the movie only when visitors click the movie's icon or on the Play button.

Embedding a Movie with HTML

To embed a 120x160 QuickTime movie, select the No or False option for starting the movie automatically when the page loads. Loop the movie once, and type the following HTML code:

```
<EMBED SRC="video/MyMovie.mov"
WIDTH="160" HEIGHT="138"
LOOP="1" AUTOSTART="False">
```

Yegads! What's That?

If you embed a movie with a graphical Web page editor, you'll see something like this extremely ugly plug-in icon: 

Not to worry. Most Web page editors cannot display plug-in files and use these placeholders instead. If you view your page in a Web browser, your movie player will launch and play your movie.

Creating a Web Page Slide Show

Want to try some instant multimedia? Create a Web page **slide show** like the one shown in **Figure 7.10**.

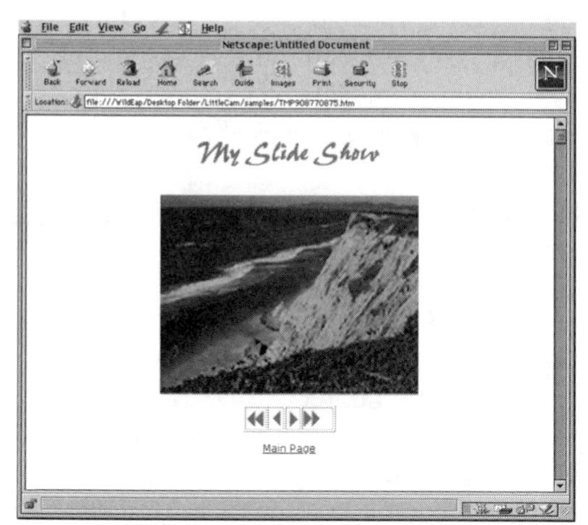

Figure 7.10
A page in a slide show.

Here's how it works. First, you create a set of Web pages that display one picture each. Decide on an order in which to display the pages. Then set up each page to automatically progress to the next page after a certain number of seconds. In Web lingo, this is called **document redirection.**

A Bit of HTML

With some Web page editors, you can redirect Web pages from the Page Properties dialog box. Alas, however, most programs require you to enter the HTML code yourself in the HTML Source Code view. Fortunately, it's only a *teeny* snippet of code that you enter at the very beginning of your HTML document.

Steps for Making a Slide Show

To redirect a document:

1. Open your Web page with a text editor, or in the source code view of your Web authoring software.
2. Scroll to the top of the Web page and find the <HEAD> tag.
3. After the <HEAD> tag (but before the </HEAD> closing tag), enter the following code:

   ```
   <META HTTP-EQUIV="Refresh" CONTENT="10";
   URL="NextPage.html">
   ```

   In this example, **10** is the number of seconds that you want the current page to stay displayed before the next page loads, and **NextPage.html** is the name of the next page that you want displayed after the 10-second interval.
4. Save your work, open your page in a browser, and see what happens.

When you have this process down pat, you can do the same thing with the rest of your Web pages.

Please be a nice host. Give people some tools so they can move forward and backward within the slide show, or leave it if they want. You can find lots of attractive Back and Forward buttons, like the simple ones shown here, plus many other cool clip-art goodies, at the Icon Bazaar at **http://www.iconbazaar.com/**.

Fun with DHTML

Have you heard about **DHTML** yet? It stands for **Dynamic HyperText Markup Language**—a sort of supercaffeinated version of regular old HTML. Graphic designers appreciate DHTML because it provides improved page-layout options. You'll like it because DHTML lets you do new and exciting things with the pictures you take with your cam. Now, you can create eye-popping Web-page animations, work with layers of images and text, use fancy fonts, and more.

So how do you learn DHTML? You don't have to. Many new Web programs, including FrontPage 2000, make it easy to create DHTML pages with special effects. Netscape Navigator and Internet Explorer versions 4.0 and higher support DHTML. For some cutting-edge examples of what you can do with DHTML, visit the DHTML Zone at **http://www.dhtmlzone.com/**.

Getting Your Stuff onto a Web Server

For Web pages to get from your computer to a Web server, you **upload** your files to the server. To do this, you need a **File Transfer Protocol (FTP) program**. Windows folks can use **WS FTP** or **Cute FTP** (Windows); for Macintosh there's **Fetch,** for example. Uploading files is the opposite of downloading them—it means moving files from your computer *to* a server instead of the other way around.

Getting FTP

These FTP programs are all **shareware** that you can get from your ISP or from a shareware Web site like TUCOWS. URLs for TUCOWS and the other companies mentioned here are in the earlier section, "Recommended HTML Programs."

Other Choices

Some Web page authoring programs come with **built-in FTP** capabilities and are easier to work with than FTP programs. These ready-to-go applications include Microsoft FrontPage (Windows and Macintosh), Macromedia Dreamweaver (Windows and Macintosh), and HotDog Pro for Windows.

You can also set up the Web camming programs discussed in Chapter 8 to upload your pictures for you.

Summary

The Web gives you the perfect way to show off your cam creations—including pictures, GIF animations, movies, and a live Web cam.

- If you don't have a Web site yet, your **ISP** or **Web hosting company** can help. Many companies give you all the tools you need to get started.
- Web pages are written in HyperText Markup Language (**HTML**), a set of codes that tells Web browsers how to display text and pictures.
- You can use any text editor to create Web pages, but **Web editor software** greatly simplifies Web page creation. If you want to learn HTML while creating your pages, try a text editor. If you prefer working with pages as they will appear in your browser, start off with a graphical editor.
- Before you can put images on a Web page, you'll need to save them as **GIFs** or **JPEGs,** the image file formats for the Web.
- Most Web editors provide a helpful dialog box to help you **place a picture** on your Web page.
- If you want to display a favorite photo on a Web page, but worry that it might take too long to load straight from a Web page, try the **low-res trick.** You can set your Web page up to display a substitute picture.
- You can slim down your pages while giving visitors a preview of your pictures and movies. Try creating a page with **thumbnails** (images) that link to larger images or movies.
- If you want to display a movie straight from your Web page, you can **embed it.** However, visitors with older browsers or without the correct plug-in won't be able to play your movie or view your Web page properly. Another option is to **make a link** to your movie, so visitors can choose whether or not to play it.
- You can create a **Web page slide show** with pages that display for a certain amount of time, then automatically change to a different page. Web designers call this technique **document redirection.**
- **Dynamic HTML (DHTML)** is a new technology that lets you do more exciting things with pictures and Web pages. With newer Web page editors like FrontPage 2000, it's easy to design cool pages with animated special effects—without writing a single line of code!

- Once you create a Web page, you need to upload it to your server using **FTP**. Many Web page editors have built-in FTP tools that make it easy to get pages onto the server. Or you can download an FTP program from one of the shareware Web sites.

Now that you've had an introduction to Web pages and acquired a few tricks for making them, you can move on to Chapters 8 through 10, which tell you all about setting up your own live Web cam.

Part Four
Web Cams

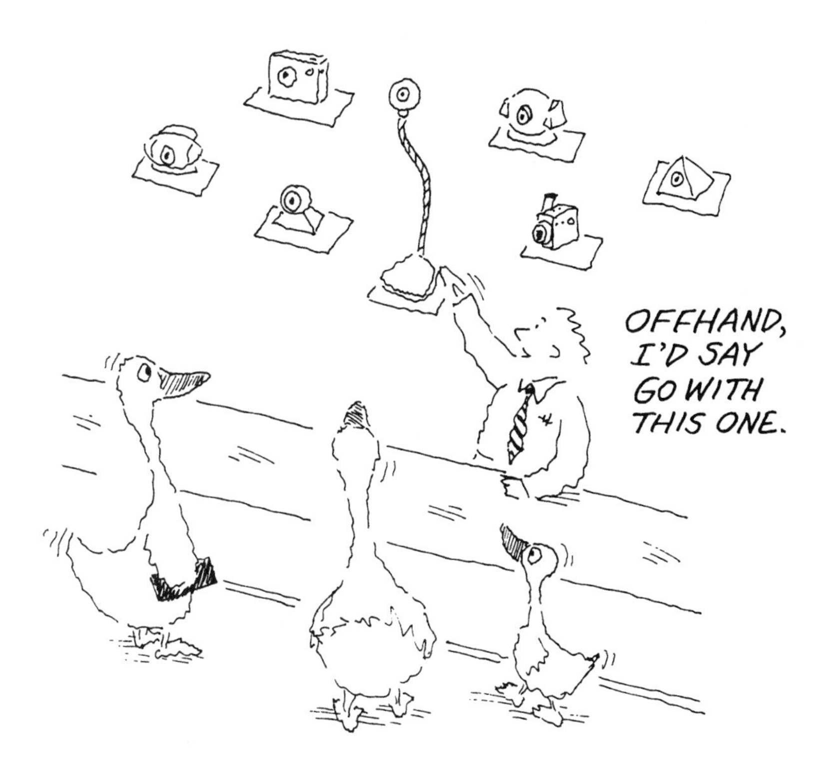
OFFHAND, I'D SAY GO WITH THIS ONE.

8 Web Cams: Examples, Ideas, and Inspiration

This chapter takes you on a quick tour of some of my favorite Web cam sites so you can have fun, get some ideas, and see how other people deal with the challenges of camming. Some of these sites use expensive technical setups and involve a lot of programming. Others cam with nothing more than QuickCam and a clever idea.

In this chapter:

- Find your inspiration
- Where the Web cams are
- Outdoor cams
- Pet and animal cams
- Home and office cams
- Miscellaneous cams
- Other Web cam ideas

Find Your Inspiration

Now that you've decided to set up a cam, you need to find an idea that works for you. Sure, we'd all like to do something breathtakingly clever, but we also have to consider the limitations of our equipment, connections, and budget.

For example, do you want people looking at your mug all day, or would you rather point the cam out your window and have more privacy? You also have to figure out the logistics—after all, your cam and your phone line do need to connect to your computer. With those considerations in mind, go ahead and get creative. Lots of people are out there creating and maintaining popular and imaginative cams with the same equipment you've got.

Remember, too, that you don't need an action-packed scene to make your Web cam interesting. If you point the cam toward your yard so people can watch your dog, and Spot wanders away from the camera's view, so what? You can offer still images and movies so your visitors have something to look at until Spot comes back. Even cammers who've got tons of equipment and the perfect setup can't guarantee an exciting masterpiece for every snapshot. Unpredictability is part of the fun.

Do You Need a Longer Cable? If your cam just won't go far enough, you don't have to rearrange your entire house. Call your local computer or video camera store and see if you can get a longer cable or an extension. You can then run the cable under the rug, or use guides to run it along the wall so people (and pets) don't trip over it.

Look Up Some Cams

Once you've explored the cams in this chapter, you might want to find some Web cams on your own. The Web sites in the following sections will get you started. They offer links to lots of Web cams, along with plenty of camming tips, information, and online stores where you can buy software and equipment. When you get your cam up and running, you can go back to these Web sites and fill out their forms to add your new cam to their listings. Who knows—maybe you'll win an award.

Be patient when you visit Web cams and related Web sites. The images can take a couple of minutes to load, and many of these Web sites also run advertisements.

The Digital Camera Network (DCN)

http://www.dcn.com/

Take a tour of Web cams around the world, and space cams too. You'll also find an online forum for cammers and a featured Cam of the Day. DCN also makes Cam Runner—Web cam software for $39.95—which you can download or take for a spin. Like most Web cam shareware, in DCN the company logo displays on your pictures until you pay for the program.

WebCam Central

http://www.camcentral.com/

WebCam Central, shown in **Figure 8.1**, links to its recent FeatureCam award winners from its main page. This site offers an extensive listing of cams organized by category and location. Or try the Random Cam for a new and exciting surprise.

Figure 8.1 *Web Cam Central.*

Virtual Cams

http://www.dreamscape.com/frankvad/cams.html

Dreamscape's Virtual Cams page lists thousands of cams organized by categories. In addition, owner Frank Vad can hook you up with all kinds of goodies on the Net. You'll find extensive lists of shareware, chat, how-to's, and other Internet resources.

Web Cam Network

http://www.webcam.net/WebCamNetHome.html

Need more information about camming? The Web Cam Network recommends products, resources for getting help, and, of course, links to other cool cams.

Tommy's List of Live Cams World Wide

http://chili.rt66.com/ozone/cam.htm

Take a tour around the world, or check out cams in the good ol' US of A. If you need pictures of tarantulas and other odd insects, or an engraved silver belt buckle, you can view and order them from Tommy's Gallery.

WeatherNet's Weather Cams

http://cirrus.sprl.umich.edu/wxnet/wxcam.html

If you're a weather junkie, believe me, you aren't alone. Whether you're planning a vacation, a trip to the beach, or an alternate route to work when the weather's bad, stop in here for up-to-date weather cams and forecasts all around the world. You can even set up your own weather cam by pointing your camera out your window.

Outdoor Scenes

Outdoor scenes are one of the easiest types of cams to set up. After all, you probably have a window somewhere near your computer, and it's likely there's almost always something interesting going on outside. If the scenery looks kind of blah, you can make it more compelling by setting up a bird feeder, planting a garden, hanging up some wind chimes, or buying a pinwheel or wind sock. And hey, if you're really determined, you can always move somewhere more lively! But with a little imagination, that shouldn't be necessary.

Olivet Intersection Webcam

http://webcam.olivet.edu/int/main.htm

Not much happens at this sleepy intersection of Routes 102 and 45 in rural Illinois, but it's still fun to watch the cars go by. Students at Olivet College use the cam to check the line at the Dairy Queen before heading over there for their fast food fixes.

Dave's Deck Cam

http://www.marsweb.com/dave/view.htm

Montana has some of the most beautiful scenery in the world, with dramatic skies, lush forests, and tall mountains. Check out Dave's Deck Cam for a lovely view of his front yard and a mountain.

Kremlin Kam

http://www.kremlinkam.com

You might want to put off your trip to Russia 'til things settle down over there. Fortunately, our cheery hostess, Oksana, assures us that despite Russia's troubles, the Kremlin Kam is perfectly safe, as shown in **Figure 8.2.** Launched as a joint venture by Russian high-tech companies Mosenergo and Multi-Page, the cam features snapshots of the Kremlin and St. Basil's Cathedral. Since the area is well lit, you can even see the Kremlin at night.

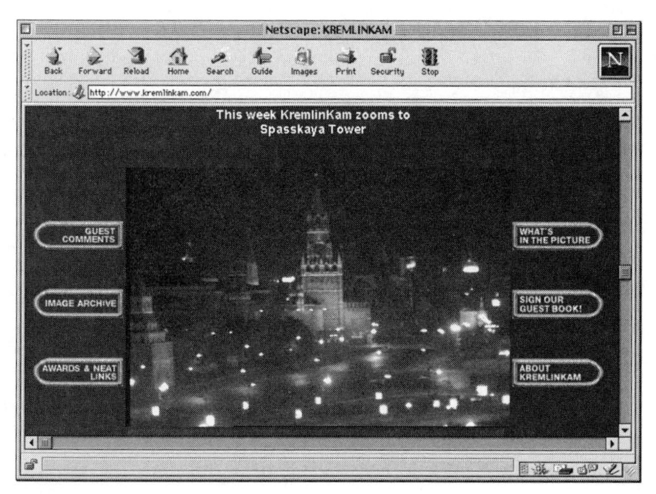

Figure 8.2 *Kremlin Kam.*

http://www.rearden.com/live/current/default.html

Rearden Technology's Bay Bridge Cam

The makers of SiteCam, the popular Macintosh camming software examined in Chapter 9, run a cam that gives you a panoramic view of downtown San Francisco and the Bay Bridge. If you've got the latest version of Netscape Navigator or Internet Explorer, check out the Pan Tilt Cam (at **http://www.sitezap.com/**), complete with controls so you can move the camera around. If you're wondering how they did it, read Chapter 10 for an interview with Brad Lowe.

http://freespace.virgin.net/kevin.croucher/gardencam/

Kevin's Garden Cam

English gardens are renowned for their charm. Since you probably don't have time to move to England and set up your own garden, visit Kevin's instead. And he's even planning to put in *more* flowers for your viewing pleasure.

http://www.dmssoft.com/live.htm

Courthouse Square Live Action Cam

At this site you've find a view of a park from the second or third story of a building in Courthouse Square, Morgantown, West Virginia. You can also follow a link to Virtual Morgantown and take a tour of the town.

Tips for Camming In the Great Outdoors

- **Keep your windows clean.** Otherwise you won't get a good picture. Since San Francisco generally has a mild climate and very few insects, I avoid the clean-window issue altogether for my own Street Cam (**http://www.byteit.com/cam/StreetCam.htm**) by just leaving the window open. But if you don't live in a place that's blessed with a mild climate, you may not have the luxury of doing that.

- **Adjust your image settings.** QuickCam and other desktop video cameras get finicky when it comes to bright outdoor light. Unless you live in a cloudy climate like Seattle's, you may need to experiment with the image settings (details in Chapter 2).
- **It's OK to stop the cam.** If you live in the city or leave the porch light on, your cam may look cool even at night. But most places just look *dark* at night. When you go Web-cam surfing, you'll see that plenty of people shut their cams down at night. When you stop your cam, the last image remains displayed.
- **Read the interview with Brad Lowe.** Sure, Brad Lowe of Rearden Technology has a more expensive setup than most. But he offers some tips that all of us can use (Chapter 10). His San Francisco Bay Bridge and Pan Tilt cams are listed in this section.

Pets and Animals

Lots of people like to set up Web cams starring their pets. Naturally, this works best with animals that don't move around very much because they live in a cage or maybe have a special napping spot and take lots of naps. Birds, gerbils, hamsters, guinea pigs, and fish make for perfect camming because they're fun to watch and they don't go anywhere.

But cat, dog, and wildlife lovers shouldn't give up. Lots of people on the Web have found ways to keep their animals near the cam often enough to make their Web pages interesting.

Lisa Violet's Cat House

http://www.lisaviolet.com/cathouse/page3.html

Lisa Violet has 18 cats running around the house, and she puts the camera near their favorite chair. So you're just about guaranteed to see something interesting on the Cat House Web Cam, shown in **Figure 8.3.** You can also send online postcards to your cat-loving friends and family, meet the cats (all 18 of them), play Java cat games, listen to MIDI music files, visit the chat room, and more. Naturally, all this stuff takes a long time to download, but it's worth the wait. To learn Lisa Violet's camming secrets, read the interview in Chapter 10.

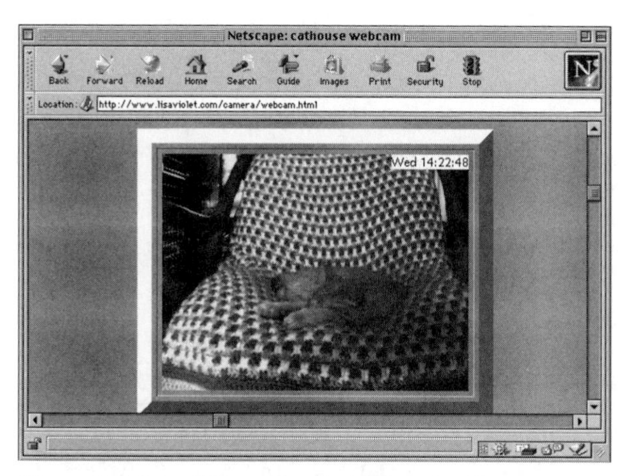

Figure 8.3 *One of 18 cats at Lisa Violet's Cat House.*

http://www.shgroup.com/gerbilcam/gerbil_cam.htm

Safe Harbor Group Gerbil Cam

Visit Blackie, Nukem, and Max, the Griffin household's gerbils, for hours of entertainment. The gerbils live in a cage, but sometimes they escape or the family lets them out to run around. Dad's a computer consultant, so the setup is pretty cool. Depending on your connection speed, you can view the Gerbil Cam at various image sizes, and there's a Reset button you can click to view new images whenever you want.

http://www.wbu.com/feedercam_home.htm

Wild Birds Unlimited Bird Feeder Cam

My neighbor set up a hummingbird feeder, but no hummingbirds came. As far as I can tell, only the pigeons ever visit our apartment building here in San Francisco. If this sounds like your situation, check out the Bird Feeder Cam during daylight hours for constant live bird action. If it inspires you, you can order everything you need from Wild Birds Unlimited to set up your own bird feeder.

http://www.employlaw.com/CatNap.htm

Cat Nap Cam

See if you can catch Nikita, the purebred Abyssinian, taking a nap on her embroidered pillow. Follow links to her pals, drop by her haunted house, and check out some photos of Nikita as a kitten.

http://www.si.edu/organiza/museums/zoo/hilights/webcams/molerat1/elecam/elecam10.htm

National Zoo Elephant Cam

Watch the elephants at the National Zoo in Washington, D.C.; take a tour of the elephant house; and read more about the elephants. The best times to view the Elephant Cam are between 6:00 and 9:00 A.M. or between 3:00 and 4:00 P.M. Eastern Standard Time.

Scooter's Electric Digs

http://www.geocities.com/~scooter_hound/webcam1.html

Drop by Scooter the Basset Hound's Electric Digs and see if he's playing in the yard. If he's not there, you can drop by the chat room for Basset Hound lovers, watch some Scooter movies, or flip through an electronic photo album. The cam turns off at night because it's too dark to see anything and Scooter goes inside. But you can turn on the Scooter TV and see what the ol' pooch is watching.

Africam

http://www.africam.com/

Go on an African Safari in the world's first virtual game reserve. There's one cam set up at the local watering hole, where animals frequently stop by for a drink; and there's a mobile cam that takes you to various other locales, depending on what's happening. For example, one day the mobile cam might take you hunting with the lions, or you may get to witness an elephant giving birth.

Ginger's Wolf Cam

http://www.nidlink.com/~ugholl/pages/wc1.html

Ginger and her husband Urnie live in Iowa, where they've been raising wolves for the past nine years. You can watch the wolves playing or lolling around in their tree-filled compound. Ginger also provides links to other cams, other wolf-related Web sites, and information about herself, her family, and their wolves Angus and Brianna.

Here are some suggestions for camming with pets and animals:

- **Watch your pet's habits**. Cats and dogs have favorite hangouts just as you do. The animal and pet cammers mentioned in this chapter generally put their cameras near a favorite pillow or by the food bowl. If your animals stay in the yard during the day, like Ginger's wolves and Scooter the Bassett Hound, you can focus your camera on the spot where they go most often.
- **Move the cam around**. When you're home, you can move the camera around to catch your pets in various activities and locations.
- **Watch those wires and cables!** Cats and dogs can get pretty rambunctious—many cat and dog cammers caution visitors that if the cam isn't working, Pumpkin or Fifi probably knocked it over. You can run cables under your rug so your pets (and you) don't trip over them, or use a staple gun to secure them along the moldings between your walls and floors.

- **Lure roaming animals within camming range.** You might not see them much, but just about every area has some sort of wildlife nearby. You can easily attract birds, squirrels, and deer by leaving food out for them, as the people who run the Bird Feeder cam do. Of course, you should be careful if lions, tigers, and bears (oh my!) live in the neighborhood.

Home and Work

Face it—Web cams appeal to the snoop in all of us, and many of the most popular cams focus on real live people. If you're an extrovert, go ahead and put your cam in your living room or on your desk. Otherwise, you can focus the cam in an area that bustles with activity but isn't as private, like a kitchen, hallway, or near the office water cooler. And remember that you can always turn off your cam or point it somewhere else.

JenniCam

http://www.jennicam.org/

Imagine if everyone in the world could see you schlepping around in your bathrobe, working at your computer, getting dressed, or...? Welcome to JenniCam. Jenni launched a cam sensation when she first set up her 24-hour-a-day, uncensored Web cam. Besides the cam, her Web site has lots of other cool stuff. She keeps a dream diary, writes poetry, publishes a FAQ about her and her Web site, and designs Web pages.

WozCam

http://wozcam.woz.org/

When you visit Steve Wozniak's office, the text below the picture nicely asks "Be nice. Don't fight over the controls." Sure enough, the legendary co-founder of Apple Computer, lover of gadgets and gizmos, has set up a PanTilt cam that lets you control the camera and explore Woz's office in real-time. You can also visit his classroom (he teaches computer skills to grade-schoolers), check out the gorgeous view of Silicon Valley from his balcony, or dive into his pool.

The Amazing Dave Cam

http://ranier.oact.hq.nasa.gov/staff/davecam.shtm

Poor Dave. He must work awfully long hours, because he almost always seems to be there (though not when I took the picture shown in **Figure 8.4**). You can also check out Dave's office map, with pointers to everything in his office (including a NASA strategic plan). If you've got the QuickTime VR plug-in, you can even take a panoramic tour. (If not, go get it from Apple's QuickTime Web site at **http://quicktime.apple.com/**.)

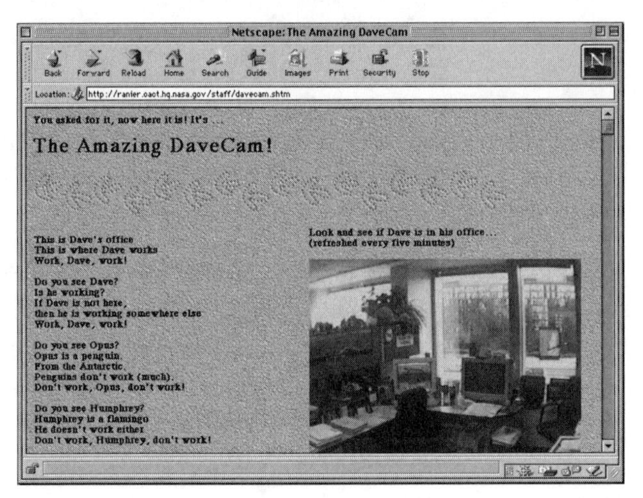

Figure 8.4 *The Amazing Dave Cam.*

Netscape's Cams

Since Netscape developed the server and browser technologies that made camming possible, it's only natural that their Amazing Netscape Fish Cam made Web headlines back in 1995. You can watch the fish swim around in their tank at

http://fishcam.netscape.com/fishcam/fishcam.html

While you're in the neighborhood, drop by the Engineering Sign cam at **http://www.weissman.org/sign/**

This cam displays a bus sign in the Netscape Engineering department. You can change what the sign says by entering a few words of text (keep it down to 2–4 words at a time, or your message won't fit on the sign). To find out about the people behind the Netscape Cams, read Chapter 10.

James and Kevin World

http://www.cableregina.com/users/jamesandkevin/livecamera2.htm

Watch out, Jenni, guys can cam too. See what's happening in James and Kevin's messy pad in Toronto, surf through the photo archives, or download and watch a few videos. You can also read biographies of the stars at James and Kevin World, read what other people have to say about their Web site, and drop by their fan club.

Café Cam

http://www.aloha-cafe.com/

Live from Honolulu, Hawaii, it's the 24-Hour Cyber Café Cam. Depending on your browser and connection speed, you can surf the basic version of the Aloha Café Web site, or the highly caffeinated version with Java, QuickTime movies, and other bells and whistles. Once you get into the site, you can drop by the café and watch people hanging out (and sometimes waving to the camera). You can also say hello to everyone by typing something in the form. A PowerMac sitting in the café speaks your message out loud to whomever happens to be there.

The Pad Cam

http://www.internetad.net/connections/

Hang with Amber, Amanda, Nick, and Dan in their living room in Southfield, Michigan. You can even page them if you use ICQ (a program that tells you when friends are on the Internet and lets you send instant messages). Plans are underway to set up a chat room.

The Amazing Ironing Cam

http://www.bogan.com/bogan/webcam/

Watch live-action laundry at all hours of the day and night! I guess the Web design consultants at Bogan.com don't like their local laundromat, because they do their laundry at work instead. If someone isn't ironing, you'll see a Mr. Potato Head instead. Or you can read the FAQ and explore Bogan's laundry links for recommended products and Web sites (Black and Decker for a "Real Man's Iron"; Niagara Heavy Spray Starch for perfect creases).

Here are some suggestions for your home and office cams:

- **Put the cam where the action is.** Some areas of a home or office—like the living room, kitchen, or coffee machine—tend to have more activity than others.
- **Put pictures and movies on your Web site.** This is a good tip for anyone who runs a Web cam. If you put plenty of interesting and fun stuff on your Web site that relates to your cam, visitors won't mind if the cam doesn't show anything particularly exciting.
- **Tell people a little about yourself.** You don't have to give your life story, but visitors do get curious about the person behind the cam.
- **Keep "office hours," if you want.** If you don't want the cam snapping pictures of you day and night, you can run it just during certain hours and post those hours on your Web page.

Inanimate Objects

Even if you don't have a window near your computer, you don't keep pets, and you prefer not to cam yourself, don't let that stop you from camming. Ordinary household and office objects—appliances, house plants, gizmos, toys, kitsch items, collectibles—just about anything can have its 15 minutes of fame! So go ahead and plop something on your desk, turn your camera toward it, and fire up your cam. What could be easier?

Trojan Room Coffee Machine

http://www.cl.cam.ac.uk/coffee/coffee.html

This cam has been around forever. Is the coffee pot at the University of Cambridge's Computer Laboratory half full or half empty? That depends on whether you're an optimist or a pessimist.

The Peeling Paint Web Cam

http://www.mich.com/~rrreibel/paintcam.htm

Whether you want to reminisce about the shabby dwellings of your youth, or you *still* live in a shabby dwelling and take comfort in the fact that other people live in crummy places, too, take a gander at the Peeling Paint Web Cam. This image updates every 60 seconds, though you'll probably have to watch it for a couple of years before anything changes.

Mold Cam I: Night of the Living Strawberries

http://reality.sgi.com/dlai/mold.1/mold.1.html

Eeeew. Someone at Silicon Graphics left a glass bowl full of strawberries in the refrigerator and they've been left to moulder since August 1996. Someone finally noticed them in September 1996, and voilà! The Mold Cam was born.

The Infamous Lava Cam

http://www.newtonline.com/HOMEPG/lava.cgi

For the people at Newton Online Business Solutions, Lava Lamps aren't a cheesy holdover from the sixties. They're a way of life. Check it out—the Lava Lamp keeps a-bubbling night and day, as shown in **Figure 8.5**.

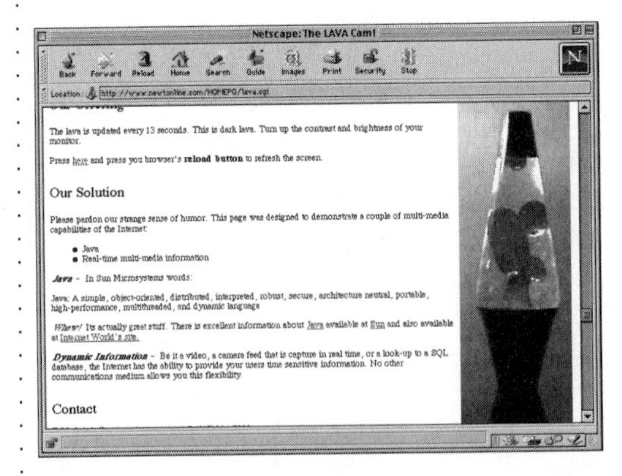

Figure 8.5
The infamous Lava Cam.

A few suggestions for Inanimate Object Cams:

- **A sense of humor** goes a long way. If you've got a funny idea, people will visit.
- **Use objects that change sometimes**—or that you can change yourself.
- If you're a collector, you can **show a different item** from your collection every day.

Other Web Cam Ideas

Sure, cams are fun. But they also come in handy for a variety of practical purposes.

If you want to put your cam to serious use, then you may need to spend more money on your cam setup. For example, if you want a live video feed, then you'll need a dedicated high-speed line that stays connected to the Internet all the time. Many local phone companies offer ISDN and ADSL access to home and business users for $80 to $300 per month.

You may be planning to put your cam outside or in a public area. If so, you should consider buying a mounted security camera with motion detection.

Windows only

Windows users: Cam anywhere! Having to keep your cam tethered to your computer can definitely cramp your Web camming style. With the $399 **FoneCam,** Windows users can cam anywhere. Once you set up the FoneCam and connect it to a phone line, you can control it remotely from a computer in the next room, or thousands of miles away. For more information, visit the FoneCam Web site at **http://www.fonecam.com/**.

Macintosh only

For Mac folks, there's SiteZAP: For *serious* camming, take a gander at the $2700 SiteZAP cam for Macintosh users, from Rearden Technology. SiteZAP is a mounted security camera with motion detection. It comes with software for setting up a Web cam with controls that appear on the Web page next to the image. You can use the controls to change views, zoom in, zoom out, or follow moving objects. For more information—and to see some SiteZAP cams in action—visit **http://www.sitezap.com/**. Also, you'll find an interview of Brad Lowe, creator of SiteZAP and SiteCam, in Chapter 10.

Useful Cams

Here's a list of a few useful (and clever) types of Web cams:

- **Kid cam**: Launch your Web browser and keep an eye on your baby or toddler (and the sitter!) while you're at work or otherwise away from home. Many childcare centers and schools have Web cams nowadays.
- **Security cam**: If you travel a lot or have a vacation getaway, you can keep an eye on things at home while you're gone.
- **Remote work-site cam**: Web cams can help you survey a remote work site and see how things are going—for example, a home or office under construction, or an interior decorating project.

Summary

Now that you've taken this tour of Web cams, you probably have some great ideas cooking. So let's get to work! Chapter 9 tells you how to set up your own live Web cam. You can try some variations of the following types of cams explored here in Chapter 8:

- **Outdoor Scene**: Got a computer near a (clean!) window with a good view? Point your cam out the window, and voilà! A cool outdoor cam. You can also *make* your view more interesting by putting a pinwheel, some wind chimes, or a bird feeder nearby.
- **Pets and Animals**: Critter cams are irresistible—if you can figure out a way to keep your furry, feathered, and scaly friends in front of the cam so visitors can see them! Sometimes it works to point the cam toward Pepper's favorite hang-out, such as her food dish or pillow. Parakeets, gerbils, and fish make for easy pet-camming because you can simply put your cam near their cage or tank.
- **Home and Work**: Ready for your fifteen minutes of fame? Put a cam in your living room or on your desk! For privacy, you can always turn the cam off.
- **Inanimate Objects**: Not to worry if you don't have a view, pets, or anything interesting happening in your home or office. With a sense of humor, you can turn just about any object into a subject for your Web cam.

9 Setting Up a Web Cam

And now, the chapter you've been waiting for: How to set up your Web cam!

Back in the bad old days, you had to be a programmer with direct access to a server in order to get a Web cam up and running. Boy, have things changed! Now all you need is your cam, some inexpensive Web cam software, a Web page, and this book. The Web cam software will do all kinds of stuff for you, automatically—like taking your pictures and uploading them to your Web site. This chapter tells you everything you need to know about getting cam software, setting up a Web cam, and creating your Web cam page.

TO SET UP CAM:
① DOWNLOAD CAM SOFTWARE.
② LAUNCH IT.
③ PREVIEW & ADJUST PHOTOS & VIDEO.
④ SET SOFTWARE FOR FREQUENCY OF SHOTS.
⑤ TEST, AND HAVE AT IT!
TO DEMONSTRATE THE IMPORTANCE OF PROPER CAM POSITIONING, WE'VE CHALLENGED OURSELVES WITH THIS FEED TO AN EXCITING NEW WEB SITE, <JOHNSBALDSPOT.COM>.
IT GREW!

Steps to Setting Up a Web Cam

1. Download, install, and start up **ISpy for Windows** or **SiteCam for Macintosh** (the recommended Web cam programs for this book).
2. Preview your pictures.
3. Choose a picture size and color depth.
4. Select brightness, contrast, and color settings (optional).
5. Determine where to save Web cam images on your computer.
6. Choose settings for image quality.
7. Tell your Web cam program how often to take pictures.
8. Give your Web cam program your Web server's FTP information, so the Web cam can upload your pictures.
9. Test your Web cam and make sure the program successfully uploads your images to the server.
10. Put a timestamp on your pictures (optional).
12. Create a picture history with a series of pictures (optional).
13. Create your Web pages and place your images.
14. Sit back and enjoy!

Getting Web Cam Software

Do you want to sit at your computer all day, take pictures, and upload them to your server? Of course not. That's why you need some **Web cam software.** By Web cam software, I mean the program that automatically takes snapshots and uploads them to your Web site—as opposed to the *cam* software that ships with the cam itself.

There are lots of great shareware programs waiting for you out there, ready to be downloaded from the Web and put to work right away. After I took several Web cam programs for a spin, I chose ISpy for Windows and SiteCam for Macintosh as the subjects of this chapter. They combine great features with ease of use, they're reliable, and they work with just about any type of cam.

Figure 9.1 *Camming with ISpy for Windows.*

- **ISpy for Windows**: ISpy by WebNet costs $49 if you like the program and choose to register it. You can download ISpy, shown in **Figure 9.1**, from **http://www.ispy.nl/**.

Web cam software *is the program that takes snapshots and uploads them to your Web site. It's separate from the cam software that comes along with your cam.*

- **SiteCam for Macintosh**: SiteCam, shown in **Figure 9.2**, costs $129 if you choose to register it ($99 for students, teachers, and schools). In addition, plans are under way for a low-cost QuickCam version. SiteCam is available at the Rearden Technology Web site at **http://www.rearden.com**.

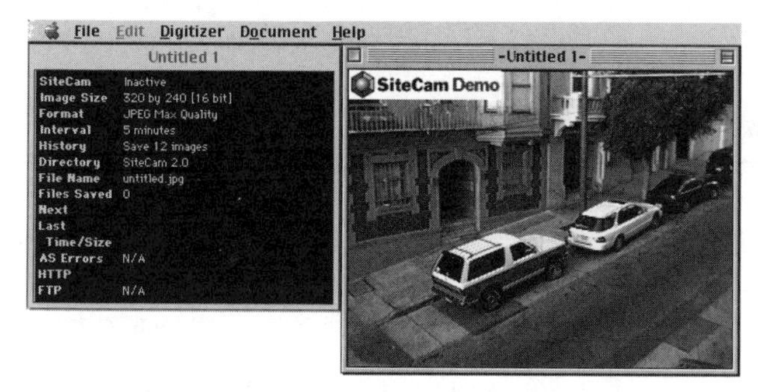

Figure 9.2 *Camming with SiteCam for Macintosh.*

Trial versions available

You'll be able to get a feel for ISpy or SiteCam before you pay for the program. The trial versions are fully functional. But you'll have to do a little free advertising until you pay, because the programs automatically stamp their logo on your pictures. When you register and send payment, you'll receive a registration code by e-mail so you can unlock your software.

Other Cam Software

On a budget? Here are some alternatives: WebCam32 for Windows, and StripCam for Macintosh.

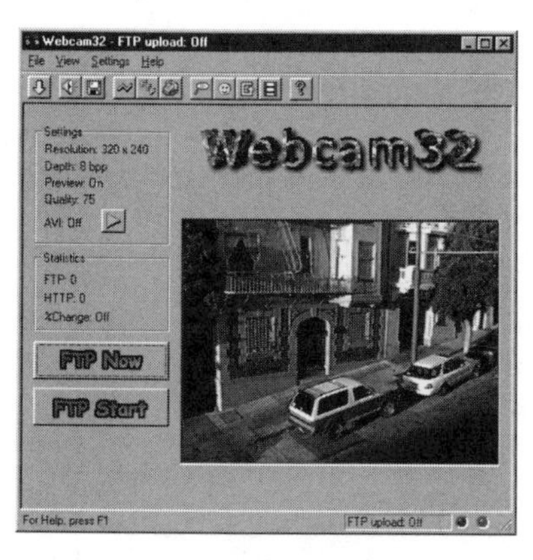

Figure 9.3 *WebCam32 for Windows.*

- **WebCam32** (for Windows) by Neil Kolban, shown in **Figure 9.3**, costs $25 and does everything that ISpy does. So what's the catch? It only works with QuickCam and Snappy, and it isn't *quite* as easy to use as ISpy. You can download WebCam 32 from **http://www.kolban.com/**.

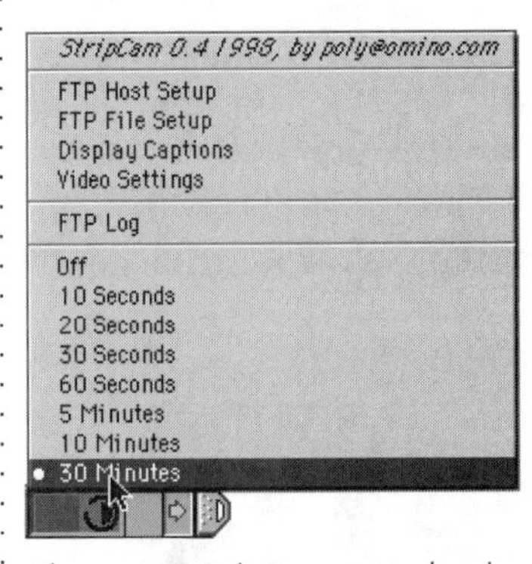

***Figure 9.4** StripCam control-strip module for Macintosh.*

- **StripCam** (for Macintosh) by David VanBrink is a clever freeware utility that works as a control-strip module with a menu you can use to choose your options, as shown in **Figure 9.4**. But, like most other things in life, you get what you pay for. StripCam doesn't have SiteCam's many features, does not work well with System 8.5, and has been known to freeze up some people's systems (though others have no problems with it). You can download StripCam from **http://www.stripcam.org/**.

Launching ISpy for Windows

Windows only

Ready to go? After you download, unzip, and install ISpy, launch it by opening the ISpy folder from within the Program Files folder (see **Figure 9.5**), then double-clicking the ISpy.exe icon. While you're there, you can drag the ISpy.exe icon to your desktop to create a shortcut, if you want.

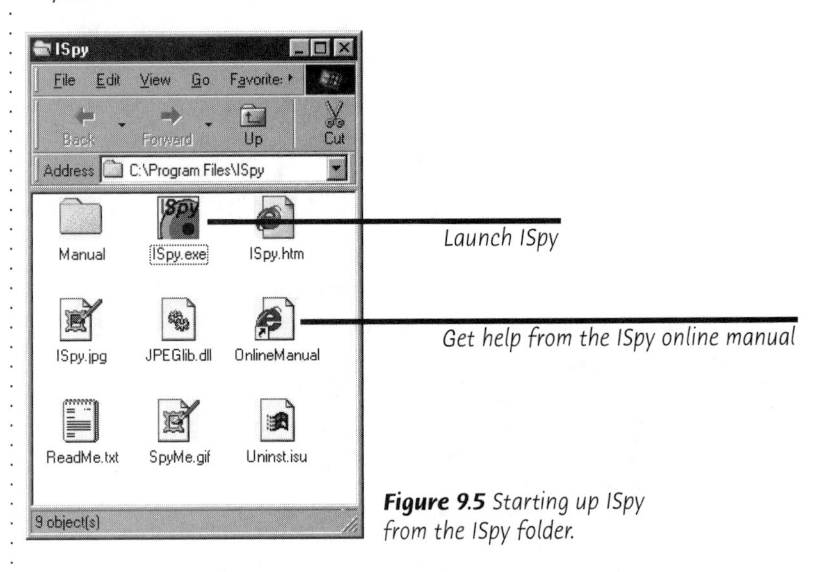

***Figure 9.5** Starting up ISpy from the ISpy folder.*

When ISpy starts up, a welcoming dialog box appears (**Figure 9.6**). Click the OK button, and you get the Settings dialog box. Skip your Web cam settings for now (we'll discuss them in detail throughout this chapter), and click OK to display the application window that you saw back in **Figure 9.1**.

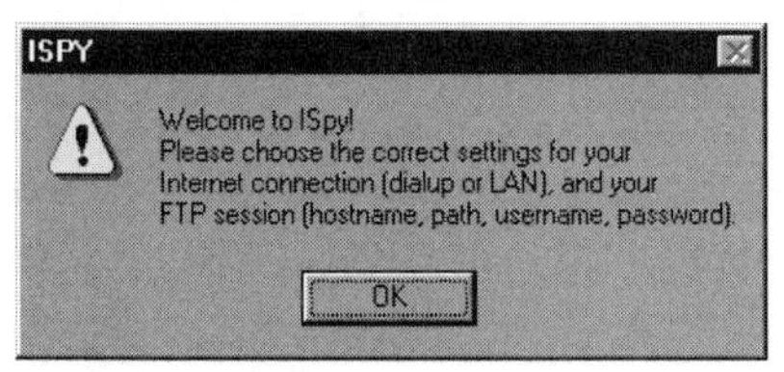

Figure 9.6
ISpy's welcoming dialog box.

Launching from Windows Start Menu

When you finish installing ISpy, you'll need to restart your system. You can then fire up ISpy from the Windows Start menu. Click the Start button, choose Programs, select the ISpy folder, and then select ISpy WebCam.

Need Help with ISpy?

If you get stuck, not to worry. WebNet includes plenty of documentation with the ISpy application. Return to the ISpy folder, and double-click the **ISpy.htm** icon to display an introduction and links to other helper documents in your Web browser. The ISpy.htm document is ISpy's manual, which is formatted as as Web page. You can also go to ISpy's Web site for updates.

Launching SiteCam for Macintosh

Macintosh only

After downloading, unstuffing, and installing SiteCam, you're ready to roll. Open up the SiteCam folder (see **Figure 9.7**), double-click the SiteCam icon, and...get ready for a math pop quiz!

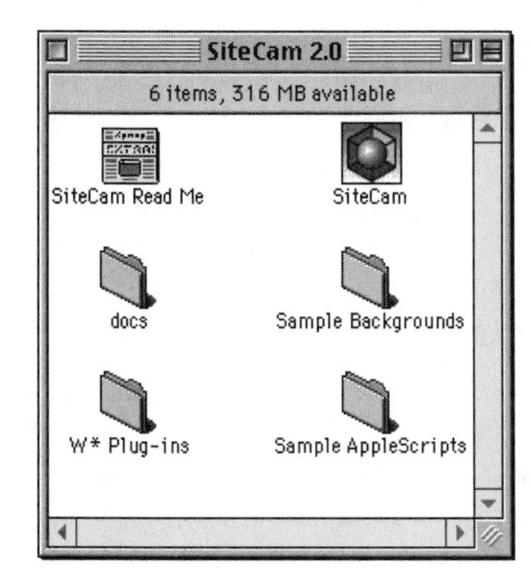

Figure 9.7 *Launching SiteCam from the SiteCam folder.*

If you've downloaded SiteCam 3.0, released as this book was going to press, the math problem dialog box will not appear.

At this point, older versions of SiteCam will ask you to solve a simple math problem, as shown in **Figure 9.8**. Indulge the programmer's quirky sense of humor, add up the numbers, enter your answer in the box, and click OK. When the SiteCam dialog box appears, you can either read the registration information or click the Close box to make it go away.

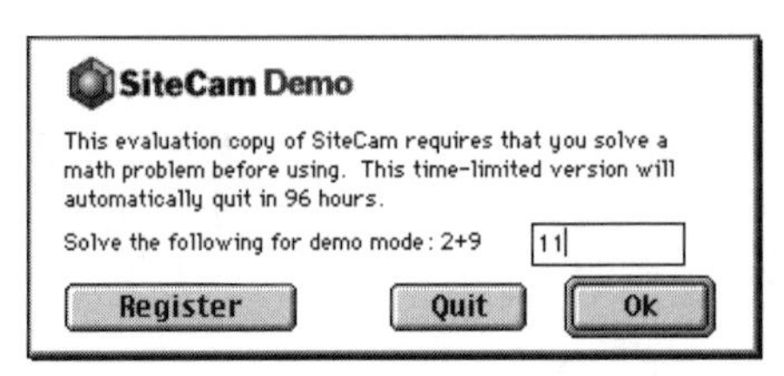

Figure 9.8 *Solve the little math problem in the SiteCam Demo dialog box.*

Before You Begin with SiteCam

SiteCam requires two system extensions that come with your Macintosh operating system: AppleScript, and either Open Transport PPP or Free PPP if you connect to the Internet through a modem.

- **AppleScript** is Apple's **programming language** for running the scripts that tell your system to do things automatically. Unless you or someone else has done something funny, like changing the settings on your computer and somehow disabling AppleScript, the feature should be ready, willing, and able.

If you have a dedicated connection to the Internet, then you don't need either Open Transport PPP or Free PPP.

- **Open Transport PPP and Free PPP** are control panels for dialing up your Internet account. The setup programs for some ISPs install other types of extensions and control panels for this purpose, so you may not be able to get SiteCam to upload your files. If this happens, call your ISP's tech support or your network administrator and ask them to walk you through the process of setting up Open Transport PPP.

Getting Started with SiteCam

How does SiteCam work? It uses AppleScript—a special programming language that works on all Macs—to generate the scripts that run your cam. You won't have to do any programming; SiteCam does it all for you.

But to get started with SiteCam, you *do* have to create a new file. Select New from SiteCam's File menu. When the Untitled window appears (**Figure 9.9**), select File | Save to display the Save dialog box. Enter a name for your file (such as **mydoc** or **WebCam**) in the Save File As box. Then browse for a folder in which to store this new file (preferably the folder where you plan to store the Web cam images), and click the Save button. SiteCam creates the JPEG images automatically, using the document's name. You should therefore use a short document name that doesn't contain spaces or periods, so the images will display properly on your Web page.

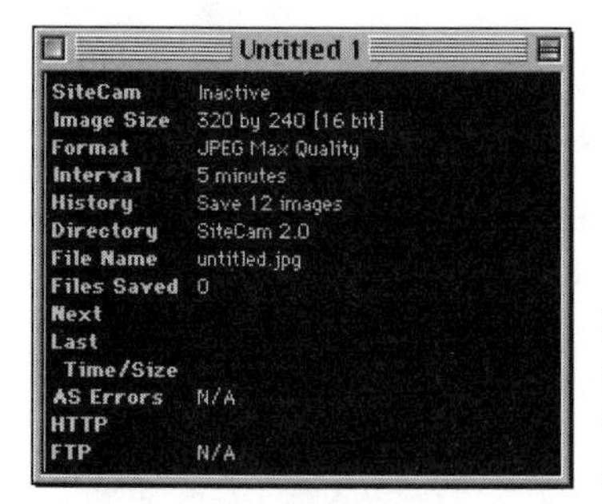

Figure 9.9 *The SiteCam Untitled window tells you whether the cam is active, how often it's taking pictures, and whether your pictures are uploading properly.*

"But wait," you might be thinking. "You promised this would be *easy*, and now I'm stuck looking at this yucky box thing." Don't worry about the box. It displays a list of all your cam settings, but you don't actually have to do anything with it. In fact, it will come in handy when you want to see what's going on with your cam. Keep reading, and you'll see.

Need Help with SiteCam?

SiteCam comes with plenty of documentation if you get stuck. The help files are set up as Web pages located in the SiteCam folder's **Docs folder**. To view the help files, launch your browser and select the option for opening a Web page on your computer (not on the Web). Open the SiteCam folder, then the Docs folder, and then the default.html document. If you use Netscape Navigator as your default browser, you can simply double-click the default.html document to launch it in Navigator. You can also find updated information on Rearden Technology's Web site at **http://www.rearden.com/**.

Previewing Your Pictures

If you're one of those people who fiddles with your TV set to get the picture *just* right, you'll like this section. It's only natural to want to see what your cam is seeing, so you can make the necessary adjustments. With the help of your Web cam software's **preview** feature, you can move the cam around and tilt it at different angles to get just the shot you want.

Setting Refresh Rates

Part of a good preview is the setting you choose for the **refresh rate**. This determines how quickly the preview **refreshes** (or **updates**) the shot. For example, if your preview refreshes at 30 frames per second, your preview will be moving almost in real time. At that rate, if you point your cam out the window you'll be able to watch the cars drive by. On the other hand, this faster preview rate demands a lot from your system and doesn't make your Web cam pictures look any better. So try out various settings; you can always change them later. Live it up a little!

Preview rates, refresh rates, frame rates...

What's the difference between these terms? Not much—they all mean pretty much the same thing: the number of pictures your cam records within a certain amount of time, or the number of pictures that are displayed within a certain amount of time. In multimedia, time is generally measured in seconds, hundredths of seconds, or milliseconds. The terminology depends on which application you're using (GIF animators, video editors, Web cam programs, or the software that comes with your cam).

Previewing Pictures with ISpy

Windows only

When you launch ISpy, the application window displays a preview right away, as shown in **Figure 9.10**. As mentioned earlier, if you haven't registered ISpy yet, the program stamps a promotional boilerplate on your picture that does not appear in the preview. You can see this in **Figure 9.10**.

Figure 9.10 *Previewing an image with ISpy for Windows.*

To change the frame rate for your preview:

1. Select Video | Preview Rate.
2. Choose a frames-per-second (fps) rate from the menu, as shown in **Figure 9.11**.

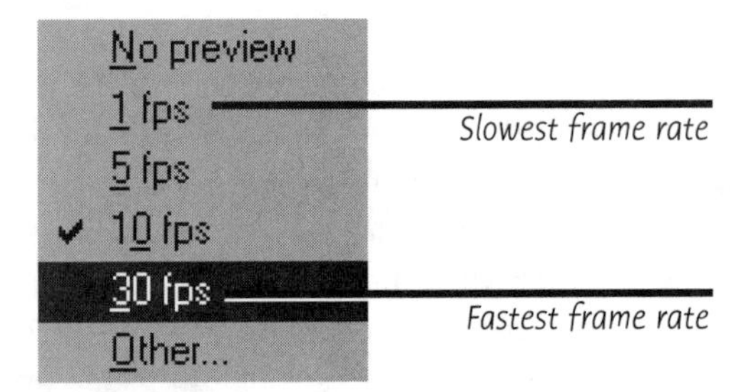

Figure 9.11 *Choosing a frame rate for the preview in ISpy for Windows.*

The most realistic preview rate is 30 frames per second (fps). At the other end of the scale, 1 fps will look somewhat choppy. Select Other if you want to experiment with some other frame rates.

Previewing Pictures with SiteCam

Macintosh only

For SiteCam users, a picture preview is only a menu away. Select Document|Preview Window, and voilà—SiteCam displays a window with a preview, as shown in **Figure 9.12**. Like ISpy, SiteCam displays the SiteCam Demo graphic on the image preview until you register.

Figure 9.12 *SiteCam Preview window.*

The preview also has a timestamp if you have chosen to have one. To find out how to put a timestamp on your Web cam pictures, see the "Timestamping Your Pictures" section later in this chapter.

To change the frame rate for your video preview:

1. Select Document|Video Refresh.
2. When the Settings dialog box appears with the Video Refresh options displayed, as shown in **Figure 9.13**, adjust the frame rate for the preview window by typing a number in the Refresh Delay box.

Fewer ticks = a faster frame rate

SiteCam measures the frame rate in **ticks**—a more precise measurement than frames per second. The default value is 45 ticks, or one frame for every 3/4 second. To speed up the frame rate for a more realistic display, enter a lower number. To slow down the frame rate and put less strain on your computer, enter a higher value.

3. Click the Save button to save your changes, or click Cancel if you've changed your mind.

If these frame rate/tick options confuse you, leave SiteCam's Refresh Rate at 45 ticks. And if you *really* want your image to update more quickly, set it to 0. Rearden Technology plans to simplify the Video Refresh dialog box for SiteCam version 3.1. Check their Web site for upgrades.

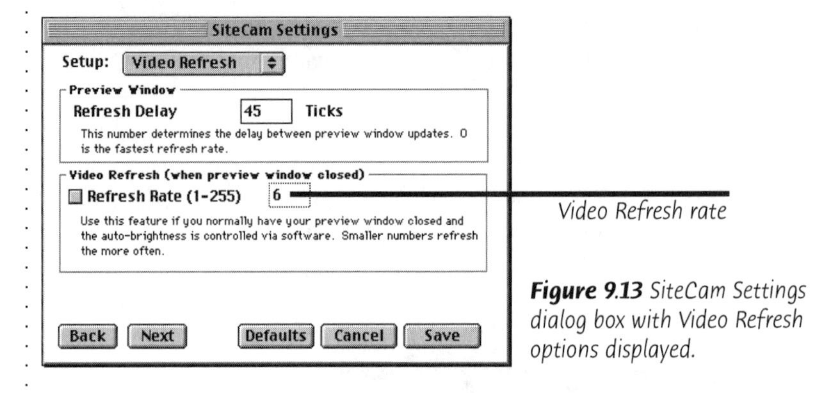

Figure 9.13 *SiteCam Settings dialog box with Video Refresh options displayed.*

Setting Video Refresh Rate

Most cams automatically adjust brightness and contrast levels, depending on the amount of light. This way, you don't need to worry about fiddling with the brightness and contrast settings yourself, as covered later in this chapter. But what if you use a video camera that doesn't come with any special cam software? Let SiteCam help.

To tell SiteCam to adjust the brightness and contrast levels, display the Video Refresh dialog box and click the Refresh Rate (1-255) checkbox. To determine how often SiteCam changes your settings, type a number in the box to the right. Lower numbers refresh brightness/contrast more frequently; higher numbers refresh less frequently.

If your own cam software has a setting for automatically adjusting the cam's brightness and contrast levels, then you don't need to use SiteCam's Video Refresh Rate settings for your Web cam. On the other hand, **if you've got a video camera with no camming software**, then SiteCam's Video Refresh Rate options will come in handy.

Picture Size and Color Depth

Remember our discussion of image sizes and color depth back in Chapter 2? Now's the time to decide what picture size and color depth you want for your pictures. The larger your pictures and the more colors you use, the better your images will look—just remember that you'll have correspondingly larger file sizes.

For best results, I recommend using the **320x240** picture size and **16-bit color** (thousands of colors). The 16-bit color almost always looks as good as 24-bit color (millions of colors), but the files are quite a bit smaller.

ISpy Size/ Color Settings

Windows only

To change the picture size and color depth in ISpy:

1. Select Video|Format to display the Video Settings dialog box. The available settings depend on the type of cam you use. If you use QuickCam, as I do, then the dialog box will be the one shown in **Figure 9.14**. Even if you use a different cam, the options will be similar to the ones described here.

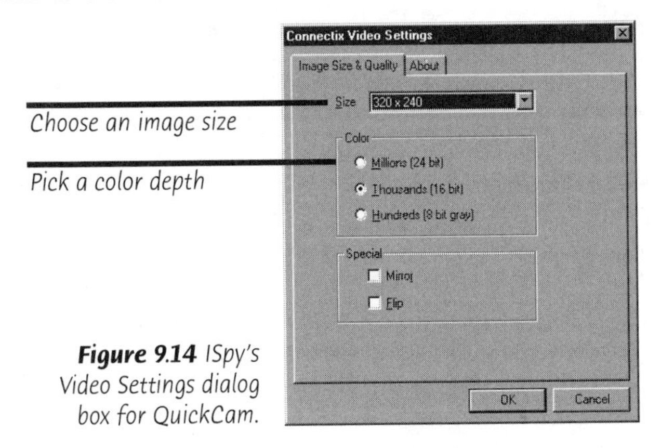

Figure 9.14 *ISpy's Video Settings dialog box for QuickCam.*

2. Pick a size (either 160x120 or 320x240) from the Size list.
3. Choose a color depth by clicking a radio button in the Color list.
4. Click the OK button.

Special effects, anyone? QuickCam and other Web cam programs allow you to apply special effects, such as flipping or mirroring the picture. With QuickCam, you select special effects by clicking checkboxes on the Special Effects list. Even more of these options may be available if you've got a high-end video card.

SiteCam Size/ Color Settings

Macintosh only

To change the picture size and color depth in SiteCam:

1. Choose File|Settings. Then choose Output Format from the Setup list.
2. **Figure 9.15** shows the Output Format options. In the Video Capture Size list, choose 50% for a 320x240 picture; or select 25% for a 160x120 picture.
3. Choose a color depth from the Colors list.
4. Click the Save button to save your changes.

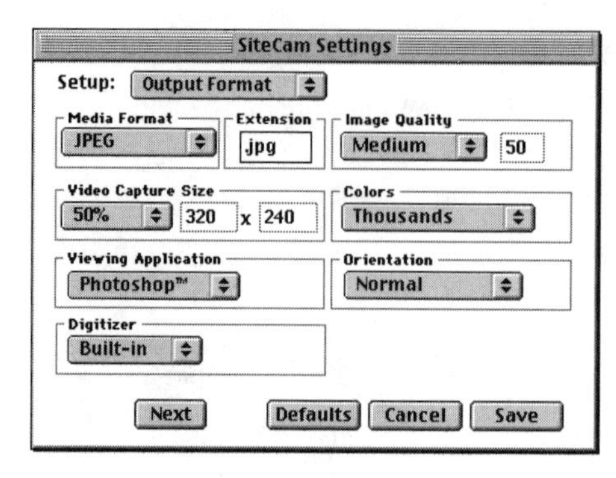

Figure 9.15
SiteCam's Output Format options.

More SiteCam Output Format Options

Advanced settings are available in the Output Format dialog box. To view a picture by opening it in the Finder, choose your favorite image editor or viewer from the Viewing Application list. To rotate or flip your picture, select an option from the Orientation list. If you've got another video source (such as a different cam), you can pull it down from the Digitizer list. If your picture dithers too much, try clicking the Reduce in Half checkbox.

Contrast, Brightness, and Color

Most cams are set up to make automatic adjustments to the brightness, contrast, and colors when taking pictures. These adjustments compensate for too much or too little light. However, if your cam is focused on a spot where the light level generally stays the same, **you can tweak your Web cam settings** to get the best picture.

The new brightness/contrast/color settings will override your cam software's default settings. Nevertheless, the cam will continue to automatically adjust for different amounts of light based on the new settings. With some types of cam products, you can disable the automatic adjustments feature and have complete control over the light levels for your pictures. For example, with Color QuickCam for Windows, you can deselect the Auto Brightness and Auto Hue checkboxes in the Video Settings dialog box with the Camera Adjustments tab selected (as shown in **Figure 9.16**).

Many available Web cam settings—including contrast and color—depend on the capabilities of the software that comes with your cam. For more about **basic cam settings**, see Chapter 2.

Camera Adjustments with ISpy

Windows only

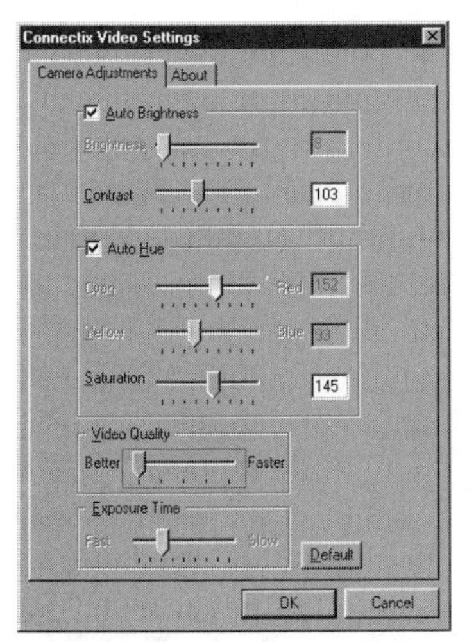

Figure 9.16 *Accessing QuickCam's video settings through ISpy.*

With ISpy it's easy to change your cam's brightness, contrast, and color settings. Choose Source from Video menu to access the video options for your cam display. If you use QuickCam, the dialog box will look something like the one shown in **Figure 9.16**. That's because the available image and video options depend on the type of cam you use and the software that comes with it. Adjust your settings and click OK to return to ISpy.

Camera Adjustments with SiteCam

Macintosh only

Like ISpy, SiteCam's brightness, contrast, and color-level options depend on the type of cam you use. However, the options shown in **Figure 9.17** are fairly standard for QuickCam and other types of cams.

To make adjustments, select File|Configure Digitizer. When the Video dialog box appears (**Figure 9.17**), select Image from the list box, and make your changes. Click OK when you're happy with what you see in the preview area. For more details about the image options, see Chapter 2.

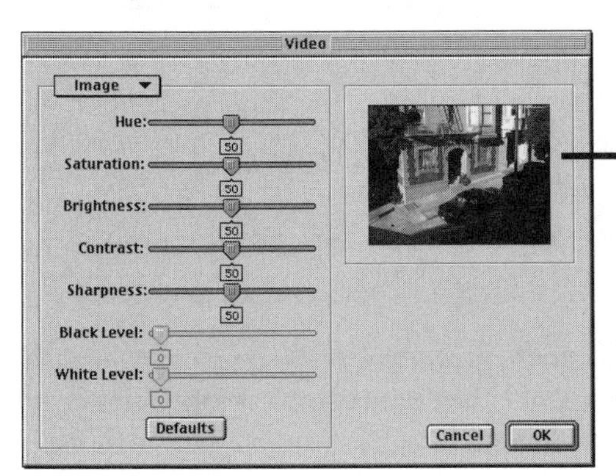

Figure 9.17 *You can use SiteCam's Video dialog box (with the Image option selected) for making camera adjustments.*

Saving Pictures to Your Computer

First things first: Before you can upload pictures to your server, you need to save them to a folder on your computer.

Ideally, you should tell ISpy or SiteCam to put your pictures in the **Images folder** for your Web site. This way, you can preview your Web cam page when you set it up. Your Web cam software then automatically takes the pictures, saves them to a folder, and uploads them to your server.

Saving Pictures with ISpy

Windows only

To tell ISpy where to save your pictures:

1. Select File|Settings. When the Settings dialog box appears, click the Image tab, shown in **Figure 9.18**.

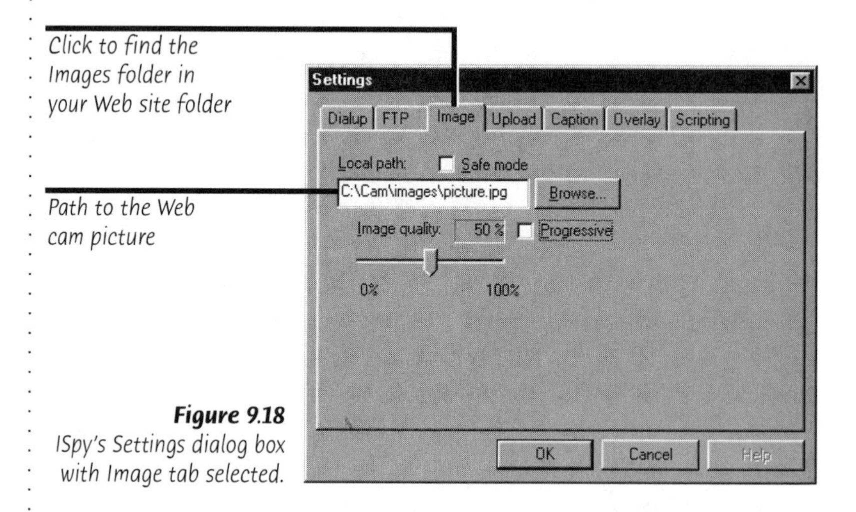

Figure 9.18
ISpy's Settings dialog box with Image tab selected.

2. Click the Browse button to display the Open dialog box so you can hunt around for your folder. (This is just like browsing for a file or folder in any other Open dialog box.)
3. Select the folder for the images, and click OK to return to ISpy's Settings dialog.

What's a directory? *No big deal—it's the same thing as a folder.*

When the directory path (location of your folder) and picture filename appear in the Local path box, you can **rename your image file** if you wish. ISpy automatically names it picture.jpg, but you can select that name and change it. Whenever ISpy takes a new picture, it automatically names the image and replaces the old file.

Saving Pictures with SiteCam

Macintosh only

To tell SiteCam where to save your pictures:

1. Choose Document|Destination. The SiteCam Settings dialog box appears, with the Destination options displayed (**Figure 9.19**).

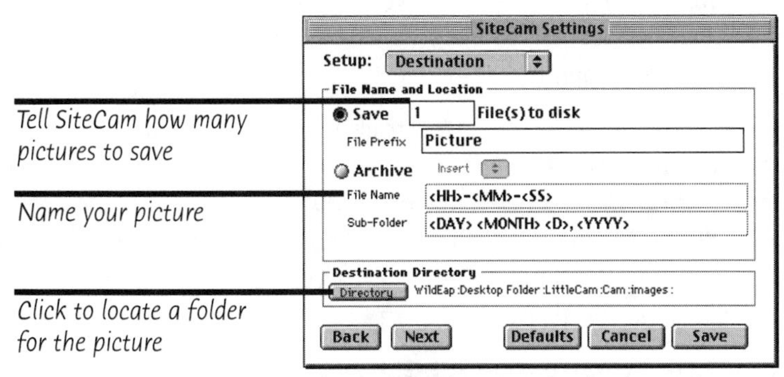

Figure 9.19 *SiteCam's Destination options.*

2. Click the Directory button to display the Select Directory dialog box (**Figure 9.20**).
3. Hunt for your folder, and when you find it click the Select button. When you return to the SiteCam Settings dialog box, the directory path (location of your folder) appears next to the Directory button.

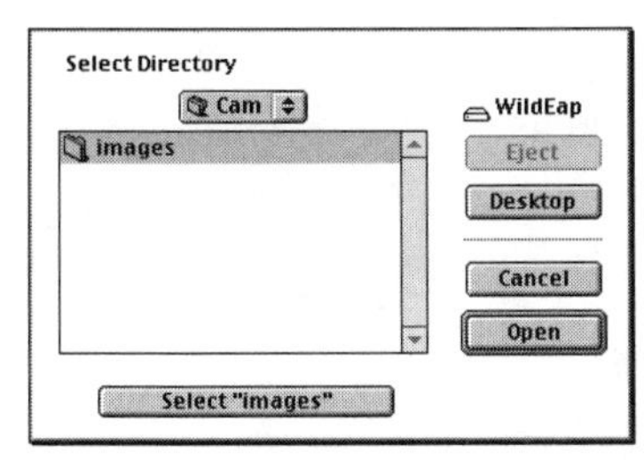

Figure 9.20 *Telling SiteCam where to put your pictures.*

4. In the File Name and Location section, click the Save radio button and enter the number 1.
5. Type a name for your image in the File Prefix box.
6. Click the Save button to save your changes.

Whenever SiteCam takes a new picture, it automatically names the image and replaces the old file.

Image Quality

If you've looked at a lot of Web cams, it's a safe bet that you've noticed great-looking pictures usually take longer to download. File compression shortens download, and the JPEG file format (most Web cam images are JPEGs) allows various levels of compression. Although highly compressed images are smaller, however, they don't look as good as larger, minimally compressed images.

When it comes to Web cams, the trick is to get the **highest-quality image at the smallest file size**. Most Web cam programs let you choose among various levels of image quality. Typical settings range from Highest, Maximum, or 100%, to Least, Low, or 0%. Usually, the midlevel setting (Medium or 50%) gives you images of decent quality with reasonable file sizes.

Avoid progressive JPEGS! Some WebCam programs let you format your pictures as **progressive JPEGs**. These files load into the browser a little faster, but they look blocky while the image is gradually focusing itself. I don't recommend progressive JPEGs as an alternative because some Web browsers can't display them at all. Why put all this work into your Web cam if some people can't see it?

ISpy Settings for Images

Windows only

Choose File|Settings and click the Image tab. Move the Image Quality slider to the right to improve image quality, or to the left to decrease it. Image quality is measured in percentages, and the percentage appears in the box above the slider.

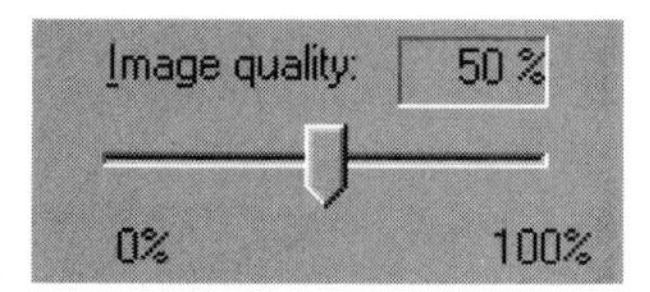

SiteCam Settings for Images

Macintosh only

To adjust the image quality with SiteCam, choose Document|Output Format. When the SiteCam Settings dialog box appears, select an option from the Image Quality list and click OK.

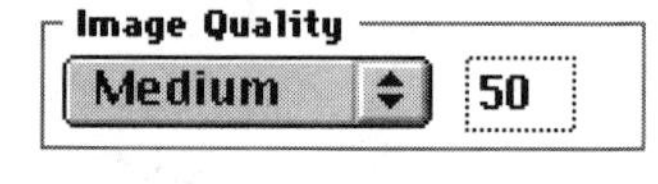

Updating Your Pictures

And now for the big question—how often do you want your Web cam to take pictures and upload them to your server?

Some cams update every few minutes or so. But do you really want to listen to that screeching modem noise every five minutes? And if you don't have a separate line for your Internet account with a dedicated connection, you won't want your Web cam to interrupt important telephone conversations! To preserve your sanity, space your uploads 30 minutes apart or more.

Psst! I've got a secret for you. Most cammers only update their pictures during certain hours—usually when they go to work and don't need to use their computer or telephone line. Most Web cam programs give you lots of control over updating your images. You can tell the cam how often to take pictures and when to stop. Would you like your cam to update images every two hours while you're away at work—say Monday through Friday from 8:00 A.M. to 5:30 P.M.? No problem. There's no reason for your Web cam to cramp your style.

Be smart about the timing of your cam updates

Updating Pictures with ISpy

Windows only

To tell ISpy when to update your pictures:

1. Select File | Settings. In the Settings dialog box, click the Upload tab (**Figure 9.21**).

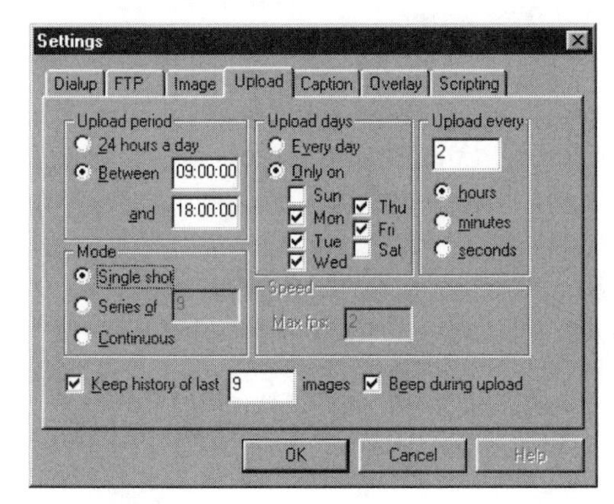

Figure 9.21 *The Upload settings in ISpy.*

2. **To upload your pictures day in and day out,** click the 24 hours a day radio button under Upload Period. Or you can click the Between radio button and enter a start time and end time. (ISpy uses a 24-hour clock, so 18:00:00 means 6:00 P.M.)

   To upload pictures every day of the week, click the Every Day radio button under Upload Days. Or you can choose the Only On radio button and select checkboxes for the days on which you want your cam to run.

3. In the Mode section, choose Single Shot.
4. Next, specify the amount of time between uploads. In the Upload Every section, enter a number in the box, and choose the Hours, Minutes, or Seconds radio button.
5. When you're satisfied with the upload settings, click OK.

Updating Pictures with SiteCam

Macintosh only

To tell SiteCam when to update your pictures:

1. Select Document|Interval to display the SiteCam Settings dialog box with the Interval options, as shown in **Figure 9.22**.

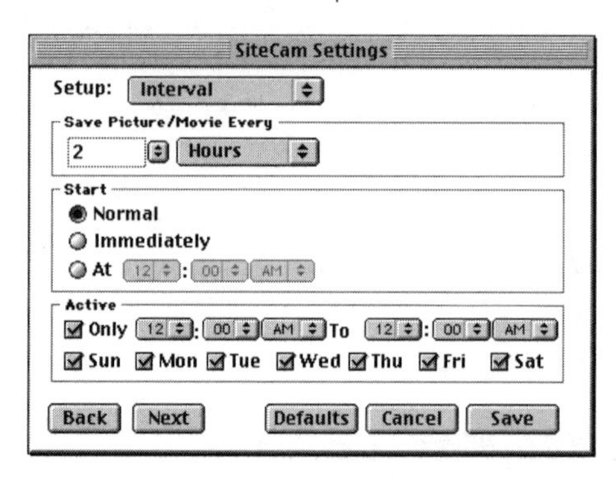

Figure 9.22 *SiteCam's Interval options.*

2. Use the Save Picture/Movie Every options to determine how often SiteCam saves your pictures. In the lists provided there, select a number (or choose Other to type a number), and select a unit of time (hours, minutes, or seconds).
3. To activate your cam, choose Normal from the Start options. (I'll tell you more about activating your cam in the "Starting Up Your Cam" section later in this chapter.)
4. **If you want to run your cam only during certain hours,** click the Only checkbox in the Active section. Choose numbers from the pull-down lists for starting and ending times. Don't forget to also select A.M. or P.M.!

   If you want to run your cam only during certain days of the week, click the appropriate checkboxes to select days.
5. When you're satisfied with the Interval settings, click the Save button.

Uploading Pictures to Your Server

Now let's set up your Web cam program so it can upload pictures to your Web site.

- First you tell the program how to **dial up your Internet account.**
- Then you **enter your FTP settings.** If you already have a Web site up and running, then you already know about FTP. FTP (File Transfer Protocol) supports the transfer of your files to the server. When you FTP files to your Web site, your server asks for a user name and password, so you'll need to supply that information to your Web cam program.

- In addition, you can tell your Web cam program to **put your pictures in a particular directory on your server.**

  Many ISPs and Web hosts will give you a Web folder named **public_html**. If so, you must include that in your directory path.

  If you don't know your FTP information, you can get it from your ISP, Web host, or system administrator.

With this structure in place, your Web cam program will take pictures, and automatically dial up your account and upload the files to the server.

Uploading with ISpy

Windows only

To tell ISpy how to upload your files:

1. Select File | Settings and click the Dialup tab, as shown in **Figure 9.23**.

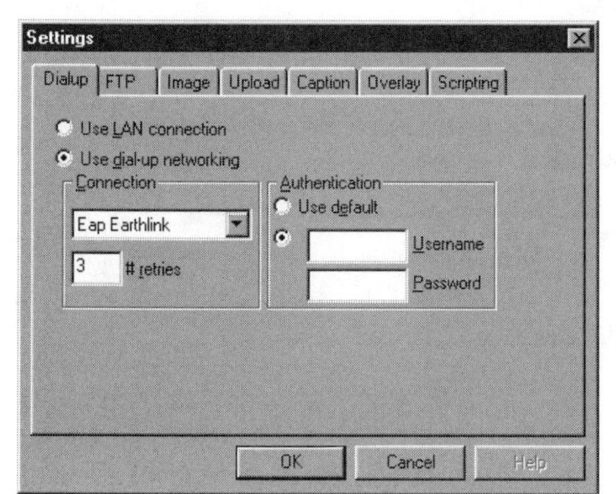

Figure 9.23 *ISpy's dial-up settings for uploading to the server.*

2. If, like most people, you connect to the Internet **through a dial-up ISP,** select the radio button for Use Dial-Up Networking Connection, and choose a dial-up account from the Connection list. If you have only one Internet account, then only one item appears on the list.

   If you connect **through a network** at work or school, select the option for Use LAN Connection.

3. On occasion, your dialer may not be able to connect to your server successfully. You can tell ISpy to try again, and how many times it should try before giving up. To do this, enter a number in the # Retries box.

4. When you dial up your Internet account, the server asks for your **user name and password**. Usually, the dialer stores these items for you, and you can click the Use Default radio button. If for some reason you didn't enter a user name and password in your dialer (maybe you and the other people who use your computer have separate accounts with your ISP), you'll have to click the second radio button under Authentication. Then enter your user name and password in the appropriate boxes.
5. Click the FTP tab at the top of the Settings dialog, to display your **FTP settings** (**Figure 9.24**).

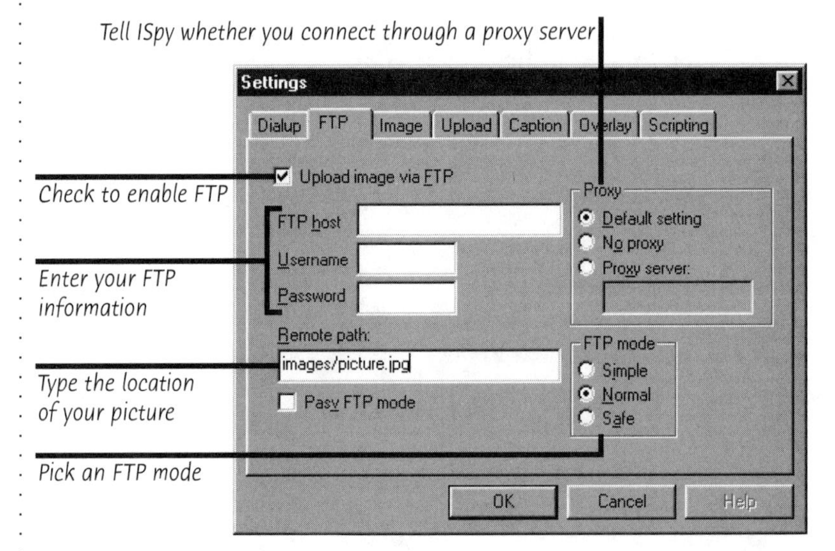

Figure 9.24 *ISpy's FTP settings for uploading to the server.*

6. Make sure the checkbox for Upload Image via FTP is selected. Then enter the FTP host name, your user name, and your password in the appropriate boxes.
7. If you store your pictures in a folder, enter a path name in the Remote Path box; for example, **images/yourpicture.jpg**.

Never put a forward slash (/) at the beginning or end of the Remote Path entry. Your server won't understand it when ISpy tries to upload your pictures.

8. For faster uploads, check the Pasv FTP Mode checkbox. Some servers don't like this, but if you have any problems, you can always come back and turn this off. With passive FTP mode, ISpy

connects to your server through the first available port (entryway) rather than the one specifically assigned for uploading files.

9. Next, choose a **Proxy** setting. In most cases, you'll do just fine if you select Default Setting.The Default Setting options uses information from your computer to determine how to upload your files. If you know for sure that you do not connect to the Internet through a proxy server, then you can click the No Proxy button.

   Note: If you dial out through school or work, your organization may have a **firewall** for security reasons; in this case, select Proxy Server and enter the name of the proxy server in the text box. (Your network administrator will have this information if you need it.)

10. Choose an **FTP mode.**
    - With **Normal** FTP mode, ISpy gives your picture a temporary name while uploading the file, so visitors won't have problems if they happen to be viewing your Web cam while the picture changes.
    - If an online service such as Microsoft Network or GeoCities hosts your Web site, select the **Simple** mode.
    - Some servers, however, don't like to rename files in midtransfer. So if you have problems uploading files with either the Normal or Simple FTP mode, come back to this dialog and choose the **Safe** option.

Which FTP mode should I use? If you're skittish about calling tech support, you can avoid problems by just using the Safe option for FTP mode. You can also ask your Web host's tech support department whether "the FTP server enables the Rename command." (They'll be so impressed with your technical prowess!) If the answer's Yes, choose the Normal option; otherwise, pick Simple or Safe as your FTP mode.

11. When your FTP and Dialup settings are ready, click OK to save your choices and return to ISpy.

Uploading with SiteCam

Macintosh only

To tell SiteCam how to upload your pictures:

1. Choose File | PPP Setup to display the PPP Setup dialog box (**Figure 9.25**).

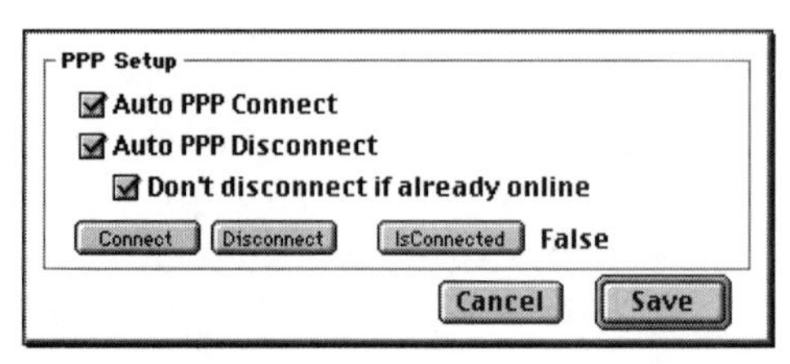

Figure 9.25 *PPP Setup dialog box in SiteCam.*

2. Check the Auto PPP Connect checkbox to automatically dial up your Internet account.
3. Check the Auto PPP Disconnect checkbox if you want SiteCam to hang up when it finishes uploading your pictures.
4. Check the Don't Disconnect If Already Online option to prevent SiteCam from disconnecting if you happen to be online while a picture uploads.
5. Click Save to save your settings and close the dialog box.
6. Select Document | FTP Setup to bring up the SiteCam Settings dialog box with the FTP options displayed, as shown in **Figure 9.26**.

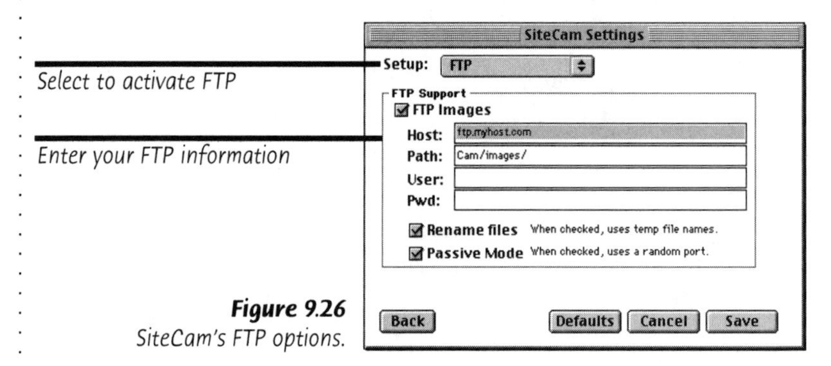

Figure 9.26
SiteCam's FTP options.

7. Click the FTP Images checkbox to tell SiteCam to upload your images.
8. Enter the FTP information. SiteCam needs to know your host address (Host), the path to your images, a user name (User), and a password (Pwd).

   The Path entry tells SiteCam where to find your pictures. If you—like most people—put your pictures in a folder called Images, type **images**. If you have a separate folder for your Web cam pages with an image folder inside, type in the path to that folder, perhaps something like **Webcam/images**.

Never put a forward slash (/) at the beginning or end of the Path entry. If you do, your server won't understand it when your ISpy tries to upload your pictures.

9. Click the Rename Files checkbox. This tells SiteCam to give your picture a temporary name while uploading the file, so visitors won't have problems if they happen to be viewing your Web cam while the picture changes. (If an online service such as Microsoft Network or GeoCities hosts your Web site, this setting might not work. If that's the case, leave the checkbox unselected.)

Rule of Thumb: You can call your Web host or ISP's tech support department and ask whether the "FTP server enables the Rename command." If they say Yes, check the Rename Files checkbox. If they say No, leave it unselected.

10. Click the Passive Mode checkbox to upload your images through your Web host's first available port (entryway), rather than waiting for the FTP port to become available. This generally makes your pictures upload to the server more quickly. Note, however, that **some servers do not allow you to use passive mode**. If you have trouble uploading your files, turn off passive mode or call your ISP for more information.
11. When your settings are ready, click the Save button.

Testing Your Web Cam

Ready to see if your Web cam works? Let's take it for a spin.

- In ISpy, select Upload Now from the Session menu.
- In SiteCam, select Take Picture Now from the Document menu.

If either ISpy or SiteCam encounters problems when it's uploading your image, the program will let you know. In ISpy, you'll see an error message; SiteCam will display a message at the bottom of the black window to tell you the status of your upload.

Problems?

Here are some **suggestions for solving problems** that occur when you're testing your cam:

- Check your FTP settings and make sure they're correct.
- Read the latest version of the Web cam program's manual, and any FAQs (frequently asked questions) on the program's Web site. Most cam software designers put this commonly needed information on the Web site so it's available to everyone.

- Call your ISP or Web host's tech support line, or ask your system administrator. Servers tend to have their own quirks, but you can get around them with a little help.

Activating Your Cam

Web cam programs usually start running your cam as soon as you enter all of the settings we've examined in this chapter. To keep your cam running, you'll have to **leave the program open**. (If the window gets in your way on the desktop, you can hide it.) If at any time you want to stop your cam, you can do so by closing the program.

And There's More!

Once you've got a basic cam up and running, you'll have the opportunity to experiment and fool around doing other cool stuff, like stamping your pictures with the date and time. Try creating a picture history so visitors can look at previous pictures you've taken with your cam. Most cam software includes advanced features for people who know how to program server scripts, or who have a direct hookup to their Web server.

The following sections discuss some of these options.

Timestamping Your Pictures

When you create a **timestamp** (date and time) for your Web cam, you can tell your visitors when the current picture was taken. The Web cam program automatically adds the date and time to your images. Usually Web cam programs provide options for a font and font color for the timestamp, and let you decide where the caption will appear on the picture. Depending on your cam program, the timestamp caption may not be visible in the preview window, but it does appear on the image itself.

Make Your Timestamp Legible. Otherwise people might have trouble reading it. Make the text 12 or 14 points, use boldface, and choose a contrasting text color for best results. For Web cams with changing light levels, such as outdoor cams, a lime green generally shows up well against both light and dark backgrounds. Or you can also pick a background color for your timestamp.

Adding a Timestamp with ISpy

Windows only

To add a timestamp with ISpy:

1. Select File|Settings and click the Caption tab, as shown in **Figure 9.27**.
2. Click the Show Caption in Picture check box.
3. To choose a font and font color, click the Set Font button to bring

up the Font dialog box. You can then choose your font styles and colors and click OK to return to the Settings dialog box.

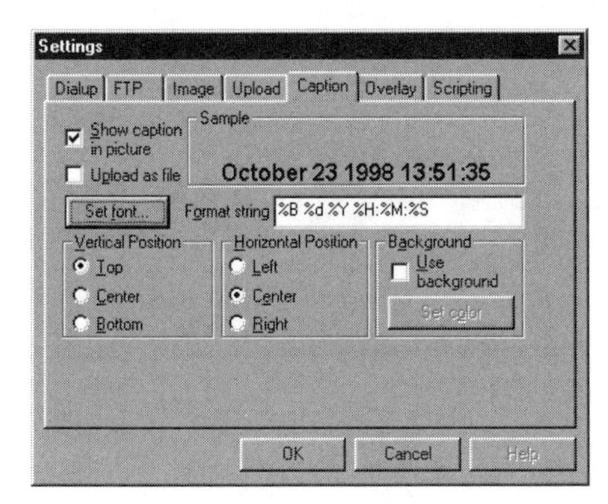

Figure 9.27 *In ISpy, use the Caption settings to make and position a timestamp.*

4. If you want your timestamp to display against a colored background, click the Use Background checkbox in the Background section. Then click the Set Color button to display the Color dialog box. When you select a color, you can click OK to return to the Settings dialog box.
5. To position your timestamp, select options from the Vertical Position and Horizontal Position sections. The vertical position determines whether the caption appears on the top, center, or bottom of your picture. The horizontal position aligns the caption to the left, center, or right.
6. When you're satisfied with the Caption settings, click OK to apply your timestamp.

To add a timestamp with SiteCam:

Adding a Timestamp with SiteCam

Macintosh only

1. Select Document|Caption 1 from the Document menu. When the Caption Setup dialog box appears (**Figure 9.28**), choose a date format and a time format by clicking the appropriate checkboxes in the Insert Timestamp section.
2. Pick a font, size, and font style by selecting them from the lists at the top of the dialog box.

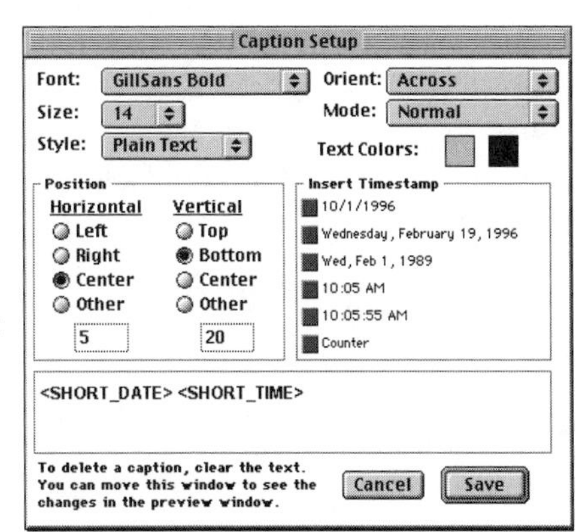

Figure 9.28 *In SiteCam, use the Caption Setup dialog box to choose attributes for a timestamp.*

3. To choose a text color (and a background color if you want), click one of the Text Color boxes to display the color picker. The color box on the left sets the font color; the color box on the right sets the background color.
4. To position your timestamp, choose the appropriate options from the Horizontal and Vertical lists. The horizontal position determines whether the caption aligns to the left, center, or right. The vertical position determines whether the caption appears on the top, center, or bottom of your picture.

   Or you can manually position your text, pixel by pixel, by selecting Other and entering values in the number boxes.
5. Click the Save button to save your settings.

Creating a Picture History

You may have noticed that some Web cam pages also provide links to the last 10 or 20 pictures. Pretty neat, but how do they do that? It's called a **picture history**, and it's easy to do.

First you tell your Web cam program how many pictures to save. The program then **automatically** names the image files, renames them when it takes a new picture, and uploads all of the pictures to your server. The Web cam program can also cycle your pictures so that the first image is always the most recent one, the second image is the second most recent one, and so on. Whenever your Web cam takes a new picture, it automatically renumbers all the other pictures, too.

Creating a Picture History with ISpy

Windows only

When you create a picture history with ISpy, it automatically numbers your pictures by adding a period and a number to the image's filename, as in picture.jpg, picture.1.jpg, picture.2.jpg, and so on. You need to remember these filenames when you create Web pages for your pictures.

To create a picture history with ISpy:

1. Choose File|Settings. When the Settings dialog box appears, select the Upload tab.
2. At the bottom of the dialog box, click the Keep History... checkbox and type the number of images you want in your history into the box provided. For example, the entry in **Figure 9.29** tells ISpy to keep the 9 most recent images as the picture history.

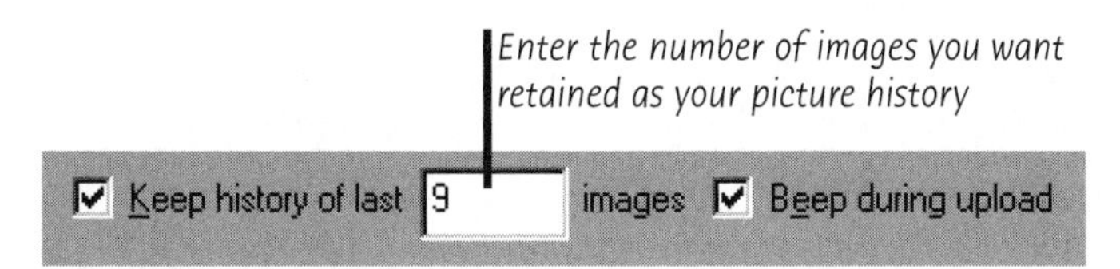
Enter the number of images you want retained as your picture history
Keep history of last 9 images
Beep during upload

Figure 9.29 *Creating a picture history in ISpy's Upload settings.*

3. If you want, you can click the checkbox for Beep During Upload to tell ISpy to alert you whenever it uploads your pictures.
4. Click OK to save your settings.

Creating a Picture History with SiteCam

Macintosh only

When you create a picture history with SiteCam, it automatically numbers your pictures by adding the number to the end of your file name, as in picture.jpeg, picture1.jpeg, picture2.jpeg, and so on. The images are renamed so that the first image is always the most recent image. You need to remember these filenames when you create Web pages for your pictures.

To create a picture history with SiteCam:

1. Select Document|Destination to bring up the SiteCam Settings dialog with the Destination settings.
2. To specify the number of images you want to save in your picture history, enter that number in the Save File(s) to Disk box, as shown in **Figure 9.30**. (Make sure the Save radio button is selected.)
3. Click OK to save your settings.

Enter the number of images you want retained as your picture history

Save 10 File(s) to disk

Figure 9.30 *Creating a picture history in SiteCam's Destination Settings dialog box.*

SiteCam also supports **image archiving**, which lets you save a history of images that are not automatically replaced. Archived images are saved with a timestamp filename, such as 1-1-1999.jpeg.

Creating Your Cam Web Page

Congratulations! You're almost finished. Now all you have to do is create a Web page to display your Web cam picture—which isn't any different from creating a regular ol' Web page with an image.

First, take a picture or a series of pictures with your Web cam. (You can make your cam program take pictures right away, as explained in the "Testing Your Web Cam" section earlier in this chapter.) Then you can **insert one or more of these pictures on Web pages**. Chapter 7 tells you about putting pictures on Web pages and refers you to some books that teach you how to create Web pages.

Once you put your pictures on your pages and upload all needed files to your Web site, you can sit back and enjoy your Web cam. Since the Web cam program keeps taking new pictures and giving them the same filenames, you won't need to do anything else to your Web pages.

If you've set up your Web cam program to create a history of pictures, it's best to **put each picture on a separate Web page** and make links to each page. Otherwise, the pictures take forever to load.

Name Your Files Correctly!

When you create Web pages for your pictures, make sure to name your image files correctly. **This includes pointing to the correct folder|directory**. If your Web site's folders aren't set up exactly like the ones on your server, or if you don't specify the correct path in your Web cam program's FTP settings, your pictures won't display correctly.

Advanced Web Camming

If you're ambitious, you can get plenty creative and come up with some pretty cool stuff with your cam. But you'll need a direct hook-up to a Web server for this advanced work, and a little programming knowledge wouldn't hurt, either.

ISpy and SiteCam, as well as other cam programs, have the features you'll need to produce *way* more advanced results if you've got the time and inclination. I won't get into this stuff in detail here, because you'd fall asleep and this book would become too heavy to lift. Here's just a quick run-down to get you started on your own path to serious Web camming.

Advanced Web Camming Features

Feature	Capabilities
Live Video Feed	Sends a constant stream of pictures to the server, so the Web cam page updates as frequently (or almost as frequently) as your Web cam program's preview window. Or you can stream your Web cam as an AVI or QuickTime movie.
CGI Scripting	CGI scripts let you customize how your server handles stuff—including your Web cam pictures. You don't necessarily need a direct server hook-up to run CGI scripts, but some ISPs and Web hosts don't allow CGI scripting. SiteCam can even generate a few scripts for you, if you've got access to the right type of server.
Archiving Pictures	SiteCam lets you automatically save and name pictures by date and time rather than by filename. Theoretically, you can keep all of your pictures from the past year and let visitors search for them. Of course, this would mean doing a little programming to automatically generate Web pages for each image and the links for these pages, so archiving is not for the faint of heart. Plus, it takes up a lot of disk space.
Time Lapse	You can set up your cam to capture a series of images and turn them into a movie. You don't need a direct server connection or programming skills to do this, but you do need substantial disk space and some time to experiment.
Image Overlays	Some Web cam programs let you put your logo on your pictures; you can also layer your picture over a background image. These options usually require solid knowledge of the HTML 4.0 <Layer> tag, which is used to layer images. If you want to experiment, keep in mind that layering is supported only in version 4.0 and later browsers. You won't need a direct server hook-up or programming knowledge, but you do need a little Web design knowledge.

Want To Run Your Own Server?

Running your own server may sound far-fetched to you, but if you like tinkering and don't mind the learning curve, you can do it. Lots of folks out there are using Macintosh, Windows NT, and Linux computers as servers—all you need is a normal PC with plenty of RAM and a decent processor speed, a dedicated connection, some server programs (many are free) and a high-speed, dedicated connection. Computer prices keep falling, and more and more local telephone companies offer high-speed Internet connections like ISDN and ASDL for as little as $80 per month, plus a one-time installation fee. Go for it!

Summary

Congratulations—you now know how to set up your own Web cam page. Enjoy your 15 minutes of fame!

- **ISpy for Windows** and **SiteCam for Macintosh** make it easy to get your cam up and running. You can download these programs and start using them right away.
- You can **preview** your pictures and make adjustments. ISpy and SiteCam allow you to **change your cam's settings** for picture size, color depth, brightness, contrast, color settings, and image quality. For a more detailed discussion of these settings, see Chapter 2.
- Your Web cam first **saves** pictures to a folder on your computer, and then **uploads** the pictures to your server. You can tell your cam where to save your pictures, and how frequently to take them. Whenever your Web cam takes a new picture, ISpy and SiteCam upload the pictures to your server.
- You'll also need to provide your server's **FTP information** so ISpy or SiteCam can upload the Web cam pictures to your Web site.
- In order for visitors to your site to see the pictures taken with your Web cam, you'll need to create a **Web page** for your image. You can also set up your cam to take a series of pictures, create a Web page for each picture, and make links to each picture from the main page.

The next chapter features interviews of experienced Web cammers. Learn how they set up their cams and find out about a few special tips and tricks.

How Do They Do It?

Interviews with Web Cammers

"So how do you do it?" I ask this question whenever I stumble on a particularly cool cam. Some cammers have elaborate setups with fancy video cameras, their own servers, and custom programs that do everything but take out the garbage. Other cammers just get a great idea one day, hook up the ol' QuickCam to their computer, and a new Web cam is born. The most interesting Web cammers come from all walks of life, but they've got a couple of things in common: a concept that attracts visitors, and the creativity and determination to make their cams work. I talked with three of my favorite Web cammers, and in this chapter you'll find their stories and some of their camming secrets.

- **Terry Weissman**
  Netscape Engineering Sign cam at
  http://www.weissman.org/sign/
- **Brad Lowe**
  San Francisco Bay Bridge cam and the SiteZAP system at
  http://www.rearden.com/ and
  http://www.sitezap.com/
- **Lisa Violet**
  Lisa Violet's Cat House at
  http://www.lisaviolet.com/

Terry Weissman

Got something to say? Tell the **Netscape Engineering Sign**, shown in **Figure 10.1**. You'll find it at **http://www.weissman.org/sign/**.

This cam shows a sign in Netscape's Engineering Department, and you never know what the sign will say next. That depends on what visitors like you submit through the sign's handy-dandy Web form.

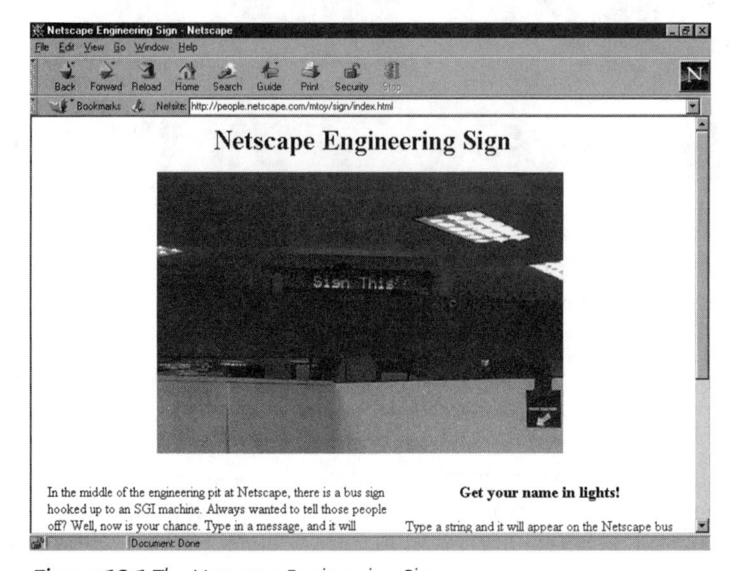

Figure 10.1 *The Netscape Engineering Sign*

"Very cool," you might be thinking. "Why haven't I heard about this before?" Shhh! The Engineering Sign is one of the techno-hip crowd's best kept secrets.

Tips for Using the Engineering Sign:

- The sign doesn't have room for full sentences, so you'll have to post longer messages two or three words at a time.
- Read the whole Web page, and remember to click the link to show the current sign.
- The amount of time it takes for your message to appear on the sign depends on how many people posted messages before yours.

Engineering Sign Cam Setup

Here are the elements of Terry's Netscape Engineering Sign cam:

- **Type of cam**: Video camera
- **Computer**: UNIX machine with Netscape Server software (what else?)
- **Cam software**: Custom CGI scripts
- **Other**: Bus sign rigged up to computer

About Terry Weissman

Terry Weissman programs and maintains tools that keep mozilla.org up and running. Mozilla.org serves as a clearing house for Netscape's free programming source code. Whew! This may sound pretty high-falutin' to us nontechnical folks, but Terry's work helps all of us in the long run. Other programmers *need* these source code snippets so they can create plug-ins, server software, Web page editors, and other stuff that enrich our experiences on the Internet.

In addition to the Engineering Sign Cam, Terry has worked on serious projects like Netscape Mail and News. He's also been on the teams for Bugzilla, Bonsai, and Tinderbox, which developers use to report bugs and check for the latest source code updates.

On a more personal note, Terry lives in a geodesic dome with his wife Amy, their newly arrived twins Amy and Jacob, and three dogs. When he isn't juggling career and family, Terry juggles other stuff...bowling pins, for instance. Amy juggles too, and their dog Pipsqueak can ride a skateboard. For more about Terry Weissman, and lots of pictures, visit **http://www.weissman.org/**.

The Interview

How did you come up with the idea for the Engineering Sign?

Well, John Giannandrea (we call him JG) had this sign lying around. So he and Phil Karlton (who passed away last year) managed to cobble together some software and a cable so that we could use a computer to program the sign. For a while, it was just set up so that us Netscape engineers could see it, and any of us could put up a message. But we ran out of imagination. For a week or two, I ran a program which would run `fortune` [a UNIX program] and put a random fortune up on the sign every hour. But that got old too. So, someone (probably JG, or maybe Michael Toy) had the idea that we should put it up on the Web. Michael Toy hacked the scripts together—I may have helped a bit, I don't remember—and the sign was born.

Soon, though, we realized that people out on the Net would want to see it, as well as post to it. So, I got together with Lou Montulli, and he

Terry Weissman's Interview *(cont.)*

helped me modify his FishCam stuff so that we could get it to work with the sign too. This must have all happened in the summer or fall of '95.

Can you tell us how the sign works?

The only complicated part, really, is from the firewall [server security software]. Netscape has a pretty strong firewall to protect ourselves from people on the Internet getting into our internal network. Which is all well and good, but the Sign and SignCam are hooked up to machines on our internal network, and we needed a way through the firewall to let external people [people outside of Netscape] put data on it [post messages], and to show the current image to people externally [on the Web]. We worked it out.

Do people use the sign to holler for help with Netscape?

Probably. But, realistically, nobody pays attention to the sign. If you're walking down the hall, and you have nothing better to do, then you might look up and see if there's anything entertaining there.

I have some speech-synthesis software on my machine [which converts text to speech]. I once hooked it up so that whenever a new posting appeared on the sign, it was read out loud to me. That was entertaining, but pretty distracting. I stopped after a few days.

Got any stories about the Engineering Sign?

We've had a couple of marriage proposals. Someone once posted the entire text of *Green Eggs & Ham* [by Dr. Seuss]—I really respect that.

"We've had a couple of marriage proposals. Someone once posted the entire text of Green Eggs & Ham—I really respect that."

A couple of years ago, there was a campaign by users of the OS/2 operating system to get Netscape to port to their platform [create an OS/2 version of Netscape Navigator]. Which did eventually happen, but not noticeably as a result of this campaign. Part of their effort was to flood the sign with messages about how wonderful OS/2 was and how we ought to run there. This became so annoying that we installed software to censor out any message containing "OS/2." This is the only form of censorship we've ever put on the sign. More "normal" offensive messages containing all varieties of four-letter words appear all the time, but it wasn't nearly as bothersome as the never-ending stream of messages containing the four-character word OS/2. The censorship is now gone.

But the best story is a bit of a geeky one. I remember looking up once or twice and seeing that someone had posted an 8-digit binary number to the sign. You know, something like "01101001." I was very mildly amused at this nonsense, and forgot about it.

Several days later, for some reason or another, I was looking at the log file of things that had been sent to the sign. And I noticed that in fact there were a whole bunch of 8-digit binary numbers that had been posted one right after another. And I got suspicious [because it looked like a hacker was trying to break into the server].

Most computer programmers are very familiar with ASCII, which is a standard way of representing text as numbers. And 8-digit binary numbers are exactly the size that are used by ASCII. So, I quickly wrote a program to translate that bunch of 8-digit numbers as if each one was an ASCII character.

Sure enough, the result was: *If found, email mumble@fumble.com—reward offered.* (The address wasn't actually "mumble@fumble.com." I won't give out anyone's e-mail address without their permission. If you want to talk to them, send me a message and I'll forward it.)

So, I sent him mail, and he sent me this cool little scorpion made out of resistors and a computer chip. The scorpion now hangs out near the sign.

Some Web cams aren't born; they evolve.

You can always change or fine-tune your cam, and you don't need to be a programmer. Look for ideas, software, preprogrammed shareware Java applets, and CGI scripts that you can tweak to work with your cam. As Web cams grow more popular, you'll find more and more great stuff out there.

How many hits does the Sign get per day?

About 200 per day. The most interesting thing is that it doesn't vary. I had the sign down for a couple of months, when I moved offices. When I finally got it back up—pow!—we instantly got the usual number of messages that day. I figure that there is absolutely no repeat business. People randomly surf the 'Net, come across the sign, send it a message, say to themselves "that's cool," and *never come back*. When the sign was down, they saw the message saying it was down, said to themselves "oh well," and *never came back*. Same amount of traffic, whether it works or not.

How much time do you spend maintaining the site?

Zero. I get a few messages a week saying "The camera is misaimed" [pointing the wrong way], but they're generally wrong. These days, I just delete those messages without checking. If the camera really gets misaimed, I'll get a bunch of messages on the same day, and then I'll actually check it.

Do you see cams as useful, or just for fun?

Oh, I dunno. There have been a few useful cams (like ones that point at known hot-spots on the freeway, so you can see if there's a traffic jam). But mostly, I think this is just a neat way for people to be creative. It's a different world now. These days, you can just buy a package that does it all for you. We had to cobble our cam [and the software to run it] together ourselves.

Terry Weissman's Bookmarks

I asked Mr. Weissman about *his* favorite cams, but he said he's been too busy to do much Web surfing lately. Fortunately, he saved his bookmarks from more carefree days. They pointed me to a couple of *way* cool cams that Chapter 8 doesn't cover. (No, I didn't crack Netscape's firewall and snoop around on anyone's computer. Mr. Weissman publishes his bookmarks on his Web site at **http://www.weissman.org/bookmarks.html**.)

- **The Exploratorium:** Rainy day? You can count on the Exploratorium—an interactive science museum for kids (and grown-ups, too)—for a fun afternoon. One cam gives you a peek at today's exhibits so you can explore the museum. And when you're ready for a break, you can check out their other cam for a lovely view of the San Francisco Bay.

  http://www.exploratorium.edu/

- **USC Mercury Project:** Thinking of growing a garden? Try the virtual Telegarden first. You can view a picture of the garden and control a robotic arm that waters the plants, weeds the garden, and performs other gardening tasks. Terry has a link to the Mercury Project at **http://www.usc.edu/dept/raiders/** which originally launched the Telegarden at **http://www.usc.edu/dept/garden/**.

Other Netscape Cammers

Did you know that Netscape hosted the **second Web cam ever** in the world? That makes sense, since Netscape developed the server and browser technologies that make camming possible.

Back in 1995, **Lou Montulli** set up the **Amazing Fish Cam** (**Figure 10.2**) at **http://www.netscape.com/fishcam/fishcam.html**.

Netscape's techno-guru, **Michael Toy,** also played a major part in getting the Amazing Fish Cam and the Engineering Sign up and running. To meet the other people who contributed to the Engineering Sign, visit **http://people.netscape.com/mtoy/sign/credits**.

You can also find out more about the Amazing Fish Cam, as well as what fish live in the tank and how it works, at **http://fishcam.netscape.com/fishcam/fishcam_about.html**.

And what was the first Web cam? *That distinction goes to the Trojan Room Coffee Machine described in Chapter 8* ***(http://www.cl.cam.ac.uk/coffee/coffee.html)***.

Figure 10.2 The Amazing Fish Cam.

Brad Lowe and the Bay Bridge Cams

Equipment, technical knowledge, his own company, and a great view of San Francisco—**Brad Lowe** of Rearden Technology has it all. He wrote MacWebCam, one of the first Web cam programs, back in 1995. Since then, the program has evolved into two popular products: **SiteCam**, which I covered in Chapter 9; and the **SiteZAP Cam**.

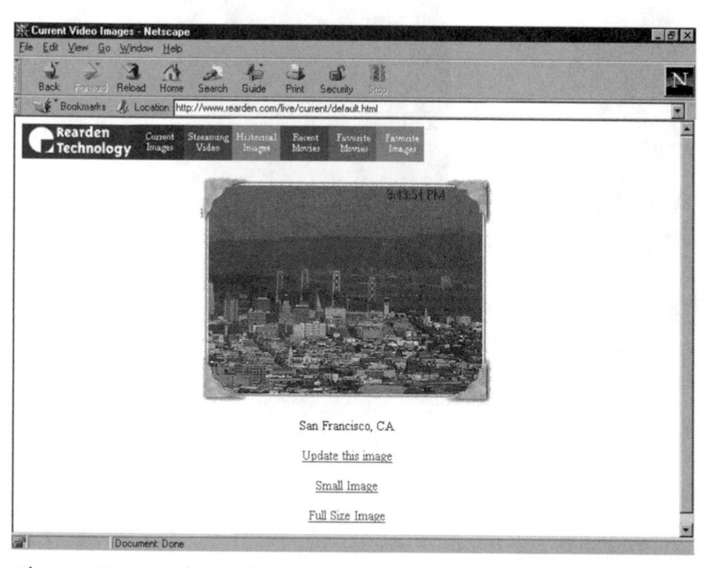

Figure 10.3 Rearden Technology's SiteCam view of the Bay Bridge .

SiteZAP is an amazing contraption with a programmable security camera, motion detection, a live video feed, and software that lets Web site visitors control the cam. You need your own server and about $2,000 (not bad, since it includes a pan, tilt, zoom camera, cables, and software). But SiteCam is way more affordable: Anyone with a Macintosh and a cam can use it.

Brad's Setup

Lowe's home office is a gadget freak's paradise. It has a few computers (including two servers and a laptop); several video cameras; a balcony with a stationary camera running on SiteCam software, and a SiteZAP camera that Web browsers can control remotely; and a tangle of cables. He is currently experimenting with a cat-scratching-post cam that sounds an alert and takes a picture when the cat goes to scratch. I don't know if Brad plans to put the scratching-post cam online, but you can check out the Bay Bridge cam, shown in **Figure 10.3**, at **http://www.rearden.com/live/**.

And if you really want to have some fun, drop by the SiteZAP Web site at **http://www.sitezap.com/** and take a spin around the city, as shown in **Figure 10.4**.

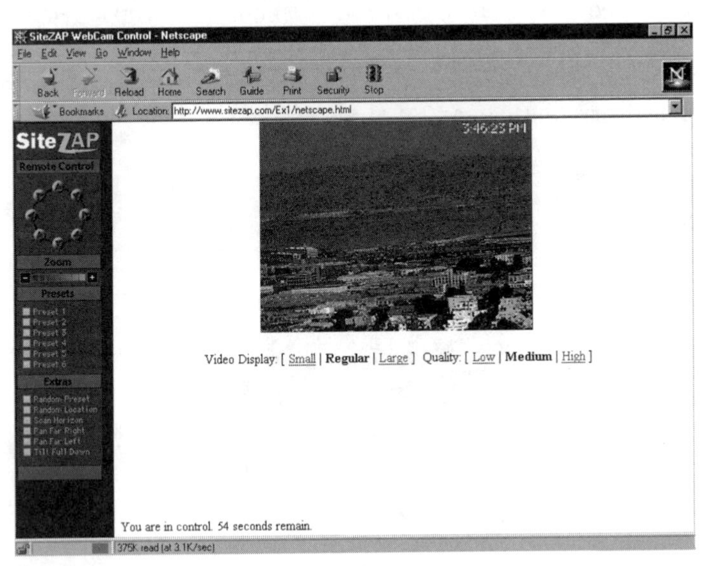

Figure 10.4 *Rearden Technology's SiteZAP Cam.*

Tips for Using the SiteZAP Cam:

- To move the camera, click the arrows on the Remote control.
- To zoom in and out, click the Zoom + or – buttons.
- For the best views, click one of the Presets options.
- Click one of the Extras options and see what happens.
- Share the controls! SiteZAP puts you on a timer and bumps you off so other people can use the cam. Text at the bottom of the Web page tells you how much time you've got left.

Bay Bridge and SiteZAP Cams Setup

Here are the elements of Brad Lowe's cams:

- **Type of cam**: A Sony HandyCam for use with the SiteCam software, and the SiteZAP Pan/Tilt/Zoom controllable camera that is mounted outdoors in a weatherproof enclosure. (Lowe sells optional outdoor enclosures for his SiteZAP camera packages.)
- **Computer**: Macintosh with video-input card and direct Internet connection.
- **Cam software**: Rearden Technology's SiteCam and SiteZAP
- **Other**: A fabulous view

The Interview

What got you into camming?

I had a programming job in Texas for six months in 1995 and was playing on the Web. So I wrote some cam software for the Mac because I thought it was cool. At first the cam software only worked if you had a full-time Internet connection, but now SiteCam is good for anyone with a Mac, a modem, and a regular Internet connection.

What's your background?

I went to Chico State [in California] and got a degree in Computer Science with a Business minor. So I'm actually doing what I went to school for!

What is the SiteZAP Cam, exactly?

SiteZAP is a Sony security-grade video camera that you can control using software. Sony sells [the cameras] to developers who write software for them. Unlike consumer-grade video cameras, security cameras can detect motion, follow people when they're walking around, and you can mount [the cameras] on a wall or outside more easily. With the SiteZAP software, you can create QuickTime VR panoramas on-the-fly, time-lapse movies, and let visitors control the cam from a browser like Netscape or Internet Explorer.

What's QuickTime VR?
It turns QuickTime movies into three-dimensional, virtual reality worlds. A QuickTimeVR movie offers a 360° photographic environment. You can view the entire panorama by dragging your mouse across the image. Get this plug-in from Apple's Web site at ***http://www.quicktime.com/****.*

Who are some of your clients?

I work with NASA on weather observation and conditions at remote sites, and also the Jet Propulsion Laboratory (JPL). I also have a list of links to some users of SiteCam and SiteZAP on my Rearden Technology Web site [**http://www.rearden.com/links/**].

What are some good uses for Web cams?

If you have a separate telephone line for your Internet connection, Web cams work well for videoconferencing. You can talk on the phone [because audio quality on the Internet still isn't up to snuff] and look at each other in your Web browsers. Some of my clients do that. They're also great for parents who want to check in on their children at a daycare center. The center can password-protect the site so only the parents can look in. Or you can view progress on a constuction site remotely [Mr. Lowe then showed me the Virginia Tech Building Construction Site Cam at **http://sitecam.arch.vt.edu/website/sitecam1.html**]. They're also good for weather observatories.

Have you got any favorite cams?

I like the trainspotting cams, like the Tehachi Rail Cam at **http://www.trainorders.com/cameras/**. The Tehachapi cams use SiteCam's motion detector to take a picture when a train comes by. It turns out that train watching is a popular activity—the site is very popular with "rail fans."

Got any camming tips?

First consider what you want to spend, and get up to speed with HTML and FTP [File Transfer Protocol for uploading files to your server]. Setting up a cam isn't hard, but it requires commitment to keep it running and build a following.

Brad Lowe's WebCam Tips

Brad offers the following suggestions for your Web camming efforts:

- Change the view [move the camera] to keep things fresh.
- Keep track of your visitors and their domains [most ISPs offer server statistics]. Sometimes people may "hijack" your cam [display *your* picture on *their* page—SiteCam's documentation talks more about deterring cam hijackers].
- Consumer-grade video cameras make good cams. QuickCam's fine but doesn't like bright light. Sometimes you can find a video camera with a broken tape drive and buy it cheap. You don't need the tape drive for camming.

- Make sure the camera doesn't shift into Sleep or Demo mode [during periods of inactivity]—and that there's a way to turn that feature off.
- You can find outdoor enclosures designed for small cameras [for setting up a cam outside]. But make sure the enclosure is the right size. Security cameras mount better, but they're more expensive.
- If you set up a cam that takes pictures through a window, you can reduce reflections from the window by putting a cardboard box around the camera.
- Give visitors options for various picture sizes and use SiteCam's image archiving to let them see what the view was in the past.

Lisa Violet

Okay, we've talked with a couple of renowned cammers who program, who have their own servers and other resources at their disposal. But you don't need a fancy setup and a degree in programming to set up a way-cool cam. **Lisa Violet's Cat House** cam (**Figure 10.5**) at **http://www.lisaviolet.com/** gets lots of visits, and she has a regular PC and dial-up Internet account just like the rest of us. (Though Ms. Violet freely admits that having 18 cats definitely helps keep the cam interesting!)

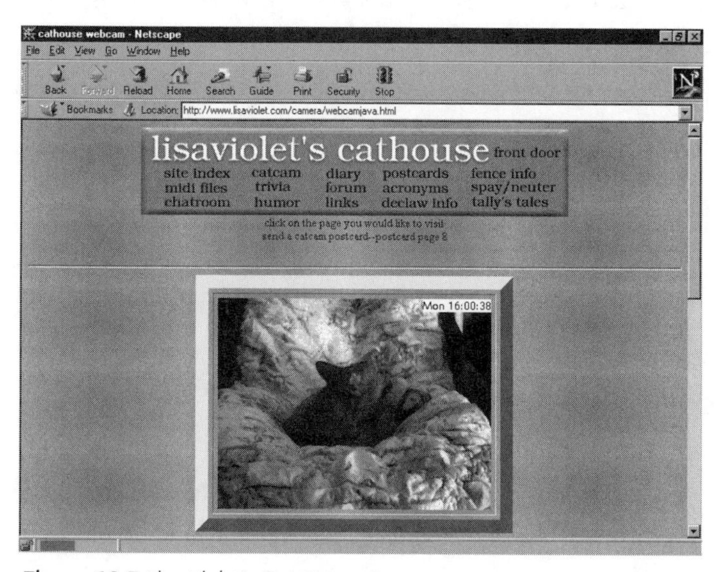

Figure 10.5 *Lisa Violet's Cat House Cam.*

And while you're in the neighborhood, why not stay a while? There's plenty to do at the Cat House. You can send friends souvenir postcards with MIDI music, like the one shown in **Figure 10.6**. Play Java cat games, read about the cats, and more—definitely one of the most fun Web sites around.

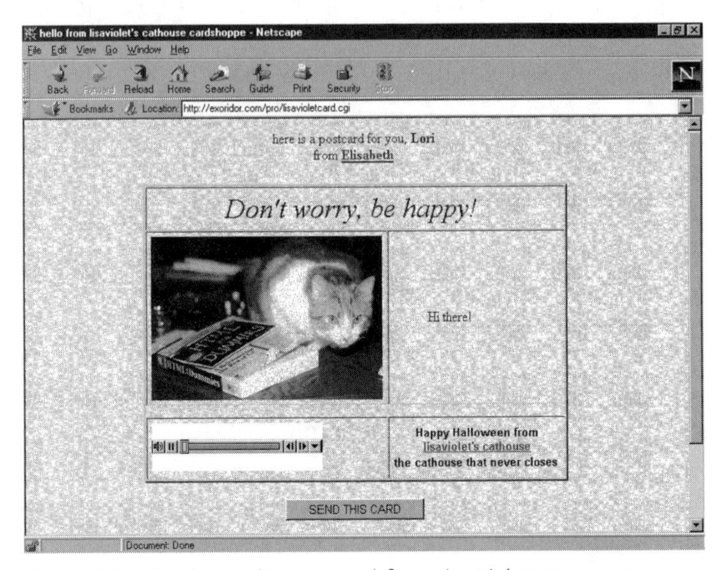

Figure 10.6 *Send an online postcard from Lisa Violet's Cat House.*

You can create online postcards, too. Try using your own pictures as Web postcards. Visitors to the Cat House can pick a picture and a MIDI music tune, and fill out the form with their e-mail address and the recipient's e-mail address. When the recipient gets an e-mail message announcing that the postcard is waiting for them, he or she can click the link to get their postcard. Find out how at **http://mypostcards.com/**.

Lisa Violet's Cat House Cam Setup

Here are the elements of Lisa's cam setup:

- **Type of cam**: Connectix Color QuickCam (Logitech now owns QuickCam)
- **Computer**: Windows 95 PC with dial-up Internet connection
- **Cam software**: WebCam 32 (as mentioned in Chapter 9)
- **Other**: 18 cats and a comfy chair

The Interview

Eighteen cats! Where did you get all of them?

Well, we had four when we got married (I made a vow after one bad relationship, no more *serious* things unless he loves these guys as much as I do, and I'm glad I held out). When we moved to our current home, one [cat] ran away. We looked all over for him, went to animal control, searched the neighborhood, knocked on doors, and we never did find him. The others just kind of came to us. By twos. Since we've lived here, we have only lost one, and that was our youngest, five days before Christmas 1993. She got into the yard of a cat-hating dog and her back was broken. After that, we decided that the cats weren't leaving the yard, and my husband came up with a way to modify our existing fence to keep them in. It's worked pretty good so far. (With the exception of Benny, our intrepid explorer, but I think we have that well in hand.)

The last two we got are feral, totally wild. One of them, Red Rafter, we had to trick onto the premises, because he was wise to the trap from the time we caught him and got him neutered. He lived in our garage rafters (hence the middle name Rafter) for over a year. Our cats have come into our lives from garbage trucks, to the side of the road, to an unscrupulous woman who sold sick kittens and puppies (I put her out of business). Oh, and we actually bought one. A Maine Coon pedigree named Maggie Xuxa.

How do you lure your cats to the chair?

Nothing to it. They like to be with a human. And I spend many hours in the office, working on my Web site and helping others out with their cats. Also, it's a very comfortable spot for them. They were sleeping in the chair long before I had the camera set up. We have a cat feeder in here, as well as water and a litter box. All the comforts of home, you might say [smiles].

"They were sleeping in the chair long before I had the camera set up. We have a cat feeder in here, as well as water and a litter box."

What inspired you to start camming?

Geez. The first time I saw one, I loved it. It was the camera that focused on a cat's food dish, I think. I wanted one. And I noticed that very few people ever saw the cat.

"Well, heck," I thought to myself, "We have 18 cats and I know there's a bigger chance of seeing *them* than *one* cat."

And so started my quest for the CatCam.

How did you set it up?

The story of the camera is a great one, I think. I had my site at GeoCities [**http://www.geocities.com/**], where I am a GeoPlus member

Lisa Violet's Interview *(cont.)*

[GeoCities is free, and GeoPlus is their paid service]. Having GeoPlus, if you get so many visits to your site a month, your visitors actually pay for the GeoPlus cost [through increased advertising]. And the additional GeoPoints accumulate. With these accumulated GeoPoints, you can buy stuff at the GeoStore.

A camera was 2350 points. I needed about 1000 more to get the camera, and I got busy advertising my site. It took me six months to get enough and boy was I happy. I ordered the camera and I set it up the minute I got it. It was a Connectix Color QuickCam. I downloaded the software to upload the pictures from **http://www.kolban.com/**.

You can imagine my disappointment when the camera didn't work. It took many phone calls to the manufacturer to finally get the problem resolved, four months later. They sent me a new camera. And it worked right away. I was ecstatic. I set up the camera and I pointed it at the chair. And the rest is history.

What other software do you use?

I now use Notepad and Wordpad [text editors that come with Windows] to update my site. Paint Shop Pro [a Windows imaging program available from **http://www.jasc.com/**] is what I use for my graphics.

How do you keep all those cats from knocking over the cam?

"I had to get Red Rafter down [from the rafters]."

Well, the way the camera is now set up, they *can't* knock it over. It's attached with a clamp to the desk. They do interfere with the lighting, by walking in front of the window, but that's no big deal.

How did you get into computers and technology?

I've always liked to play games on the computer. My husband is self-employed and we got our first computer so that I would have an easier time keeping his records. I got online because we could. I was connected for at least three months before I started to surf. And my first real exploration was to a cat bulletin board, to find out how I could get Red Rafter down [from the rafters]. He had been here all of two weeks and I was worried about getting him down.

The advice I got didn't help at all, and it was a good year later before he joined the rest of us at ground level, but by that time I was hooked on the Internet. I joined GeoCities (free Web pages), so that I would have a place to put pictures so that I could show off my cats to other people on bulletin boards. Then I added the cats' stories. Then I added links. And I just kept adding. Finally, I moved my site off of Geo Cities (which is a great place for beginners, but I was past that and they have way too much advertising) after I got my own domain.

Declawing issue

Do you hear from people who visit your Web site?

Yes, I do get a lot of e-mail. My favorite comments are the ones from people that say because of what they have read, they won't declaw their cats. And I really like the comments that people are going to start a movement to make animal cruelty a felony in their state because of what they have read on my site. Makes me feel my time spent on my Web site is actually doing something to help our furred critters.

About how many hits do you get?

All pages? Between 1000 and 2000 a day.

How much time do you spend maintaining the cam?

The camera doesn't really take a lot of time, once it's set up. But for the remainder of my site, I usually spend two to four hours a day on it.

What do people talk about in your chat room?

Um... [they say] "Hello, is anybody here?" [laughs].

What's your favorite Web cam?

There's one by the name of LaddieCam. It's a little Sheltie pup. He's a real cutie. [LaddieCam is at **http://cx45564-a.chnd1.az.home.com/myweb/laddie/Default.htm**.]

Have you got any tips for would-be Web cammers?

Well, if you are really into Web pages, a Web cam (for me, at least) is the ultimate fun thing. Be prepared to lose your life. Try not to let the litter box overflow while you test some new Java games for your visitors' pleasure.

Summary

So what can you learn from Terry Weissman, Brad Lowe, and Lisa Violet? That where there's a will, there's always a way. With low-cost equipment and a little creativity and determination, you can set up a Web cam that brings lots of visitors to your Web site.

- **Terry Weissman's Netscape Engineering Sign** cam went through several phases before Weissman and his coworkers found the right idea and a way to make it work. You, too, may need to experiment a little with your Web cam to get it up and running the way you want.
- **Brad Lowe** of Rearden Technology has a couple of outdoor cams that overlook the **San Francisco Bay Bridge**. Being a programmer with a server and fancy video cams certainly helps, but when it comes to setting up a Web cam, it's amazing what you can do with a regular ol' consumer-grade, handheld video camera and your computer.
- **Lisa Violet** shows what you can do with QuickCam, an Internet connection and Web site, some interesting subject matter, creativity, and a willingness to experiment. Of course, having 18 cats gives her an edge, since it increases the likelihood of visitors' seeing one of the kitties at any given time. In addition, Lisa's Web site offers lots of other cool **cat-related stuff**—pictures, movies, cat stories, helpful information about caring for cats, and online picture postcards that you can e-mail to your friends.

Part Five
Cams & Videoconferencing

HI, AND WELCOME TO OUR FIRST ANNUAL FAMILY REUNION BY VIDEOCONFERENCE.
ON YOUR SCREENS, SET "FAMILY CONFLICT CATCHER" ON LEVEL 10. ... JUST KIDDING! HEY, HOW THE HECK IS EVERYONE?

Videoconferencing with White Pine CU-SeeMe

11

Videoconferencing is fun, and it can save you money, too. If you've got a cam, a microphone, and speakers, you can talk face-to-face with friends, family, and coworkers—even when they're thousands of miles away. Or you can explore the large (and still growing!) CU-SeeMe community. There are lots of conference rooms where you can meet people with common interests and discuss a variety of topics. Check out the big variety of electronic broadcasts and educational resources. And since you can connect over the Internet, videoconferencing costs less than a phone call or plane ticket!

TO MAKE AMENDS FOR ANY PROBLEMS YOU MAY HAVE EVER EXPERIENCED WITH MY SOFTWARE, I'M RETIRING TO DEVOTE MY LIFE TO ANIMALS, ESPECIALLY DOGS... BUT NOT CATS—DON'T CARE MUCH FOR CATS...

So what are you waiting for? CU-SeeMe by White Pine Software is an easy and inexpensive way to get started. It costs $89 ($69 if you download the program and pay online), and it runs on both Macintosh and Windows.

In this chapter:

- Downloading, installing, and setting up **White Pine CU-SeeMe**.
- Group, point-to-point, cybercast, and multicast **videoconference types**.
- **Group videoconferencing**: Dialing reflectors from the Phone Book's contact list; reflector etiquette; sending and receiving text chat, audio, and video; and getting information about conference participants.
- **Conferencing with individuals**: IP addresses and ILS servers; making and receiving phone calls.
- **Managing your contacts with CU-SeeMe's Contact List**: Creating new groups and contacts; adding people from an ILS; organizing the Contact List.
- **Customizing CU-SeeMe settings**: Video window layout; send and receive settings; Contact Card information; choosing an ILS.

Why White Pine Cu-SeeMe?

You'll have no trouble finding plenty of videoconferencing products out there. Many cams, including QuickCam VC, come with videoconferencing software. You can download NetMeeting or iVisit for free (see Chapter 12). So why should you pay for CU-SeeMe? Because it's well worth the money.

After taking a few programs for a spin, I found White Pine CU-SeeMe to be the most reliable and easy to use. It runs on both Windows and Macintosh and works with most types of cams and video cards. And remember that you can't videoconference alone! CU-SeeMe has a vast community with millions of users. When you launch the program, you'll find a long list of servers that host public conferences. In addition, White Pine's Web site lists exciting events, broadcasts, and other resources. For more about finding out where the CU-SeeMe action is, see Chapter 13.

CU-SeeMe comes with VideoLabs's PlanetView videoconferencing system (as mentioned in Chapter 2), and with White Pine's CU-SeeMe Cam Kit.

If you'd like to explore a bit and get your feet wet before diving in and paying for a videoconferencing program, Chapter 12 tells you about the freebies and where to get them. But if you want to start talking with people right away, download and register White Pine CU-SeeMe.

Isn't CU-SeeMe free?

Yes, there is a freeware version of CU-SeeMe, developed at Cornell University back in 1993. It's still around, and it's discussed in Chapter 12. However, since White Pine now owns the rights to Cornell CU-SeeMe, you can expect big changes ahead for this freebie edition.

Coming soon: CU-SeeMe Pro! White Pine plans to release CU-SeeMe Pro for Windows soon. This enhanced version of the program will work similarly to the version of CU-SeeMe covered in this chapter. But you can also expect some improvements, including a sleeker design and the ability to do point-to-point conferencing with people who use NetMeeting, PictureTel, Intel Pro Share, Intel Team Station, LiveLAN, and a host of other popular videoconferencing programs.

Let's Get Started

Let's go to **White Pine's Web site (http://www.wpine.com)**, shown in **Figure 11.1**, and download CU-SeeMe. Then we'll walk through installing the program and setting it up, and take it for a spin. You can try out CU-SeeMe for 30 minutes. After that, the program stops working and you'll need to register in order to continue using it.

Figure 11.1 *White Pine's Web site.*

Downloading CU-SeeMe

To download CU-SeeMe, visit White Pine's Web site, click the Get Software Link, then click on the Request to Download Evaluation Software link. When the Web form appears (**Figure 11.2**), type in your information and click the Evaluate button. You can then click on one of the links for the Windows or Macintosh version.

When downloading the CU-SeeMe demo, make sure that you get the correct version for your computer system!

Platform ○ Windows 95/98/NT 4.0 ○ Mac OS
First Name
Last Name
Title
Organization
Phone
E-mail
Address
Address (cont.)
City
State or Province
Zip or Postal Code
Country
Request Evaluation

Figure 11.2 *White Pine's form for requesting evaluation software.*

Get the manual, too!

When you download CU-SeeMe, be sure to download the **manual**, too. Once this chapter gets you started with the program, you can learn more about it from the manual. Note that the manual is formatted as a .pdf file, which you can view with the free Adobe Acrobat Reader. Download the Acrobat Reader from Adobe's Web site at **http://www.adobe.com**.

Installing CU-SeeMe

1. Double-click the CU-SeeMe installation file.

   Windows: You'll see the InstallShield Self-extracting dialog box, then the Setup dialog box, and then the Software License Agreement dialog box.

   Macintosh: The CU-SeeMe splash screen appears. Click the Continue button to display the Software License Agreement.

2. Accept the Software License Agreement by clicking the Yes button (Windows) or Accept Button (Macintosh).

   Windows: The CU-SeeMe Serial Number dialog box appears (shown in **Figure 11.6** a little later in this chapter). If you have paid for the program, enter your name, company, and the serial number, and click OK. Otherwise, click the Demo button. The Setup Type dialog box appears, as shown in **Figure 11.3**.

   Macintosh: The CU-SeeMe Installer dialog box appears (**Figure 11.4**).

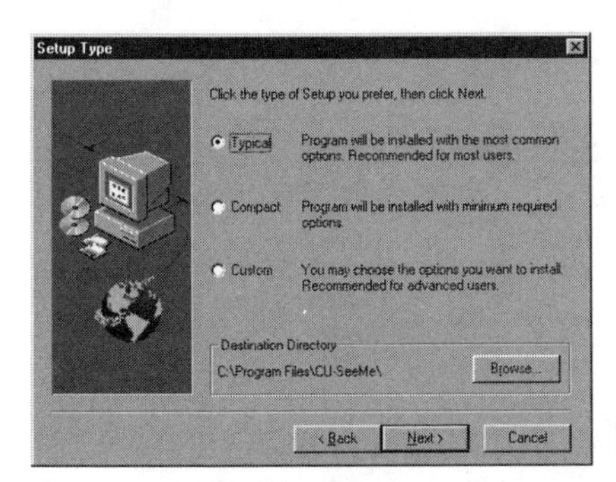

Figure 11.3 *Installing CU-SeeMe in Windows.*

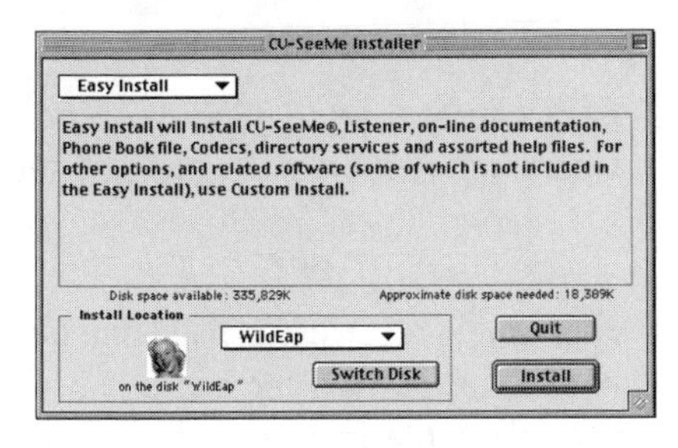

Figure 11.4 *Installing CU-SeeMe on the Macintosh.*

3. Choose an installation option.

   Windows: Select the Typical radio button from the list of options, and click Next to begin the setup.

   Macintosh: Select Easy Install from the list of options at the top, and click the Install button to begin the installation.

4. Complete the setup.

   Windows: When the Setup Complete dialog box appears, click "Yes, I want to launch CU-SeeMe" to launch CU-SeeMe immediately and try it out. Or leave the checkbox unchecked if you want to run the program later, and click the Finish button.

   Macintosh: When the Installation Sucessful dialog box appears, click the Restart button to restart your machine.

Purchasing CU-SeeMe

If you haven't yet registered and paid for CU-SeeMe, you can go to White Pine's How to Buy page at **http://www.wpine.com/buying/**. Select an option from the Purchase Option list for CU-SeeMe, as shown in **Figure 11.5**, and click the Go! button. You can pay for the program online (which saves you 20 bucks!). Or you can have it mailed to you on disk, or display a list of stores where you can purchase the program in person.

Save $20!

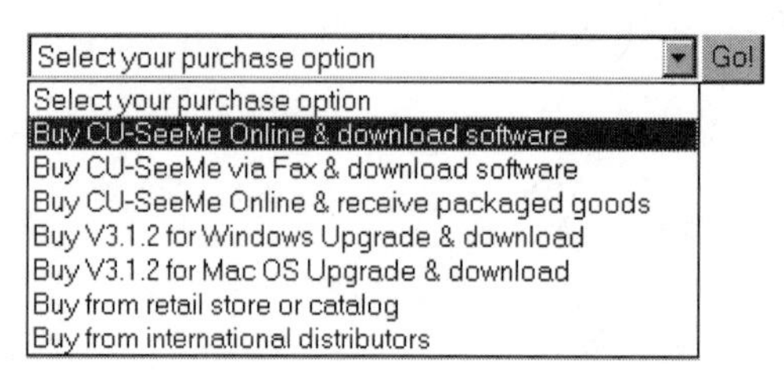

Figure 11.5 *CU-SeeMe purchase options.*

Packages That Include CU-SeeMe

CU-SeeMe also comes with the VideoLabs PlanetView videoconferencing system, as mentioned in Chapter 2, as well as 3Com's BigPicture Video Phone System.

Still need a cam? Windows users can try the CU-SeeMe Cam kit. It, too, includes the CU-SeeMe videoconferencing software and sells for about $124.

Registering CU-SeeMe

When you purchase CU-SeeMe, you'll receive a serial number that enables you to continue using the program after the demo version expires. To unlock the program, follow the instructions coming up in the next section. Once you've done this, you can register. In the Serial Number dialog box—**Figures 11.6** and **11.7**—type your information, enter your serial number, and click OK.

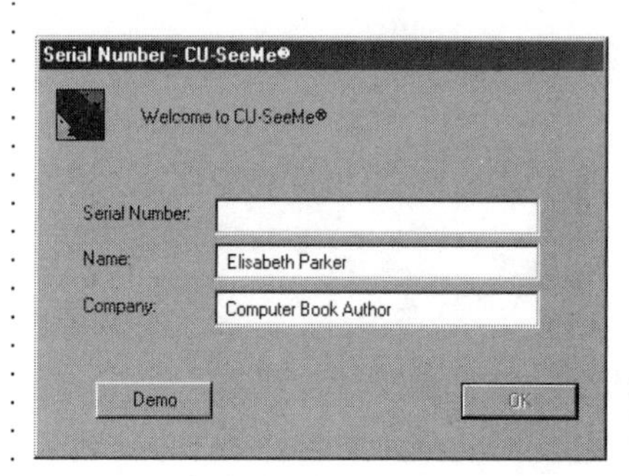

Figure 11.6 *Registering CU-SeeMe in Windows.*

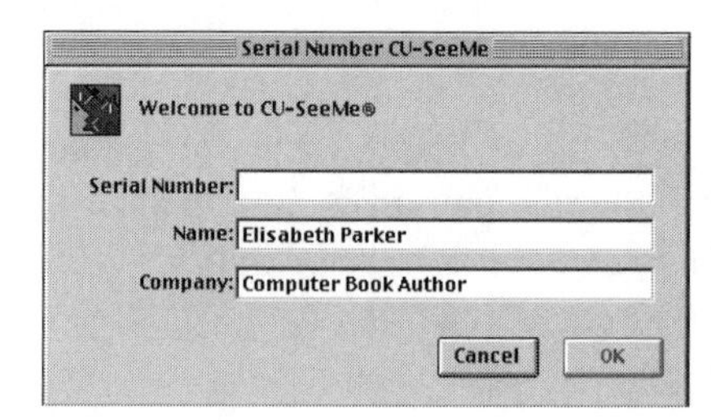

Figure 11.7 *Registering CU-SeeMe for Macintosh.*

It's never too late to register

If your 30-minute demo times out, you can still register the program. Just start up the application again, and enter your serial number when the Registration dialog box (Windows) or Serial Number dialog box (Macintosh) appears. CU-SeeMe will then be unlocked for your continued use.

Start It Up!

To launch CU-SeeMe:

- **Windows** users go to Start|Programs|CU-SeeMe, and click the CU-SeeMe application icon.
- **Mac** users double-click the CU-SeeMe icon.

Want to make CU-SeeMe easier to find? **To create a shortcut** (Windows), drag the application icon to the desktop. **To create an alias** (Macintosh), click on the application icon, select Make Alias from the File menu (or use the ⌘M key-combination), and drag it to your desktop.

Setting Up CU-SeeMe

When you first launch CU-SeeMe, you'll see a dialog box with a place to enter your program's registration number (**Figures 11.6** and **11.7** shown earlier). If you've purchased the program and already have the serial number, enter it and click OK. Otherwise, click the Demo button.

The Setup Assistant then launches and guides you through the setup in five steps. Follow the instructions and click the Next button after each step until you're finished. The Setup Assistant also displays dialog boxes in between each step, showing your progress so far. (Since the Windows and Macintosh versions of CU-SeeMe look almost identical, I will show mostly Windows illustrations for the rest of this chapter.)

Does setup count against demo time? If you're using CU-SeeMe in demo mode and haven't registered yet, don't worry about the time it takes to get the program set up. Setup Assistant time doesn't count toward the 30 minutes allotted to your demo.

Step 1

Provide information.

The first Setup Assistant dialog box (**Figure 11.8**) asks you to provide information about yourself. This information identifies you to other CU-SeeMe users when you join a group conference. Enter your first name, last name, your CU-SeeMe name (a short nickname), and your e-mail address. If you want, you can also tell people what city, state, and country you live in. Your CU-SeeMe name will appear on the title bar of your video window, and is also used if you choose to list yourself with an ILS server, as explained in Step 2.

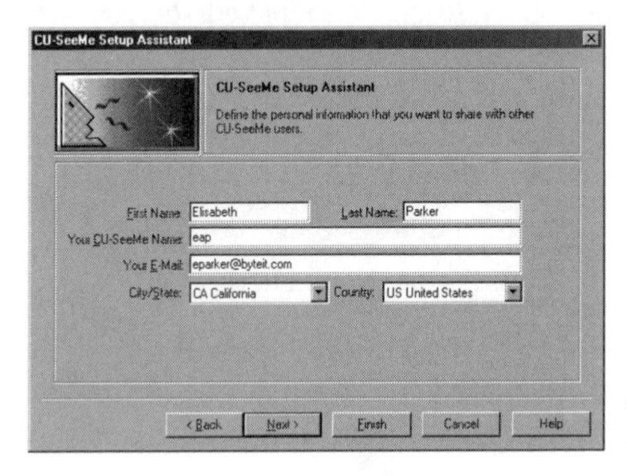

Figure 11.8 *Step 1 of the CU-SeeMe Setup Assistant.*

Step 2 **Help other users connect to you.**

The Setup Assistant asks if you want to make your CU-SeeMe name and e-mail address available to an Internet Locator Service (ILS), as shown in **Figure 11.9**. This enables other CU-SeeMe users to search for you and your e-mail address so they can call you. You'll read more about how ILS servers work later in this chapter.

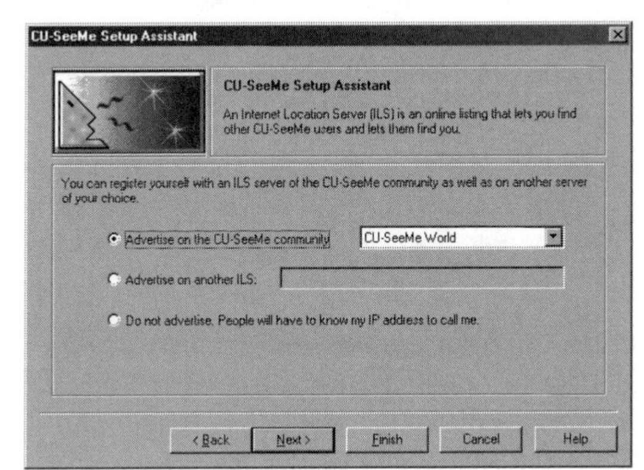

Figure 11.9 *Step 2 in CU-SeeMe setup.*

Choose one of the following ILS options:

- **Advertise on the CU-SeeMe community.** This option adds your CU-SeeMe name and e-mail address to an ILS server for CU-SeeMe users. You can choose a server from the list box. I recommend that you choose **ils.cuseeme.com**, the default ILS server.

- **Advertise on another ILS.** If you know of another ILS server or need to list yourself with one at work or school, choose this option and enter the URL (such as **ils.myserver.com**).
- **Do not advertise. People will have to know my IP address to call me.** If you're a more cautious type and prefer not to give out your e-mail address, select this option.

If you haven't decided whether or not to buy CU-SeeMe, don't list with an ILS server yet. When your name appears on an ILS, others may try to call you. And if you don't use CU-SeeMe (or Microsoft NetMeeting, which also supports ILS), they won't be able to reach you.

Define your network configuration.

Step 3

Next, the CU-SeeMe Setup Assistant needs to know how you connect to the Internet (through a modem or a network) and your connection speed (such as 33.3 Kbps or ISDN). From the Network list, select the option that describes your connection and connection speed. If you're not sure which settings to enter, or you don't see any options on the list that describe your Internet setup, or if you connect to the Internet through a firewall (as explained in Chapter 13), ask your ISP or network administrator to help with this step.

Define your video source.

Step 4

The Setup Assistant next asks you to define your video source, shows you a preview of your video, and creates your Contact Card, as shown in **Figure 11.10**. If your picture isn't displaying properly, click the Device button to display your cam settings so you can make adjustments (covered in Chapter 2).

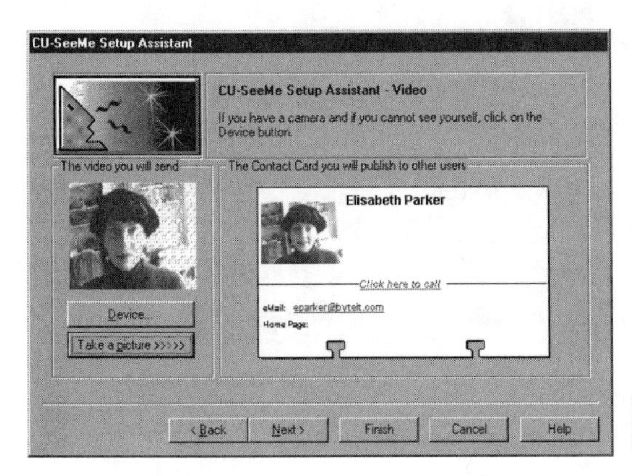

Figure 11.10 *Setting up video for CU-SeeMe.*

To put your picture on your Contact Card, click the Take a Picture button. **Contact Cards** are like cyberspace business cards. When you conference with people, you can exchange Contact Cards and put them in your Phone Book, as covered later in this chapter.

Step 5 **Define your audio source.**

In this step, the SetUp Assistant helps you define your audio source—which means testing your microphone and speakers to make sure they work, as shown in **Figure 11.11**. To test your microphone, start talking. If the audio indicator (above the Microphone Volume control on the left side of the dialog box) displays sound waves in neon green, your microphone is working. To test your speakers, click the Test button (at the bottom of the Speaker control area), and a test message will play for you.

You can also adjust your audio settings. To set the sound levels, slide the Microphone and Speaker volume controls to the right (louder) or left (softer). Additional settings are available for both microphone and speakers, available by clicking the Device buttons. For now, however, in most cases I recommend that you make your life easier and just stick with the default sound settings. Chapter 14 tells you more about the various audio settings and what they mean.

Figure 11.11 *Setting up audio for CU-SeeMe.*

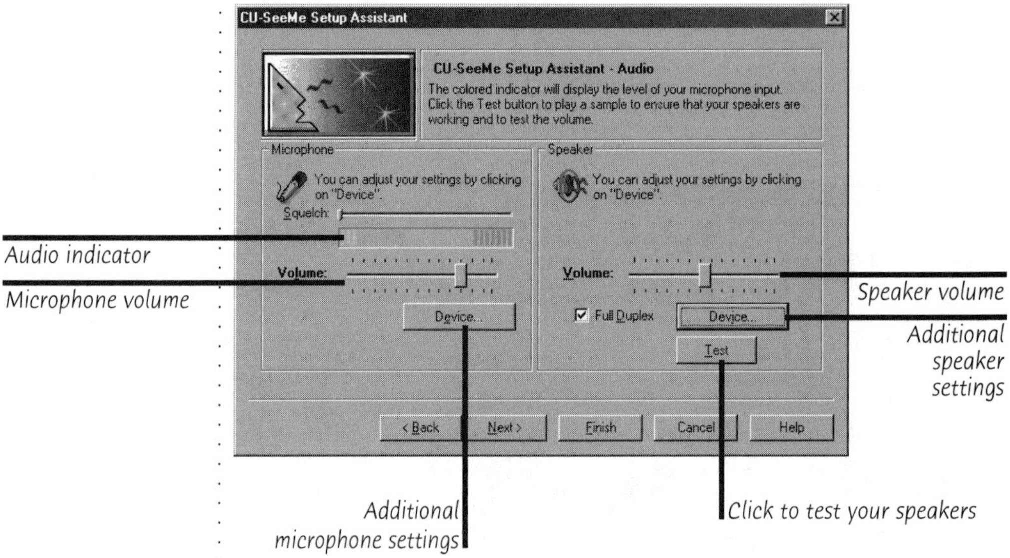

Audio indicator

Microphone volume

Speaker volume

Additional speaker settings

Additional microphone settings

Click to test your speakers

If Your Microphone and Speakers Don't Work... Make sure your microphone and speakers are properly connected—you'd be surprised at how often people disconnect them by mistake! Luckily, many computers come with built-in microphones and speakers these days, which eliminates that problem.

Step 6

Ready to Roll!

When you finish Step 5 and click the Next button, a dialog box appears and says "Congratulations! You are now ready to run CU-SeeMe." Click the Finish button to launch the program and begin videoconferencing.

Launching CU-SeeMe

Once you've set up CU-SeeMe, you can start it up any time by going to Start|Programs|CU-SeeMe, and then selecting the CU-SeeMe icon from the cascading menu (Windows), or by double-clicking the CU-SeeMe application icon (Macintosh). Depending on your Internet settings, your computer will either dial up your Internet account or display your dialer application and ask if you want to connect to your account.

Once you're connected, CU-SeeMe launches and the QuickStart & Tips dialog box appears, as shown in **Figure 11.12**. To display additional helpful tips, click the Next button. (If you'd prefer to stop the Tips screen from appearing in the future, deselect the checkbox for Show This Welcome Screen next time...)

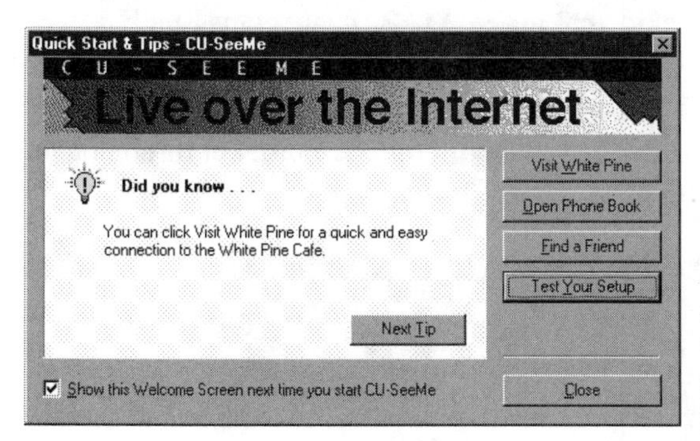

Figure 11.12
QuickStart & Tips dialog box (shown in Windows).

Open the Phone Book

From the QuickStart & Tips dialog box, click the Open Phone Book button to display the Phone Book window. Since all videoconferences start with a phone call, the Phone Book window is where you'll begin.

Videoconference Types

When it comes to videoconferencing, there are four basic types of conferences. Some videoconferencing programs only support one or two types of conferencing. With CU-SeeMe, you can participate in any of the following:

Point-to-Point Conference: In this conference you'll talk one-on-one with an individual, as you would with a phone call. To call someone, you need to know their e-mail address (if both of you are listed on the same ILS server, as explained later in this chapter) or their IP address (also covered later in this chapter).

Group Conference: Think of group conferences as online chat rooms; they have audio and video, as well as text chat. You can meet with many people at once at a group conference. In order to participate, you need to connect to a server that hosts conference groups. The CU-SeeMe Contact List gets you started with a list of public conference servers.

Cybercast: Cybercasts are similar to television broadcasts—the host talks and displays his/her video, while visitors simply watch and listen. Cybercasting is ideal for online teaching, training, and presentations.

Multicasting: In a multicast, a CU-SeeMe user can set up or join a group conference with other CU-SeeMe users without going through a server.

Making Your First Call

With CU-SeeMe, making your first phone call is easy. The CU-SeeMe Phone Book, illustrated in **Figure 11.13**, even comes with a list of Contact Cards to help you get started. For this example, let's start off connecting to a group conference from the CU-SeeMe Phone Book's list of Contact Cards. We'll talk about point-to-point conferencing later in this chapter, so you can call up Grandma, too.

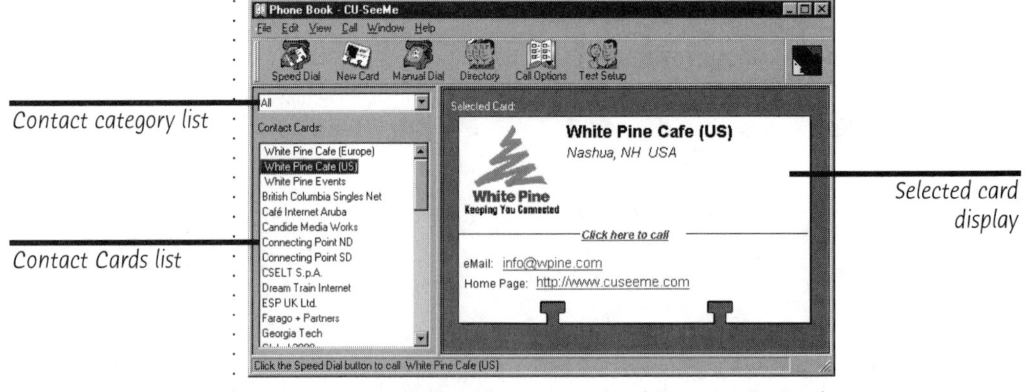

Figure 11.13 *The CU-SeeMe Phone Book (shown in Windows).*

Phone Book window elements:

- **Contact Category**: A drop-down list with categories of Contact Cards, similar to the folders in which you store your Netscape Navigator bookmarks or Internet Explorer favorites. Later you'll see how to create your own Card categories.
- **Contact Cards**: A scrolling list of Contact Cards with information for connecting to group videoconferences. You can add your own Contact Cards for group conferences, cybercasts, and individuals.
- **Display for Selected Card**: Shows the card you select from the Contact Cards list. Information may include a name, a logo or photograph, and links to the individual or organization's conference server, e-mail address, and/or Web site address.

Joining a Group Conference

Group conferences and cybercasts are hosted on **reflectors**—servers that are set up especially for hosting CU-SeeMe group conferences and cybercasts. The term "reflector" comes from an old server product from White Pine. Although that product has been replaced with White Pine's MeetingPoint Conference Server, most CU-SeeMe users still refer to conference rooms as reflectors.

When you connect to an individual, you can only talk to one person at a time (although CU-SeeMe's multicast conferencing feature also lets you set up your own group conferences with other CU-SeeMe users, without a reflector). Reflectors, on the other hand, can handle hundreds of users at once.

To connect to a group conference:

1. Select an item from the Category list (since you haven't created any categories yet, leave All selected for now).
2. Click on an item from the Contact Cards list. For now, choose White Pine Café (US).
3. When the selected Contact Card appears, click on the Click Here to Call link. The Connection dialog box appears and displays a list of conferences (**Figure 11.14**).
4. Select a conference from the list, and click the Join button. The Connection dialog box will then usually display a message (generally referred to as a **Message of the Day**, or **MOTD** for short). See **Figure 11.15**.

Feeling Shy?
If you want to get a feel for videoconferencing but aren't up to meeting other people yet, connect to the White Pine server and select the Self Reflector Test 1 or Test 2 conference room. The test rooms make it easy for you to get your feet wet without the pressure of talking to other people.

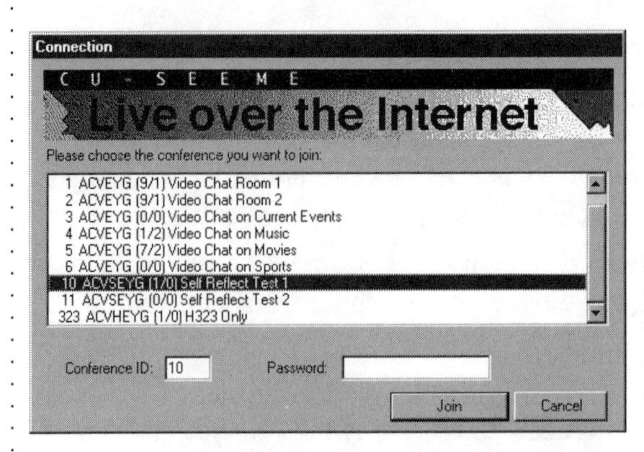

Figure 11.14
Connection dialog box with list of conferences displayed (shown in Windows).

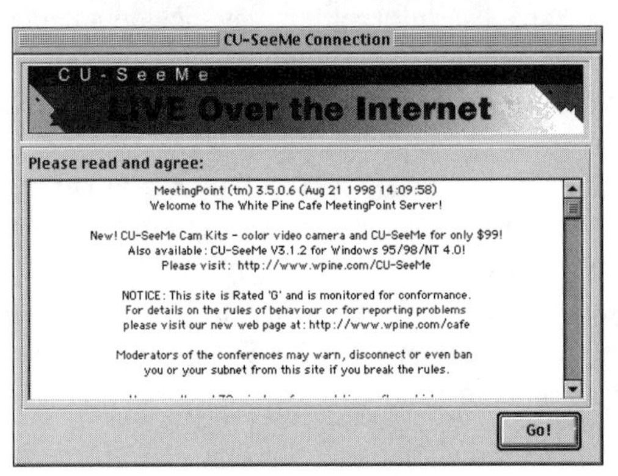

Figure 11.15
Connection dialog box with a Message of the Day displayed (shown in Macintosh).

What about the Conference ID and Password boxes?

The conferences on the Contact List that comes with CU-SeeMe are all open to the public, and do not require entry of a Conference ID or Password in the Connection dialog box. If you connect to a private conference offered through work, school, or a subscription service, the server administrator will assign you a Conference ID number and Password for that conference.

5. Click the Agree button to indicate that you have read the MOTD and agree with the rules and guidelines listed for the conference.

The MOTD generally provides a description of the conference and the rules for participating, or it may announce upcoming events, products, and services offered by the organization that runs the server. In some cases, you may be asked to change your Send and Receive rates.

Congratulations! You've entered the Conference Room. After a quick discussion on Reflector Etiquette, I'll show you how to find your way around the conference room and talk to people.

Reflector Etiquette

Group conferences are a lot like real-life social gatherings. You don't just barge in. Instead, you hang back a little to see what people are talking about. Then you look for an opening and politely step in and introduce yourself. This also gives you time to get a feel for the conference room and decide whether you want to join the conversation.

> **Squeaky Clean.** If you're a concerned parent, or you simply prefer not to encounter stuff on the 'Net that you consider offensive, you can relax. The Contact List that comes with CU-SeeMe will hook you up only with Web sites that are suitable for most folks. In addition, most reflectors display a Message of the Day that describes conference topics, so you can decide for yourself whether or not to join in.

Now let's take a look at the guidelines for participants' behavior in group conferences.

Mind your p's and q's

If you're new to chatting online, remember that you always need to **make an extra effort to be nice**. You're probably thinking, "Of course I'll be nice—I'm always nice!" But instant face-to-face communication has its drawbacks. You don't have as much time to think, for instance, as you do when composing an e-mail message. And it's harder for people to gauge one another's body language when they're talking via a computer screen. Humor (especially deadpan sarcasm) may be misunderstood as bad-mouthing, insulting, critical, and so forth. Even the mildest negative comments can come across *way* more harshly than you intended!

Follow the rules

As mentioned, reflectors often publish a Message of the Day that appears before you log on. In most cases, the person running the conference posts a **list of guidelines** for people participating in the conference. Make sure to read the rules carefully! Sometimes the MOTD simply lists topics, conference hours, and upcoming events. Other reflectors require you to change some of your settings (as explained later in this chapter) in order to conserve bandwidth.

Don't be a bandwidth hog

Bandwidth refers to resources, such as connections and servers, that handle all the data people send back and forth over the Internet and through servers. People who run free public reflectors do so out of the goodness of their hearts—they sure don't get paid for it. So don't stay around and yak away forever, and avoid sending lots of high-bandwidth audio messages back and forth unless you're invited to do so.

What's In a Conference Room?

When you enter a conference room, a new window appears with the name of the conference on the title bar and a toolbar with common videoconferencing functions. In addition, you'll find a list of participants, video windows, controls for sending and receiving audio messages, and a Chat window for typing and reading text chat messages. **Figures 11.16** and **11.17** illustrate conference rooms from the Windows and Macintosh versions of CU-SeeMe.

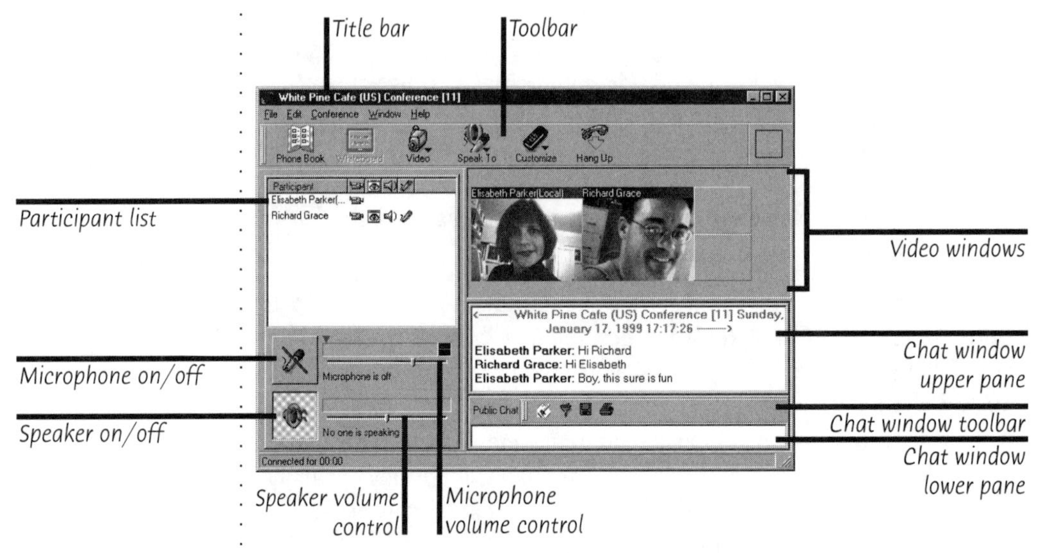

Figure 11.16 *Conference room shown in Windows.*

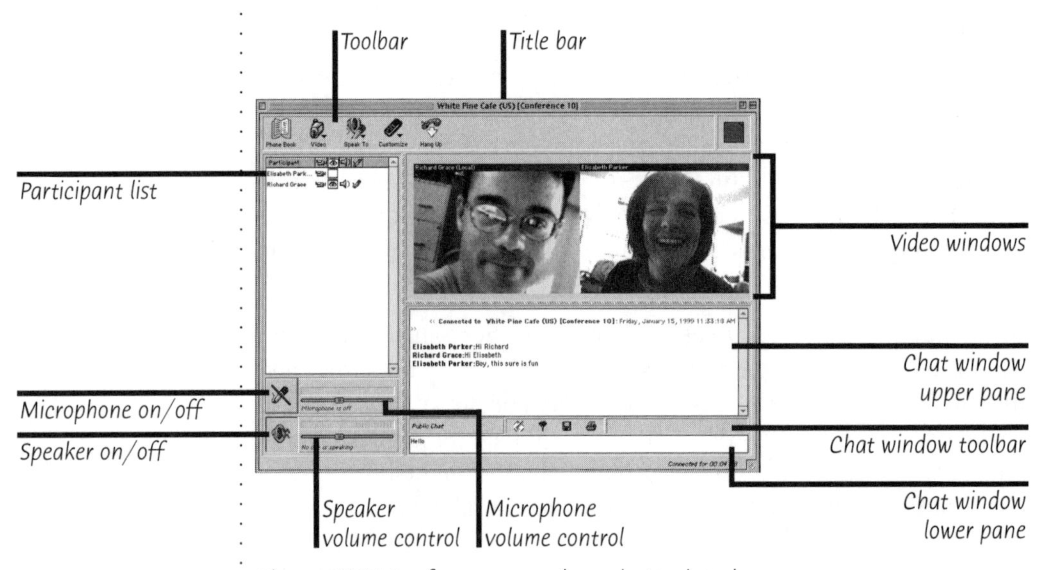

Figure 11.17 *Conference room shown in Macintosh.*

Conference room elements:

- **Title bar:** Displays the name of the conference room.
- **Toolbar:** Icons for frequently used videoconferencing functions.
- **Participant list:** Shows a list of people in the conference room and provides information about their videoconferencing setups (as explained later in this chapter).
- **Video windows:** Images and CU-SeeMe names of people in the conference room who have their video turned on.
- **Chat window:** In this area there's a place to see text chat messages, a box for typing in chat messages, and some icons for frequently used chat functions.
- **Microphone on/off switch**
- **Microphone volume control:** For adjusting the volume on your outgoing audio messages.
- **Speaker on/off switch**
- **Speaker volume control:** For adjusting the volume on incoming audio messages.

Text Chat

If you plan to do videoconferencing on reflectors, you may wind up using the Chat window a lot. That's because some conference hosts discourage visitors from sending audio messages (it slows down the server). If you've checked out chat rooms on America Online or on the Internet, then the CU-SeeMe Chat window, as shown in **Figure 11.18**, should look familiar to you. Text chat is the simplest means for instant communication via the Internet.

Figure 11.18 *Chat window (shown in Windows)*

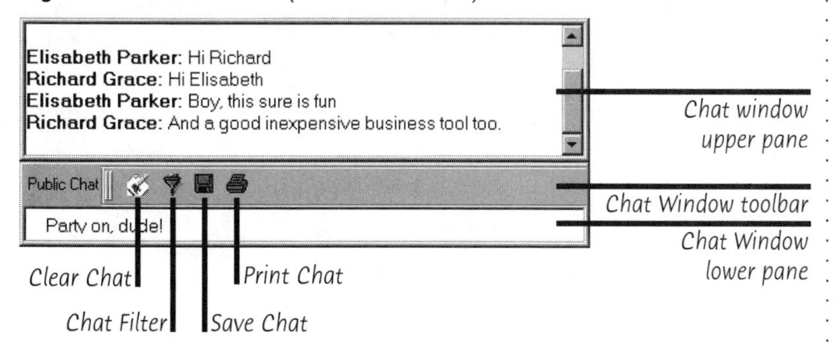

Chat window components:

- **Chat window upper pane**: For reading text chat messages. Each message is preceded by the sender's CU-SeeMe name.
- **Chat window toolbar**: Icons for executing frequently used text chat functions.
- **Chat window lower pane**: For typing and sending text chat messages.

Using Text Chat

To send a text chat message:

Type your text in the Chat window's lower pane and press Enter or Return. The text message appears in the Chat window's upper pane as it is sent.

To read text chat messages:

Messages appear in the Chat window's upper pane as people send them. To read them, scroll through the list.

To send a private text chat message:

Private text chat messages are messages you want to send to another person in the conference room without sending it to everyone else. To send a private message, select Conference|Chat to, choose a name from the cascading list, type your message, and press Return or Enter. You can then return to the general conversation by selecting Conference|Chat to again, and choose Everybody from the cascading list. A check mark appears next to your choice on the Chat to list.

To clear messages from the Chat window's lower pane:

Click the Clear button on the Chat window toolbar, and you'll have a clean slate.

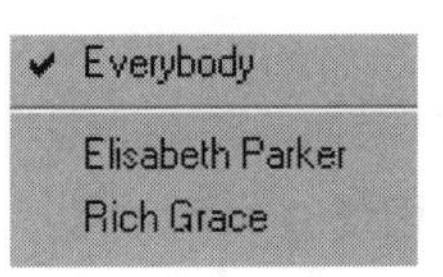

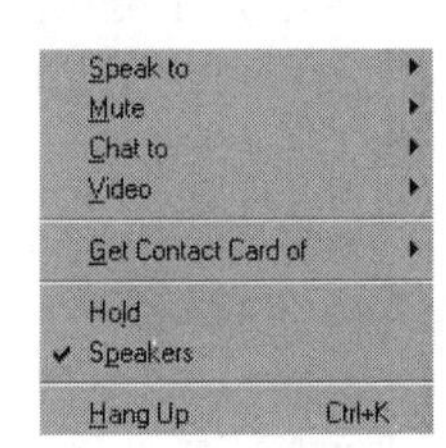

Unwanted Messages

To exclude a text chat participant:

If you find a particular conference participant annoying, you can use the Chat Filter feature to exclude their messages. Here's how it works:

1. Click the Chat Filter button in the Chat window toolbar. The Customize dialog box appears with the Chat Extensions tab selected, as shown in **Figure 11.19**.
2. In the Include List on the left, select the conference participant you want to exclude.
3. Click the Exclude button to move the selected participant over to the Exclude list on the right.
4. Click OK to save your changes and return to the conference.

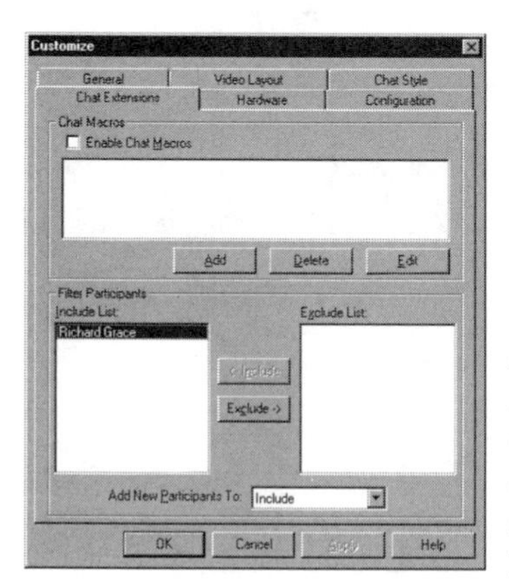

Figure 11.19 *Use the Chat Extensions tab of the Customize dialog box (shown here in Windows) to block a participant's messages from your Chat window.*

Saving and Printing Chats

Sometimes a conference gets so interesting that you've just gotta save it. Or maybe you meet online with people from work—usually it's a good idea to save the meeting's text chat transcript.

You can **save a transcript** of the current conference by clicking the Save button in the Chat window toolbar. When the Save dialog box appears, name your file and save it to a folder. You can open the file later in a word processor or text editor.

Printing out a transcript of the current conference is just as easy—click the Print button in the toolbar.

Sending and Receiving Audio

CU-SeeMe makes it easy for you to start talking online. The Audio window, as shown in **Figures 11.20** (Windows) and **11.21** (Macintosh), contains controls for turning your microphone and speakers off and on, as well as various status indicators and status messages.

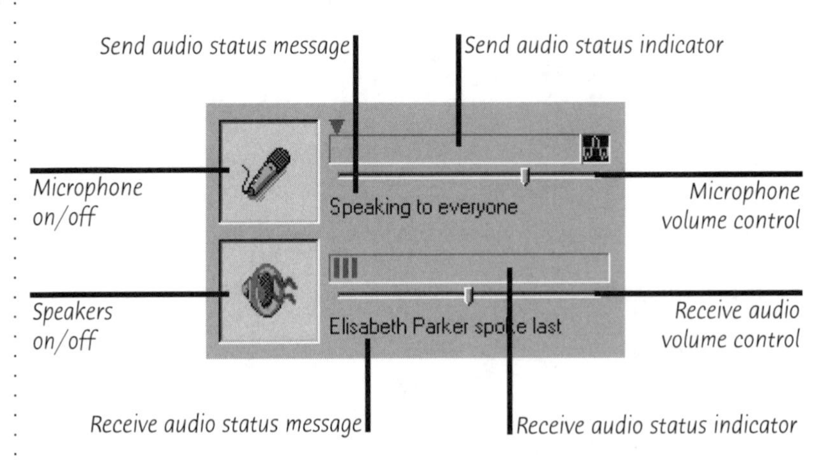

Figure 11.20 *Audio window (shown in Windows).*

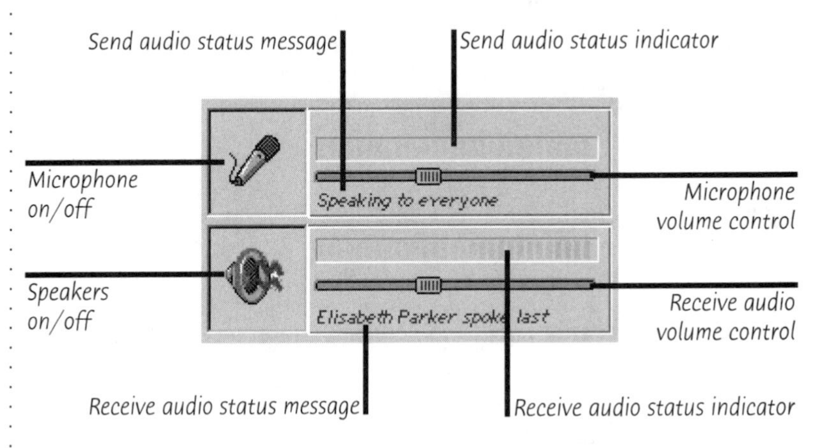

Figure 11.21 *Audio window (shown in Macintosh).*

The Audio Window

Audio window components:

- **Microphone on/off**: For turning on your microphone so you can send audio messages.
- **Send audio status indicator**: Displays a sound wave when you talk.

- **Microphone volume control**: For adjusting the volume on your outgoing messages.
- **Send audio status message**: Indicates whether you're sending audio messages to the entire group (Everyone), or a private message to someone in the conference room.
- **Speakers on/off**: For turning your speakers on or off. You need to turn your speakers on in order to hear incoming audio messages.
- **Receive audio status indicator**: Displays a sound wave when someone sends you an audio message.
- **Receive audio volume control**: For adjusting the volume on incoming messages.
- **Receive audio status message**: Displays status messages that tell you who's talking (when someone is sending audio) or who last spoke.

To receive audio messages:

In order to hear incoming audio messages when other people speak to you, make sure your speakers are on by clicking the Speakers On/Off button. When the speakers are turned on, the button looks as though you've pressed it down. A red diagonal line appears on the button when the speakers are off.

To send audio messages:

In order to send an audio message, turn your microphone on by clicking the Microphone On/Off button. When the microphone is turned on, the button looks as though you've pressed it down. A red diagonal line appears on the button when the microphone is off.

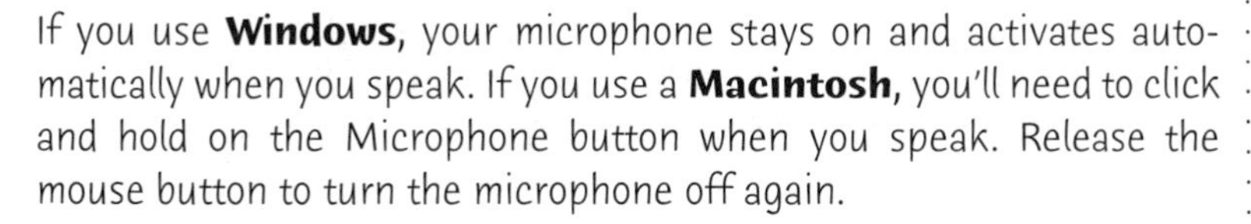

If you use **Windows**, your microphone stays on and activates automatically when you speak. If you use a **Macintosh**, you'll need to click and hold on the Microphone button when you speak. Release the mouse button to turn the microphone off again.

To send a private audio message:

As with text chat messages, you can send private audio messages to individuals in the conference room. To talk with someone privately, select Conference|Speak to, choose a name from the cascading list, and start talking. When you're ready to return to the general conversation, select Conference|Speak to again and choose Everybody from the cascading list. A check mark appears next to the name you choose.

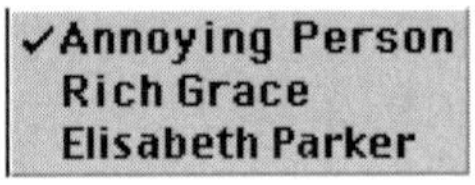

✓Annoying Person
Rich Grace
Elisabeth Parker

To turn off someone's audio:

Well, you can't *really* turn someone else's audio on or off. Just because you can connect to people via the Internet doesn't mean you can control their computers! But you *can* keep people from sending *you* audio messages. Why would you want to do a mean thing like that? There are a couple of reasons: Once in a while, someone may use audio settings that your sound card doesn't support—which means you can't hear them anyway. Or maybe you just find someone downright annoying.

To turn off someone's audio, select Mute from the Conference menu; then select the person's name. To turn their audio back on, select their name from the list again. When you mute a person, a check mark appears next to their name.

Sending and Receiving Video

When you enter a conference room, CU-SeeMe displays video windows for people in the conference room. Each video window, displayed within your main video window, has its own title bar with the person's CU-SeeMe name on it. In addition, you'll see your own video window in the upper-left corner of the main window. Your own video window is called the **local video window**. Other people's windows are called **remote video windows**.

To show and hide video windows:

Naturally, you'll want to see the people with whom you're conferencing. In most situations, you'll want to see everyone's video windows when you visit a conference room. But too many open video windows can slow your system down. And sometimes you won't be able to see everyone in the conference room unless you close a few video windows first.

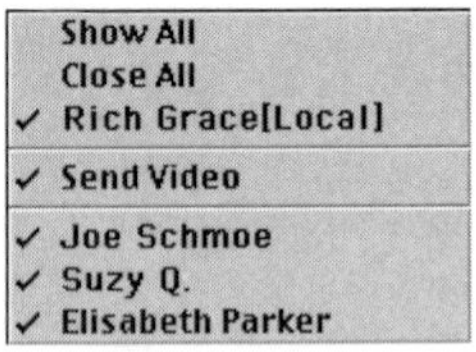

Show All
Close All
✓ Rich Grace[Local]
✓ Send Video
✓ Joe Schmoe
✓ Suzy Q.
✓ Elisabeth Parker

Luckily, it's easy to show and hide video windows. In CU-SeeMe's main toolbar, click the Video icon to display the Video menu (or select Video from the Conference menu. Then choose an option from the list. You can select Show All or Close All to display or hide everyone's video windows, or select the name of one or more specific participants. When a check mark appears next to a person's name, the video window is displayed. Shown here is the Video menu on a Mac; the Windows version is virtually identical.

Who's There?

Feeling a little nosy? When you connect to a conference, you can find out more about the people with whom you're conferencing. And you can relax—CU-SeeMe won't reveal those "permanent records" that grown-ups threaten their kids with when they misbehave. But you *can* find out the person's nickname, or whether they can send and receive audio and video, and which version of CU-SeeMe they use.

The Participant List

Let's see how to find out about conference participants. First, look at your Participant list, as shown in **Figure 11.22**. Participants come in three flavors: **visible users, hidden users, and lurkers.** Visible users send video, and you can see their remote video window on your computer screen. Hidden users are also sending video, but you don't have their remote video window open for some reason (perhaps you turned it off, as explained in the preceding section).

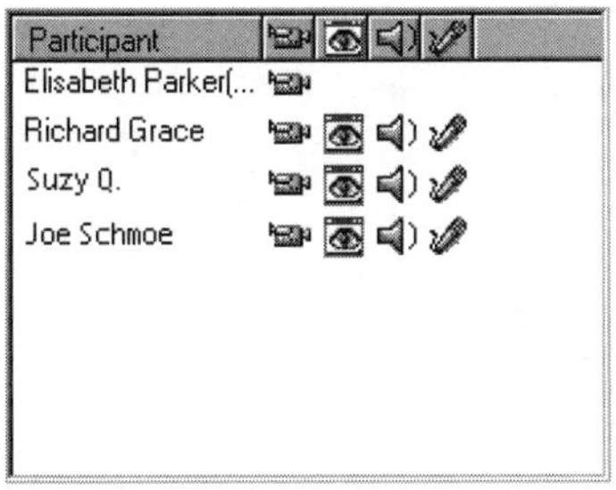

Participant
Elisabeth Parker(...
Richard Grace
Suzy Q.
Joe Schmoe

Figure 11.22
Participant list (shown in Windows).

The following table explains the icons you see beside participants' names.

Participant List Icons

Icon	Tells You This About the Participant
	Sends video: The participant has a cam and is sending video.
	**Is displaying your video window:** The participant has your video window displayed on their computer.
	**Has hidden your video window:** The participant isn't viewing your video window, possibly because there are many people in the conference room and the participant only wants to display certain video windows.
	Is receiving audio: You can send audio to the participant. The participant has speakers and has not muted your audio.
	Can send audio: The participant has a microphone and can send audio messages.

You can tell who the lurkers are.

The term *lurkers* sounds kind of creepy, but it'll be familiar to you if you've been in any Internet chat rooms. It simply refers to people who aren't fully participating—in this case, not sending video or audio, possibly because they don't have a cam. You can tell who the lurkers are because audio or video icons (or both) won't be displayed next to their names on the Participant list.

Getting More Information

When you want to know even *more* information about someone in the conference, you can check out the person's **Info window**. In **Windows**, right-click a name on the Participant list and select Info from the shortcut menu. **Macintosh** users can display the Info window by clicking a name in the Participant list and selecting Conference|Get Participant Info.

From the Info window, you can display various types of information by selecting the following tabs:

Version: Tells you which videoconferencing program and operating system the person is using, as shown in **Figure 11.23**. The Version tab also displays the person's IP address, as explained later in this chapter.

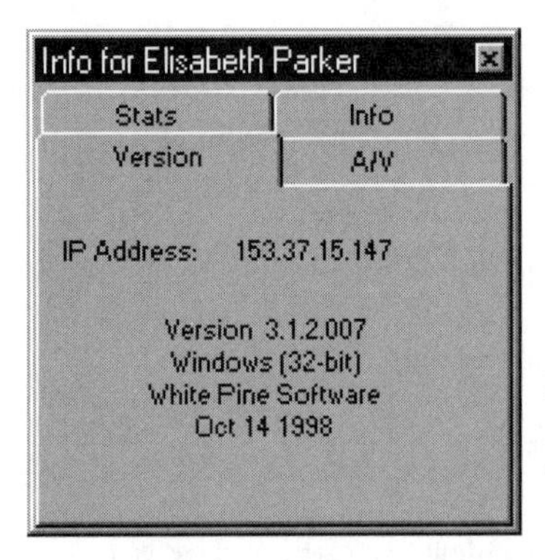

Figure 11.23 *Participant information dialog box with Version tab selected (shown in Windows).*

What's a Codec?
Codec *is short for* ***co****mpressor/****dec****ompressor—software that compresses audio and video files for storage or transmitting over the Internet, and then decompresses the data when the audio and video are played. Most programs for recording and editing audio and video, including QuickEditor, come with codecs. For more about video codecs, see Chapter 6; and for audio codecs, see Chapter 14.*

A/V: This tab, shown in **Figure 11.24**, displays information about the person's audio/video codecs (see sidebar). With White Pine CU-SeeMe, the default video codec is White Pine MJPEG, and the default audio codec is Delta-Mod. These standard settings allow just about anyone to see and hear one another. If you're in a conference and find that you cannot see or hear someone, check their A/V information. They may be using a codec that your computer doesn't understand.

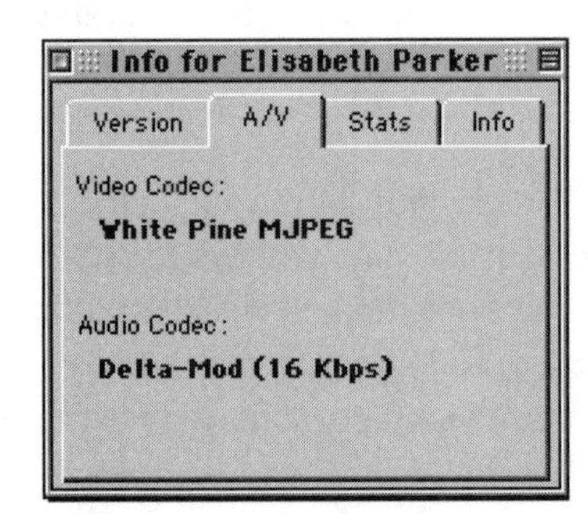

Figure 11.24 *A participant's audio/visual information in the Info window (shown in Macintosh).*

Getting More Information (cont.)

Stats: This tab shows the rate at which the participant is sending and receiving data (**Figure 11.25**). CU-SeeMe sets up your sending and receiving rates based on your modem's speed. This information may not look terribly exciting, but it can help experienced users to troubleshoot problems when they occur during a conference.

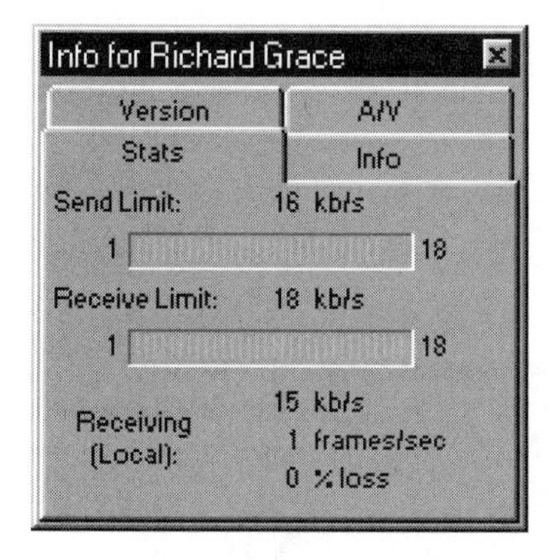

Figure 11.25 *The Stats tab of a participant's Info window (shown in Windows).*

Info: If you ever forget what those icons mean on the Participant list, you can look it up here (**Figure 11.26**). Select a participant, display the Info window, and click the Info tab.

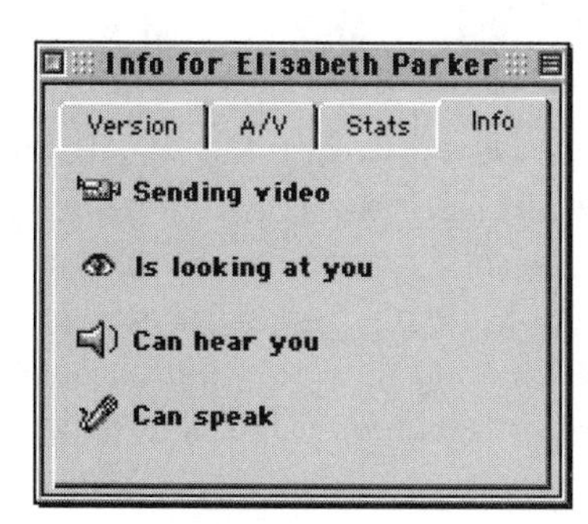

Figure 11.26 *The icons on the Participant list are explained in the Info tab (shown here in Macintosh).*

Point-to-Point Conferencing

Point-to-point conferencing gives you an easy way to stay in touch with friends and family, or talk with coworkers who live far away. However, calling up individuals is a little trickier than calling up a reflector. First, you need to catch someone while they're sitting at their computer. And secondly, you either have to know the person's IP address, or be listed on the same ILS server (which allows you to call a person by entering their e-mail address). For more about IP addresses and ILS servers, read on.

Making a Call

To call an individual:

1. In CU-SeeMe's toolbar, click the Manual Dial button, or select Manual Dial from the Conference menu. This displays the Manual Dial dialog box (**Figure 11.27**).
2. Open the General tab of the Manual Dial dialog box. Type the IP address, then click the Manual Dial button.
3. The Connection dialog box will be displayed until the other person accepts your call. If the other person answers, you'll see the Go! button. Click the Go! button to start conferencing. If the person does not answer, click the Cancel button to end your connection attempt.

Figure 11.27 *Manual dialog box with General tab selected (shown in Windows).*

Macintosh only

Richard Grace (Local)

Elisabeth Parker

Attention Mac Users: If you use CU-SeeMe on a Macintosh, the icons on your Participant list will look different when you do point-to-point videoconferencing. Not to worry—you can still get information about the person with whom you're talking. Simply display the Info window by clicking the person's name and selecting Get Participant Info from the Conference menu, as you would during a group videoconference.

What's My IP Address?

IP addresses are sets of numbers used on the Internet to specify locations for all the servers and computers that are out there. Every computer connected to the Internet, including yours, has an IP address.

If you want people to call you, then you need to give them your IP address. To find out your own IP address, follow these steps:

Windows only

If you use Windows—

1. Dial up your Internet account.
2. Click the Start button, and select Run to display the Run dialog box.
3. Type **winipcfg** in the Open box, and click OK.

The IP Configuration dialog box appears, as shown in **Figure 11.28**, and displays your IP address in the IP Address box. (My computer is connected to a network via Ethernet, so your dialog box may not look exactly the same as the one shown here.)

4. Click OK to close the IP Configuration dialog box—after jotting down your address, of course!

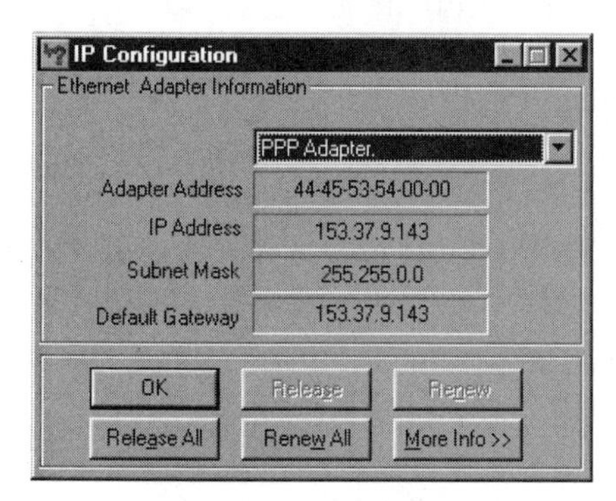

Figure 11.28 *Get your IP address from the Windows IP Configuration dialog box.*

What's My IP address?

Macintosh only

If you use a Macintosh—

1. Dial up your Internet account.
2. Select Control Panels from the Apple menu.
3. Select TCP/IP from the cascading menu to display the TCP/IP dialog box (**Figure 11.29**).
4. Look for the number that appears next to the IP Address item, and jot it down.
5. To close the TCP/IP dialog box, click the Close box on the upper-left.

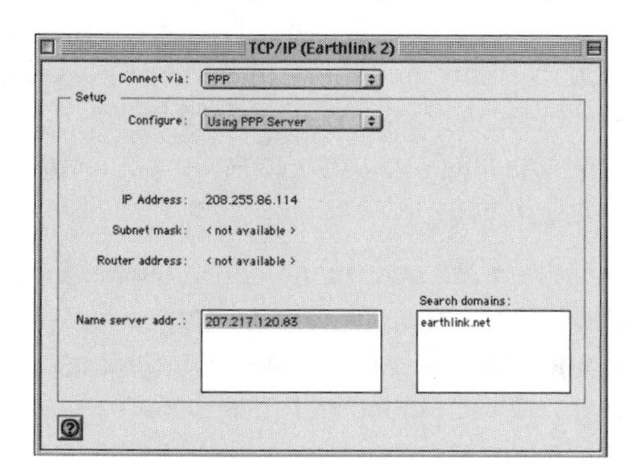

Figure 11.29 *TCP/IP dialog box with IP address (in Macintosh).*

Attention Network Users: If you're on a network, then **you've got two IP addresses**—one for the network and one for the Internet. If you run into problems understanding the two addresses, ask your system administrator for help. Also, Chapter 13 helps you troubleshoot CU-SeeMe if you get stuck.

Coping with Dynamic IP Addresses

Unfortunately, there's a problem with IP addresses—there aren't enough to go around for everyone on the Internet. To solve this, most ISPs assign IP addresses **dynamically**—which means that your IP address changes every time you connect. Needless to say, that's pretty darned annoying. (I mean, how would you like it if your phone company changed your phone number every time you made a call? People wouldn't be able to call you!)

Fortunately, there are two ways to get around this nuisance in videoconferencing. One solution is to use an ILS server and get everyone with whom you videoconference to use the same one, as explained in "Using an ILS Server" later in this chapter. Or you can use a freeware program called **ICQ** to set up conferences on the fly. Let's take a look at ICQ.

Rendezvous with ICQ

The ho-hum way to hook up with friends, family, and coworkers for a videoconference is to exchange traditional e-mail or phone messages to arrange a time. But that can sure take the fun out of things. On the other hand, ICQ (pronounced "I seek you") from Mirabilis and America Online comes to the rescue with a way to get connected that's a lot more spontaneous!

When you connect to the Internet, ICQ tells you if your buddies are online, too (if they have ICQ). You can send them an **instant message** and arrange a videoconference. ICQ comes in especially handy if your ISP assigns IP addresses dynamically—you can look up your current address and send that along with your instant message.

Instant messages announce you

What's an instant message? When you and the person you want to talk to are both online and have ICQ running, instant messages mean you can **exchange text messages in real-time.** When you type text and send it to someone, it appears on their computer in less than a second. America Online users are already accustomed to exchanging instant messages with other AOL members. Now ICQ brings this convenient way of communicating to the rest of us.

Getting ICQ

What if your pals and family don't have ICQ? That's not too likely with 20 million ICQ users and growing, but you can tell people who aren't yet connected to go and get it. At the time of this writing, the program is free and runs on Macintosh, Windows 95/98, Windows NT, Windows 3.x, and Linux. So there's no excuse for not having it! To download ICQ, learn how to use it, hook up with online communities, and more, visit the ICQ Web site (see **Figure 11.30**) at **http://www.icq.com/**.

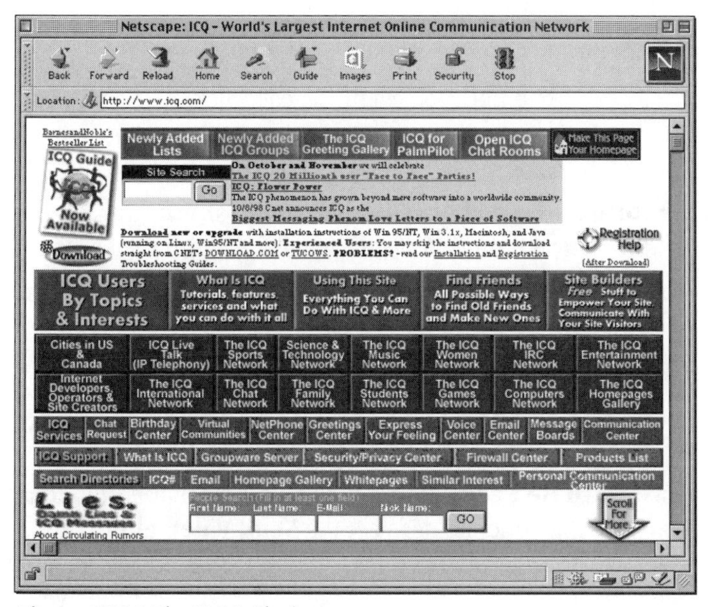

Figure 11.30 The ICQ Web site.

Receiving a Call

CU-SeeMe accepts calls from people whenever you're online—even if you don't have the program running. When you're online and someone calls you, CU-SeeMe makes a ringing sound and displays the Listener Status dialog box (for Windows, shown in **Figure 11.31**) or the Connection Request dialog box (for Macintosh, shown in **Figure 11.32**).

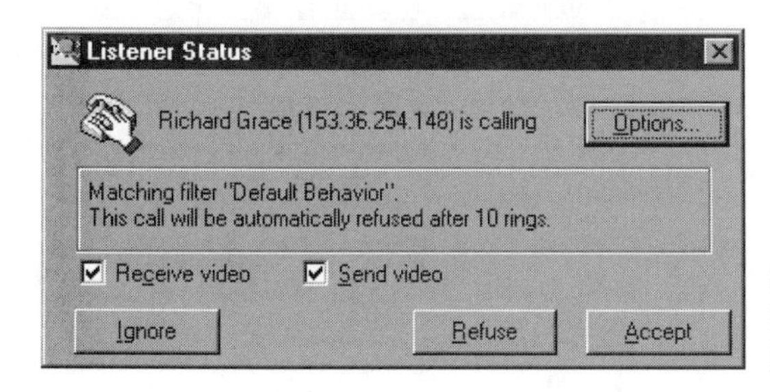

Figure 11.31 The Listener Status dialog box (Windows).

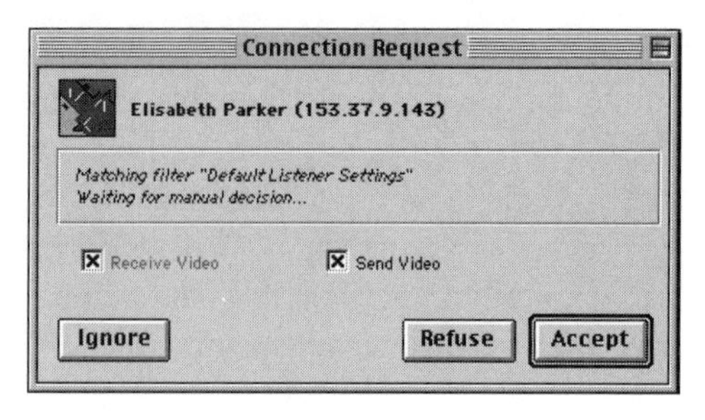

Figure 11.32 *The Connection Request dialog box (Macintosh).*

When receiving a call, you can do the following:

- **Accept the call**: To accept the call, click the Accept button. The Conference window then appears, so you can begin conferencing.
- **Refuse the call**: If you don't want to answer the call, click the Refuse button. A message will appear in the caller's Connection dialog box and tell them that the connection was refused.
- **Ignore the call**: You can also click the Ignore button to **refuse the call more politely**. No message will appear, and the caller will think you aren't online or aren't at your desk.

The polite way to refuse a call

Other Options for Receiving

Don't Want to Be Seen? Before clicking the Accept button to take a call, you have the option to deselect the **Send Video checkbox**. (Both Windows and Mac users have this option.) This comes in handy if you're having a bad hair day and don't want the caller to see you!

Turn Off Audio. If you want to conserve system resources, you can also deselect the **Send Audio checkbox** and stick with text and audio chat for your conference.

Calling Through an ILS

The IP address shortage, as explained earlier, kind of puts a damper on videoconferencing. Wouldn't you rather call someone for a chat using their e-mail address instead? You can do that with other CU-SeeMe users through an **Internet Locator Service (ILS)**. ILS servers store people's names and e-mail addresses. When you call someone through an ILS server, the ILS figures out the person's IP address so you don't have to. In order to call someone through an ILS, you need to know which ILS the person uses.

Dialing Up through an ILS

If you know the URL for someone's ILS server and their e-mail address, you can call them the same way you would call using an IP address. Unlike those dynamic IP addresses, though, ILS server names and e-mail addresses always stay the same! ILS server URLs begin with the letters **ils**, as in **ils.server.com**. Here are the steps to call someone through an ILS server:

1. From the Phone Book, click the Manual Dial icon in the toolbar, or select Manual Dial from the Call menu.
2. When the Manual Dial dialog box appears, type the person's ILS server and e-mail address, separated by a forward slash, like this: **ils.server.com/name@e-mail.com**
3. Click the Manual Dial button to put your call through.

Looking People Up

Whenever you aren't sure whether someone is listed with an ILS, go ahead and **look them up on the server.** Here are the steps:

1. From the Phone Book, click the Directory icon on the toolbar, or select Directory from the View menu. This displays the Directory dialog box (**Figure 11.33**).

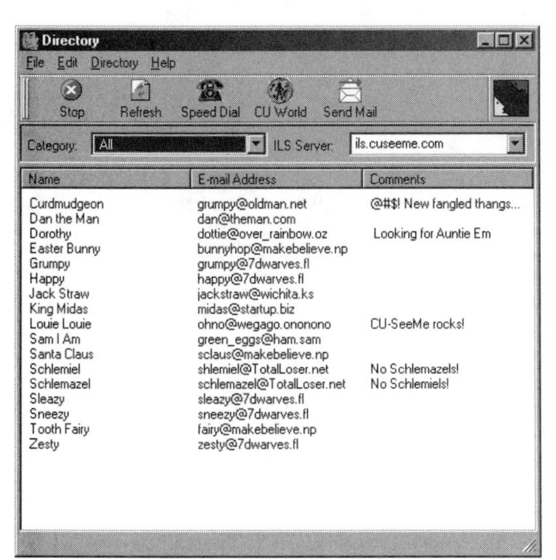

Figure 11.33 *Use the Directory dialog box to find someone on an ILS.*

2. Select an ILS server from the list.
3. Select an ILS from the ILS Server list. If the one you're looking for does not appear, you can add it to the list by typing the URL directly into the ILS Server box. Wait for the names and addresses to appear.

> *Many CU-SeeMe users are registered with* ***White Pine's ILS (ils.cuseeme.com)****, since the Setup Assistant automatically advertises you on that server unless you choose a different option.*

Note: When you load information from an ILS for the first time, it can take several minutes.

4. When the names and e-mail addresses finish loading, scroll down and look for the name and address you need.

Speed Search: If you know the person's name and/or e-mail address, and you just want to see if they are advertised on the ILS server, here's a faster way to do it. To search for the person **by name**, click the Name column heading in the Directory. To search for the person **by e-mail address**, click the E-mail Address column. Then begin typing the name or e-mail address you're looking for.

Once you've selected the person you want to contact, you can call them right now by selecting their name in the Directory and clicking the Speed Dial icon in the CU-SeeMe toolbar. Or, you can click the Send Mail button to send them an e-mail message.

Listing Yourself on an ILS Server

So how do you advertise yourself with an ILS server? When you start up CU-SeeMe for the first time, the **Setup Assistant** asks you to choose an ILS server—you may recall this from Step 2 of setting up the program. CU-SeeMe then automatically publishes your name and e-mail address with your specified ILS server. Other people can then access the server and call you by entering your e-mail address instead of an IP address.

Help people find you

If you have not yet published your information with an ILS server, you can do it through CU-SeeMe by changing your default ILS (this is explained later, in the section on changing Contact Cards). When you choose a default ILS, CU-SeeMe automatically advertises your information with that server.

I recommend that you choose **ils.cuseeme.com**—White Pine's ILS for CU-SeeMe users. There are also many other public ILS servers that you can register with, as covered in Chapter 12.

Getting Access to a Private ILS

If you only plan to do videoconferencing with certain individuals for business and academic purposes, and prefer not to make your e-mail address accessible to the whole online world, consider signing on with a **private ILS**. Your school, business, or employer may have a private ILS, and some ISPs also offer access to an ILS servers for their customers. Unlike the public ILSs, only authorized users have access to private ILS servers. Ask your network administrator or ISP for more information.

Managing Your Contacts

Typing people's e-mail or IP addresses into the Manual Dial dialog box gets to be a drag after a while. Luckily, you don't have to type your most-used ones over and over again. Instead, you can add people to your **Contact List**, or you can create new **Contact Cards** for individuals and group conferences.

The Contact List

The Contact List works sort of like Netscape Navigator bookmarks and Internet Explorer favorites. You create entries for the people you call most often, and then get in touch with them as easily as clicking a button. In order for your Contact List to work properly, the people you list there need to have an IP address (people who work at universities, large corporations, and Internet-related organizations, or who run their own servers, often do) or be registered with an ILS.

Select Contact List from the View menu. As shown in **Figure 11.34**, the Contact List window has a toolbar at the top, with icons for creating new groups and contacts, speed-dialing a selected contact, and displaying the Directory dialog box to access an ILS. In the main part of the window, you'll see folders for groups of contacts—for example, family, friends, and coworkers—as well as entries for individuals.

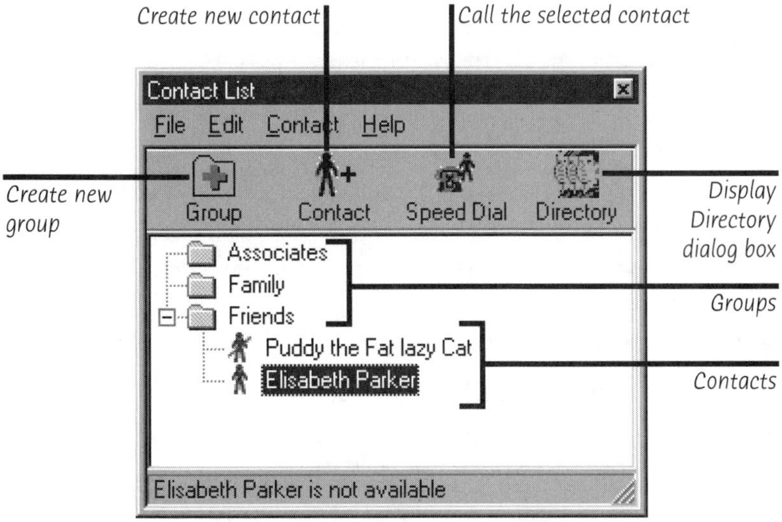

Create new contact

Call the selected contact

Create new group

Display Directory dialog box

Groups

Contacts

Figure 11.34 *Contact List (shown in Windows).*

Can we talk?

Once you've added contacts to your list, the icons beside their names tell you whether or not the person is online and available to conference with you. When you go online, display the Contact List and look at the icon to the left of each person's name.

Icon	Status
	This person is online and available for a videoconference call.
	This person is either not online or not available for a videoconference call.

Speed dialing from the Contact List

If you've added someone to your Contact List, and they're available to talk, you can call them straight from the Contact List window. Simply select their name and click the **Speed Dial** icon in the toolbar to put a call through.

Creating New Contacts

You can look someone up on an ILS through the Directory dialog box, as covered earlier in this chapter, and add them to your Contact List. You can also add a brand-new contact from scratch.

To create a new contact from an ILS directory:

Follow the earlier instructions for looking someone up on an ILS through the Directory dialog box (see "Looking People Up"). Then add them to your Contact List following these steps:

1. From the Contact List dialog box, click the Directory button to display the Directory dialog box.
2. Select the appropriate ILS server from the ILS Server box (or type in a new ILS server to add it to the list, and select it).
3. In the main window of the Directory, locate the name and e-mail address you need.
4. Drag it to the Contact List window.

To create a new contact from scratch:

1. From the Contact List dialog box, click the Contact icon in the toolbar to display the New Contact dialog box, shown in **Figure 11.35**.
2. Enter the person's nickname in the Nickname box.
3. In the ILS/E-mail box, enter the person's IP address (if they have one), or type their ILS server and e-mail address, separated by a forward slash, like this: **ils.server.com/person@e-mailaddress.com**
4. Click OK to return to the Contact List window.

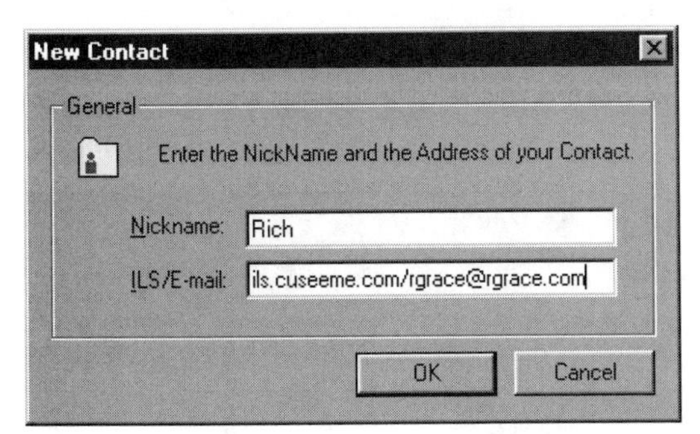

Figure 11.35
Adding a new contact.

Creating a New Group

You can create groups to organize your contacts. When you create a new group, CU-SeeMe adds a folder to your Contact List window. You can then move your contacts into the appropriate folder.

From the Contact List dialog box, click the Group icon in the toolbar. CU-SeeMe adds a new folder to the Contact List window, names it "Untitled," and highlights the name. Type a new name for the group folder, and your new group is ready for use.

Organizing Contacts

Once you create your Contact List folders and entries, you can organize and display them in the following ways:

- **Organize contacts into groups**: To move a contact into the appropriate group (folder), just select the contact and drag it into a folder.
- **Display a list of the contacts in a group**: To display a list of contacts in a particular group, click on the folder icon for a group. The folder then expands to show the list of names. Groups that contain contact names appear with a + symbol next to the folder. An expanded folder will have a – symbol next to it.

- **Hide a group of contact names**: You can also hide (collapse) the list of names for a group by clicking on the – symbol next to the folder.
- **Delete names and folders**: To remove a contact name or entire folder, select the item and press Del, or select Delete from the Edit menu.

Using Contact Cards

Remember the CU-SeeMe Phone Book and list of Contact Cards? As you explore the world of videoconferencing and start discovering new group conferences, you can create

Contact Card Info: *There's a section on changing information on Contact Cards, coming up.*

new Contact Cards for them. From the Phone Book, click the New Card icon in the toolbar, and the Contact Card Assistant will take you through the steps.

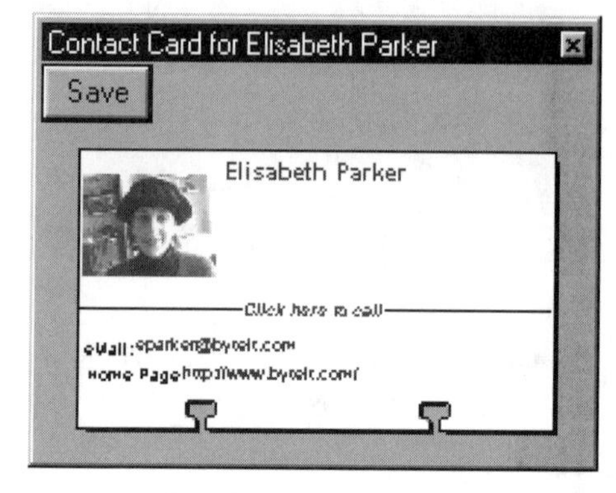

Exchanging Contact Cards: If you like someone you meet during a videoconference and want to talk with them again, you can exchange cards just as you do in real life! When participating in a video conference, grab a participant's Contact Card by selecting Conference|Get Contact Card Of and selecting a name from the cascading list. When the Get Contact Card dialog box appears with the person's Contact Card, click the Save button to add the card to the Contact Card list in your Phone Book.

Customizing Your Settings

When you use the CU-SeeMe Setup Assistant, it automatically configures CU-SeeMe according to your information. It's unlikely you'll ever have to change your settings, since the CU-SeeMe Setup Assistant knows what's best for your type of cam and connection to the Internet. Nevertheless, it's still useful to know what the customization settings look like and how to use them, just in case you need them.

Video Window Layout

When you join in a group videoconference, you may want to change the layout for the video windows. The **video window layout** determines the number of video windows that you can display at one time, and their size.

The CU-SeeMe Setup Assistant generally sets up your video window layout based on your computer system and Internet connection speed. Displaying larger video windows or keeping many video windows open at once demands more from your computer and your Internet connection. By the same token, fewer video windows shown at smaller sizes requires less from your system and helps things run more quickly.

To change your video window layout:

1. **While participating in a videoconference,** choose Customize from the Edit menu to display the Customize dialog box.

2. Click the Video Layout tab to display the video window's Layout options, as shown in **Figure 11.36** (Windows) and **11.37** (Macintosh).

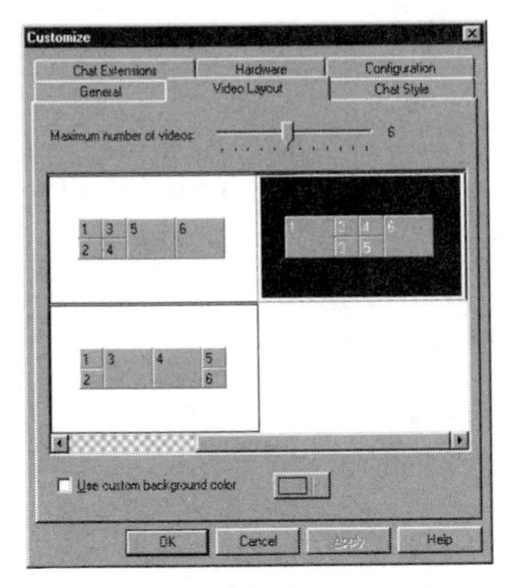

Figure 11.36 *Video layout settings (Windows).*

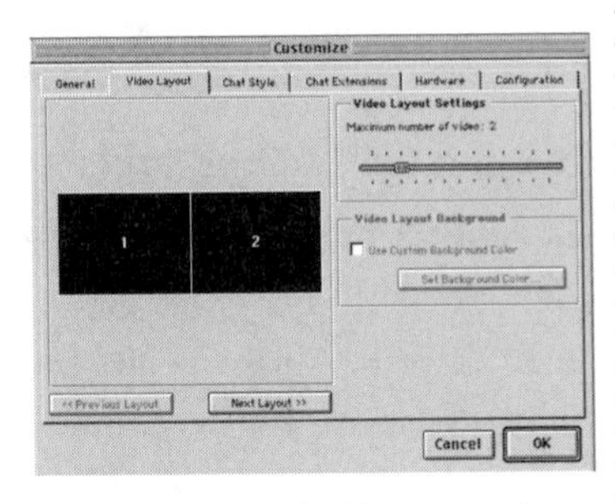

Figure 11.37 *Video layout settings (Macintosh).*

3. To set the maximum number of video windows that CU-SeeMe can display at once, move the slider to the left (for fewer windows) or to the right (for more windows).

   Remember—increasing the maximum number of video windows allows you to see more people at once, but also demands more from your computer system.

4. Choose the layout for your video windows.

   Windows users: Choose a layout by selecting one from the layout area. To view more layouts, slide the scroll bar to the right or left.

   Macintosh users Display different layouts by clicking the Next Layout and Previous Layout buttons. When you see the layout you want, leave it displayed.

5. You can also change the background for your video layout. Select the Use Custom Background Color checkbox, click the Set Background Color button, and choose a color from the pop-up palette.
6. Click OK to return to the videoconference.

Send and Receive Settings

Occasionally, a reflector may ask you to **adjust your Send and Receive settings** to improve performance and conserve bandwidth. As mentioned earlier in the chapter, the Message of the Day sometimes tells you what your settings should be; at other times the person hosting the conference may ask you to change your settings. This happens most

Send and Receive Settings *(cont.)*

frequently to people who have high-speed connections (56.6 Kbps or more), which send and receive data more quickly than the server can handle. The Send settings determine how quickly you send out audio and video, and the Receive settings determine how quickly you receive other people's audio and video.

To adjust your Send and Receive settings:

1. **From a videoconferencing room,** select Customize from the Edit menu.
2. In the Customize dialog box, click the Hardware tab to display the Hardware settings, as shown in **Figure 11.38**.

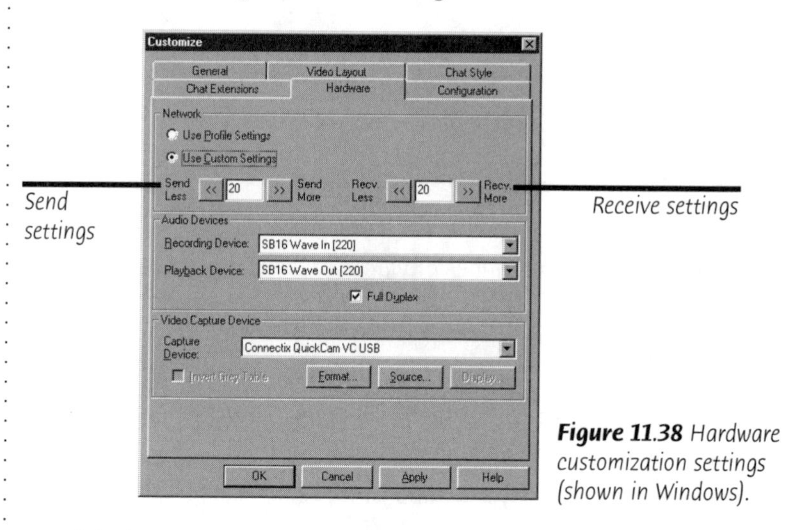

Figure 11.38 *Hardware customization settings (shown in Windows).*

3. Click the Use Custom Settings radio button.
4. Adjust your Send rate by clicking the Send Less or Send More button until the desired number is displayed.
5. Adjust your Receive rate by clicking the Send Less or Send More button until the desired number is displayed.
6. When you finish, click OK to return to the conference room.

Your Own Contact Card

You may want to change the information on your own personal Contact Card to display a better picture of yourself than the one you took with the Setup Assistant, or to include the URL for your Web site with your telephone and fax number and other information. Here are the steps:

1. From the Phone Book, select Edit|Personal Profile.
2. When the Personal Profile Editor dialog box appears, click to open the Card Personal Info tab, as shown in **Figure 11.39**.

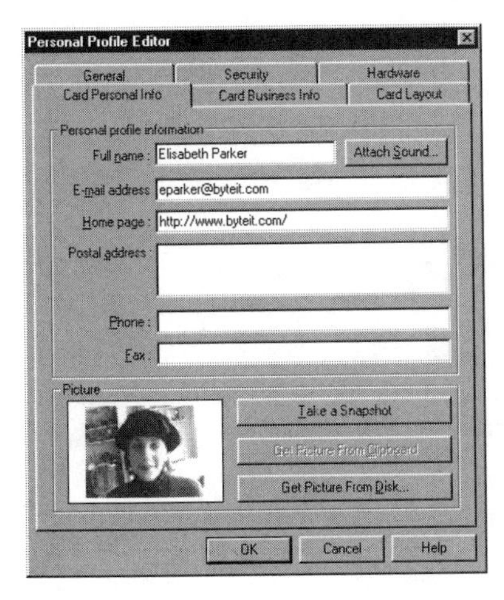

Figure 11.39 *Use the Personal Profile Editor to change your personal Contact Card info (shown here in Windows).*

3. Enter your new information.
4. If you want to **change the picture** that displays on your Contact Card, strike a stunning pose and click the Take a Snapshot button. Or you can browse for an existing picture that you like by clicking the Get Picture from Disk button.
5. Feel free to click other tabs in the Personal Profile Editor if you need to view or enter additional information.
6. When you finish, click OK to return to the Phone Book.

Changing Your Default ILS

As you know, when you choose an ILS with the CU-SeeMe Setup Assistant, it publishes your contact information to that ILS and also makes it your default ILS. Then, when you display the Directory dialog box, CU-SeeMe automatically connects you with that ILS. Unless you select a different ILS during setup, the **Setup Assistant chooses** White Pine's ILS as the default for CU-SeeMe users.

To change and publish yourself to a different ILS:

1. From the Phone Book, display the Contact List window by selecting View | Contact List.
2. In the Contact List window, select Edit | Preferences. If necessary, click to open the General tab.
3. In the Directory section of General tab (see **Figure 11.40**), make sure the Advertise On radio button is selected, and choose a server from the Advertise On list.

***Choosing Another ILS** (cont.)*

You can also choose a server that is not on the list. Click the Advertise with Another ILS radio button, and enter the ILS's URL in the box provided, like this: **ils.nameofserver.com**

4. Click OK to return to the Contact List window.

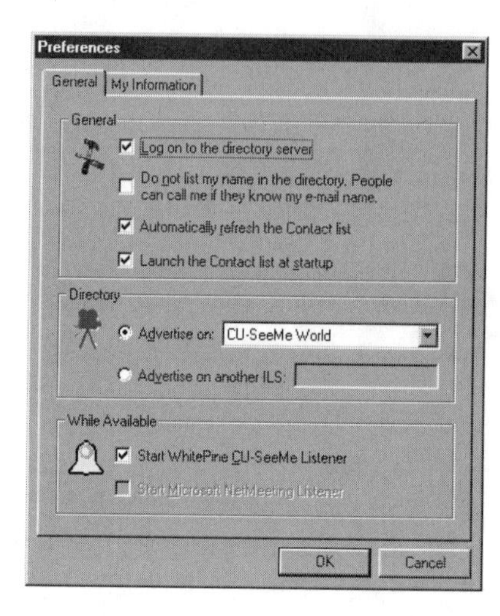

***Figure 11.40** Setting Directory preferences for the Contact List window (shown in Windows).*

More Cool Stuff

You can also do lots of other cool stuff with White Pine CU-SeeMe. For more information, refer to the manual that you downloaded along with the CU-SeeMe software. Or visit White Pine's CU-SeeMe Web site at **http://www.cuseeme.com/** or the CU-SeeMe support site at **http://support.wpine.com/cuseeme/**.

Here are a few of White Pine's other goodies:

- **WhitePine Board**: This free CU-SeeMe add-on (available for Windows only) adds a **whiteboard** feature to CU-SeeMe, so you and others can work on documents together while videoconferencing. To download the WhitePine Board, go to **http://www.wpine.com/Software/Downloads/cu31-wpb-download.html**.
- **Multicast Videoconferencing**: Chat with groups of your relatives, coworkers, or buddies—without having to go through a reflector. To enable Multicast Videoconferencing, go to the Phone Book and select Edit|Current Profile. In the General tab of the Personal Profile Editor, click the Enable Multicast Connections checkbox.

- **Web browser support**: You can set up CU-SeeMe to launch from your Web browser whenever you click a link to a CU-SeeMe conference from a Web page. Chapter 13 tells you how.
- **Integration with other videoconferencing programs**: Plans are underway at White Pine for better compatibility with other videoconferencing programs. In the future, you'll be able to use CU-SeeMe to videoconference with just about anyone, regardless of what program they use! Check the CU-SeeMe Web site at **http://www.cuseeme.com/** for more information

Talk to NetMeeting Users!

If you use Windows, you can use CU-SeeMe to talk with **NetMeeting** users. NetMeeting is **Microsoft's videoconferencing program**, and it comes with Windows. To set this up, go to the Contact List window (select View|Contact List) and display the Preferences dialog box (select Edit|Preferences). At the bottom, in the While Available area, click the Start Microsoft NetMeeting Listener checkbox.

With this option turned on, CU-SeeMe will detect when a NetMeeting user calls you and will launch NetMeeting for you. For more about NetMeeting, see Chapter 12. Alas, NetMeeting is not available for Macintosh users.

Summary

Whew! That was sure a long chapter. By now, you not only know how to work with CU-SeeMe—you've also learned enough to get you up and running with pretty much any old videoconferencing program.

- Although there are many good videoconferencing programs out there, I highly recommend **CU-SeeMe**. It's easy to set up and use, it works with both Windows and Macintosh, and it has a large community of users and conference rooms that you can visit.
- In a **group conference,** you connect to a reflector and meet with other people. A **point-to-point conference** is established when one person calls another person. **Cybercasts** are like television shows or radio broadcasts, in that participants gather together on a reflector, one person talks, and everyone else listens. **Multicast conferences** allow groups of people to talk together without going through a reflector.
- You can **connect to a group videoconference** by selecting a conference from the Contact List in the CU-SeeMe Phone Book. CU-SeeMe comes with a list of Contact Cards for lots of interesting and informative conferences and cybercasts on general topics. Of course, you can create new Contact Cards for other conferences that you encounter.
- You call individuals for point-to-point conferences through the **Manual Dial** dialog box. One way to connect is via the person's **IP address,** but a more reliable method is to use a person's e-mail address through an **ILS server**. For callers to find one another on an ILS, you and they must be published on that ILS.
- When someone calls you, and you're connected to the Internet and available for conferencing, the Listener Status dialog box (Windows) or Connection Request dialog box (Macintosh) appears so you can **choose whether or not to accept the call**.
- CU-SeeMe comes with a **Contact List**. You can add people to your list, organize them into groups, see whether or not they're available for conferencing, add names from an ILS, and speed-dial people from the list. While you're participating in a conference, you can add people's **Contact Cards** to the **Phone Book**.

- The **CU-SeeMe Setup Assistant** configures your settings according to your computer's capabilities, connection speed, and the information you provide. However, you can also customize your settings to adjust the video window layout, the send and receive settings, your own Contact Card information, and the default ILS you use.
- CU-SeeMe also lets you set up and participate in **multicast** conferences; has a **whiteboard** feature that you can download; allows you to **launch a videoconference from a Web page** link; and is integrated with other videoconferencing programs (including **NetMeeting**).

The next chapter takes you further along in your experience with videoconferencing.

12 Videoconferencing Freebies

Maybe you're wondering if there's a way to get your feet wet with videoconferencing before plunking down money for a program. That's understandable. Sure, White Pine CU-SeeMe (as you learned in Chapter 11) offers great business and personal conferencing features, plenty of tech support, and access to a wide community of users. But that 30-minute CU-SeeMe demo doesn't give you much time to explore. Not to worry. This chapter introduces you to popular freeware videoconferencing ("video chat") programs that you can take for a spin, and explains the advantages and disadvantages for each program. Go ahead and try 'em all!

TODAY'S TOPIC:
"STRATEGIZING FOR
WORLD DOMINANCE."
BOB, YOU WANNA TAKE
A CRACK AT IT?

In this chapter:

- A collection of basic video chat concepts
- BoxTop Software's iVisit
- Microsoft NetMeeting
- Freeware (Cornell) CU-SeeMe
- Videoconferencing software that comes with your cam

Video Chat Basics

Before we take a look at the free videoconferencing programs available to you, let's quickly go over some fundamentals of videoconferencing itself.

If you want to know more, Chapter 11 covers many of these concepts from a more specific point of view, showing you how it's done with White Pine CU-SeeMe. Most video chat applications work similarly.

Types of Videoconferences

Videoconferences come in four flavors:

- **Point-to-point** conferences, for individuals
- **Group** conferences, in conference rooms through a conferencing server such as White Pine Reflector or MeetingPoint
- **Multicast** conferences, in which a group conference can be set up on-the-fly, without going through a server)
- **Cybercast** conferences, group conferences in which the host conducts a video lecture and visitors watch and listen

For more details about these videoconference types, see the "Videoconference Types" discussion in Chapter 11. White Pine CU-SeeMe and NetMeeting both support all these conference types. The freeware CU-SeeMe and iVisit programs support all except multicast conferencing.

White Pine's upcoming **CU-SeeMe Pro** offering, which allows point-to-point conferencing between CU-SeeMe and NetMeeting users, will only be available for Windows users.

Video Windows

Video chat applications display **local** and **remote video windows.** The local window shows you how your conference participants are seeing you, and the remote windows show the other conference participants (see **Figure 12.1**). For better performance and viewing, you can generally close and resize video windows, and also change the video window layout.

Figure 12.1 *Remote video windows (in iVisit for Windows).*

Video windows usually have the following elements:

- A title bar that displays the person's name
- A status bar that displays participants' *send and receive rates* (the speed at which video transfers back and forth, as measured in frames per second)
- A row of icons that tell you whether the person can receive your audio and video
- Options for displaying more information, including the person's IP address and which program (and program version) they're using.

Audio Chat

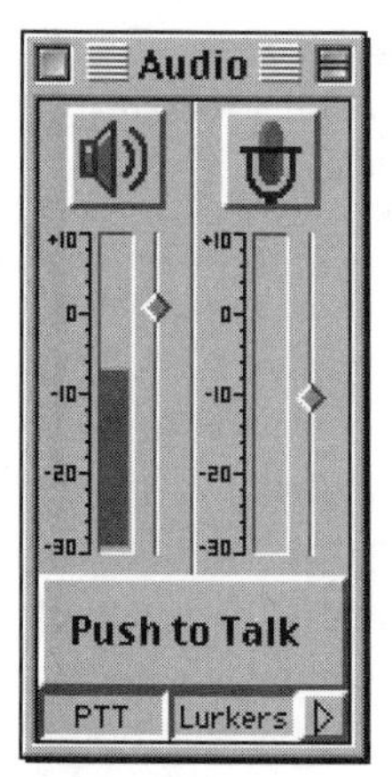

Figure 12.2 *Audio controls (in freeware CU-SeeMe for Macintosh).*

Figure 12.2 shows a typical set of the controls provided for **sending and receiving audio chat messages.** You'll see a button that you can click to begin talking, and volume controls for your microphone and speakers. In Windows-compatible video chat applications, you can usually send audio messages by simply talking into the microphone. Macintosh programs usually require that you click on the Talk button first. When you're in a group conference, the way you generally send private audio messages to an individual participant is by selecting the person from a menu or from a participants list.

Incoming Calls: *If you're connected to the Internet and someone calls you, your videoconferencing program automatically launches and displays a dialog box so you can choose whether or not to accept the call.*

Text Chat

If you've ever used a text chat program such as ICQ (discussed in Chapters 11 and 13) or AOL's Instant Message, and if you've ever visited chat room Web sites such as World Without Borders (**http://www.worldwithoutborders.com/**) and Talk City (**http://www.talkcity.com/**), then your videoconferencing application's chat window will look quite familiar.

For a look at White Pine CU-SeeMe's text chat setup, see Chapter 11.

Because it uses up less bandwidth than audio, text chat is popular in the videoconferencing world. All the videoconferencing programs mentioned in this chapter come with a **text chat window** like the one shown in **Figure 12.3**. Text chat windows provide an area for typing a message, which is sent by pressing Return or Enter. Another pane in the window lets you scroll through and read messages from others. Most programs also allow you to exchange private text messages, and to save chat transcripts to your computer as a text file.

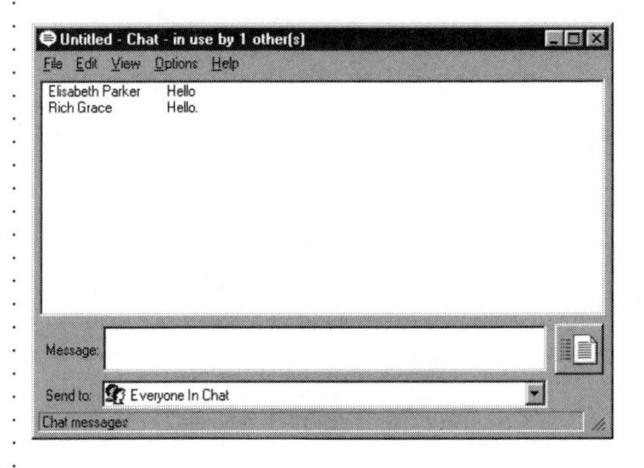

Figure 12.3 *Text chat window (in NetMeeting for Windows).*

Participants List

When you videoconference (chat) with an individual or in a chat room, a list of participants is displayed for you, as shown in **Figure 12.4**. This list tells you **who's in the conference room,** with icons that tell you whether each person can receive audio, video, and chat messages, and whether they have your video window open. By selecting someone in the participants list, you can click menu items or toolbar buttons to display additional information about the participant, or to send them private messages.

Figure 12.4 *Participants list (in freeware CU-SeeMe for Windows).*

Contacts List

All videoconferencing programs come with some sort of contact list or phone book so you can save lists of your **favorite conference rooms and people** with whom you frequently conference. Once you've added items to your list (see **Figure 12.5**), you can connect to people and conference rooms by selecting a name or place from the list.

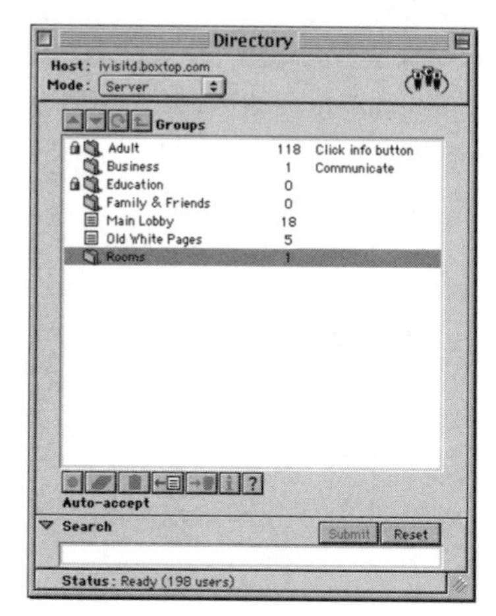

Figure 12.5 *Contacts list (bookmarks) in iVisit for Macintosh.*

Shared Whiteboard

Want to show Mom and Dad a picture of the grandkids? Or review that spreadsheet with your finance committee and get their comments? **Shared whiteboard** features fit the bill. NetMeeting and White Pine CU-SeeMe both provide shared whiteboards. (To use White Pine CU-SeeMe's offering, you'll need to download the White Pine Board application from White Pine's Web site at **http://www.wpine.com/**).

When a conference participant opens the whiteboard window, like the one shown in **Figure 12.6**, all other participants' whiteboard windows launch, too. Participants can then take a snapshot of something displayed on their computer screen (such as a photo or an Excel spreadsheet), put it on the shared whiteboard, and show it to everyone who has access. Participants can then use the text, highlighter, and drawing tools to make comments and notes in the whiteboard window.

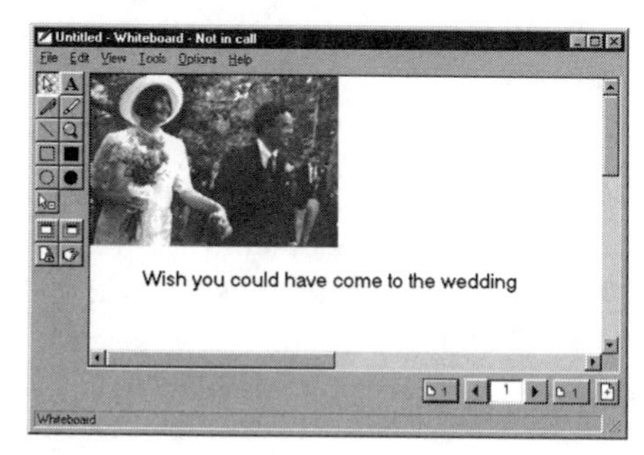

Figure 12.6 *NetMeeting for Windows Whiteboard window displayed with picture and text.*

> ***Sorry, Mac Users!***
> *Alas, when it comes to videoconferencing software, Mac users are still getting the fuzzy end of the lollipop. I haven't found any Macintosh videoconferencing programs that offer shared whiteboards and applications, or other business-friendly features.*

Application Sharing

NetMeeting and White Pine CU-SeeMe (with White Pine Board installed) also support **application sharing**. This means you and other conference participants can open files and work on them together —provided that you all have the same videoconferencing application. For example, if one participant enables the application sharing feature and then opens a document in Microsoft Word, the application will launch the other participants' computers with the shared document displayed, so that everyone can discuss it and make suggestions and changes jointly.

Avoid Slower Modems!

Are you considering shared applications or thinking about trying multipoint conferencing? **Before you leap, consider your hardware.** Application sharing and multipoint conferencing work best over high-speed connections of 56.6 Kbps or faster. It's not recommended that you try to use slower modems for these videoconferencing activities. Another advantage of high-performance computers is that they will produce video and still allow you to run other programs. On slower computers, a video display slows other tasks to a crawl.

Cross-Platform Considerations

If you are looking into videoconferencing and online collaboration options for an office environment, it may be that you need to accommodate both Windows and Macintosh users. This may seem difficult, but it's not impossible. With the right combination of communication and server products, you can make it work.

Netopia's Timbuktu Pro (**http://www.netopia.com/**) simplifies the process of allowing Windows and Mac users to share applications and files. Also, the White Pine CU-SeeMe works on both platforms. Both White Pine and Netopia offer server products to support NetMeeting users.

Coping with IP Addresses

Normally, when you call someone for a point-to-point videoconference, you have to enter their IP address—a combination of numbers that points to the other person's computer. This has become a problem because most of today's ISPs give you a different IP address every time you connect to the Internet.

*For more about **IP addresses** and how to find yours, see "What's My IP Address?" in Chapter 11.*

You can get around this issue by using an instant messaging "buddies" program such as **ICQ** to contact people. You tell them your IP address and set up a conference using the ICQ arrangement. Look for details on this kind of connection in the "Rendezvous with ICQ" section of Chapter 11, and "Find Your Buddies Online" in Chapter 13.

ILS Servers

ILSs are also called ***directory servers*** *or* ***user location servers (ULSs)*** *by some conferencing programs.*

Yes, you *can* avoid the dreaded IP address problem. White Pine CU-SeeMe, iVisit, NetMeeting, and ICQ all support **Internet Locator Services (ILS)**. ILS servers store people's names and e-mail addresses. Instead of having to know an IP address, you can make calls using their e-mail address and the URL for their directory server. Programs that support ILS provide a window like the NetMeeting directory shown here, in which you can search for people by name or e-mail address. For more information, see "Calling Through an ILS" in Chapter 11.

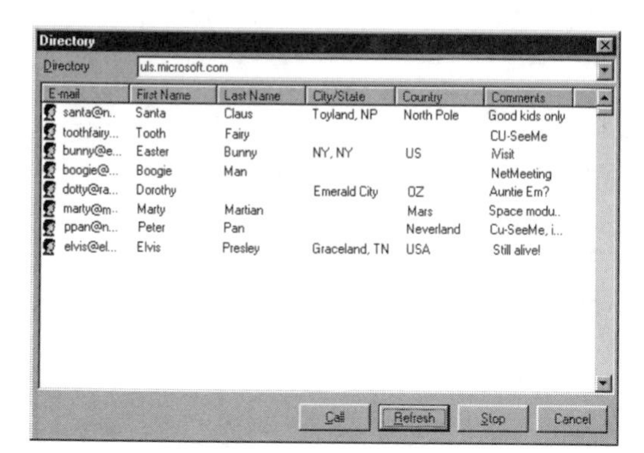

Listing Yourself with an ILS

Unless you specify otherwise, videoconferencing programs with directory server features automatically **publish your name and e-mail address** to their default servers. If you want, you can include your city, state, and country in this published information. (You can suppress this publishing through the program's preferences, or during the setup process.) In addition, there are several public directory servers on the Web that you can sign up with.

You can list yourself ("publish") with as few or as many ILS servers as you want. However, you only need to register with the default ILS for the videoconferencing and chat applications you use, and also with a public ILS via the Web.

Public ILS servers

Anyone can access and list their name and e-mail address with a **public ILS**. Simply visit the ILS's Web site, follow the instructions, and fill out a Web page form. Public ILSs—like the Yahoo! People Search site—also offer search forms for looking up other people's e-mail addresses, as shown in **Figure 12.7**. Once you sign on and receive your user ID and password information, you can give friends your e-mail and ILS addresses, so they can add you to their ICQ buddies list and their videoconferencing program's phone book.

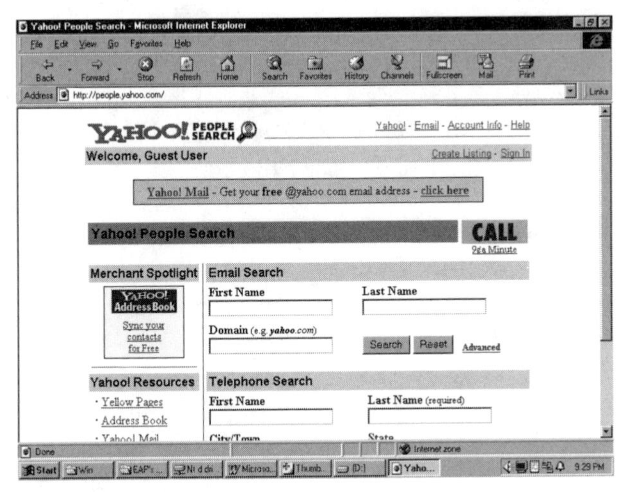

Figure 12.7 *Yahoo! People Search—a popular ILS.*

Public ILS Servers

ILS	Web Address	ILS Address
Yahoo! People Search (formerly Four11)	**http://people.yahoo.com/**	**ils.four11.com**
WhoWhere	**http://www.whowhere.com**	**ils.whowhere.com**
Big Foot	**http://www.bigfoot.com**	**ils.bigfoot.com**

Private ILS Servers

If you videoconference through school or work, or have signed on with an ISP that supports ILS, then you may have access to a **private ILS server.** If you're on a private ILS, ask your network administrator *before* giving out your ILS address. The answer may be yes. But in many cases, people will not be able to access your address from the private ILS and get hold of you. So if you've got access to a private ILS, it's a good idea to sign on with a public one, too.

Giving Information to an ILS

When you sign up with an ILS through your videoconferencing program's setup program, or by filling out a form on an ILS Web site, you'll be asked for your first and last name, contact information, a nickname, and some comments about yourself. Just remember that *you don't have to provide any more information than what you feel comfortable giving.* Most ILS servers only require a first name or nick-name and an e-mail address.

You may want to receive calls only from people who speak in your language. If so, it's a good idea to include your country of residence in the info that you give the ILS and in the Comments that the ILS will publish for you. (There's more about Comments coming up.)

Listed or Unlisted?

Most ILSs (through their Web page form or a dialog box in your videoconferencing program) also allow you to have an **unpublished listing**. This is a lot like having an unlisted telephone number. People who know your e-mail address will be able to call you through the ILSs where you're registered, but your name and information will not appear in the directory list. If, on the other hand, you'd like to make new friends online, you can choose to publish your information.

How to Avoid Unwanted "Adult" Chats: You can have lots of fun and make new friends through videoconferencing. But some people's interests are not exactly PG-rated. One way to protect yourself from this is to remain unpublished by your ILS, or you can put Comments in your listing to indicate your interests (or lack thereof). When looking for people to chat with, read their Comments before calling them. People who are into the adult chat scene typically indicate their preferences through specific comments about themselves, their gender and lifestyle, or the people they'd like to talk to (for instance, "27-year-old male").

Comments

Most videoconferencing programs and ILS Web sites provide a **Comments area** when you sign up with an ILS. Here, you should list the videoconferencing program(s) you use, topics of interest to you, and your limitations. For example, if you use CU-SeeMe and NetMeeting, and you don't want to discuss "adult" topics, you can publish a comment such as "CU-SeeMe, NetMeeting, General topics only."

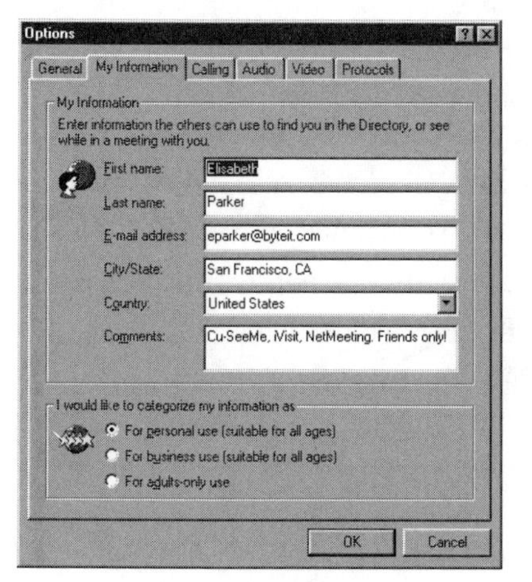

Changing Your ILS Info

To change the information you provide to an ILS at any time, go to the ILS Web site and resubmit the Web form. Or you can do this through your videoconferencing program's Preferences or Options dialog box. (Choose File|Preferences in CU-SeeMe and iVisit, or Tools|Options in NetMeeting.) When you change the information for your default ILS, the ILS automatically updates your listing the next time you connect with your videoconferencing program.

Other Videoconferencing Software

Now let's get to those freebies. The sections that follow offer descriptions of and suggestions for using three free programs that have been successful in today's videoconferencing arena: **iVisit** from BoxTop software; **NetMeeting** from Microsoft; and the **freeware version of CU-SeeMe,** also known as the Cornell version.

Chatting with iVisit

BoxTop software's iVisit is a friendly little program created by Tom Dorsey, who is best known for his work on the Cornell CU-SeeMe project. iVisit's conference rooms aren't as active or well-populated as CU-SeeMe's, and it doesn't provide the collaboration features that serious business users want. However, iVisit is available for both Windows and Macintosh and is great for keeping in touch with your friends and family. To download iVisit, go to **http://www.ivisit.com/**.

What You Get...

iVisit offers the following advantages:

- Available for Windows and Macintosh.
- Easy to install and use.
- Provides a list of iVisit conference rooms, to which you can add you own choices.
- Supports ILS and gives you access to the iVisit directory server.
- Allows you to record local and remote video from your chats.
- Displays a message when you connect, telling you about upcoming events and program upgrades.

...and Don't Get

iVisit has the following limitations:

- Poor video performance for lower-speed connections (28.8 and 33.3 Kbps modems), as compared with NetMeeting, White Pine CU-SeeMe, and freeware CU-SeeMe. Also, iVisit video slows overall performance on even relatively fast computers.
- Lacks important business conferencing features such as whiteboard, application sharing, and multipoint conferencing.
- Not supported by White Pine MeetingPoint servers, which allow users of White Pine and Cornell CU-SeeMe and NetMeeting to join group conferences and talk to one another.

Getting Started with iVisit

When you install iVisit, the setup program takes you through a series of dialog boxes that guide you through the process and register you with BoxTop software. When you first launch the application, you'll need to **set up your preferences** before you make your first call.

Setting iVisit Preferences

1. Select Settings | Preferences to display the iVisit Preferences dialog box, shown in **Figures 12.8** and **12.9**. (Windows users need to select the Personal Info tab.)
2. Enter your nickname, e-mail address, and a short comment in the appropriate boxes. iVisit automatically publishes this information to the iVisit directory server. This is the easiest way to ensure that other iVisit users can call you.

   Note, however, that you can choose another default ILS by entering its URL in the Directory Server box. (Windows users: Click the Connection Management tab to get there.)

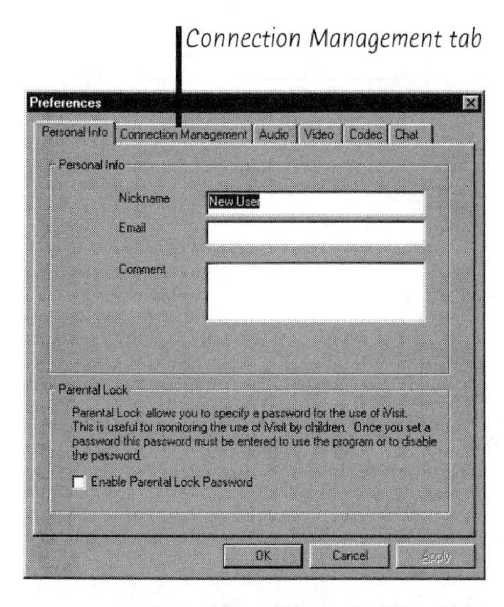

Figure 12.8 *iVisit Preferences dialog box shown in Windows.*

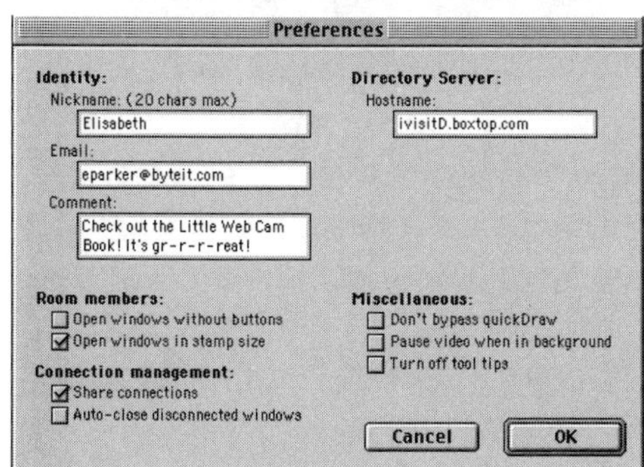

Figure 12.9 *iVisit Preferences dialog box shown on Macintosh.*

Making a Call with iVisit

iVisit comes with a **Directory** of conference rooms that you can visit, and also lets you save your favorite conferences and people as **bookmarks** in the Directory list. As shown in **Figure 12.10**, you can connect to a group conference, search for an iVisit user on the directory server, or connect to a person or conference room that you've bookmarked.

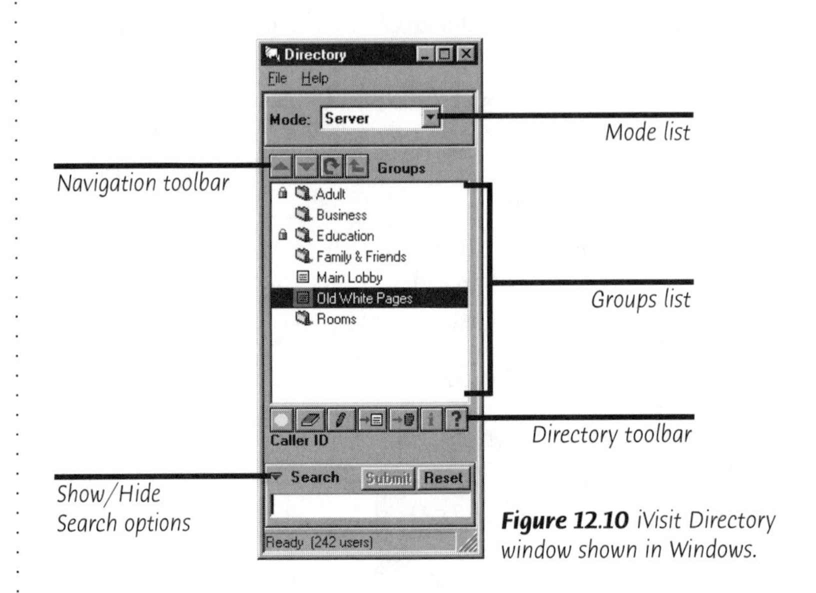

Figure 12.10 *iVisit Directory window shown in Windows.*

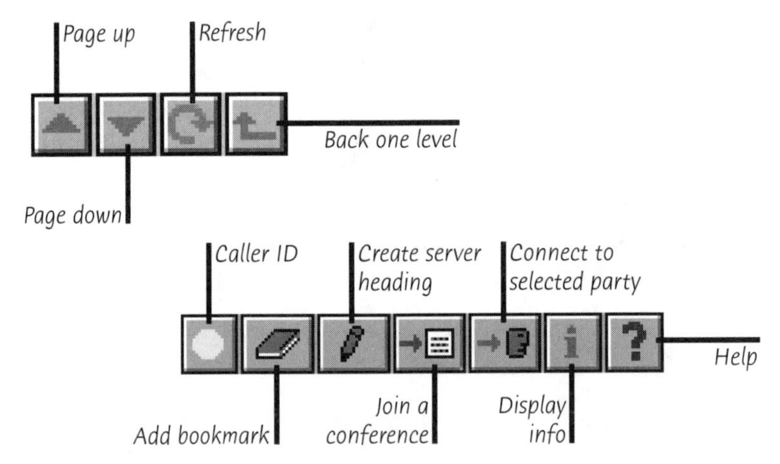

To a Group Conference

To connect to a group conference on the Directory list, choose Server from the Mode list, open a folder, and double-click on a conference. When the list of participants displays, click the **Join Conference** button to enter the conference room.

To an Individual

To connect to an individual, just select the name from the Directory list and click the **Connect to User** button.

You can also search for someone on a directory server and then call them. First make sure the **Search options** are visible at the bottom of the Directory window, by clicking the button to Show/Hide Search Options. Then select Server from the Mode list, type an e-mail address or nickname in the Search box, and click the Submit button. If your party is found, it appears in the Directory list. You can then double-click the name to make your call.

To a Bookmark

After you've created bookmarks in iVisit, you can connect to those persons and conferences by choosing **Bookmarks** from the Mode list, opening the Saved folder, and double-clicking the person or chat room you want to connect to.

Search a Different ILS: Unless you've specified a different ILS server in your iVisit Preferences, the program automatically searches the iVisit ILS. You can search a different directory server by displaying the Preferences dialog box and entering a new URL.

Using iVisit Bookmarks

Creating a bookmark is easy. When you search the directory server for an address or connect to a group conference, select an item from the list in your Directory window and click the **Add Bookmark** button. To display your bookmarks, select Mode | Bookmarks. iVisit automatically saves bookmarks to the Saved folder. In addition, the program creates bookmarks for the participants in your most recent conference and saves them to the AutoLog folder.

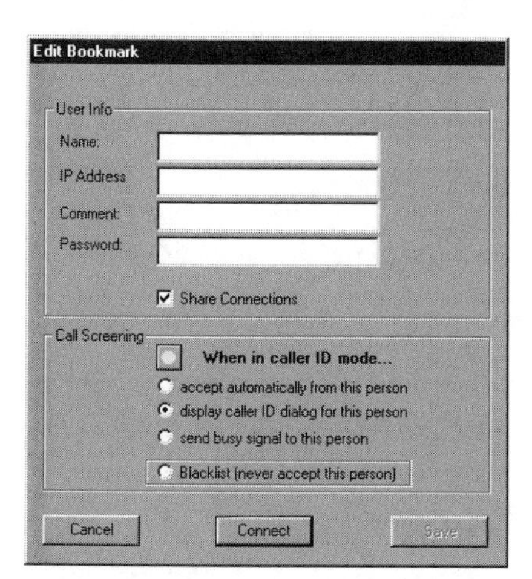

Figure 12.11 *iVisit Edit Bookmark dialog box (shown in Windows).*

Connecting to an IP Address

If you can't find someone on the iVisit ILS but you *know* they have the iVisit software, you can try connecting to their IP address. Choose File | Connect IP to display the Edit Bookmark dialog box, shown in **Figure 12.11**. Type the person's nickname in the Name box and their IP address in the IP Address box, and click the Connect button. This automatically adds the person to your bookmark list.

If the party you're trying to reach doesn't have a permanent IP address, you should delete them from your bookmarks list after the conference. Select their name in the list, and click the Delete Selected Bookmark toolbar button (it looks like a trash can and only appears when you select a bookmark).

IVisit's Video Windows

Let's start with the **local video window, Figure 12.12**.

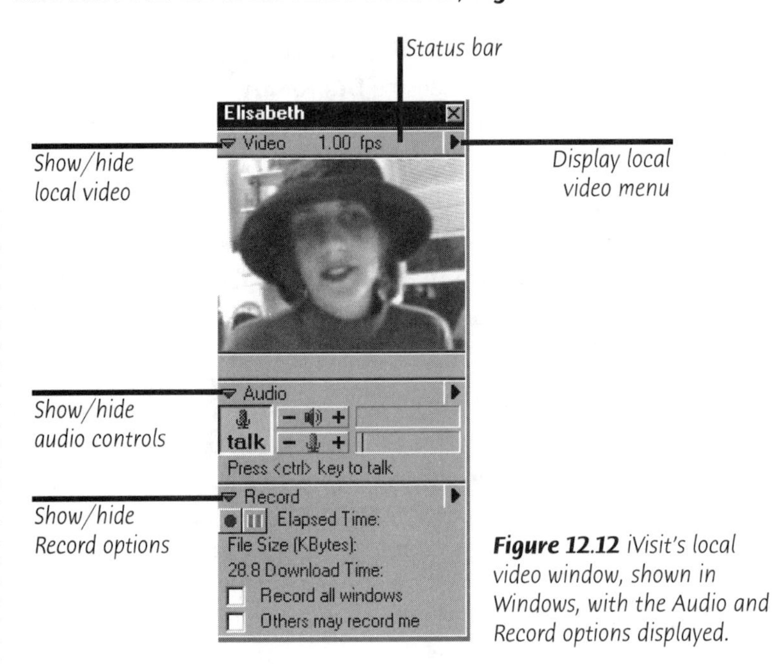

Figure 12.12 *iVisit's local video window, shown in Windows, with the Audio and Record options displayed.*

Local Video Window

The local window contains your audio controls and displays your send and receive rates, in frames per second (fps), in the status bar. Click on the small arrow buttons on the left side of the video window to display or hide iVisit's various features.

To show/hide your video:

You may want to hide your local video window to save room on your computer screen.

To select local video options:

You can pause your video or resize the video window. Also, you may want to paste an image into the window from the Clipboard to display instead of your video picture. Click on the Display Local Video Menu arrow button to make these options available.

To send and receive audio:

To display audio controls for each video window, click the Audio arrow button to make the controls visible. Press the Ctrl key or click the Talk button to send audio to the other person. (Of course, for this to work, you need a microphone hooked up to your sound card or sound input.)

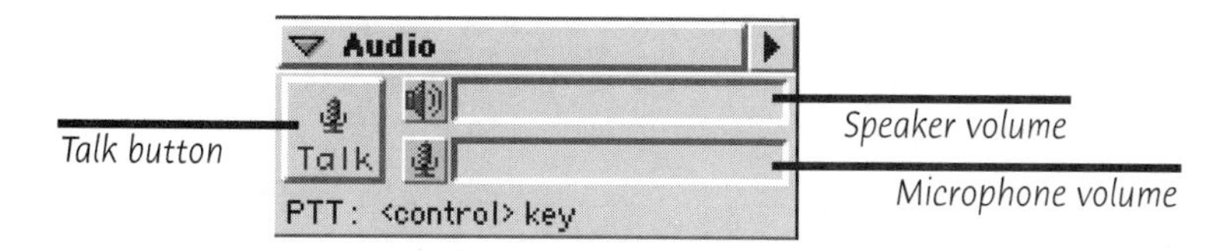

Recording from the Local Window

iVisit lets you **record video from your videoconferences.** First, click the arrow button on the right to open the Record options. Then check the Record All Windows checkbox.

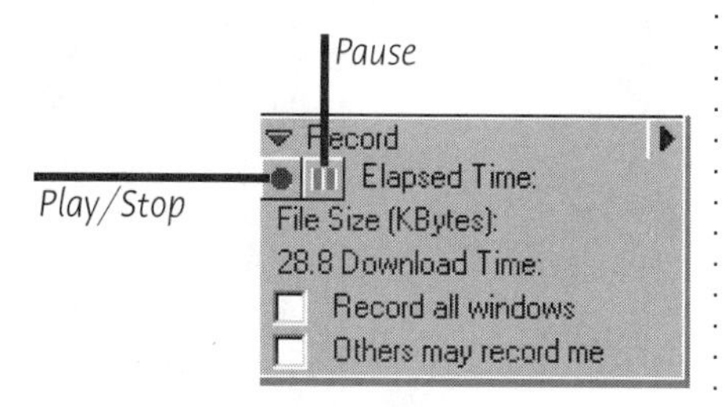

To begin recording, click the Record/Stop button, and click it again when you're ready to stop your recording. (There's a Pause button, too, if you need it.) When the Save As dialog box appears, you can name your video file and save it. You can also click the Others may record me checkbox so your friends can make movies when chatting with you.

To play your videos, select Play File from the File menu, and then browse for a movie in the Open File dialog box appears (iVisit videos have the **.ivf** filename extension). Unfortunately, iVisit saves the video to its own file format, so you won't be able to share your movies with non-iVisit users. However, when you play your videos, you can save individual frames as pictures.

Remote Video Windows

Remote video windows look a lot like local video windows: They have a title bar, status bar, and arrow buttons for showing/hiding the video window and display menu options (see **Figure 12.13**). In addition, there's a toolbar and icons to show information about the participant.

Remote Video Windows *(cont.)*

On the **toolbar**, you can change your incoming chat/conference arrangement by clicking buttons to stop receiving video, stop incoming chat, and/or stop incoming audio (see **Figure 12.13**). This lets you **block the messages** of someone in a conference room if you prefer not to see or hear those messages.

It may happen that you want to know **more information** about a person you're conferencing with. To see their IP address and which version of iVisit they're using, click the arrow button to show/hide more info. A row of icons appears at the bottom of the video window, telling you whether the participant has their video, chat, and audio enabled, and the type of conference that you're currently participating in.

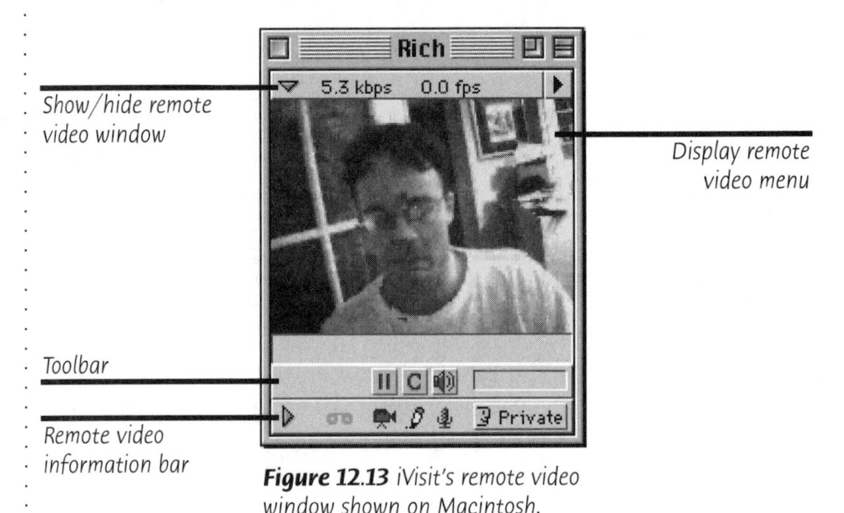

Figure 12.13 *iVisit's remote video window shown on Macintosh.*

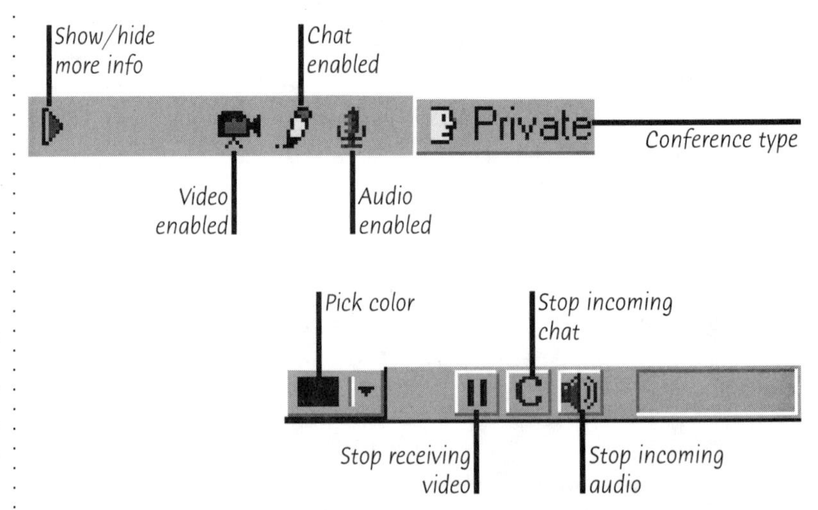

Click the ***Pick Color*** *button to display a color palette and change the color for the remote video window's title bar.*

iVisit's Chat Window

iVisit also comes with a handy little Chat Window, as shown here from the Macintosh version of the program. Chat windows work similarly in most videoconferencing applications: To send a text chat message, type it in the upper pane of the Chat Window. To read messages from others, scroll through them in the lower pane.

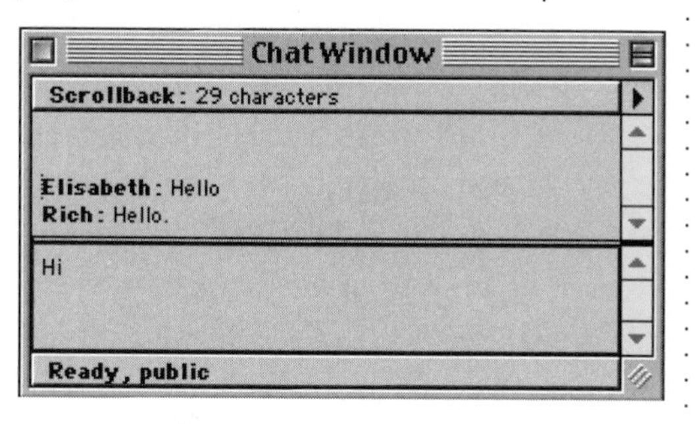

Taking NetMeeting for a Spin

Windows only

If you plan to run videoconferencing among Windows-only computers, you'll like **Microsoft's NetMeeting**. This everything-and-the-kitchen-sink program comes packaged along with Internet Explorer 4.0 and higher, and the Windows 98 operating system.

> If you don't have the latest version of NetMeeting, you can always visit Microsoft's NetMeeting Web site at **http://www.microsoft.com/netmeeting/**.

For a free videoconferencing program, NetMeeting offers a huge collection of features and is great for anyone getting started with videoconferencing. If you're a Windows user and none of your pals uses a Mac, then NetMeeting may be all you ever need.

What You Get...

NetMeeting offers the following advantages:

- Easy to set up. Wizards guide you through the setup process. (Performance isn't bad, either.)
- Provides access to Microsoft's directory server so you can contact people using an e-mail address.
- Excellent business videoconferencing features, with a built-in whiteboard, application sharing, and multipoint conferencing so you can set up and join meetings.
- Gives you access to the White Pine and freeware CU-SeeMe community, too! You can now visit thousands of CU-SeeMe chat rooms hosted by White Pine MeetingPoint servers. In addition, the soon-to-be-released **CU-SeeMe Pro** will allow point-to-point conferences between CU-SeeMe and NetMeeting users.

...and Don't Get

NetMeeting has the following limitations:

- NetMeeting is Windows-only, so I don't recommend it if you conference with many Mac users. (You can, however, talk to Mac CU-SeeMe users in a White Pine chat room and share files with Mac people who use Timbuktu Pro through a Timbuktu server, as explained in the section on cross-platform considerations earlier in this chapter.)
- To use NetMeeting's application sharing and multipoint conferencing, you need a high-speed connection (56.6 Kbps or faster). These features do require a fair amount of bandwidth. Luckily, high-speed connections through cable modems and ADSL are becoming less expensive and more widely available.

Getting NetMeeting

If you're running Windows 98, simply check the Start menu. NetMeeting should be waiting and ready to go, under Programs | Internet Explorer. If you're running Windows 95 or Windows NT, you have a couple of options. You can go buy an inexpensive Internet Explorer CD (which will include NetMeeting) from CompUSA or another retailer, or you can download the latest version of NetMeeting from Microsoft's Web site. Installation is just a matter of double-clicking the Setup icon, sitting back, and letting the Setup Wizard guide you through the steps.

Setting Up NetMeeting

Once you install NetMeeting, you'll need to set it up so you can use it. Depending on whether NetMeeting was installed with Internet Explorer or separately, click through one of the following series of commands:

- Start | Programs | Internet Explorer | Microsoft NetMeeting

  or
- Start | Programs | Microsoft NetMeeting

When you first launch NetMeeting, a wizard for the Microsoft Internet **User Location Service (ULS)** starts up to help you enter your basic contact information

To ULS or Not to ULS?

As explained earlier, a ULS is just another type of ILS or directory server. When you first launch NetMeeting, you'll need to decide whether you want other NetMeeting users to be able to contact you through Microsoft's User Location Server. (This is the second step in the wizard, as shown in **Figure 12.14**.) Unless you choose otherwise, NetMeeting establishes **uls.microsoft.com** as your default directory server, and adds your information to that server so that other NetMeeting users can call you.

The ULS isn't necessary if you plan to connect to specific users and you already know their IP addresses. However, keep in mind that since most people's IP addresses change every time they connect to the Internet, it's far easier and more reliable to connect to people using an e-mail address and a directory server.

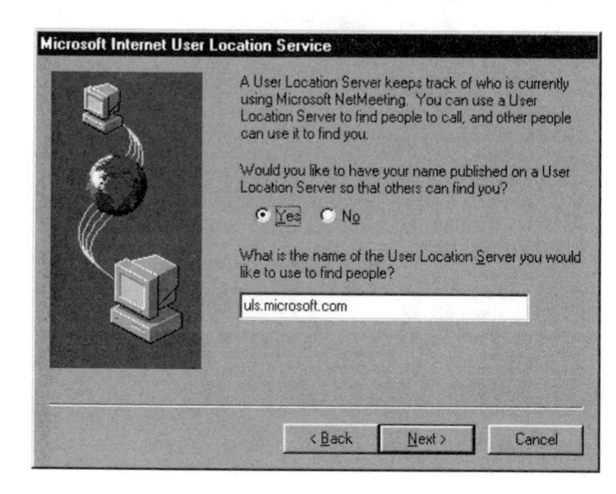

Figure 12.14
Selecting a ULS (User Location Server).

Testing and Tuning

The next step in setting up NetMeeting is to tune your audio settings for the best possible speed and performance. The **Audio Tuning Wizard** (**Figure 12.15**) detects your installed sound card and lets you define recording settings. The Wizard then asks you to choose a modem speed so it can adjust your audio and text settings for better performance.

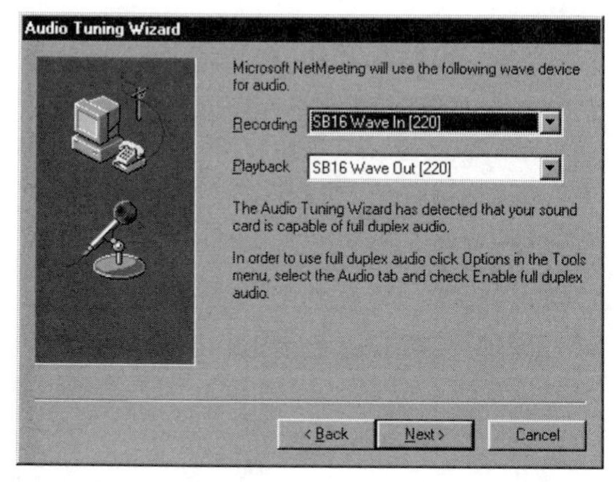

Figure 12.15
The Audio Tuning Wizard detects your installed sound card and lets you adjust your recording settings.

Making a NetMeeting Call

Once you've installed and set up NetMeeting, you're ready to start using it to call people. NetMeeting launches and dials up your Internet connection and displays listings from your default ILS, as shown in **Figure 12.16**.

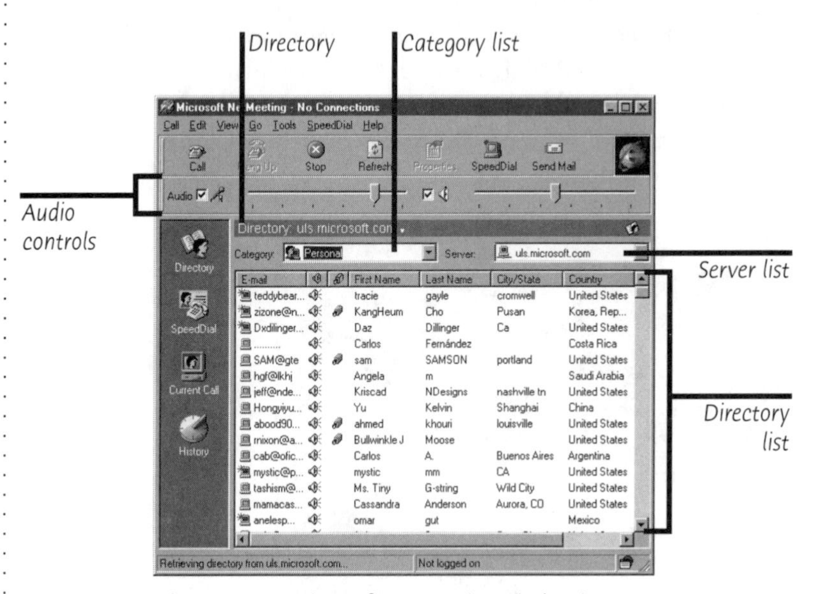

Figure 12.16 *Microsoft NetMeeting window in the Directory view.*

Setting Up a Conference

To call someone from the ILS list:

Select a category from the Category list, **choose an ILS server** from the Server list, and wait for the directory to load. In the directory list, select the person you want to connect to, and click the Call button in the main toolbar. When the Call dialog box displays, click the Call button.

To call someone manually:

If you have a person's ILS and e-mail address, you can call them directly. Click the Current Call icon on the left side of the NetMeeting window; this switches you to the **Current Call view**. Click the Call button in the main toolbar to get the New Call dialog box. Type in the URL for the person's ILS server, followed by their e-mail address in the Address box, as shown here, and click the Call button. If you have only the IP address for the person you're calling, type it in the Address box.

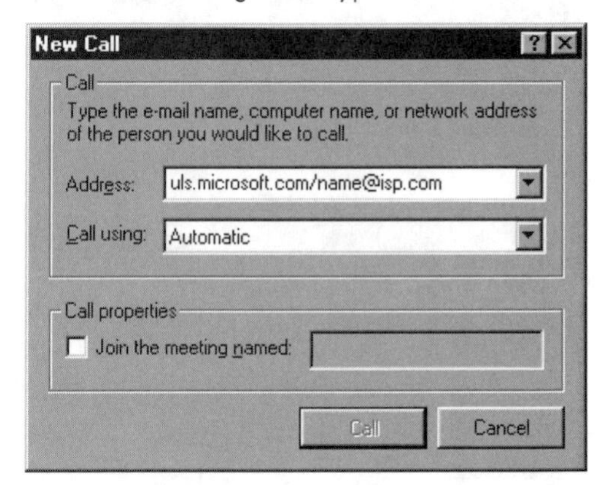

To set up a multipoint conference:

With a high-speed Internet connection, you can conference with several people at once. Choose **Host Meeting** from the Call menu. The Microsoft NetMeeting dialog box appears with a little information about hosting meetings; click OK to move on. (You may want to check the Don't Show Again check box so you won't see this message any more.) When you have Host Meeting enabled, people can then connect to your meeting by calling you as they would for a regular point-to-point conference.

> **Adaptive Toolbars.** NetMeeting gives you several views of its interface, including the Directory (for ILS directories); SpeedDial (with a list of people you frequently call); Current Call (for conferencing); and History (with a list of previous conferences). As you switch among these views, the main toolbar's buttons change and offer you all the tools you need for that view. These "dynamic" toolbars are called **adaptive toolbars.**

Conferencing with NetMeeting

When you call someone, NetMeeting automatically switches to the Current Call view (**Figure 12.17**) if necessary. A list of participants appears, with icons indicating their status for sending and receiving audio and video, and whether they can run the whiteboard, chat, and application-sharing features.

Figure 12.17 *NetMeeting window in the Current Call view.*

Exchanging Messages

To send and receive audio and video, sit back (but not out of your cam's range, please!) and start talking. NetMeeting automatically sends and receives both video and audio, unless you or the other person doesn't have video capabilities.

To exchange text chat messages, click the Chat button in the Current Call view's toolbar.

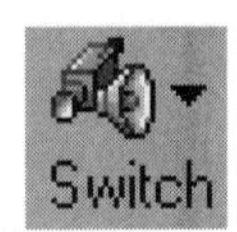

Disconnecting and switching connections: If you're a multitasking kind of person, you can switch among connections by clicking the Switch button in the main toolbar. This displays a list of available conferences and individuals, and you can select a connection from the list. To disconnect from a conference, click the Hang Up button in the toolbar.

Whiteboarding and Sharing Applications

To launch the whiteboard, click the Whiteboard button in the main toolbar. When you're in a conference, the whiteboard feature automatically launches on other participants' computers, too.

To share an application and a file, open the application and file, click the Share button in the main toolbar, and choose an application from the list. If the other person has the same application available, it will launch on their computer and display your file. If you want to let other participants make changes to your file so you can work on it together, click the Collaborate button in the toolbar.

SpeedDialing with NetMeeting

People whom you plan to call frequently can be listed in the **SpeedDial view,** so you don't have to enter their ILS server and e-mail address every time you give them a jingle. NetMeeting's SpeedDial works similarly to White Pine Cu-SeeMe's Contact List and iVisit's Bookmarks.

To call a person on your SpeedDial list, click the SpeedDial icon on the left of the window and select the desired name from the list. Click the Call button in the main toolbar to display the Call dialog box, and click the Call button there to connect.

Adding to SpeedDial

To add someone to your SpeedDial list, right-click on their name from the Directory view or Current Call view (*while* you're conferencing with them), and choose SpeedDial from the shortcut menu.

You can also create a SpeedDial list entry from scratch. From the Directory view, click the SpeedDial button in the toolbar. When the Add SpeedDial dialog box appears, type the person's directory server URL and e-mail address just as you would when making a call from the New Call dialog box (see "Making a NetMeeting Call" earlier in this chapter). When you finish entering your information, click OK.

Freeware CU-SeeMe

The CU-SeeMe program was originally developed as an experimental project at **Cornell University**. Over the years, it grew popular and began to take on a life of its own, as millions of people started using freeware CU-SeeMe and creating resources to support it. Thanks to the volunteer efforts of CU-SeeMe fans all over the world, the Internet abounds with CU-SeeMe chat rooms, technical-support Web sites, and spiffy add-on shareware programs. Chapter 13 mentions a few of them.

The "original" CU-SeeMe is still free

If you want to take freeware CU-SeeMe for a spin, you can download it from the CU-SeeMe Cool Site at **http://www.rocketcharged.com/cu-seeme/**. The Windows and Macintosh versions are shown in **Figures 12.18** and **12.19**, respectively.

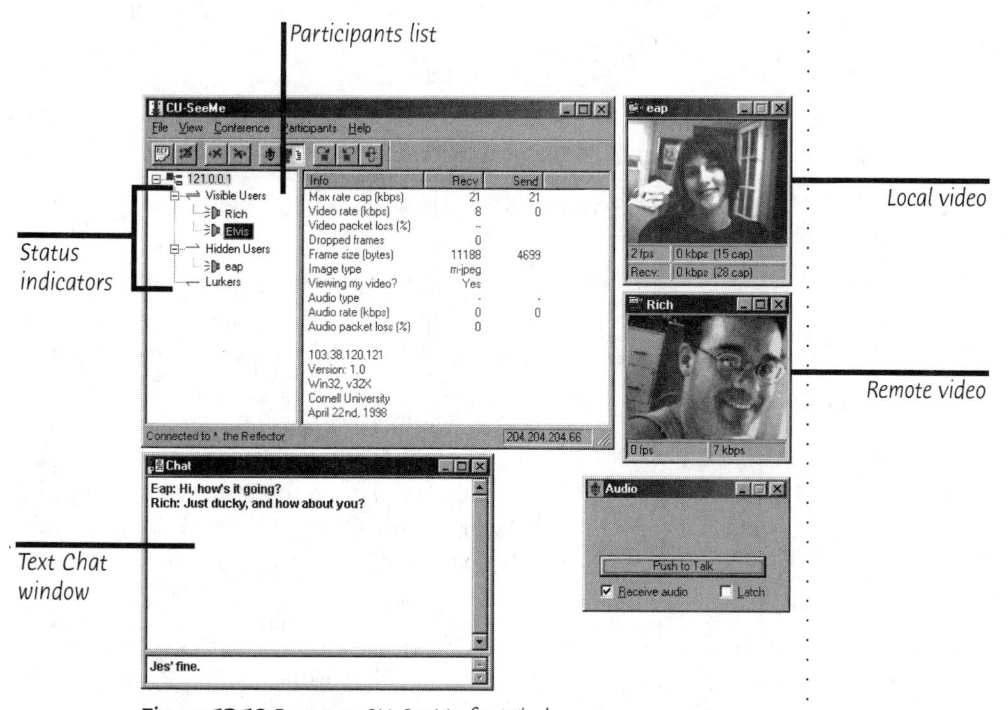

Figure 12.18 *Freeware CU-SeeMe for Windows.*

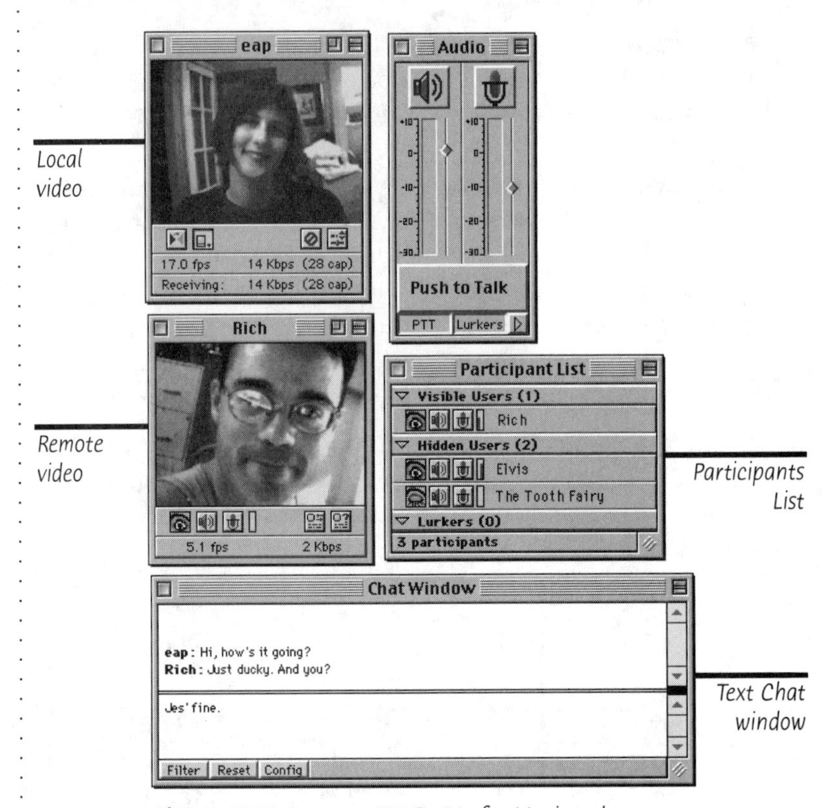

Figure 12.19 *Freeware CU-SeeMe for Macintosh.*

It's Compatible!

Freeware CU-SeeMe fans include programmers, who have created versions of the program for a variety of operating systems—which means freeware CU-SeeMe users can **talk to just about anyone!** This version of CU-SeeMe is available for most types of computers, including Windows 95/98, Windows 3.1, Macintosh, Linux, and even the defunct (but still alive and kicking) OS/2 and Amiga. In addition, you can conference with individuals or visit group chat rooms hosted by White Pine Reflector and MeetingPoint servers (where you can also talk with White Pine CU-SeeMe and NetMeeting users). And of course, you can't beat the price!

A Shaky Future

So why didn't I mention the freeware version of CU-SeeMe in the first place? Why is there a whole chapter written about the $89 (or $69) version? After taking the freeware CU-SeeMe program for a spin, I decided that for computer, Internet, and camming novices, it might be more trouble than it's worth. Freeware CU-SeeMe has many limitations, as you'll see in the upcoming long list of its shortcomings. On top of that, the freeware version may not be around much longer.

White Pine has a long history with the Cornell CU-SeeMe project. They acquired the rights to create a commercial version of the program back in the early days, and have designed server products that allow users of both White Pine and freeware CU-SeeMe to join conferences on White Pine's reflectors. In the fall of 1998, the Cornell project came to an end, and White Pine acquired full rights to the freeware version of the software as well.

This development puts the future of freeware CU-SeeMe in doubt. At the time of this writing, the people at White Pine were in the process of figuring out a way to strike a workable balance between developing cutting-edge videoconferencing technologies while continuing to support the freeware CU-SeeMe community.

What You Get...

Why freeware CU-SeeMe is cool:

- It's available for a variety of operating systems, including Windows, Macintosh, Linux, and even OS/2 and Amiga.
- You get access to a wide community of users (White Pine CU-SeeMe, freeware CU-SeeMe, and NetMeeting) through chat rooms hosted by White Pine MeetingPoint servers.
- It supports group conferences hosted on White Pine reflector or MeetingPoint servers.

...and Don't Get

Freeware CU-SeeMe's shortcomings:

- Often proves more difficult to get up and running, although the CU-SeeMe Cool Site and several other sites do provide tutorials, FAQs, and message boards (see Chapter 13).
- If you're on a network, freeware CU-SeeMe may confuse your network IP address with your Internet IP address and display error messages when you try to connect to individuals and chat rooms (Chapter 13 talks about this problem).
- Incompatible with many of the newer cams and video products (although it does work with QuickCam, Comp Pro Dcam, Snappy, and other well-established hardware).
- Doesn't support directory servers. To connect to individuals and group conferences, you need to know their IP address.
- Only supports grayscale video. (The Windows version does support color video, but installing the codec and getting it to work can be tricky.)

- Lacks important business-conferencing features such as whiteboard, application sharing, and multipoint conferencing. (You can, however, download separate whiteboard shareware applications from the Cu-SeeMe Cool Site.)
- In group chats, it doesn't allow you to see remote video windows for White Pine CU-SeeMe or NetMeeting users, although you can still exchange voice and text chat messages.

Free with Your Cam

Last but not least in this chapter are the videoconferencing products that ship with many cam products. For example, the CU-SeeMe cam and VideoLabs's PlanetView conferencing system come with CU-SeeMe; and Logitech's QuickCam VC comes with its own VideoPhone program.

Cam-specific videoconferencing programs like VideoPhone do have their good points. Because they're made especially for the cam that goes with them, you may get better video and audio performance and quality. Unfortunately, custom programs like VideoPhone let you conference only with people who have the same type of cam. But QuickCam VC is a popular product, so you may already have friends, family, and coworkers who also use VideoPhone. You won't have access, however, to the wider videoconferencing community unless you use a more common product, such as CU-SeeMe, iVisit, or NetMeeting.

Summary

In this chapter, you got acquainted with basic videoconferencing concepts and three popular freeware videoconferencing programs: iVisit, NetMeeting, and the freeware (Cornell) version of CU-SeeMe. Once you've mastered one videoconferencing program, you can get the hang of the other ones, since most video chat applications have similar features.

- There are **four types of video conferences**: point-to-point (for individuals), group (through a chat room hosted on a conferencing server), multicast (a group conference that doesn't require a server), and cybercast (one person talks and the rest watch and listen).
- Most videoconferencing programs have **similar features**, including video windows, audio controls, text chat, a participants list, and a contacts list. NetMeeting for Windows also features whiteboard and application sharing features for online business meetings and collaboration.
- **iVisit**, by BoxTop Software, makes point-to-point conferencing easy for Windows and Macintosh users. If all you want is to keep in touch with friends and family, iVisit is ideal. You can download it from **http://www.ivisit.com/**.
- **NetMeeting** is easy to use and has all the features you need for personal and business conferencing. Unfortunately, it is only available for Windows users. You can download it from **http://www.microsoft.com/netmeeting/**.
- The popular **freeware version of CU-SeeMe** allows you to conference with users of White Pine CU-SeeMe and NetMeeting in CU-SeeMe chat rooms. Unfortunately, it isn't always easy for Internet, cam, or computer novices to make this freeware program work properly. If you'd like to try it out, you can download it from the CU-SeeMe Cool Site at **http://www.rocketcharged.com/cu-seeme/**.
- Many cams come with CU-SeeMe or their own videoconferencing software. Although custom programs like QuickCam VC's VideoPhone combine good audio and video quality with user-friendliness, they limit your video-chat social circle to people who have the same cam as you.

Next, in Chapter 13, we'll take a look at sources for help when things don't quite go as planned, as well as a handful of other freeware products that'll add to your videoconferencing experience.

13 Troubleshooting, Online Help, and Fun Stuff

So, have you got your videoconferencing program up and running yet? If not, and the reason is that something isn't working right, this chapter has the answers to some common glitches that people run into. If your videoconferencing software works just dandy, then you're ready to go beyond the basics. This chapter helps out with that, as well, pointing you toward online help and valuable resources where you can find more information, meet other cammers, and download some cool shareware that helps you get the most out of videoconferencing.

In this chapter:

- **Troubleshooting** your videoconferencing program: Dealing with annoying error messages, firewalls, and common videoconferencing glitches.
- **Online help and resources**: Places to go, things to see, and where to get help.
- **Other stuff you'll need**: Helpful shareware programs that enhance your videoconferencing.

Troubleshooting

Can't get your videoconferencing program to work right? When you think about it, videoconferencing is amazingly complex and sometimes things can go wrong. If that happens, don't despair! Most of the problems people encounter are pretty straightforward and easy to fix. Just read the following sections. And if you *still* run into a problem not explained here, read the "Online Help and Resources" section later in this chapter. Chances are good you can get the answer to your question from other people in the videoconferencing community.

Connection Problems

Let's start with issues you might encounter when trying to connect with someone for a videoconference.

IP Address Errors

IP address errors happen when there's a problem with your ISP or Internet settings. As you'll recall from Chapter 11, videoconferencing programs use IP addresses to identify people on the Internet. When a server or the person you're trying to call can't get your IP address, you'll get an error message like the one shown in **Figure 13.1**. Although the various videoconferencing programs show their own versions of error messages, the word "IP address" should tip you off about what's wrong.

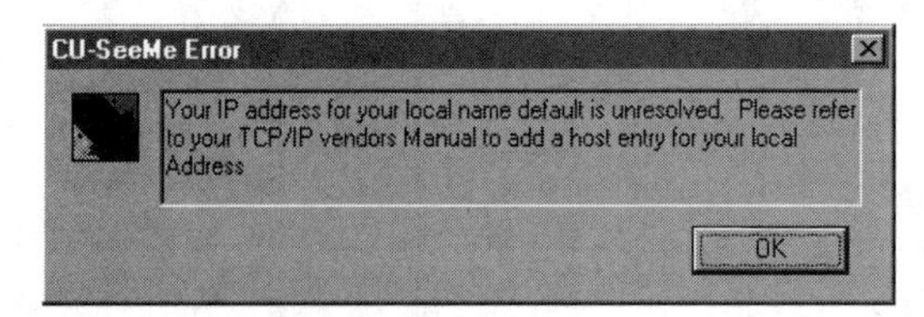

Figure 13.1 *An IP address error message in CU-SeeMe.*

If you're on a network

If you're hooked up to a network, you can have IP address issues there, too. Every computer that connects to other computers through a network or over the Internet has an IP address. When you network your computers, you've got *two* IP addresses: one for your network and one for the Internet. When you connect to another computer (such as a server, or a friend's computer for a point-to-point conference), the other computer wants to know your Internet IP address. If your computer sends your network IP address, the other computer will reject it.

Re-install Internet software

To solve ISP address problems, try re-installing your Internet software. This might be on the disk or CD-ROM that your ISP gave you, or it might be software that came with your operating system. Your videoconferencing program will generally recognize whichever IP address you installed most recently, so this should take care of the error. If it persists, contact your ISP or system administrator.

> **Use an E-mail Address Instead**. In order to call someone up, you need to know their IP address. And IP addresses generally change every time a person connects to the Internet. It's easier to contact someone for a videoconference using their e-mail address—but this only works when the party is listed with an ILS server. For more about IP addresses and ILS servers, review Chapter 11.

No Response

A "no response" message, like the one shown for CU-SeeMe in **Figure 13.2**, means that no one's home. Either you've called an IP address that doesn't exist, or you've called a person or server that doesn't have a videoconferencing setup.

Figure 13.2 *No-response message shown in CU-SeeMe.*

Host Errors

With some videoconferencing programs, Windows users sometimes get a pesky "Get Host by Name" error message when they try to connect. If you're having this problem, I've got a quick fix for you. First, do a Find and locate your **winsock.dll** file. It probably lives in either the C:\Windows folder or the C:\Windows\System folder. Next, create a file named Hosts and store it in the same folder. Once you create a Hosts file, you shouldn't get the error message anymore.

To create a Hosts file:

1. Launch that trusty little text editor, NotePad, by clicking Start | Programs | Accessories | NotePad.

2. When NotePad opens, type your IP address followed by the term **localhost**, as in 000.0.0.0 localhost. (If you don't know your IP address, Chapter 11 tells you how to get it.)

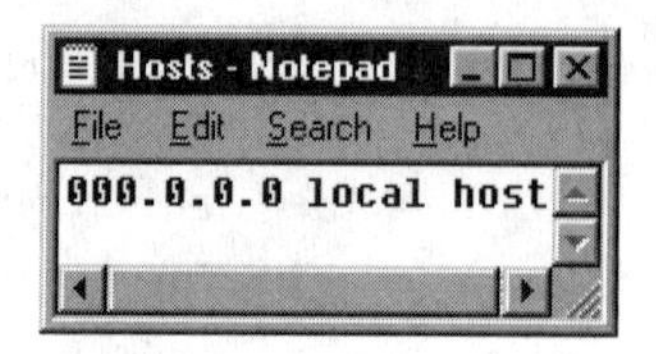

3. Save your little text file to the folder that contains your winsock.dll file, and type **"Hosts"** in the File Name box. *Be sure you type the quotation marks, too,* or Windows will automatically add the .TXT filename extension—and your new Hosts file won't work.

Watch Those Dynamic IP Addresses! If your ISP assigns IP addresses dynamically—and most do—then you'll need to view your IP address (as explained in Chapter 11) and retype the IP address in the Hosts file.

Differing Videoconference Software

"My friend has a different program," you say? Yes—unfortunately, today's videoconferencing applications can't talk directly to one another. Point-to-point and multicast conferences require that you and your correspondents all use the same program. However, White Pine does offer a server product called MeetingPoint, which allows CU-SeeMe and NetMeeting users to talk on a reflector. MeetingPoint reflectors also support several other popular videoconferencing products, including Intel's VideoPhone, ProShare, and Team Station.

To solve the incompatibility problem, you and the people you want to conference with should all start using the same program (NetMeeting and iVisit are free), or figure out a way to meet on a White Pine MeetingPoint reflector. Some public conferencing rooms do support MeetingPoint and allow you to set up your own conferences. Other reflector owners rent space on their servers.

Talk with Anyone...Very Soon! White Pine plans to release a version of CU-SeeMe that will allow point-to-point or multicast conferencing with *any* videoconferencing program that conforms to the H.323 standard, including NetMeeting. The H.323 standard is a set of guidelines for capturing, compressing, sending, and receiving video over networks. Most hardware and software companies comply or plan to comply with the H.323 guidelines.

Looking for a Server

People who use CU-SeeMe and NetMeeting can join group conferences on CU-SeeMe reflectors. In addition, NetMeeting users can hang out on NetMeeting servers. But how do you figure out where the action is?

Both programs come with a built-in list of public reflectors and conferences that you can connect to.

If you're looking for more, try RocketCharged's Reflector List to find general (and adult) CU-SeeMe reflectors, as well as places that rent out reflector space so you can host private conferences. RocketCharged is at **http://www.rocketcharged.com/cu-seeme/reflectors.html**.

You can also check out White Pine's Video Chat Directory at **http://www.wpine.com/Products/CU-SeeMe/VCD/index.html**.

In addition, the "Online Help and Resources" section later in this chapter points you to other starting points for exploring the world of videoconferencing.

For NetMeeting Only

The **NetMeeting Place Server List** has links to the 50 best NetMeeting servers—although, unfortunately, they don't separate the adult sites from the general sites. They also provide a long list of ILS servers.

My Video Won't Display

Desktop video can get awfully finicky sometimes, and you may need to exit the videoconferencing program and check your cam's settings. CU-SeeMe and NetMeeting do work with most types of Web cams and video cards, and iVisit and the freeware version of CU-SeeMe support most popular camming products, so don't get discouraged. Here are a few common video problems with some fixes.

This list of checkpoints applies to both Windows and Macintosh users

Things to check when the video won't display:

- **Ooops! It's unplugged**. Make sure your cam is still connected securely to your computer. They do get unplugged occasionally.
- **Old cam or video camera software**. If you bought your cam or your video card a long time ago, the videoconferencing program might not work with the software you installed with your cam. That's okay. Most manufacturers let you download the latest software and drivers from their Web site.
- **Corrupted cam software**. Sometimes, if your cam software gets corrupted, CU-SeeMe won't recognize your cam. Correcting this problem may be as easy as re-installing the cam software.
- **Incompatible cam software settings**. Check your cam software's settings. Some cams come with video codecs (such as QuickCam's Videc compression) that aren't supported by

most videoconferencing programs. Also, some cams allow you to capture pictures and video at sizes that aren't supported by most other videoconferencing programs. Make sure that your image size setting (as covered in Chapter 2) is set to 160x120 (quarter-screen).

- **Another program's using your cam**. Cams can only work with one application at a time. If another program is using your cam, your videoconferencing program will display an error message when you try to start it up. For example, if you have a Web cam running, you'll need to exit the Web cam program before you can begin videoconferencing.
- **Incompatible cam or video card**: CU-SeeMe, NetMeeting, and iVisit work with most types of cams and video cards. But there's always an exception to the rule. If you've tried everything and still can't get your video to work, then your videoconferencing software may not work with your video card or cam. If this happens, try another videoconferencing program, or buy another cam or video card.

Reflector/Browser Problems

When looking for CU-SeeMe reflectors on the Web, you'll find that some people provide links to the reflector. Click these links, and your browser will launch CU-SeeMe as a **helper application**. But for this to work right, you need to tell your Web browser how to recognize CU-SeeMe. (**Windows** users may not need to do this, because Windows applications generally recognize each other through the Registry.) The following steps take you through the process of introducing your browser to reflector links.

I'm going to show you these steps with Netscape Navigator 4.0 for Macintosh, but the process is similar regardless of browser or operating system. The exception is when you're using Internet Explorer 4.0 or higher with Windows 98; in that case, Windows automatically sets up your helper applications for you.

To tell your browser how to recognize reflector links:

1. Display your browser's options or preferences, usually by selecting Options or Preferences from the Edit menu.
2. When the appropriate dialog box appears, display the Applications options. **Figure 13.3** illustrates the options for Netscape Navigator 4.0 for Macintosh.

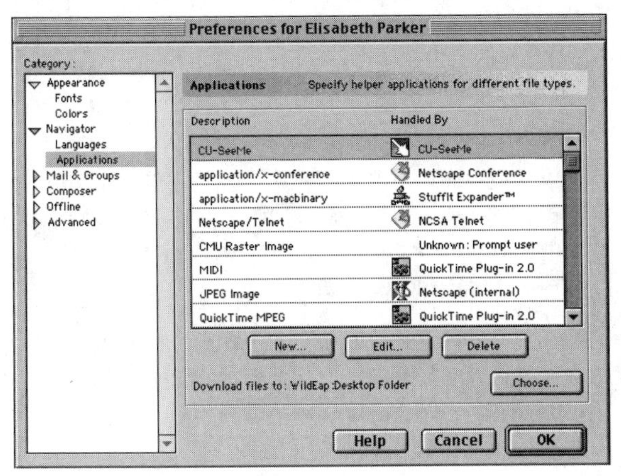

Figure 13.3 *Preferences dialog box in Netscape Navigator 4.0 for Macintosh, with Applications options displayed.*

3. Click the New button to display the Edit Type dialog box, as shown in **Figure 13.4**.
4. Type **CU-SeeMe** in the Application box, **Application/x-cu-seeme** in the Mime Type box, and **.cu,.csm** in the Suffixes box.
5. Now you need to browse for your CU-SeeMe Helper application (**Macintosh**) or the CU-SeeMe application file (**Windows**). Click the Choose or Browse button, select the file, and click Open.
6. When you return to the dialog box with your application's preferences or options displayed, click OK to save your changes.

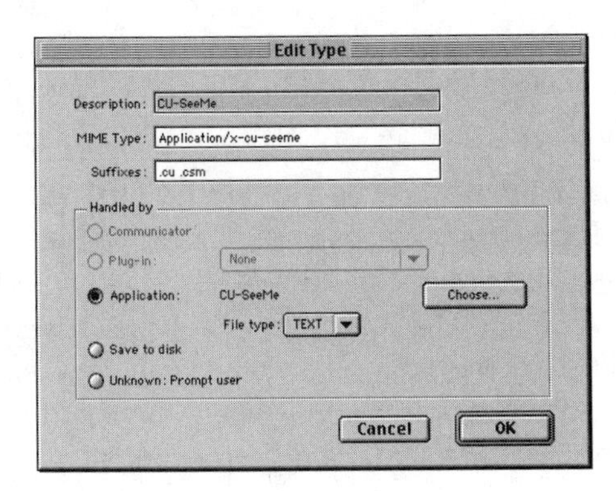

Figure 13.4 *Telling a browser to recognize CU-SeeMe (in Netscape Navigator 4.0).*

Behind the Firewall

If you access the Internet through work, school, or another location, then you probably have to deal with **firewalls** (also called **proxy servers**). Firewalls keep your organization's system safe from hackers who try to mess around with the network. The drawback is that firewalls may not be set up to let people run videoconferencing programs. Go to your network administration staff and ask *very nicely* to have the firewall set up so you can videoconference. If they don't know how to do that, send them to the Web for more information.

- **CU-SeeMe**: White Pine's Web site has a searchable tech support page that has the answers to most questions. Go to **http://support.wpine.com/cuseeme/**.
- **NetMeeting**: Microsoft's NetMeeting page offers lots of information for users, and a free Resource Kit for network administrators that makes it easier to set up a server so people can use NetMeeting. You can find it at **http://www.microsoft.com/netmeeting/**.
- **iVisit**: The troubleshooting document that comes with iVisit has information about iVisit and firewalls.

Mean ol' Network Administrators!

In some situations, your organization's network administrators may not want to allow videoconferencing with CU-SeeMe. Before you start whining "Gee, that's no fun," put yourself in their shoes and multiply the amount of time you spend trying to get things to work on your computer by however many computers there are in your organization! The network administrator is likely to be overworked, short on patience, and reluctant to deal with a technology that may cause more headaches.

You'll need to do some serious persuading, and your boss or department head can probably help you. **Approach it as you would any other business proposal.** After all, many companies, schools, and nonprofits spend big bucks on videoconferencing because the lower phone bills and travel expenses save time and money in the long run. With today's low-cost cams and CU-SeeMe, your organization can do videoconferencing for peanuts. Who knows? Your network administrator may get so enthusiastic, she'll want to set up a reflector, too!

I Don't Have a Cam!

Maybe your cam setup doesn't work with your videoconferencing program. Or maybe you're still looking into the world of videoconferencing and haven't yet purchased a cam. But don't let a silly little detail like that stop you from exploring!

Most videoconferencing programs do allow you to use the audio and text chat features, even if you don't have video capabilities. You can also use SoftCam for Windows or Imposter for Macintosh. These programs let you use a folder that contains still images as your video source, instead of a cam. The "Bad Hair Day?" section later in this chapter tells you more about these programs.

Online Help and Resources

If you're looking for help with your videoconferencing, a place to chat, the latest news, nearby videoconferencing events, and/or other resources, you'll have no shortage of information. You can find lots of helpful Web sites that are well organized, frequently updated, fun to visit, and packed with useful information and tidbits.

General Resources

Want to find out where the action is, or get general information about videoconferencing that isn't focused on a particular type of cam or product? Try the ImeetU, Cammunity, and RocketCharged Web sites.

ImeetU.com

Find out about cool videoconferencing events—or schedule time on ImeetU.com's reflector and host your own! **ImeetU.com** also has live chat, a message board, and links, so you can meet other people who like to videoconference. And best of all, it's free. Visit the iMeetU Web site, shown in **Figure 13.6**, at **http://www.imeetu.com/**.

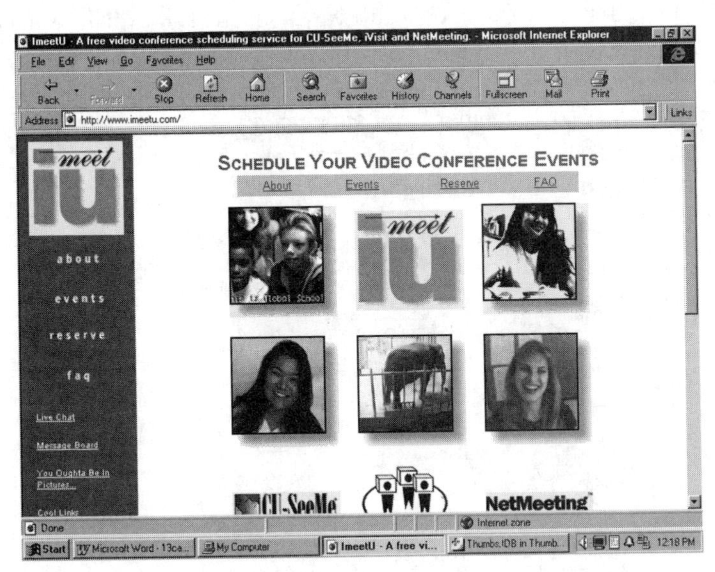

Figure 13.6 *ImeetU Web site.*

Cammunity

Cammunity is a great general resource for cammers, with links to cool Web cams, a free e-mail newsletter, and software/hardware recommendations. In addition, they offer a variety of online forums, including a CU-SeeMe discussion group. They host live video events, too. Go to **http://www.cammunity.com/**.

RocketCharged

RocketCharged, a vendor of videoconferencing solutions for schools and businesses, also has informative Web sites and message boards for CU-SeeMe and iVisit users. Start off at the RocketCharged Talk site at **http://www.rocketcharged.com/talk/**.

CU-SeeMe Help

Millions of people around the world use either the White Pine (commercial) or Cornell (freeware) version of CU-SeeMe. Users of these programs can even conference with one another on the same reflectors. As a result, the Web abounds with fans who post information on using and troubleshooting CU-SeeMe. Since White Pine CU-SeeMe is easier to set up and use, most of these resources focus on the far more feisty Cornell version.

White Pine's CU-SeeMe Pages

Want to get help, find out about cool events, meet people, and keep up on CU-SeeMe news? White Pine hosts a special Web site for the CU-SeeMe community and the videoconferencing/camming world at large. **CU-SeeMe World,** as shown in **Figure 13.7**, helps answer the question, "Now that I have videochat software, what do I do with it?" You can register (it's free) and become a CU Citizen. This gives you access to members-only features, including directories of video chat rooms, listings of your fellow members, announcements of online events, user forums, Web-based ILS searches, tips, news, and more. Point your browser to **http://www.cuseeme.com/**.

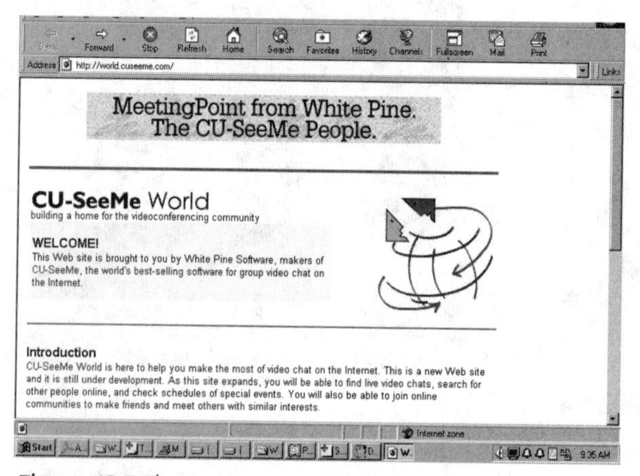

Figure 13.7 *The CU-SeeMe World site.*

FAQs

White Pine's excellent FAQ pages offer a good list of common questions with links to detailed answers. If your problem doesn't appear on the list, you can use the search form to see if White Pine has the answer to your question in their database. White Pine offers separate support pages for Windows and Macintosh users. The Macintosh support page is shown in **Figure 13.8**. Here are the two URLs:
http://support.wpine.com/cuseemewin/
http://support.wpine.com/cuseememac/

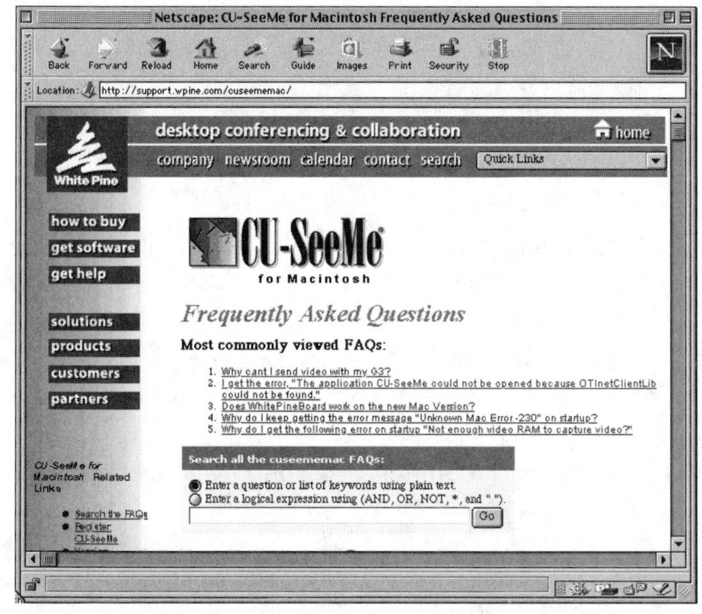

Figure 13.8 *White Pine's CU-SeeMe for Macintosh FAQs page.*

CU-SeeMe Cool Site

RocketCharged also hosts the CU-SeeMe Cool Site, which has lots of useful information, along with a message board, for White Pine and Cornell users. Go to **http://www.rocketcharged.com/cu-seeme/**.

CU-SeeMe Network

The freeware CU-SeeMe crowd hangs out on the CU-SeeMe Network at **http://www.cu-seeme.net**. If you dig around, you'll find the freeware CU-SeeMe download, Bill (a.k.a. "Squeek") Woodland's manual and FAQs from the Cornell server, SpiderChris's freeware CU-SeeMe add-ons, and more. See **Figure 13.9**.

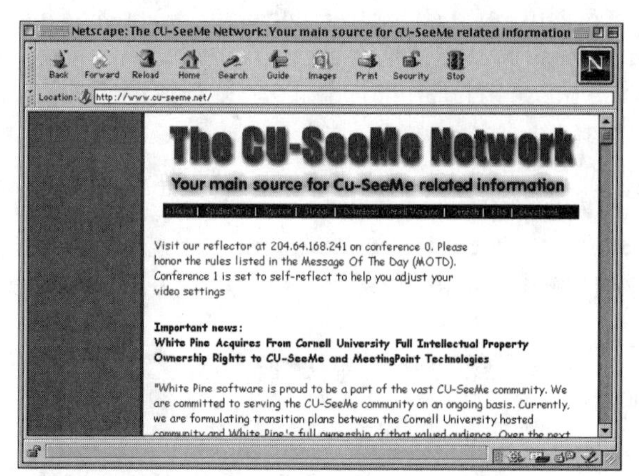

Figure 13.9 *The CU-SeeMe Network.*

NetMeeting Help

Following are some resources for NetMeeting users.

Microsoft's NetMeeting sites

- Microsoft provides two Web sites to help you with NetMeeting. The **Home User site** and the **Business User site**. Both provide tutorials, product information, questions and answers, and more.

  http://www.microsoft.com/netmeeting/nm2/
  http://www.microsoft.com/netmeeting/corp/

Meeting By Wire

- At the Meeting By Wire site (**http://www.meetingbywire.com/**) you can sign up for their mailing list and exchange tips, tricks, and advice with other NetMeeting fans. Or follow the links to Web pages to keep up-to-date on the latest NetMeeting news and events. See **Figure 13.10**.

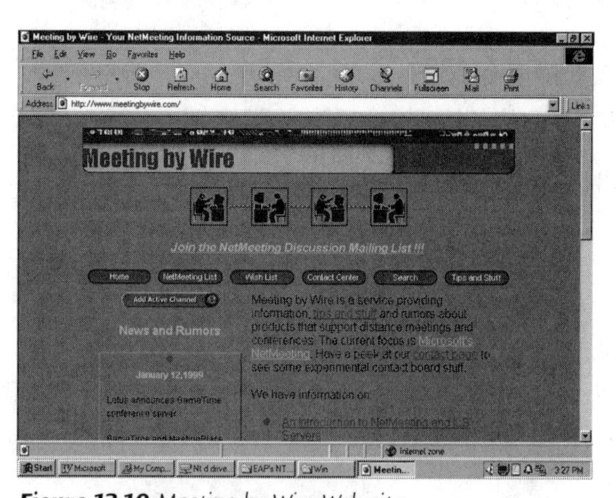

Figure 13.10 *Meeting by Wire Web site.*

- Check out the NetMeeting Place at **http://www.netmeet.net/**. Here, you'll find all sorts of offerings you won't find on the "official" site, including how to use NetMeeting with ICQ and other buddy-list programs. The site maintains lists of ILS servers, too, and links to other Web sites.

The NetMeeting Place

iVisit Help

Want to learn more about iVisit? Drop by the iVisit Web site. They have a FAQ, a User Guide, and a Message Board where users post questions and answers, as shown in **Figure 13.11**.

http://www.ivisit.com/faq.html
http://www.ivisit.com/guide.html
http://www.ivisit.com/support/

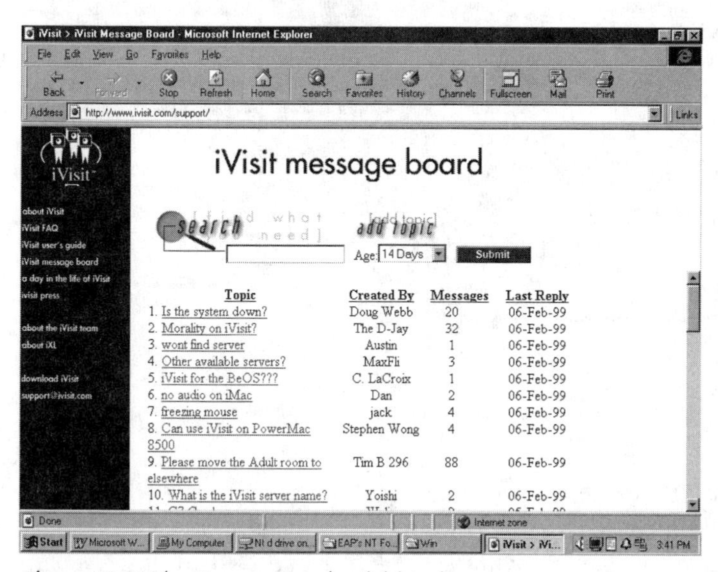

Figure 13.11 *The Message Board at iVisit's site.*

Other Stuff You'll Need

Hey, you've worked pretty hard to get your videoconferencing program up and running, right? Now it's time to reward yourself with a couple of nice downloadable shareware treats that extend your videoconferencing program's capabililities. First, you should get ICQ, a freeware program to help you find out when your friends are online. You also might want to pick up SoftCam for Windows or Imposter for Macintosh.

Find Your Buddies Online

It's a lot easier to connect with folks for a videoconference chat if you know when they're online. **Mirabilis's ICQ** (pronounced "I seek you") **for Windows and Macintosh** tells you when your buddies are online at the same time you are, and lets you send them an instant message so you can hook up for a chat.

If you are or have been a subscriber to America Online, then ICQ should look familiar to you (in fact, AOL now owns Mirabilis and ICQ). With ICQ, you create a "buddies list," as shown in **Figure 13.12**. When you're connected to the Internet and someone on your list goes online, the icon next to the person's name changes to notify you.

ICQ: freeware for instant messaging

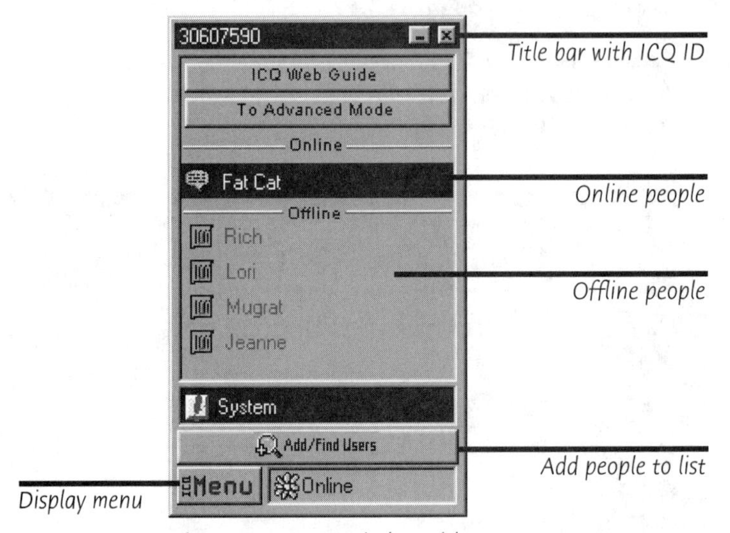

Figure 13.12 *ICQ window with "buddies list" (shown in Windows).*

Like CU-SeeMe and NetMeeting, ICQ looks up the e-mail address on an ILS to see whether or not someone is online. This means you and the people you want to conference with will need to advertise yourselves on a public ILS. **ICQ has its own ILS, too,** and helps you publish your information during the setup.

To download the program, view a tutorial, and get more information, visit **http:www.icq.com/**.

Learn More About ICQ. There's plenty of information on the ICQ Web site if you'd like to learn more. Or, you can purchase the *ICQ Guide* (published by ICQ, Inc.) from Barnes and Noble's Web site at **http://www.barnesandnoble.com/**.

Bad Hair Day? Or No Cam?

Maybe you still can't get your videoconferencing program to work with your cam for some reason. Or maybe your cam works fine but you don't *always* want people to see the real you! Try SoftCam for Windows or Imposter for Macintosh.

SoftCam: $8
Imposter: $20

SoftCam and Imposter let you create slide shows with pictures. You can create a special folder for these pictures and use them, instead of a real cam, as a video source for CU-SeeMe. If you've got a recalcitrant cam that doesn't work with CU-SeeMe, SoftCam can also grab the video for you. So why not try one of these programs and put your best face forward!

- **SoftCam** by Luminositi, Inc. costs $8, and you can download it from **http://www.luminositi.com/**.
- **Imposter** by Michael Eskin costs $20; it's available for download from the CU-SeeMe Cool Site's Plug-Ins page at **http://www.rocketcharged.com/cu-seeme/plugins.html**.

Summary

This chapter aims to help you solve your videoconferencing glitches, or at least point you to the right places to go for more information.

- You can get rid of **IP address problems and host-related error messages** by making some simple changes to your Internet and network configurations.
- In general, you cannot do point-to-point or multicast conferencing unless the people involved have the same videoconferencing program. However, White Pine's **MeetingPoint** servers do allow people who use CU-SeeMe, NetMeeting, and a few other videoconferencing programs to get together for group conferences.
- CU-SeeMe comes with a list of **Contact Cards** for popular group conferences, and Web chats and events.
- If the **video on your videoconferencing program isn't working**, you can often fix it by downloading the latest version of your cam software or changing your cam software's settings. Make sure that some other program isn't using your cam. You may need to replace an incompatible cam or video card.
- You can access a CU-SeeMe reflector through a link on a Web page by **configuring your Web browser** to recognize CU-SeeMe.
- A **firewall** (proxy server) can cause you problems when it comes to videoconferencing. Ask really nicely, and your system administrator may change the proxy server settings so you can videoconference.
- Looking for the **cool stuff?** Whether you need help or just want to make new friends, you can find lots of videoconferencing information **on the Web.**
- Once you get your videoconferencing program up and running, check out **ICQ and SoftCam or Imposter.** ICQ tells you when your friends are online so you can send an instant message and meet for a conference call. SoftCam (Windows) and Imposter (Macintosh) display pictures in your local video window, so you can hide!

Next, in the final chapter, we'll talk about cams and audio.

Cams and Audio

14

What does audio have to do with camming? Well, you don't have to know anything about audio at all in order to take pictures or set up a Web cam. However, a basic understanding of digital audio will come in handy when you're making movies (Chapter 6), putting sounds on your Web pages to go with your pictures (Chapter 7), and videoconferencing (Chapters 11–13).

In this chapter:

- Sound file types, audio codecs, and quality settings
- Changing your cam's audio settings
- Exporting audio from a movie
- Recording audio with **Sound Recorder** for Windows and **Simple Sound** for Macintosh
- Converting audio files with **SoundApp** (Macintosh only)
- Getting free sound files from the Web

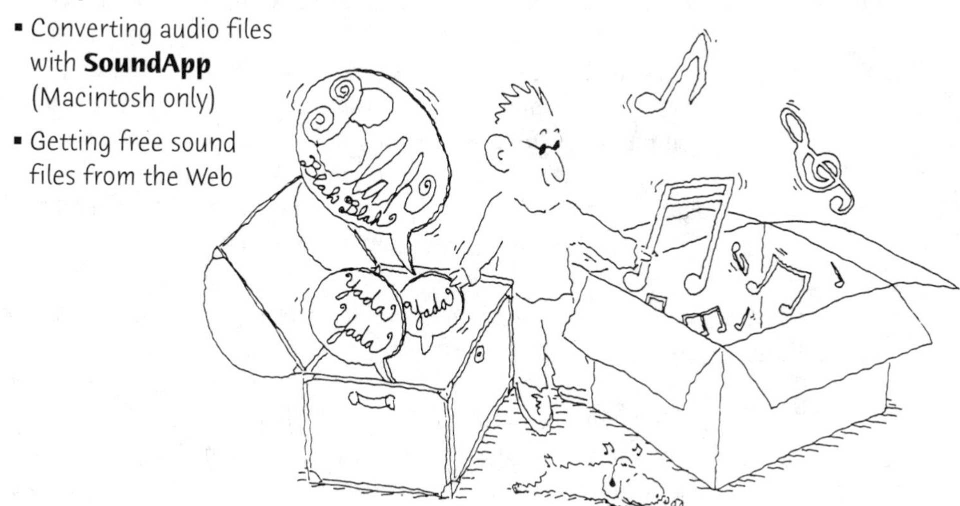

What You Need

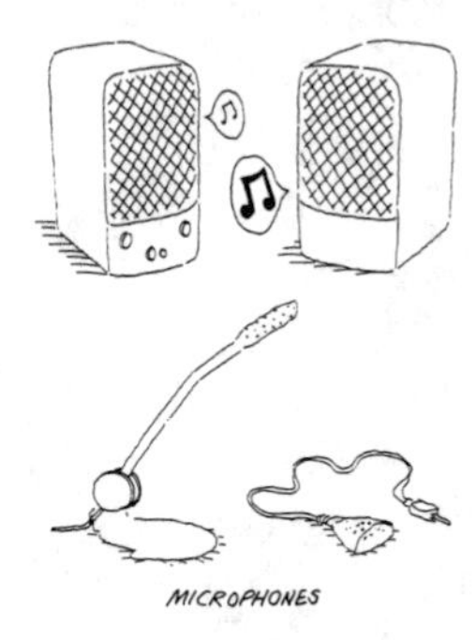

Before you begin recording and playing audio, you need a **sound card,** a **microphone,** and **speakers** for your computer. Luckily, most computers come with sound cards and built-in microphones and speakers these days. If for some reason yours doesn't, you can purchase all these items inexpensively from a local computer store. Sound cards vary in price, depending on the level of quality you want, and a microphone and speakers can be had for well under $100.

You also need software for recording and playing sounds. Luckily, Windows comes with the **Sound Recorder** and **Multimedia Player** applications for recording and playing sounds, and Macintosh comes with **Simple Sound**.

Macintosh only

Macintosh users will also need to download Norman Franke's freeware **SoundApp** in order to convert and play various types of sound files. We'll talk more about SoundApp later in this chapter.

Audio 101

Audio can **liven up your Web pages and movies** in many ways. For example, your Web page can feature a snapshot of Rover that barks when a visitor clicks on the picture. Or spice up your movies with background music and sound effects using QuickEditor (as covered in Chapter 6 and later in this chapter). Whether you plan to grab sound files from the Web or record them yourself, it helps to know about common audio formats—including file types, bit depths, codecs, and sample rates. That way, you won't feel bewildered by the mechanics of saving a sound file, or when choosing which files to download from a Web site.

Some Definitions

Analog, Digital, and Digitize. *Analog* means "not on a computer." Pictures in your photo album, a letter from a friend, the sounds you hear, your brand-new automatic peach defuzzer, and other real-world objects and happenings are all analog data. The word *digital* refers to information that lives on a computer. *Digitizing* means converting analog data to a format that your computer understands. In fact, you digitize images and sounds every time you use your cam and microphone. Whew! I prefer the word *camming*, don't you?

Types of Sound Files

When you start recording sounds and cruising the Web for sound files, you'll come across a variety of popular sound file formats that you can download and play. In addition, Web browsers are capable of playing several types of audio files. QuickEditor, SoundApp for Macintosh, QuickTime, and other multimedia applications let you save recorded sounds to various file formats. The following table tells you more about the most prevalent sound-file types, the applications that support them, and when you should use them.

Common Sound File Types

File Type	What Is It?	Supported By	When to Use It
AU	Stands for Audio UNIX. This oldie-but-goodie was originally developed by Sun Microsystems for UNIX machines.	Netscape Navigator Internet Explorer QuickEditor Windows Multimedia Player SoundApp	When adding sound effects and brief recordings to Web pages (Chapter 7) and movies (Chapter 6).
AIFF	Stands for Audio Information File Format, developed by Apple Computer.	Netscape Navigator Internet Explorer QuickEditor Windows Multimedia Player SoundApp Photos4Us	When adding sound effects and brief recordings to Web pages (Chapter 7) and to screen savers created with Photos4Us for Macintosh (Chapter 3).
WAV	Short for WAVeform. Microsoft made this sound file format part of the Windows operating system, and the format is also supported by most Macintosh multimedia applications.	Sound Recorder and Multimedia Player for Windows SoundApp for Macintosh QuickTime QuickEditor A+ ScreenSaver Creator for Windows QuickTime or SoundApp for Macintosh	For recording sounds with Windows and adding them to Web pages, movies, screen savers, and other multimedia projects. Sound Recorder for Windows only saves files to the WAV format. Since SoundApp, QuickTime, and QuickEditor support WAVs, Macintosh users can use WAV files, too.
Macintosh System Sound	The format to which Macintosh audio is saved when a Macintosh user records with Simple Sound.	QuickEditor for Macintosh and Windows can import System Sounds. However, since we live in a Windows world, very few applications support this format.	You can record audio on a Macintosh with Simple Sound and convert the file to WAV, AU, or AIFF using SoundApp, or import it into QuickEditor and use it in a movie.
MIDI	Stands for Musical Instrument Digital Interface. Enables creation of complex music arrangements with small file sizes. Only works for computerized (digital) audio; cannot be used for recording live (analog) sounds.	Netscape Navigator Internet Explorer QuickTime QuickEditor (when formatted as a QuickTime movie) Windows Multimedia Player SoundApp	Perfect for adding a musical sound track that plays on a Web page or during a movie.

Other Audio Files

In addition to the formats charted just above, you may come across the following types of audio files:

- **QuickTime, AVI and MPEG**: The QuickTime, AVI (Audio Video Interleaved) and MPEG (Motion Pictures Expert Group) formats are generally used for making movies. However, they have also become popular for audio files—especially the QuickTime and MPEG formats. You can make movies with sound and then use QuickEditor to export the sound track as a movie or as a sound file.
- **MP3 (MPEG 3)**: MP3 has rapidly become popular for distributing and listening to high-quality musical recordings. However, the cams and video software covered in this book do not support it. For more about MP3, and some cool free downloads, go to **http://www.mp3.com/**.
- **RAM, RA**: Real Networks's special format for streaming audio and video broadcasts over the Internet. For more information or to download the Real Player, visit **http://www.realnetworks.com/**.

Recommended Audio File Types

Yep, that's a lot of sound file formats. Luckily, you really only need to think about three of them when it comes to Web pages and movies. For sound effects, voice recordings, and music clips, stick with WAV or AU files. They're popular, and most Web and multimedia applications support them. For background music in your movies and Web pages, try some MIDI music. MIDI files take up very little disk space and you can find them on the Web, as described later in this chapter.

More About MIDI: If you're a musician, you can have lots of fun with creating and editing your own MIDI sound tracks. Windows users can try out CakeWalk's $129 Home Studio. Download it from **http://www.cakewalk.com/**.

Macintosh users can download Masao Maeda's $20 MIDIgraphy from **http://ux01.so-net.or.jp/~mmaeda/indexe.html#Works_mg**.

Audio Codecs

Audio applications offer a bewildering array of **audio codecs** that you can use when videoconferencing, or when recording and saving sound files. Codec stands for **co**mpressor/**dec**ompressor or, as some people say, **co**der/**dec**oder. A codec compresses audio or video data when it's saved to disk or transferred over the Internet, and then decompresses the data so it can be heard.

There are many popular audio codecs. However, if you're just getting started with audio and want to make sure that everyone can play your sounds and hear you, then you only need to worry about the following:

- **PCM**: When in doubt, choose PCM. This is the most common setting for recording sounds. It works for audio at all sample rates and bit depths (these terms will be explained shortly).
- **ADPCM**: This format shrinks audio files from 16 bits to 4 bits—three-quarters of their original size—and the result is generally a good level of sound quality.
- **MACE 6:1 and MACE 3:1**: MACE is a Macintosh codec that significantly decreases file sizes, but it can also diminish the sound quality. MACE 6:1 compresses files to one-sixth of their original size, and MACE 3:1 takes them down one-third.
- **CCIT A-Law and μ-Law (also called Mu-Law)**: Compresses 16-bit audio down to 8-bit, with corresponding reduction in sound quality. This compression method is useless for sounds that are already formatted as 8-bit files.
- **Delta Mod**: Stick with this popular videoconferencing compression format; it works with most videoconferencing applications and computer systems.

Chapter 6 tells you about compressing movie files. You'll also encounter compressed files video when you do videoconferencing.

What's "Compression," Anyway?

Movies, sounds, and images can take up humongous chunks of disk space, so you have to compress them somehow. Images can be saved to a compressed file format such as GIF or JPEG, but audio and video files must be compressed with a codec.

There are two types of compression: **lossy** and **lossless**. Lossy compression schemes result in greater file-size reductions, but data is lost in the process. Lossless compression schemes compress the files without losing much (or any) data.

Some compression schemes work by reducing the file's bit depth, which results in lower quality because data is lost. Others simply eliminate data that is repeated in various video frames or audio segments. For example, if the same drum-beat pattern repeats consistently throughout a song, the compression scheme saves the pattern once and throws the rest away. Similarly, lossless video compression schemes save data that repeats from frame to frame, such as objects in the background that don't move while you're recording a movie.

Sound Quality Levels

Aside from the file format and codec settings, there are three important settings that determine the quality of an audio file: **sample rate, bit depth**, and **stereo/mono**.

The following sections explain what those terms mean. But if you just want to get to the nitty gritty, you're in luck. With most audio programs, you can choose an overall quality level instead of having to choose individual settings for sample rate, bit depth, and stereo/mono.

- **In Windows,** the sound quality settings are Telephone Quality, Radio Quality, and CD Quality.
- **On a Macintosh,** the sound quality settings are Phone Quality, Speech Quality, Music Quality, and CD Quality.

When you select a quality level, the sound program automatically applies the appropriate audio settings for you. That's a heck of a lot easier than having to decide how many Hz and bits you want!

The following table explains these standard levels of sound quality.

Standard Sound-Quality Levels

Sound Quality	Settings	File Size	Description
Telephone Quality (Windows)	11,025 Hz (11.025 kHz), 8-bit, mono	650K/ minute	Low quality, but adequate for videoconferencing and simple sound effects in Web pages and movies. Use when you need to conserve bandwidth or disk space.
Phone Quality (Macintosh)	22,050 Hz (22.050 kHz), 8-bit, mono, with MACE 6:1 compression	234K/minute	Like the Windows Telephone Quality level, Phone Quality is low quality, but adequate for videoconferencing and simple sound effects in Web pages and movies. Use when you need to conserve bandwidth or disk space.
Speech Quality (Macintosh)	22,050 Hz (22.050 kHz), 8-bit, mono, with MACE 3:1 compression	449K/minute	Sounds a little better than Phone Quality recordings, but takes up less disk space than Music Quality recordings.

Standard Sound-Quality Levels (continued)

Sound Quality	Settings	File Size	Description
Radio Quality (Windows)	Music Quality (Macintosh) 22,050 Hz (22.050 kHz), 8-bit, mono	1.3MB/minute	Medium quality. Adequate for most types of sound effects, music, and speech used in movies and on Web pages. A good compromise for decent sound that doesn't hog up bandwidth and disk space.
CD-Quality	44,100 Hz (44.1 kHz), 16-bit, stereo	10.5MB/minute	High quality. For music files that sound comparable to professional recordings. Sounds great but comes with correspondingly hefty file sizes.

Don't Be Afraid to Experiment! Go ahead and try out various settings for your sounds to see which ones get you the best quality for the least amount of disk space. For example, using the stereo instead of the mono setting for a Radio Quality file will often make a big difference in sound quality without making the file too much larger. Record a sound at the CD-Quality level and save it. You can then open the file, try different settings, and save each experimental file with a different name so you don't ruin the original file.

Sample Rate

The **sample rate** refers to the number of times per second that a sound application measures a sound wave and records a value. Sample rates are generally measured in Hertz (Hz), although some people and some applications measure in kiloHertz (kHz). A rate of 1000 Hz is equal to 1 kHz. Higher sample rates produce better sound quality and larger file sizes, while lower sample rates produce lesser sound quality and smaller file sizes.

Standard sample rates in increasing order of quality are 11,025 Hz, 22,050 Hz, and 44,100 Hz.

Bit Depth

Bit is shorthand for **bi**nary digi**t**—a number valued at either 1 or 0. All the data on your computer are created from sequences of these binary digits, including the individual segments for audio files and the pixels for images. More bits per audio segment or per pixel produces higher quality, more detail, and larger file sizes.

With images, you can have 8-bit, 16-bit, and 24-bit color, as explained in Chapter 2. Sound files work similarly, and you can record to **8-bit and 16-bit audio**. (Few people work with 24-bit audio since 16-bit audio offers very high quality.)

Stereo or Mono

If you've got a CD-player, tape deck, or radio (or maybe even a beloved record player!), then you already know what **stereo** and **mono** (for monaural or monophonic) mean. Computer sound systems, as well, have two speakers. When you record an audio file, you can format it to play on both speakers (stereo) or on one speaker only (mono). Stereo files sound better but take up more disk space, and mono files have smaller file sizes but don't sound as full.

You Can't "Upsample"! When it comes to audio, video, and images, you can scale the quality down—*but not up!* **Downsampling** means reducing the quality of a file in order to make it smaller. When you downsample a file, you lose information, and you should keep in mind that there's no way to get it back. Sure, you can save an 8-bit file up to a 16-bit format, but the details of the original file will still be lost. To be safe, when you're experimenting with sound files, save them with different names (by selecting File|Save As) to keep the original file intact.

Extra Reading: Want to learn more about digital audio? Try *The Sound & Music Work Shop for Windows*, by Richard Grace (Sybex, Inc.) and *Audio on the Web: The Official IUMA Guide*, by Jeff Patterson and Ryan Melcher (Peachpit Press).

Adjusting Your Cam's Audio

When you record video with your cam, sounds are recorded, too (if you've got a microphone). The software that comes with most cams allows you to adjust your audio settings to improve the quality of your sound track, or to lessen the quality level and save disk space. For example, QuickCam lets you switch between QuickMovie and QuickPict modes, depending on whether you want to capture video or take a picture. The audio options are available from the QuickMovie mode.

Though the menus and options vary from cam to cam, the following procedures give you at least a basic idea of how to adjust your cam's audio settings.

Changing audio settings in QuickCam for Windows:

Windows only

1. Select Settings|Movie Settings to display the Movie Options dialog box.
2. Select the Capture Sound by Setting Compression Options checkbox, then click the More button to expand the dialog box and display additional options.
3. Click the Compression Options button to display the dialog box in **Figure 14.1**.

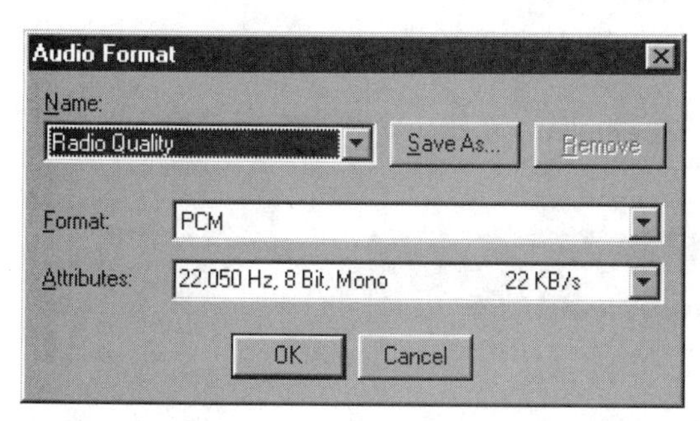

***Figure 14.1** Choosing audio options in QuickCam for Windows.*

4. Choose a quality level from the Name list, as explained in the "Sound Quality Levels" section earlier in this chapter. Or you can choose your own settings from the Attributes menu.
5. You can also choose a codec from the Format list, as explained in the "Audio Codecs" section earlier in this chapter. But in many cases, only the PCM option will be available. Choices depend on what is supported by your sound card and your cam software.

Changing audio settings with QuickCam for Macintosh:

Macintosh only

1. Select Audio|Audio Other to display the Sound dialog box.
2. Choose Sample from the menu list at the top of the dialog box. This displays the Rate (sample rate), Size (bit depth), and Use (mono/stereo) options, as shown in **Figure 14.2**.

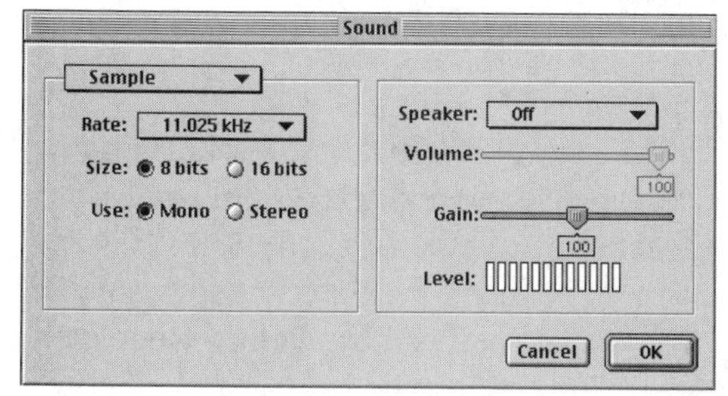

***Figure 14.2** Choosing audio options in QuickCam for Macintosh.*

3. You can also choose a codec, by selecting Compression from the menu list at the top and choosing an item from the Compressor list that appears.

Exporting Audio from a Movie

You've already learned how to add sound files to movies with QuickEditor (Chapter 6). But what if you want to take a sound track from a movie that you've recorded with your cam and export it as a sound file? You can do this with QuickEditor, too.

To export a movie sound track:

1. Open a movie with a sound track in QuickEditor.
2. Select File | Export Movie to display the Export File As dialog box (**Figure 14.3**).

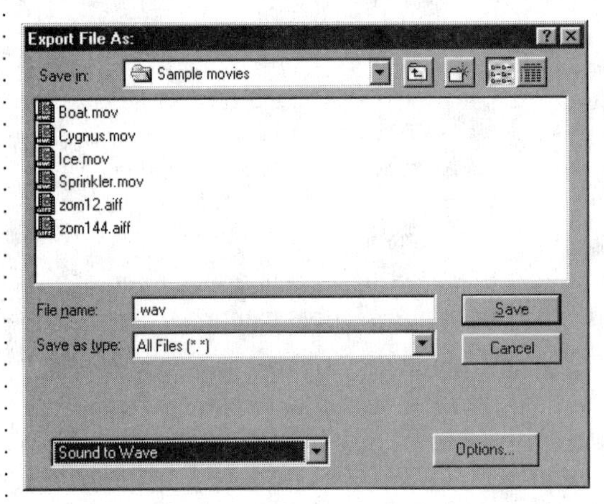

Figure 14.3 *QuickEditor Export File As dialog box (shown in Windows).*

3. Choose one of the Sound To options from the list at the bottom of the dialog box. You can export your audio as a Wav, AIFF, Macintosh System Sound, or μ-Law (AU) file.
4. Type a name for your file in the File Name box.
5. Click the Save button to return to QuickEditor.

MIDI Too! You can also work with MIDI files in QuickEditor, when they're formatted as QuickTime movies.

Recording Sounds

Want to record your own sounds? Sure, you can do it with your cam, and then open your movie in QuickEditor and export the audio (as explained in the preceding section). But when you don't want the video to ride along with your audio file, it's easier to use the sound software that comes with your system. Windows comes with the **Sound Recorder**, and the Macintosh comes with **Simple Sound**.

Sound Recorder for Windows

Windows only

The Sound Recorder records WAV-formatted audio files that you can use on your Web page or in movies. To launch the Sound Recorder, you have to burrow through a bunch of cascading lists. Click the Start button, then select Programs, select Accessories, select Multimedia, and then select Sound Recorder (whew! finally!).

To record sounds with Sound Recorder:

1. Launch the Sound Recorder, shown in **Figure 14.4**.

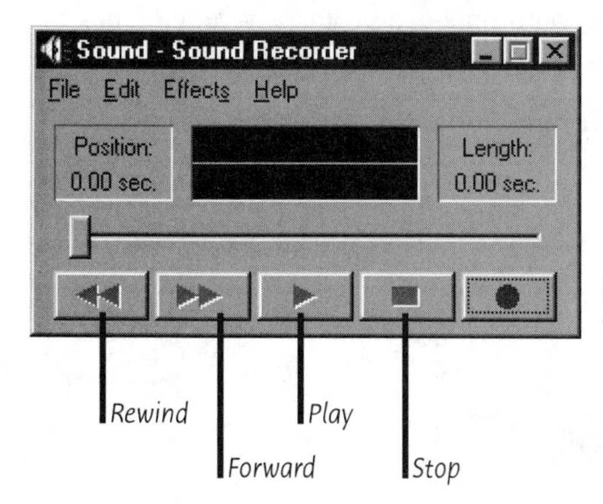

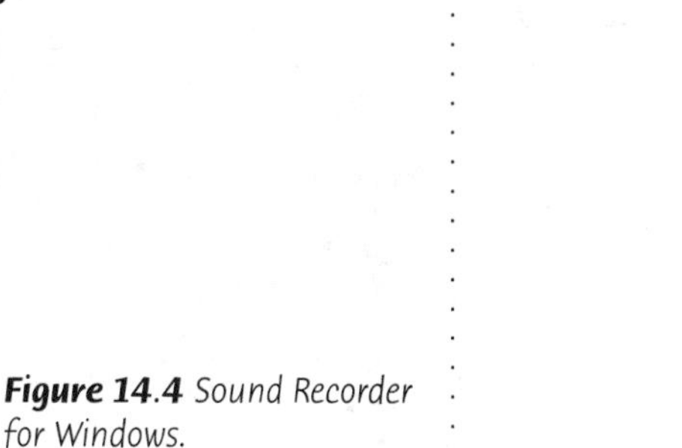

Figure 14.4 *Sound Recorder for Windows.*

2. Choose an audio quality level, as explained earlier. Select Edit|Audio Properties to display the Audio Properties dialog box (**Figure 14.5**).
3. Choose an option from the Preferred quality list (Sound Recorder defaults to Radio Quality), and click OK.
4. Click the Record button and start recording your sound. Click the Stop button when you finish recording.
5. Take your sound file for a spin. Click the Seek to Start button to rewind your sound clip, and then click the Play button to play it back.

Figure 14.5 *Sound Recorder's Audio Properties dialog box.*

6. Select File | Save and save your sound file.
7. When the Save dialog box appears, you can also reduce the quality level by clicking the Change button to display additional options.

Simple Sound and SoundApp for Macintosh

Macintosh only

Simple Sound is a handy little application for recording and playing sounds, and it comes with your Mac. There's just one catch: Simple Sound only records and plays Macintosh System Sounds, which people outside of the Macintosh world don't generally use. Luckily, you can download SoundApp, a freeware application, to play other types of sound files and to convert your Macintosh System Sound recordings.

To record sounds with Simple Sound:

1. Select Simple Sound from the Apple Menu to display the Alert Sounds dialog box, shown in **Figure 14.6**.

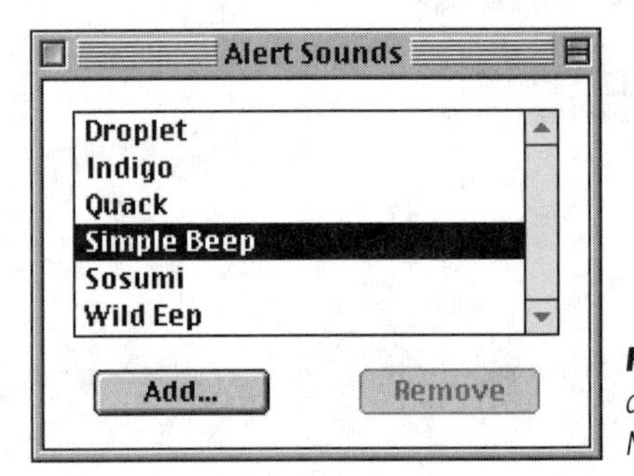

Figure 14.6 *The Alert Sounds dialog box in Simple Sound for Macintosh.*

2. Choose an audio quality level from the Sound list.
3. Select File | New to display the audio controls shown in **Figure 14.7**.

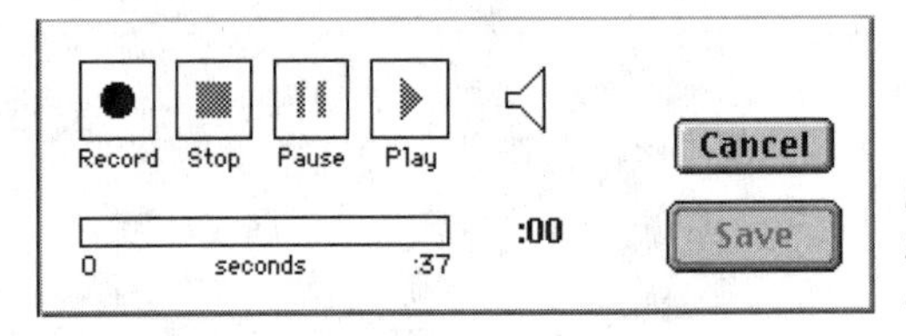

Figure 14.7 *Simple Sound for Macintosh audio controls.*

4. Click the record button to begin recording and click the Stop button when you're finished.
5. Click the Play button to play back your recording.
6. If you're happy with the sound file, click the Save button to name and save your sound.

Converting Sounds with SoundApp

SoundApp is a freeware program by Norman Franke that plays and converts sound files. It supports most common audio file types, including AU, WAV, and AIFF. To get SoundApp, go to Norman Franke's Web site at **http://www-cs-students.stanford.edu/~franke/SoundApp/** and download the program.

Once you've downloaded, unstuffed, and installed your sound files, you can convert your sound files by following these steps:

1. Launch SoundApp by double-clicking the SoundApp icon.
2. The menu bar at the top of your computer screen changes, but no application window appears. Not to worry, this is completely normal!
3. Select File|Convert to display the dialog box shown in **Figure 14.8**.

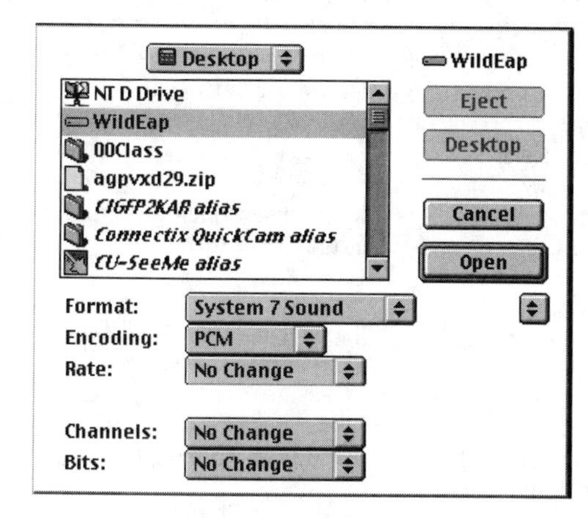

Figure 14.8 *SoundApp conversion options.*

4. Choose your options for converting the file as follows:
   - In the Format list, choose a file format.
   - In the Encoding list, choose a codec or leave the current codec selected.
   - To reduce the Sample Rate, choose an option from the Rate list.
   - To reduce a file from stereo to mono, choose an option from the Channels list.
   - To reduce the bit depth, select 8 bits from the Bits list.
5. Browse for your sound file, select it from the list, and click the Open button.

SoundApp creates a Converted File folder in the SoundApp folder and puts your newly converted file in the folder.

Experiment! Since SoundApp saves converted files to a new folder without changing your original audio file, go ahead and experiment with downsampling your files. You can then play your newly converted sounds, and see which one gives you the best sound quality for the smallest file size.

Free Sounds from the Web

If you're like most people, you probably don't have a digital sound studio or tons of sound clips. No problem—you can download lots of free sound treats from the Web. Whether you need special sound effects, clips from favorite tunes, TV jingles, bird calls, or animal noises, you can find plenty of goodies on the 'Net.

Sound Files on the Web

Site	What's There	URL
ClixSounds Sound Files	The makers of Agent Audio, a popular audio program, have all kinds of cool sound files for Mac users.	**http://www.clixsounds.com/sounds/index.html**
Geek Girl's Sites with Audio Clips	Provides links to various sound-file collections on the Web.	**http://www.geek-girl.com/audioclips.html**
The MIDI Farm Internet	Check out this enormous collection of free MIDI tunes.	**http://www.midifarm.com/**
Sun Site's Index of Sounds	Need a few beeps, animal noises, or other clips? Visit Sun Site's AU-formatted sound collection, and browse by category.	**http://sunsite.sut.ac.jp/multimed/ sounds/**
Archives of Free Sound Effects	Shareware sound and MIDI programs, and royalty-free Computer Music: MIDI tunes, WAV and AU sound effects, shareware programs, and audio tips for Windows and Macintosh users.	**http://www.partnersinrhyme.com/**
Audio Browser: Sound Files	Directory with links to sounds organized into eclectic categories, including "Bathroom," "Classical Music Midi Files," and "Cats."	**http://www.webplaces.com/html/ sounds.htm**

Summary

Now that you know a little about audio files, go to town! Audio always adds a dash of pizzazz to your Web pages and your movies.

- Before you record sounds or download audio from the Web, you should get to know a little about **common audio file types** and which applications support them. Most applications support WAV and AU files. Many also support MIDI files.
- Cams typically allow you to adjust movies' **audio settings** when you record them with the software that comes with your cam.
- You can **export a movie's sound track** using QuickEditor.
- Or you can record sound with software that comes with your system. Windows comes with the **Sound Recorder**, and Macintosh comes with **Simple Sound**.
- Macintosh users also need to download **SoundApp**, freeware that plays and converts many types of sound files. Simple Sound only records and plays Macintosh System sounds, which are not supported by many applications.
- Want some cool **audio clips and sound effects?** You can download them from the Web.

Web Camming Resources

A

Here is a collection of information about the many camming resources featured in this book, and some that were not. It includes hardware and software, printed material, Web sites, and everything else I could think of.

Cam Products

ComPro Dcam

http://www.acscompro.com/

Another popular type of cam for Windows by ACS Innovations, mentioned in Chapter 2, for about $100.

CU-SeeMe Cam Kit

http://www.wpine.com/

White Pine's $124 cam for Windows. It also comes with CU-SeeMe videoconferencing software.

FlexCam and PlanetView

http://www.flexcam.com/

As mentioned in Chapter 2, FlexCam for Windows from VideoLabs captures high-quality images and video and costs about $199. PlanetView is a complete videoconferencing system that also offers high-quality imaging, for capturing text from documents and doing online presentations. PlanetView is available for both Windows and Macintosh and costs $399.

FoneCam

http://www.fonecam.com/

This nifty little $399 Windows product from Moonlight Products was mentioned in Chapter 8. It automatically dials up your Internet connection through the nearest telephone line and uploads pictures. Once you program the FoneCam from your computer, you can take it anywhere.

GR-DVF10 Digital Cybercam

http://www.jvc-america.com/

JVC's high-end digital video camera for Windows users, as mentioned in Chapter 2, costs about $1,120.

Recommended

QuickCam Products and QuickClip

http://www.quickcam.com/

Logitech's $199 Color QuickCam for Windows and Macintosh is the camming product I used as a basis for this book. In addition, Logitech sells other cool camming products, including QuickCam VC ($139) and the $99 QuickClip, which allows Windows users to plug a video camera into their computer.

SiteZAP

http://www.sitezap.com/

A $2,000 programmable, mounted security camera with motion detection, a live video feed, and software that generates QuickTime VR movies on-the-fly. Lets Web-site visitors control the cam. Discussed in Chapter 10.

VideoBlaster WebCam II

http://www.cle.creaf.com/

Creative Labs, the well-known maker of high-end video and sound cards, also offers a Web cam, covered in Chapter 2. Cost is $99 for Windows, $149 for Macintosh.

Video Cards, Adapters, Etc.

For more about video hardware, see Chapter 2.

ATI Xclaim VR Video Card

http://www.atitech.com/

A highly acclaimed $229 video card for Macintosh users, mentioned in Chapter 2.

Buz

http://www.iomega.com/

A $199 video adapter with multimedia software for Windows and Macintosh G3 users, described in Chapter 2.

Intel Smart Video Recorder III

http://www.pentium.com/product/multimedia/svr3/

A popular video card for Windows users: $139.

Key Span

Recommended

http://www.keyspan.com

Offers $59 USB cards and other USB products for Macintosh, as recommended in Chapter 2.

Miro Video Cards

http://www.ideamedia.com.au/

Miro makes high-quality, reasonably priced video cards for Windows and Macintosh. Prices range from $735 to $1,645; high-end video editing software is included.

Video Cards, Adapters, Etc. *(cont.)*

PortXpander, iHub

http://www.macally.com/

The Mace Group's $59 PortXpander for Macintosh adds connections to the printer or modem ports so you can connect up to four devices, as mentioned in Chapter 2. Mace also sells the $79 iHub for Macintosh, which accommodates up to four devices on a USB port. Various USB products for Windows users are also available.

Snappy Deluxe

http://www.play.com/

Play, Inc.'s popular $139 adapter allows Windows users to plug a video camera into the parallel port. Snappy Deluxe, mentioned in Chapter 2, comes with plenty of video- and image-editing software.

USB Card, Bitronics Data Switch Kit

http://www.belkin.com/

Belkin Labs offers USB Card for adding USB capabilities to a Windows 95 or 98 computer ($79), as explained in Chapter 2. Belkin also sells other USB products, including The Express Bus Hub for Windows, which allows you to plug in up to four devices; and the Bitronics Data Switch Kit, also for Windows users, to plug two devices into a parallel port ($49).

Featured Software

A+ Screen Saver Creator

http://www.regsoft.com

A $14.95 shareware program for Windows users who want to assemble their own pictures into screen savers.

For more on creating your own screen savers, see Chapter 3.

After Dark

http://www.berksys.com

A popular screen-saver program for Windows and Macintosh, mentioned in Chapter 3. QuickCam's software includes an After Dark screen-saver module that displays your cam shot as a screen saver.

For more about creating Web pages, see Chapter 7.

AOL Press

http://www.aolpress.com/

An easy-to-use freeware graphical Web editor. It's ideal for AOL users, but others can use it, too.

BBEdit
http://www.barebones.com/

A text-based Web page creation program for Macintosh users, mentioned in Chapter 7. You can try out the freeware version, or pay $79 for the more capable commercial version.

Dreamweaver
http://www.macromedia.com/

A $299 graphical Web-site creation program for Windows and Macintosh users.

FrontPage
http://www.microsoft.com/FrontPage/

A popular and easy-to-use graphical Web-site design and management program for Windows and Macintosh, as mentioned in Chapter 7.

GifBuilder
http://iawww.epfl.ch/Staff/yves.Piguet/clip2gif-home/GifBuilder.html

A freeware GIF animation program for Macintosh users, explained in Chapter 5. In addition to downloading GIFBuilder from this site, you can get it from shareware sites such as **http://www.tucows.com/** and **http://www.shareware.com/**.

Graphics Converter
http://members.aol.com/lemkesoft/

Recommended

This $25 image-editing shareware program for Macintosh works great for converting and touching up pictures that you take with your cam (recommended in Chapter 2).

Home Site
http://www.allaire.com

A popular and feature-packed text-based Web editor for Windows, described in Chapter 7.

HotDog Pro
http://www.sausage.com/

A favorite text-based Web-site creation tool for Windows, $199, mentioned in Chapter 7.

Featured Software *(cont.)*

Icon Mania!
http://www.dublclick.com/

Lets Macintosh users replace plain old icons with snazzy pictures, as covered in Chapter 4. There's a demo version you can try out, but you'll need to pay before the program actually changes your icons. It's $39 if you order online, $69 in stores.

ICQ
http://www.icq.com/

How can millions of users be wrong? You can use this wildly popular instant-messaging program to meet up with your pals for a video chat. For more about ICQ, see Chapters 11, 12, and 13.

ISpy
http://www.ispy.nl

The $49 Web cam software for Windows, featured in Chapter 9. In addition, the ISpy Web site has links to some cool Web cams.

iView
http://www.scriptsoftware.com/

For Mac users; helps you track of pictures and multimedia files, as described in Chapter 2. $25 shareware.

iVisit
http://www.ivisit.com/

Freeware videoconferencing software for Macintosh and Windows by BoxTop software, introduced in Chapter 12.

Recommended

Media Blaze
http://www.dryad.com/

Multimedia cataloging shareware that helps Windows users keep track of their pictures, movies, and sound files; $14.95. Recommended in Chapter 2.

For more about creating your own icons, see Chapter 4.

MicroAngelo
http://www.impactsoft.com/

A $39 shareware program that allows Windows users to replace icons with their own pictures.

NetMeeting

http://www.microsoft.com/NetMeeting/

A freeware videoconferencing program for Windows users, discussed in Chapter 12.

PaintShop Pro

http://www.jasc.com

Recommended

This excellent image-editing program for Windows is recommended in Chapter 2. $129.

Photos4us

http://www.zoetek.com/entrance/Photos4us/

A $10 shareware program that allows Macintosh users to assemble their own pictures into screen savers.

Photoshop

http://www.adobe.com

This popular, high-end ($895) image editor comes in both Windows and Macintosh versions, as mentioned in Chapter 2.

Premiere

http://www.adobe.com/

The crème de la crème of video editing programs for Windows and Macintosh, $495. Described in Chapter 2.

QuickEditor

http://www.wild.ch/quickeditor/

For both Windows and Macintosh users, this cool $35 shareware program makes and edits QuickTime movies, as described in Chapter 6. To use it, you also need to download QuickTime 3.0 or higher (described just below).

QuickTime and QuickTime Pro

http://www.apple.com/quicktime/

For more about video, see Chapter 6.

If you plan to play or create videos, then you've gotta get QuickTime 3.0 or higher for Macintosh and Windows. Apple offers a freeware version of the program, or you can order the $29.99 QuickTime Pro for more editing, viewing, and playback features. You can also download the freeware version of QuickTime from most of the popular shareware Web sites.

Featured Software
(cont.)

Recommended

SiteCam
http://www.rearden.com/

The recommended, feature-packed $129 Web cam program for Macintosh users, covered in Chapter 9. By the way, through this Web site you can also get to the Bay Bridge and SiteZAP cams.

Recommended

SoftCam
http://www.luminositi.com/

A $12 Windows shareware program that displays a folder of images as your video source, and streams the images. Described in Chapter 13.

SoundApp
http://WWW-CS-Students.Stanford.EDU/~franke/SoundApp/

A freeware sound player and converter for Macintosh users. For more on downloading and using SoundApp, read Chapter 14.

StripCam
http://www.stripcam.org/

A freeware control panel for Macintosh Web camming, as mentioned in Chapter 9.

StuffIt Deluxe and StuffIt Expander
http://www.aladdinsys.com/

From Aladdin Systems, StuffIt Expander is a freeware decompression utility that helps Macintosh users extract files they've downloaded from the Internet. StuffIt Deluxe is a $39 program for compressing files into archives. Both programs are covered in Chapter 1.

WebCam 32
http://www.kolban.com/

This highly regarded Web cam shareware program for Windows costs a mere $25. I considered featuring it in the book, but it only works with QuickCam and Snappy.

Recommended

White Pine CU-SeeMe
http://www.wpine.com/

White Pine's videoconferencing software for Macintosh and Windows, as recommended and explained in Chapter 11. WhitePine has also acquired the rights to the Cornell (freeware) version of CU-SeeMe (Chapter 12). CU-SeeMe is $89 ($69 if you order online).

WinZip
http://www.winzip.com/

NicoMak Computing's $29 compression/decompression software for Windows users. Unzips (decompresses) files downloaded from the Internet, as covered in Chapter 1.

WWW Gif Animator
http://stud1.tuwien.ac.at/~e8925005/

A $20 Windows shareware program for creating GIF animations, described in Chapter 5.

Shareware Web Sites

Chapter 1 talks about downloading shareware.

Download.com
http://www.download.com/

CNet's searchable Web site has cool shareware, games, software demos, and other downloadable treats for Windows and Macintosh users, as mentioned in Chapters 1 and 7.

Filez.com
http://www.filez.com/

A great place to search for all kinds of files on the Web, including shareware programs, as mentioned in Chapter 7.

HotFiles
http://www.hotfiles.com/

Mentioned in Chapters 1 and 7, HotFiles is ZDNet's extensive collection of shareware and demos for Windows users.

MacDownload.com
http://www.macdownload.com/

Another ZDNet offering; this is a collection of Macintosh shareware, freeware, demos, and more. The Web site also includes reviews for most programs.

TUCOWS
http://www.tucows.com/

A well-organized shareware site for Windows and Macintosh users (as mentioned in Chapters 1 and 7). TUCOWS reviews and rates each program, also providing links to the programmer's Web site. You'll also find a section especially for Web cams.

Cool Web Cams

Africam
http://www.africam.com/
Go on a virtual safari, or watch the animals at their local watering hole.

CatNap Cam
http://www.employlaw.com/CatNap.htm
Nikita, the cat, takes frequent naps on her embroidered pillow.

CourtHouse Square Live Action Cam
http://www.dmsoft.com/live.htm
A nice view of the park.

Dave's Deck Cam
http://www.marsweb.com/dave/view.htm
A breathtaking view from Dave's deck in Montana.

Ginger's WolfCam
http://www.nidlink.com/~ugholl/pages/wc1.html
Watch Ginger and Urnie's pet wolves play, sleep, and walk around in their large compound.

James and Kevin World
http://www.cableregina.com/users/jamesandkevin/ livecamera2/htm
Who says only women can cam?

JenniCam
http://www.jennicam.org/
The woman who launched a thousand cams.

Kevin's GardenCam
http://freespace.virgin.net/kevin.croucher/gardencam/
Enjoy a day in an English garden.

Kremlin Cam
http://www.kremlinkam.com/
Visit the Kremlin in Moscow square.

Laddie Cam
http://www.cx45564a.chndl.az.home.com/myweb/laddie/
Visit the little sheltie pup.

Lisa Violet's Cat House
http://www.lisaviolet.com/camera/webcam.html

You'll almost always find one of Ms. Violet's 18 cats sitting in the comfy chair.

You can meet Lisa Violet's kitties and learn her camming secrets in Chapter 10.

MoldCam, Night of the Living Strawberries
http://reality.sgi.com/dlai/mold.1/mold.1.html

Oh, the horror! Amazing what you can do with a bowl of strawberries, a fridge, and a cam.

National Zoo Elephant Cam
http://www.si.edu/organiza/museums/zoo/zooview/exhibits/elehouse/

Visit the elephants at the National Zoo in Washington, D.C.

Netscape Engineering Sign
http://www.weissman.org/sign/

You can leave a message displayed on the bus sign in Netscape's Engineering Department. Originated by Terry Weissman.

Read an interview of Terry Weissman in Chapter 10.

Olivet Intersection Web Cam
http://webcam.olivet.edu/int/main.html

Find out what's going on at the Olivet intersection in Illinois.

Peeling Paint WebCam
http://www.mich.com/~rrreibel/paintcam.htm

Hour after hour of exhilarating live-action entertainment.

Safe Harbor Group Live Gerbil Cam
http://www.shgroup.com/gerbilcam/gerbil_cam.htm

See what those little critters are up to!

San Francisco Bay Bridge Cam
http://www.rearden.com/

A way-cool view of the San Francisco Bay Bridge, as discussed in Chapter 8. If you want, you can check out the SiteZAP cam site, at **http://www.sitezap.com/**, and take control of the camera.

Scooter's Electric Digs
http://www.geocities.com/~scooter_hound/webcam1.html

Play with Scooter the basset hound, flip through his photo album, play his videos, or drop by and watch TV with him.

Cool Web Cams *(cont.)*

Tehachi Rail Cam
http://www.trainorders.com/cameras

Watch the trains go by!

The Aloha Café
http://www.aloha-cafe.com

Drop by the coffee café and leave a message.

The Amazing DaveCam
http://ranier.oact.hq.nasa.gov/staff/davecam.shtm

See if Dave's in the office, or take a QuickTime VR tour.

The Amazing Fish Cam
http://fishcam.netscape.com/fishcam/fishcam.html

Visit Netscape and watch the fish swim around. Netscape's Lou Montulli is legendary for developing the browser and server technologies that make Web camming possible. The FishCam is the world's second Web cam.

The Amazing Ironing Cam
http://www.bogan.com/bogan/webcam/

These techies are in quest of the perfect crease.

The Exploratorium
http://www.exploratorium.edu/

Visit the Exploratorium, San Francisco's interactive science museum.

The Infamous Lava Cam
http://www.newtonline.com/HOMEPG/lava.cgi

Lava lamps aren't just memorabilia; they're a way of life.

The Pad Cam
http://www.internetad.net/connections/

Four roommates living in "The Real World."

The Telegarden
http://www.usc.edu/dept/garden/

Visit the garden and control a robotic arm that lets you water, weed, and perform other gardening tasks.

Tommy's List of Live Cams Worldwide
http://chili.rt66.com/ozone/cam.htm

A quirky home page with lists of Web cams all over the world.

Trojan Room Coffee Machine
http://www.cl.cam.ac.uk/coffee/coffee.html

Is the coffee pot half-full or half-empty? This is the world's first Web cam.

Virgina Tech Building Constuction Site Cam
http://sitecam.arch.vt.edu/website/sitecam1.html

Supervise a construction project remotely.

Virtual Cams
http://www.dreamscape.com/frankvad/cams.html

Huge list of Web cams that you can visit. You can also follow links to the rest of this Web site for other Web goodies.

WeatherNet's Weather Cams
http://cirrus.spr1.umich.edu/wxnet/wxcam.html

Going on a long commute or leaving for vacation? Check out this guide to weather cams around the world.

Web Cam Network
http://www.webcam.net/WebCamNet/

Provides links to resources for setting up a cam, where to find cool Web cams, information about camming hardware, and more.

WebCam Central
http://www.camcentral.com

Among other things, at WebCam Central you'll find links to Web cams organized by category, and frequently updated FeatureCam awards.

Wild Birds Unlimited Bird Feeder Cam
http://www.wbu.com/feedercam_home.htm

Watch the birds flutter around the bird feeder—and order everything you need to attract birds to your own yard.

WozCam
http://wozcam.woz.org

Watch the legendary Steve Wozniac at work, visit his classroom, check out his fabulous view, or take a dip in his pool.

Videoconferencing Resources

All the sites in this videoconferencing section are mentioned in Chapter 13.

CU-SeeMe Cool Site
http://www.rocketcharged.com/cu-seeme/
Offers lots of helpful information and resources for the White Pine and Cornell versions of CU-SeeMe, as discussed in Chapters 11–13.

CU-SeeMe Cool Site Reflector List
http://www.rocketcharged.com/cu-seeme/reflectors.html
A list of CU-SeeMe reflectors for general audiences, and a separate list for, um, adult audiences.

CU-SeeMe Network
http://www.cu-seeme.net/
Visit here for lots of information about the freeware version of CU-SeeMe.

Cu-SeeMe Support Page
http://support.wpine.com/
White Pine's searchable tech-support pages for Windows and Macintosh users.

CU-SeeMe World
http://www.cuseemeworld.com/
Lots of resources, news, tips, events listings, and more for CU-SeeMe users, as well as the Web camming and videoconferencing communities at large. Hosted by White Pine.

Recommended

ImeetU.com
http://www.imeetu.com *The* place to go for videoconferencing and meeting up with people. You can also host your own online events, for free.

Meeting By Wire
http://www.meetingbywire.com/
Sign up for the mailing list and exchange tips, tricks, and advice with other NetMeeting fans.

Microsoft's NetMeeting Web Site
http://www.microsoft.com/NetMeeting/
Download the NetMeeting software and find lots of NetMeeting info for home and business users.

Rocket Charged's Talk Site
http://www.rocketcharged.com/talk/

Includes links to the CU-SeeMe Cool Site and the iVisit Web sites, which offer online chat forums and other useful information.

The NetMeeting Place
http://www.netmeet.net/

Provides news, information, lists of ILS and NetMeeting servers, and other resources for NetMeeting users.

Free Goodies

All this free audio stuff is discussed in Chapter 14, and free video stuff in Chapter 3.

Archives of Free Sound Effects
http://www.partnersinrhyme.com/

A large collection of MIDI, AU, and WAV sound effects.

Audio Browser
http://www.webplaces.com/html/sounds.htm

Another popular Web site offering lots of downloadable audio files.

ClixSounds Sound Files
http://www.clixsounds.com/sounds/index.html

Free downloadable sound files, including music and sound effects.

Fun with Clip Art
http://www.nauticom.net/www/jillrh/clipart.htm

Another fun clip-art collection on the Web.

Icon Bazaar
http://www.iconbazaar.com/

Possibly the largest collection of free graphics you'll find anywhere.

Iconz
http://www.geocities.com/Heartland/1448/

An enormous collection of free pictures that you can use on a Web site or in multimedia.

Rain Frog's Web Art
http://www.rainfrog.com/

A small but worthy collection of unique, attractive images.

Sites with Audio Clips
http://www.geek-girl.com/audioclips.html

A personal Web site with lists of audio-related links to sites with downloadable sound files, tutorials, and information.

Free Goodies (cont.)

Sunsite Index of Multimedia Sounds
http://sunsite.sut.ac.jp/multimed/sounds/

A popular collection of free AU-formatted sound clips for all occasions.

The MIDI Farm
http://www.midifarm.com/

A colossal collection of free MIDI tunes. There's also lots of general information here, and resources about creating and playing MIDI files.

Virtual Free Clip Art
http://www.dreamscape.com/frankvad/free.clipart.html

A frequently updated collection of links to Web sites that offer free pictures.

Miscellaneous Web Sites

Cammunity
http://www.cammunity.com/

A great general resource for Web cammers, as described in Chapter 13.

DHTML Zone
http://www.dhtmlzone.com/

Cutting-edge examples of how to use text and pictures (which you can take with your cam) for exciting Dynamic HTML effects. For more about Web pages, see Chapter 7.

GeoCities
http://www.geocities.com/

If you connect to the Internet through school or work, you may need a home for your home page, as mentioned in Chapters 7 and 10. Move into a GeoCity online neighborhood and they'll host your Web site for free. They'll also give you an e-mail address that you can use after you graduate or change jobs.

Online PostCards
http://mypostcards.com/

Turn favorite photos taken with your cam into online postcards that you can send to your friends. Online PostCards sets you up for free!

The Digital Camera Network
http://www.dcn.com/

Links to Web cams and camming resources, a featured cam of the day, and a downloadable Web cam program for Windows users (Cam Runner).

Yahoo People Search
http://people.yahoo.com/

Formerly Four11.com, this is one of the most widely used directories for finding people's e-mail addresses.

Recommended Reading

Audio on the Web: The Official IUMA Guide
by Jeff Patterson and Ryan Melcher
http://www.iuma.com/

Tells you everything you need to know about streaming audio on the Web.

The Complete Idiot's Guide to FrontPage 2000
by Elisabeth Parker
http://www.byteit.com/books/

My nontechie guide to creating professional Web sites with FrontPage 2000, as mentioned in Chapter 7.

Dreamweaver: Visual QuickStart Guide
by J. Tarin Towers
http://beta.peachpit.com/vqs/dreamweaver/

Provides an easy-to-read guide on using Dreamweaver to create Web pages. Recommended in Chapter 7.

Hot Dog Pro: Visual QuickStart Guide
by Elisabeth Parker
http://www.byteit.com/HDPvqs/

Gets you up and running quickly with HotDog Pro, as mentioned in Chapter 7.

HTML: Visual QuickStart Guide
by Elizabeth Castro
http://www.cookwood.com/cookwood/html4bookframe.html

A good book for people who want to learn about HTML and Web-page authoring. Mentioned in Chapter 7.

The Non-Designer's Web Book
by Robin Williams
http://www.peachpit.com/titles/catalog/68859.html

Even people who don't have a graphic design background or a techie bent can create attractive Web sites, and this book shows you how.

QuickTime & MoviePlayer Pro: Visual QuickStart Guide
by Judith Stern and Robert Lettieri
http://beta.peachpit.com/vqs/movieplayer/

An excellent guide to all the cool things you can do with Apple's QuickTime Pro for Windows and Macintosh, as mentioned in Chapter 6.

The Sound and Music Workshop for Windows
by Rich Grace
http://www.byteit.com/rgrace/

If you're a musician, you can set up your own inexpensive digital recording studio. You'll learn about file formats, recording and arranging music with inexpensive shareware programs, and more.

Glossary

Numbers

8-bit color
An image that is mapped to the 256-color system palette or the 216-color Web palette; or a computer system setting capable of displaying up to 256 colors on the screen. *See also* 256-color system palette; 216-color Web palette.

16-bit color
An image captured or displayed at thousands of colors, or a computer system setting that is capable of displaying up to 67,000 colors on a computer screen. A good compromise between image quality and smaller file sizes and faster downloads.

24-bit color
An image captured or displayed at millions of colors, or a computer system setting capable of displaying up to 16.7 million colors on the screen.

216-color image
An 8-bit color image (usually a GIF) that is mapped to the 216-color Web palette so it displays properly on both the Windows and Macintosh platforms. *See also* 216-color Web palette.

216-color Web palette
The 216 colors that display correctly in all Web browsers and on both Windows and Macintosh computers. *See also* 8-bit color; dithering; 256-color system palette.

256 grays
A 256-color image reduced to shades of gray *or grayscale* (like a black-and-white photograph).

256-color system palette
Windows and Macintosh computers both come with a default 8-bit 256-color system palette. When an image is reduced to 8 bits (for example, by converting it to a GIF file), or when a display is set to 256 colors, all colors are dithered to the colors on the palette. *See also* 8-bit color; 216-color Web palette; dithering.

67,000 colors
See 16-bit color.

16.7 million colors
See 24-bit color.

A

ADSL (Asymmetric Digital Serial Line)
Offshoot of DSL (digital serial line) technology. Provides inexpensive, high-speed dedicated Internet access. Not available in many areas. *See also* DSL; cable modem.

AIFF (Audio Information File Format)
A popular sound file format created by Apple computer.

alias
On the Macintosh, an icon that you can create on your desktop (or elsewhere) so you can launch your applications and files more easily. The corresponding Windows feature is called a shortcut.

alpha software
A program or program revision that is in the first stage of development.

analog
Refers to sounds, sights, and objects in the real world. To get analog data onto your computer, a cam needs to digitize the data. *See also* digital; digitize.

Apple menu
On the Macintosh, the menu in the far-left corner that you can access by clicking on the Apple icon.

AU (Audio UNIX)
A popular audio file format created by Sun Microsystems for UNIX.

AVI (Audio Video Interleaved)
Microsoft's video format for Windows.

bandwidth
The amount of resources and disk space used when transferring files over a network or via the Internet.

beta software
A program that is still being developed but is almost ready for release. Software makers customarily allow people to try out the program during the beta stage.

bit (BInary digiT)
Image, video, and sound quality are determined by the number of bits stored per byte of data (that's where the terms 8-bit, 16-bit, and 24-bit come from).

bit depth
The number of bits per byte of data stored in a file. Images and video are stored at 8-bit, 16-bit, or 24-bit color. Audio files are stored at 8-bit or 16-bit.

black level
The amount of black (darkness) in an image or frame in a video.

blooming
A problem that occurs in images and video when your cam is overwhelmed with too much bright light.

BMP (BitMaP)
Microsoft's image file format (.bmp) for Windows.

brightness
The amount of light in an image or video frame.

browser-safe color palette
See 216-color Web palette.

cable modem
Allows high-speed Internet access through an existing cable TV connection. Cable modems download faster than they upload (like ADSL). Does not generally offer a dedicated line. *See also* ADSL; DSL; dedicated connection.

cam
A device or combination of devices that capture images and video to your computer.

cell or cel
A single frame in an animation.

chat
A general term for participating in group conferences on the Internet. Also, a feature in videoconferencing programs; allows you to send and receive text messages.

codec (COmpressor/DECompressor)
Software that compresses audio or video files for storage or transmitting over the Internet, and then decompresses the data when the audio and video are played.

color depth
The amount and level of data stored per byte in an image or movie. *See also* 8-bit color; 16-bit color; 24-bit color; bit; bit depth.

color palette
A predefined set of colors to which 8-bit (256- or 216-color) images are mapped. *See also* 8 bit images; 256-color system palette; 216-color Web palette.

compression
The process of reducing a file's size so it takes up less disk space and transfers more quickly over the Internet. *See also* codec; decompression; HTX; ZIP.

contrast
The difference between light and dark areas in an image, or in a frame of a movie.

CPU (Central processing unit)
The brain of your computer; a piece of hardware that determines the speed (measured in megahertz, MHz) at which your computer can process instructions and perform tasks.

cybercast conference
A group videoconference in which one person speaks and broadcasts video, and everyone else watches and listens but does not send audio or video.

data
Information stored on a computer or computer storage device, or transferred between computers through a network or over the Internet. Can be analog, digital, or both. *See also* analog; digital; digitize.

decompress
The process of opening a compressed file. Audio and video applications automatically open sound and movie files that have been compressed using a codec. WinZip and StuffIt archives must be decompressed by WinZip for Windows and StuffIt for Macintosh. *See also* compression; codec; HTX; ZIP.

dedicated connection
A high-speed Internet hookup that provides an exclusive IP address and enables a permanent connection to the Internet, such as ISDN, DSL, and ADSL.

desktop pattern
An image that tiles across your computer's desktop to form a pattern.

dialog box
A window launched by your operating system or an application to display a message or prompt you to select options.

digital
Describes images, movies, sounds, files, and other data formatted for a computer. *See also* analog; data; digitize.

digitize
The process of converting analog data to a digital format for use by your computer. *See also* analog; data; digital.

directory path
The location of a file in relation to your computer or Web site's main (root) directory.

directory server
A server that hosts an Internet locator service (ILS). *See also* ILS.

dithering
The process by which colors are changed (mapped) to conform to the closest available colors on a palette when a 24-bit or 16-bit image is reduced to 8 bits (usually by converting it to a GIF). Dithering also occurs when an image that is mapped to the Windows 256-color system palette is displayed on a Macintosh, because Windows and Macintosh use different colors in their system palettes. *See also* 256-color system; 216-color Web palette.

document redirection
A Web page is set up to switch to another Web page after a specified number of seconds.

download
The process of transferring files from the Internet to your computer, using a Web browser, e-mail program, FTP (file transfer protocol) software, or another client application.

download time
The amount of time it takes to transfer files to your computer, or to transfer all the text, images, and other files on a Web page. *See also* upload.

DSL (Digital Serial Line)
A technology that provides inexpensive, high-speed dedicated Internet access. Unlike its offshoot, ADSL, with DSL you get the same upload and download speeds. Not available yet in many areas. *See also* ADSL.

dynamic IP address
An IP address that changes every time you log on to the Internet, as compared to a permanent IP address assigned by your ISP or network administrator. *See also* IP address.

E

embedded
On the Web, embedded files such as movies appear as part of your Web page layout. Embedded files generally require browser plug-ins in order to launch. *See also* plug-ins.

evaluation software
A program that can be downloaded and used free for a specified amount of time. Evaluation programs have some features disabled, or stop working after a certain amount of time unless you register and pay for the software. *See also* shareware.

F

FAQs
(Frequently Asked Questions) A page or set of pages on a Web site or in a software application's documentation that lists questions frequently received from users, and the answers.

file
A collection of data that is stored on a computer, given a filename, and can be opened in an application, such as a Web browser, image-editing program, movie player, or sound player.

file format
File type. File types are indicated with filename extensions. *See also* filename extension.

filename extension
A two-, three-, or four-letter set of characters that follows the period (.) in a filename and indicates its format. On the Web, files must have a filename extension so the Web browser knows how to handle the files.

firewall
Software that protects an organization's network from hackers and other potential intruders, while allowing its users to access the Internet. You may have to ask your network administrator how to configure your Web cam and videoconferencing software to send and receive data through the firewall. Also called a proxy server.

frame
A single image in a movie. Also refers to a single cel in an animation. *See also* cell.

frame grabbing
Saving a single frame (picture) from a video file.

frames per second (fps)
The number of frames (pictures) that display per second in a movie or animation.

frame rate
See frames per second (fps).

freeware
Software that is distributed freely (usually via the Web) and requires no payment.

FTP (File Transfer Protocol)
A set of rules, technologies, and applications that enable you to upload files to a server. Also refers to the process of uploading files to a server. *See also* protocol.

GIF (Graphic Interchange Format)
A 256- or 216-color (8-bit) image file type that can be used on the Web, and which allows you to remove an image's background color or assemble a series of images into an animation. *See also* 8-bit color, 256-color system palette, and 216-color Web palette.

GIF animation
A series of GIF images assembled into an animation using a program like WWW Gif Animator or GifBuilder.

graphical HTML editor
An application that allows you to create Web pages without entering HTML source code. Instead, text, images, and other files display as they would appear on the Web page. *See also* HTML.

Graphic User Interface (GUI)
Applications and operating systems that allow you to create and manipulate files using icons, toolbar buttons, pull-down menus, and dialog boxes rather than entering arcane text commands.

grayscale
An image or video displayed at 256 shades of gray (like black-and-white photography). *See also* 256 grays.

group conference
A videoconference in which people gather in a video chat room hosted on a videoconferencing server, such as White Pine's MeetingPoint for CU-SeeMe.

H

H.263
A standard set of protocols for sending and receiving sound and video when videoconferencing. Videoconferencing programs that fully conform to the H.263 standard (such as White Pine's upcoming CU-SeeMe Pro for Windows) will allow point-to-point conferencing between people who use H.263-compliant videoconferencing programs, even if they don't use the same videoconferencing software. *See also* point-to-point conferencing, standards, and protocols.

hidden users
People who are participating in a group or multi-point conference and appear on the participants list, but are not broadcasting video.

HQX
A filename extension for files compressed with StuffIt, the compression and archiving program for Macintosh. *See also* compression; .zip.

HTML (HyperText Markup Language)
A set of codes used to format Web pages so that Web browsers understand how to display them.

HTML source code
The text-only document that contains HTML mark-up tags and supports the Web pages displayed in a Web browser. *See also* HTML.

hue
With cam and imaging software, a setting that controls the color levels (red, green, blue, black, and white) in an image.

I

Icon
On a computer, a small picture that represents a file, application, command, or process. Icons are used on a computer's desktop, inside of folders, on toolbars, and on Web pages.

ILS (Internet Locator Service)
Also called ULS (Uniform Locator Service) and directory server. An online service that stores names and e-mail addresses, for use by people using an e-mail program, videoconferencing application, or other software that supports ILS. *See also* IP address, dynamic IP address, and directory server.

inline graphics
On the Web, these are images that appear as part of the Web page layout (rather than images displayed by clicking on a link to open the image in a new window).

insert editing
When creating and editing movies, the process of replacing frames in a movie with frames from a movie clip. *See also* ripple editing.

interface
The look, feel, and visual elements of an operating system or software application.

IP address
A set of numbers that points to your location on the Internet. Since most people's IP address changes every time they connect to the Internet, Internet Locator Services (ILS) maintain directories of e-mail addresses that can be entered, instead. *See also* Dynamic IP addresses; ILS.

ISDN (Integrated Services Digital Network)
A type of high-speed, dedicated Internet connection. ISDN is losing popularity due to faster and less expensive types of connections, such as cable modems, ADSL, and DSL.

ISP (Internet Service Provider)
Companies such as Earthlink, America Online, MindSpring, and Microsoft Network that provide access to the Internet. ISP is also used as a general term for any organization (such as your school or an employer) that gives access to the Internet.

JPEG
(Joint Photographic Experts Group) A 24-bit or 16-bit image file format that can be used on the Web and offers high-quality image displays at smaller file sizes.

keyboard adapter
A device that enables a cam or other device that connects to a computer through a parallel port (Windows) or serial port (Macintosh) to draw power from the keyboard port. Also called keyboard pass-throughs.

keyboard pass-through
See keyboard adapter.

keyboard plug
A device that plugs into a keyboard adapter so you can connect it to the keyboard. These devices come with cams and other parallel/serial port devices in order to accommodate the two standard types of keyboards.

kilobits per second (Kbps)
The speed at which a modem allows you to download and upload (transfer) data, as measured in kilobits (1,000 bits) per second.

kilobyte (KB)
A unit of measurement for data and file sizes; 1,024 bits equal 1 kilobyte. *See also* bit; megabyte.

kiloHertz (kHz)
The speed at which data segments of a sound file are sampled when recording a sound. Sample rates are also often measured in megaHertz (MHz). *See also* megaHertz (MHz); sample rate.

L

local area network (LAN)
A group of computers that are networked together (usually through a server) in an office. LANs are usually inaccessible to outsiders but allow users to connect to the Internet through a firewall. *See also* firewall.

local video window
In videoconferencing, the video window that gives you a preview of what you look like when sending video.

loop
A setting that determines the number of times a movie, sound file, GIF animation, or other multimedia file on a Web page will play.

low-res
Attribute of a Web page image. Tells the Web browser to display a lower-quality (and hence smaller) image while a higher-quality (larger) image finishes loading.

lurkers
In videoconferencing, participants who are not sending video. *See also* hidden users and participants list.

M

megabyte (MB)
A unit of measurement for data and file sizes; 1,024 kilobytes (KB) equal 1 megabyte (MB). *See also* kilobyte (KB).

megaHertz (MHz)
The speed at which data segments of a sound file are sampled when recording a sound. Sample rates are also often measured in kiloHertz (kHz). In addition, refers to the speed at which a CPU can process instructions and data. *See also* kiloHertz (kHz), sample rate, and CPU.

memory
See RAM.

menu
A row of options at the top (usually) of an application window below the title bar. When you select a menu item, a list of options appears.

MIDI (Musical Instruments Digital Interface)
An audio file format for music files.

MIME type
MIME stands for Multipurpose Internet Mail Extensions, a protocol that enables transmission of nontextual data.

modem
A device that enables use of telecommunications services—such as connecting to the Internet and sending faxes—through your computer.

modem port
A port on the back of your computer that allows you to connect a modem.

MOV
The filename extension for QuickTime movies. *See also* QuickTime.

M-JPEG
(MPEG-JPEG) An increasingly popular movie file format based on a combination of the MPEG movie file format and the JPEG image format.

MPEG
(Motion Pictures Expert Group) A standard video format that has been incorporated into the QuickTime movie file format. *See also* QuickTime.

multimedia
A catch-all phrase for combinations of images, video, sound, text, and animation.

nag screen
In shareware programs, a dialog box that periodically appears and asks you to register and pay for the program. *See also* shareware.

network administrator
Manager of a network in an organization with a local area network. When doing Web camming and videoconferencing through a network, you may need to ask the network administrator how to configure your programs so you can get through the firewall. *See also* firewall; local area network.

operating system
The software that comes with a computer, tells it how to run, and determines which programs will work on the computer.

palette
A predetermined set of colors to which an image is mapped. *See also* 256-color system palette and 216-color Web palette.

parallel port
On Windows computers, a port that allows you to connect other devices, such as a cam.

PCM
The most common codec setting for recording sounds. *See also* codec.

PCI slot
(Peripheral Component Interconnect) A computer slot that accommodates video cards, USB cards, graphics accelerator cards, and other hardware that adds to your computer's capabilities.

PICT (PICTure)
The standard Macintosh image format. Macintosh cams generally let you save images as PICTs or as JPEGs that you can use on the Web. *See also* JPEG.

pixel (PIcture ELement)
The smallest unit of measurement for computer displays, and a widely used unit of measurement on the Web. Computers display images and everything else that appears on your computer screen as tiny dots. Each dot is a pixel.

point-to-point conference
A videoconference in which one person calls another person directly, without going through a chat room on a videoconferencing server.

printer port
A port that allows you to connect your computer to a printer.

processor
See CPU.

protocol
A set of rules that determine how applications, computers, and servers communicate with each other and transfer data back and forth over networks or via the Internet.

proxy server
See firewall

QuickTime
Apple Computer's popular video file format.

RAM (Random Access Memory)
Hardware that determines the task load a computer can handle without slowing down or crashing. In order to cam and work with multimedia, you should have at least 32MB of RAM.

RCA video
A widely used standard for connecting video devices (including camcorders, televisions, and VCRs).

RCA video port
A port that allows you to connect a video camera to a computer. Many types of Macintoshes come with an RCA video port. If your computer does not have an RCA video port, you can purchase a video card.

real time
Describes images, video, and audio broadcasted via the Internet while the events being recorded are actually occurring.

receiving (or reception) rate
In videoconferencing, the rate at which other people's video and audio are transmitted to your computer.

reflectors
Name for servers that host video chat rooms for CU-SeeMe users. White Pine has since replaced their reflector software with MeetingPoint, which allows NetMeeting users, too, to participate in group videoconferences.

refresh
In Web cam software, the process of displaying a new image in the preview window. Also refers to loading a new version of a Web page in a browser by clicking the Refresh button on the toolbar.

refresh rate
The frequency at which a Web cam program displays a new image (refreshes the image) in the preview window.

remote video window
In videoconferencing, refers to other people's video windows.

ripple editing
In editing movies, refers to the process of adding a clip to a movie at the Start point, and moving the other frames forward rather than replacing frames. *See also* insert editing.

sample
The process of recording a sound.

sample rate
The speed at which segments of an audio file are recorded. Higher sample rates result in better sound quality.

saturation
In cam and imaging software, a setting that controls the intensity of colors in an image.

screen saver
A program that displays a series of images (and sometimes plays sounds, too) when a computer is idle.

SEA
See HQX.

secure server
A server that automatically encrypts (scrambles) data submitted through a Web form, so you can safely provide credit card numbers and other confidential information online.

sending rate
In videoconferencing, the speed at which your video and sound are broadcasted to a conference room or an individual with whom you are chatting. *See also* receiving rate.

serial port
On the Macintosh, the serial (printer and modem) ports are used to connect cams and other devices to your computer.

shareware
Software created by (usually) individuals or very small companies, which is free to download and try before you buy. Often has a time limit or has key features disabled until you register and pay for the program. *See also* evaluation software.

shortcut
In Windows, an icon that you can create on your desktop (or anywhere you want) so you can launch an application or file more easily. The comparable feature on Macintosh computers is called an alias.

shortcut menu
An abbreviated or composite menu that pops up when, in Windows, you right-click on an object or application element; or on the Macintosh, you or click-hold, Option-click, or ⌘-click. The shortcut menu contains commands applicable to the selected object.

SIT
See HQX.

source code
See HTML source code.

standards
Rules and specifications that ensure a certain level of compatibility among file formats and associated applications (such as JPEG files, imaging programs, and Web browsers), or among devices and hardware parts (such as cams and serial, parallel, or USB ports). Standards are sometimes agreed upon by independent organizations, and sometimes evolve when a particular technology becomes popular.

Start menu
On Windows 95 and 98, the menu that appears when you click the Start button in the lower-left corner of the computer screen.

T

text chat
See chat.

text HTML editor
A program that allows you to create Web pages by entering HTML tags. Unlike graphical HTML editors, text HTML editors require that you work directly with source code files. *See also* graphical HTML editor; HTML; HTML source code.

TIF or TIFF (Tagged Image File Format)
A popular high-resolution image file format for preparing files and images for print. Most cams do not support TIFFs, and TIFF files cannot be displayed on Web pages.

tiling
The process by which a single image is repeated across the background of a Web page or a computer's desktop to form a pattern.

transitions
Animated special effects that can be added to videos and GIF animations, to appear in between frames or cels. *See also* frames; cells.

transmission rate
See sending rate.

uninstall
The process of removing a program that you've installed on your computer.

UNIX
A collection of operating systems used for running servers and performing other heavy-duty computing tasks that personal computers often cannot handle.

unlock
The process of entering a valid registration number to enable an expired or partially disabled shareware program to work. *See also* shareware.

unstuff
The process of opening an archive compressed with StuffIt for Macintosh.

unzip
The process of opening an archive compressed with WinZip for Windows.

USB
(Universal Serial Bus) An up-and-coming standard for Windows and Macintosh for connecting devices to a computer.

VFW
(Video for Windows) A newer version of AVI, Microsoft's built-in video format for Windows. *See also* AVI.

video capture
The process of recording or digitizing video. *See also* digitize.

video card
A piece of hardware that enables you to connect a video camera, television, or VCR to your computer and capture video.

videoconferencing
Real-time communications with audio, video, and text chat. *See also* real time.

video port
A port that allows you to connect a video camera or other video device to your computer. *See also* RCA video port; video card.

wallpaper
See tiled images

WAV (WAVeform)
Microsoft's audio format for Windows.

Web hosting company
A company that provides space and advanced capabilities for your Web site, but does not provide Internet access.

Web-safe color palette
See 216-color Web palette.

white level
The amount of brightness (white) in an image or a series of movie frames.

.zip or ZIP
The filename extension for files compressed using WinZip for Windows.

Index

Numbers and Symbols

A

B

Note: Page numbers in italic denote figures or screens.

N

Z